EUROPEAN SOCIAL LAW

Two week loan

Please return on or before the last
date stamped below.
Charges are made for late return.

EUROPEAN SOCIAL LAW

Noreen Burrows

and

Jane Mair

School of Law,
University of Glasgow

JOHN WILEY & SONS
Chichester • New York • Brisbane • Toronto • Singapore

First published in the United Kingdom in 1996 by John Wiley & Sons Ltd,
Baffins Lane,
Chichester,
West Sussex,
PO19 1UD

National 01243 779777
International (+ 44) 1243 779777

Other Wiley Editorial Offices

John Wiley & Sons Inc., 605 Third Avenue,
New York, NY 10158-0012, USA

John Wiley & Sons Inc., Editorial, Administration & Marketing,
7222 Commerce Center Drive, Suite 240,
Colorado Springs, CO 80919

Jacaranda Wiley Ltd, 33 Park Road, Milton,
Queensland 4064, Australia

John Wiley & Sons (Canada) Ltd, 22 Worcester Road,
Rexdale, Ontario M9W 1L1, Canada

John Wiley & Sons (Asia) Pte Ltd, 2 Clementi Loop #02-01,
Jin Xing Distripark, Singapore 0512

British Library Cataloguing in Publication Data

A catalogue record for this book is available from the British Library

ISBN 0-471-96537-5

Typeset in 10/12 Baskerville by Poole Typesetting (Wessex) Ltd, Bournemouth.
Printed and bound in Great Britain by Redwood Books, Trowbridge
This book is printed on acid-free paper responsibly manufactured from sustainable forestation, for at which at least two trees are planted for each one used for paper production.

CONTENTS

PREFACE

The class of European Social Law is offered as part of the Honours programme in European Law in the School of Law at the University of Glasgow.
It is a course jointly taught by the authors of this book. The aim of that course
is to introduce students to the complexities of the European legislative
programme and the ideas underlying the policies of the European Community
in the social field. For the purposes of our course we define social law in terms
of employment related rights. The course seeks to assist students to understand
the complex relationship which exists between European law and the laws of
the Member States. Given that directives must be implemented by Member
States, it is important to understand how the transformation of European into
national law takes place and the difficulties which can be encountered in this
process. The students who have taken part in that course have all contributed
in their own way to this book. Their questions and their comments have
proved of immeasurable help in sorting out our information and ideas. This
book is therefore dedicated to the class of European Social Law.

The book itself deals with those aspects of European Social law which have
resulted in legislation to be implemented within the UK. Each chapter takes a
particular issue and shows how European law has developed both with the
introduction of legislation and with the interpretation of that legislation by the
European Court. The chapters then examine problems which have been
encountered in the UK in the process of implementation. This book is not,
however, a full study of the implementation process since that exercise would
have taken the book into volumes rather than pages. There is a great deal
more work to be done on that process. So too is there a great deal of scope for
comparative studies of the implementation process across Europe.

Many individuals have contributed to this book and deserve our thanks. Nicole Busby was appointed as a research assistant for the book and proved to be much more than that. Her ability in finding and sorting through information at top speed must be second to none. Her commitment to the project was apparent in her generosity in sharing ideas and comments, many of which are incorporated into this book and more of which will subsequently be developed as our research goes further. Nicole's good humour saved the book on many occasions. We owe her an enormous debt of gratitude. Heather Worlledge-Andrew, the subject librarian at Glasgow University Library, was tremendously helpful in locating obscure references and assisting with electronic and other sources. Kay Munro also deserves our thanks. Her e-mails on recent developments were most helpful. Our colleagues in the Law School have been very supportive and we are particularly grateful to the Research Committee for awarding us the financial support for Nicole. Tricia McKeating, our computer manager, did the impossible in finding files lost in the depths of our computers. Without her the manuscript would not have seen light of day.

Finally, a word of thanks to our families who have lived with this book rather than with us for the past six months, particularly Aly, Andy, David, Eve and Stephen. To Carole and Steve, thanks for the discussion on occupational pensions and part-timers.

The manuscript was completed in October 1995 and the law is as we understood it on October 1st. However, the publishers have allowed some updating in this rapidly evolving area of law. Our thanks to David Wilson and his team for their encouragement and support.

November 1995

NOREEN BURROWS
JANE MAIR
School of Law
Glasgow

TABLES

United Kingdom Cases

EC Cases (alphabetically)

EC Cases (chronologically)

Statutory Instruments (alphabetically)

Statutory Instruments (chronologically)

Statutes

EC Directives

Resolutions

Treaties and Conventions

Contents of Chapter 1

INTRODUCTION

Chapter 1

INTRODUCTION

This book is about the social policy of the European Community and its impact in the United Kingdom. It sets out the legislative framework in relation to individual workers' rights. It attempts to highlight some of the problems which arise when Community policy and law meet with an established legal order. The UK legal order is an example of one such established legal order which has been confronted with the difficult task of adjusting to the harmonisation programme of the Community, sometimes in areas where UK law and policy is in contrast to that of our European neighbours.[1]

Each chapter takes one directive and examines its background, its substance, and its interpretation by the European Court where such interpretation has been given, before examining the implementation of the directive in the UK. The one exception to this pattern is Chapter 6 on atypical workers where the impact of a concept, that of indirect discrimination, has been the engine for change. This is so despite the fact that there is no directive on part-time workers as such and attempts to create such legislation at Community level have met with little success.

The place of social policy in the Community framework

Social policy did not play a major part in the original treaty framework establishing the European Economic Community. Title VIII of the Treaty

---

[1] There are two useful texts on the social policy of the Community. These texts however do not examine the implications of the law for the Member States. Nielsen and Szyszcak, *The Social Dimension of the European Community* (Handelshojskolens Forlag, 1993); Barnard, *EC Employment Law*, (Wiley, 1995).

contained only a few Articles relating to social policy. The Articles which did appear, with the exception of Article 119 relating to equal pay, were vague and provided only the challenge of co-ordination of national policy. Member States would co-operate on issues of social policy but the objective of raising overall standards of living was one which was to be met by the operation of the customs union and common market rather than by deliberate legislative policy. Equal pay was the exception, largely due to the fact that an International Labour Organisation (ILO) Convention had been adopted only seven years before the creation of the European Economic Community which explicitly linked the social dimension of equal pay with its economic counterpart, the avoidance of social dumping. Modern, well established economies which accepted progressive social policies should not be penalised as against backward looking retrograde economies which could only develop by exploiting their citizens. This was the theory in relation to equal pay but it did not seem to apply to other areas of social policy.

The real development of social policy came in 1972 when the Heads of State determined that the social policy of the Community should take equal place with the economic aims of the Treaty. The adoption of action plans in the social field led to the first flowering of social legislation based on shared values and common ideals. Legislation on equality of the sexes in the 1970s was part of an international movement towards the definition of non-discrimination. It is no coincidence that the Equal Treatment Directive was adopted within months of the end of International Women's Year. At the same time, the Community turned its attention to questions of health and safety of all workers. Again, this European development went hand in hand with developments in the ILO where interest was growing in world-wide standards of welfare of workers. The 1970s therefore was a decade of optimism for the development of European standards of employment rights.

The recession of the 1970s also led to an interest in common standards. Member States wished to develop their economies by protecting one of the main factors of production – their workforce. Women should have access to full-time, secure and well paid employment. Workers should be protected in the event of a takeover of their employer or his/her insolvency. Investment in human capital would repay itself in terms of escaping the recession.

These developments were not universally welcomed. It is apparent even within the terms of the Equal Treatment Directive, one of the strongest and least controversial Directives at the time it was adopted, that limits would be placed on European law and that exceptions to the rule of equality would be introduced where this suited the Member States. The exceptions to that Directive in relation to social security and the exceptions in the Social Security Directive for occupational pensions demonstrate the absence of a full commitment to principles of equality as well as questioning the need for Community-scale legislation.

The 1980s saw a reversal of social policy. Several Community proposals were dropped or left floundering on the table of the Council of Ministers. Two ideological opposites met and the result was disappointing legislation, poorly drafted, full of loopholes and lacking in bite or, perhaps worse, no legislation at all. At the heart of the problem was the debate on the deregulation of the labour market. The UK was intent on building business rather than barriers and reducing the role of the state in the relationship between employer and employee.[2] Freedom of contract was to replace collective bargaining. Decentralised bargaining was to replace central negotiations, and legislation which inhibited the right of managers to manage was to be repealed. Hand in hand with these developments was legislation to reduce the powers of the trade unions and the imposition of limitations on statutory rights and protections.[3] In contrast, several European countries still saw the workforce as an asset to be developed and industrial relations in terms of consensus rather than strife. In Europe, Britain's competitors were legislating for minimum standards whilst encouraging management and labour to achieve consensus on improved conditions.

One area of social law which did develop at this time was health and safety at work. The Single European Act of 1986 made certain amendments to the Treaty of Rome allowing for the adoption of Directives in health and safety on the basis of qualified majority voting. Until this time harmonising Directives in social law had to attract unanimity in the Council, which had meant that proposals on the burden of proof in sex discrimination cases, paternity and family leave, and worker participation could not be adopted. After the Single European Act there was an explosion of legislation in this area.

The completion of the Single European Market which was foreseen in the Single European Act did not, at least on paper, suggest that social policy was centre stage. It was almost an afterthought that social policy became attached to that programme. Fears that the new Europe would ignore the position of workers were allayed when Jacques Delors launched the social policy initiative which led to the adoption of the Charter of the Fundamental Social Rights of Workers in December 1989.[4] At this point the UK made its position clear. The completion of the Single Market Programme was not a matter for social policy but was only concerned with providing a level playing field for trade in goods and services. The UK abstained from the adoption of the Charter

---

[2] "Building business . . . not barriers" was the title of the government White Paper which set out the agenda for deregulation of the labour market in the UK, Cmnd 9794 (HMSO, 1986).

[3] See, on the UK position, Moher, *Trade Unions and the Law* (Institute of Employment Rights, 1995); Deakin and Wilkinson, *The Economics of Employment Rights* (Institute of Employment Rights, 1991); Ewing, *The Employment Act 1990* (Institute of Employment Rights, 1991); Hendy *A Law Unto Themselves* (Institute of Employment Rights, 1993).

[4] The text of the Charter is reproduced in full in the Appendix.

which meant that, as from this time, there was open dispute as to the place of social policy at the European level.

This dispute continued in the negotiations for the Treaty on European Union. This was to be an opportunity to transform and develop social policy but again the UK was out of step with its European partners. The solution adopted was to provide for a two-tier Europe in social policy matters with an opt-out Social Protocol and Agreement allowing the 11 members to go ahead without the UK. These procedures have been used now in the adoption of Community legislation on works councils, an area which had previously been blocked in the Council.

The Maastricht Treaty also introduced the term "subsidiarity" into the discussion of the division of competencies between the Member States and the Community. "Subsidiarity" means that the Community can move forward on legislation only if and in so far as the objectives of the proposed action cannot be sufficiently achieved by the Member States. Any action taken must be proportional to the objective to be achieved. The Works Council Directive specifically refers to this principle in the preamble and it is adopted on the basis that Community-scale undertakings should have European works councils to discuss transnational problems. In this example the Community dimension is obvious.

It is not so obvious in other matters of social policy. If it is accepted that the lack of regulation of the labour market will lead to a diversion of investment from one part of the Community to another, then the harmonisation of social policy can be seen as an imperative for the Community. Social dumping can only be avoided by common standards. This has traditionally been the rationale for social measures within the Community. As against this argument, the acceptance by the 11 at Maastricht that the UK could maintain lower standards of protection might be seen to imply that social dumping can be accepted as part of Community policy. Certainly the Commission would prefer not to go down this latter road and the Reflection Group has put onto the agenda of the 1996 Inter-Governmental Conference the issue of the UK opt-out.[5] Any solution to this problem will presumably only be found with a clear agreement that the principle of subsidiarity will be scrupulously observed and that Commission proposals for action be based on a clearly identified

---

[5] *Commission Report for the Reflection Group* (European Commission, 1995). The Report states "While the Agreement on social policy can be seen as another step towards a European social policy for all citizens of the Union, it is regrettable that not all Member States are involved because it rather blurs the Union's image with respect to social policy and creates the potential for disputes over distortions of competition" at 48.

need.[6] This is always, of course, presupposing that there is a willingness in 1996 to negotiate a solution.

Problems of harmonisation of social law

The chapters in this book concentrate on the harmonisation of national labour law to achieve common standards throughout the Community. The technique chosen is the adoption of Directives. Directives are Community provisions which lay down standards which must be transposed into national law by the Member States. A two step process is, therefore, envisaged. The adoption of the Directive is a matter for negotiation and position taking by the Member States within the Council, the Community legislature. Directives are, by definition, negotiated instruments reflecting a compromise position. The studies in this book demonstrate two things about this process. The first is that there has been a progressive deterioration in the Directives adopted by the Community in matters of social law. If the Equal Treatment Directive is compared to the Protection of Young People Directive then it is apparent that the former is written in fairly crisp language whilst the latter is full of loopholes, exceptions and derogations. A straightforward comparison would lead to the conclusion that it has become increasingly difficult to achieve agreement on the social law proposals.

The second aspect of the harmonisation process is that the transposition of Community provisions into the terms of national law is a complex process requiring both legislative and administrative changes within the Member States. This process has proved difficult for the UK and has led to deep changes in the national legal order. The term "harmonisation" implies that a certain degree of uniformity and commonality will be achieved at the end of the process. The studies in this book demonstrate that harmony may be achieved in the longer term, that is still to know, but in the shorter term the harmonisation process has been disruptive of the existing legal framework of workers' rights and industrial relations. This has been the case for the UK and it may be the case for other Member States of the Community. The harmonisation process does purport to recognise the distinct nature of national legal systems, hence each Member State is given the choice of form and methods of implementation of Community Directives. However it may be that

---

[6] On subsidiarity and the social dimension see Working Document Proceedings of the Jacques Delors Colloquium 1991, *Subsidiarity: The Challenge of Change* (European Institute of Public Administration, 1991); Duff, *Subsidiarity within the EC* (Federal Trust, 1993). See also the essays by Shaw, Szyszczak and Hervey in O'Keefe and Twomey, *Legal Issues of the Maastricht Treaty* (Wiley Chancery, 1994).

the approach of the legal systems of the Community in the area of social law is too different to achieve harmony in this way.

One factor which militates against achieving harmony is the role of the European Court of Justice in interpreting the Directives which are discussed in this book. The European Court is not always predictable nor is it always consistent in its approach. Its interpretations can be criticised as creating an additional range of problems for the courts of the Member States and their legislatures. In approaching Directives, the Court is seeking to give a meaning which is helpful to the national court which has referred the question to it and to give an interpretation which can be valid throughout the Community. This latter task is almost impossible given the range of approaches to the issues which are being discussed. Two good examples of this problem are the interpretation given by the Court to the Acquired Rights Directive and the interpretation of Article 119 to cover occupational pension schemes. The UK had significant difficulties in bringing its legislation into line with the Court's rulings in these cases. It must surely have been unforeseen that the Court's decisions on the rights of part-timers to have access to occupational pension schemes would result in a backlog of some 75,000 cases before the UK industrial tribunals. This is not achieving harmony but chaos and un-certainty.

This is not to state that the Court is the only source of uncertainty in this harmonisation process. The Member States themselves have the opportunity to implement the Directives concerned within certain agreed and negotiated time limits. Begrudging and incomplete harmonisation also introduces un-certainty into the system. National courts and tribunals are faced with conflicting rules which, on the face of it, have equal validity. They are faced with the problem of deciding which rule to choose. This situation is far from satisfactory from the point of view of employers or workers, courts or tribunals.

As the harmonisation programme progresses, some factors can be identified as requiring specific attention. The first is the need to agree on the terminol-ogy of social law. "Workers", "employees", "employer", "self-employed" are terms which lack a clear meaning in European law. "Worker" and "employ-ee", for example, appear sometimes to be used interchangeably. Any Euro-pean meaning should be internally consistent and consistent with the meaning given to these terms in the Member States. If Europe speaks with one voice on basic definitions then harmonisation will be a less painful process.

Codification of existing European and domestic law would also assist in the harmonisation process. In the UK, implementation of Community provisions could have provided the opportunity to modernise and rethink problems of labour law. Unfortunately, implementation has only had a marginal effect on such a rationalisation process, no doubt due to UK antipathy to the entire enterprise. At the European level, a certain degree of codification would be helpful. The equivalent of a Sex Discrimination Act, bringing together the legislative provisions and the decisions of the European Court, would be a step in the right direction. So too would be the codification of provisions on health and safety where there is overlap between specific and general provisions. This long-term view, however, is jeopardised by the inability to agree on policy within the Council.

The future of social policy

Certain strands of future activity are discernible in European policy. These can be summarised as being the move away from legislation to non-legal action either through social dialogue between management and labour or through policies of education and development. The second is the increasing questioning of the need for Community level activity either because of its supposed negative impact on competitiveness of Europe as against the rest of the world or because of the principle of subsidiarity. The third is balancing Community social policy as against other policies of the Community such as protection of small and medium scale enterprises. Finally, there is the need to implement existing social legislation to make it a reality for citizens of the European Union.

Non-legislative activity

In several areas it is possible to see that the Community is seeking to promote Europe-wide social dialogue, none more so than in the Maastricht arrangements.[7] How successful a policy this can be is still open to question. The first attempt to reach agreement on Europe-wide policy by the social partners failed, leaving the Commission to resort to legislation on European Works Councils. A second attempt at European collective bargaining, however, has now resulted in a draft agreement on parental leave. A further proposal for action using the Maastricht techniques is in the area of flexibility in working time and security for workers. This issue is currently with the social partners for consultation.[8] The Commission does, however, wish to pursue this element of dialogue and is proposing to assist Member States and management and

---

[7] These arrangements are explained in full in chapter 14 *infra*.
[8] See European Information Service, October 1995, 18.

labour to understand the issues involved with the establishment of a European Centre for Industrial Relations.[9]

In health and safety and in new areas of equality between men and women the Community has introduced soft-law measures with recommendations on positive action and sexual harassment or with programmes to alert employers as to how to incorporate safe working practices into the working environment.[10] It is likely that these types of activities will continue to develop in the future, perhaps side by side with legislation. This also may be the way in which new policy areas will be progressively introduced into the Community ambit.[11]

Competitiveness

In December 1993, the Commission submitted a White Paper on Growth, Competitiveness and Employment to the European Council. The White Paper outlined some of the problems facing Europe. Amongst these problems, the Commission identified low growth rates, high unemployment levels and increased competition from outside the Community as being the issues which would affect Community policy in the future. Emphasis was to be placed on the reduction of unemployment and job creation in a Community wide attempt to reduce social exclusion (poverty). In doing so, the Community would have regard to the need to develop social policy which was responsive to the needs of small and medium scale enterprises and in the light of the competitiveness of Europe with the rest of the world.

To date this has not led to a clear conception of a European social policy. Disagreements as to how to achieve lower unemployment are still apparent amongst the Member States. The impact of competing Community policies have similarly not been agreed upon. Only recently, for example, have some of the Member States begun to question the Maastricht convergence criteria for economic and monetary union to assess the likely impact of this policy on unemployment and standards of living.

Social policy takes its place beside other Community policies, in agriculture, in industry and in general economic policy. The challenge for the future is to ensure that it does not slip from the Community agenda. Social policy is always in danger within a Community context of becoming the Cinderella policy.

---

[9] Communication from the Commission to the Council and European Parliament on the establishment of a European Centre for Industrial Relations, COM (95) 445 final.
[10] Discussed in chapters 3 and 12 *infra*.
[11] See, for example, Resolution of the Council and of the Representatives of the Governments of the Member States, meeting within the Council, on the employment of older workers, OJ 1995 C 228/1.

Full implementation

It is not only in the social field that there is concern for the full implementation of Community rules. Across the whole area of Community activity is the fear that Community Directives, once adopted, will not be implemented fully. This mutual fear has caused concern for the development of future policy. In the social field, this has led to the adoption of a Council Resolution which is based on the principle of the realisation of effective Community rights for European citizens and the legal duty on the Commission to ensure effective implementation of Community provisions.[12]

In order to achieve these objectives the Commission is required to undertake adequate impact studies on existing national legislation and, in particular, to assess the impact of such legislation on implications for employment and for its effects on small and medium scale enterprises. This latter provision is in keeping with the current Community view that small and medium scale enterprises will be the prime factor in generating growth in the Community. The Commission is also asked to allow an adequate period for transposition of Community provisions into national law. Another effective way of ensuring that provisions will be applied is to ensure that adequate consultation with management and labour takes place before legislation is proposed. The rest of the Resolution is concerned with the importance of the distribution of information, suggesting that Member States should provide the Commission with information on measures taken to transpose Directives and should exchange with each other information on difficulties which they have encountered in attempting to implement Community provisions in order to draw lessons from the process.

To many people this Resolution may seem like the Council closing the stable door after the horse has bolted. It appears to be eminently sensible to study the potential impact of a legislative change before it is adopted and equally eminently sensible, if harmonisation is to be achieved, to study the difficulties which such legislation can bring within the Member States. The Community institutions, and included in this must be the governments of the Member States, must be criticised for introducing measures without an apparent concern for the difficulties which may be caused.

This book is not the place to introduce discussions on amendments which are required to the decision-making and legislative processes at Community and national level. However, the studies of implementation problems throughout the book show that poor legislation, inadequately drafted and incompletely implemented, have the potential to cause major difficulties for all

---

[12] Council Resolution on the transposition and application of Community social legislation, OJ 1995 C 168/1.

concerned in labour law, either by being governed by the rules or by having to enforce them. Legislation by negotiation behind closed doors, adopted without a clear understanding of the changes which will require to be brought about, will not lead to the harmonious development of a European social law and policy. Such an approach generates misunderstanding and disagreement. The Resolution of the Council calls for the encouragement of "the gathering and distribution of information on progress made and difficulties encountered in bringing about the effective implementation of Community legislation". This book is a contribution to that process.

Contents of Chapter 2

PAY

Chapter 2

EQUAL PAY

Background

The Treaty of Rome made very little detailed provision for social rights, with one of the most important exceptions being Article 119 which provided for equal pay for men and women. Three out of the original six Member States had ratified Convention 100 of the ILO which required equal pay for men and women for work of equal value and France, in particular, was concerned that the principle be included in the Treaty. Equal pay was accepted largely on the basis that it was not only a social issue but also an economic issue and those States who were already committed to the provision of equal pay for men and women were concerned to ensure the remaining states could not benefit from the exploitation of female workers. The principle set out in Article 119 was further defined and the precise obligations of the Member States clarified in Directive 75/117/EEC on the approximation of the laws of the Member States relating to the application of the principle of equal pay for men and women which was adopted in February 1975 (the "Equal Pay Directive").[1]

The aim of this chapter is to consider the principle of equal pay as set out in the legislation of the European Community and its development by the European Court and to discuss its implementation in the UK.

---

[1] Directive 75/117/EEC OJ 1975 L 45/19.

Equal pay – Community measures

Article 119

Article 119 was included in Title III of the Treaty of Rome which is entitled "Social Policy". Unlike the surrounding Articles, it was written in clear and specific terms and appeared to impose a precise obligation on the Member States. It has been suggested that the character of Article 119 may be explained by the fact that it had not only a vague social aim but also an important economic objective.[2]

Article 119 provides:

"Each Member State shall during the first stage ensure and subsequently maintain the application of the principle that men and women should receive equal pay for equal work.

For the purpose of this Article, 'pay' means the ordinary basic or minimum wage or salary and any other consideration, whether in cash or in kind, which the worker receives, directly or indirectly, in respect of his employment from his employer.

Equal pay without discrimination based on sex means:
(a) that pay for the same work at piece rates shall be calculated on the basis of the same unit of measurement;
(b) that pay for work at time rates shall be the same for the same job."

Initially, Article 119 had little effect and it was assumed that Member States would require to introduce implementing measures into domestic law in order to give effect to the principle. The need to do so was postponed by a Resolution of 1962[3] which provided for equal pay to be introduced in stages: pay differentials were to be reduced by 15% by 30 June 1962, a further 10% by 30 June 1963 and abolished completely by 30 June 1964. Against this background of delay and reluctance of some states to give effect to the principle, the European Court began to interpret Article 119 in a way which has made it a fundamental source of European social law. The first important development was the decision of the Court to the effect that Article 119 was capable of creating direct effects.

---

[2] For a discussion of the background to Article 119 see the opinion of Advocate General Dutheillet de Lamothe in Case 80/70 *Defrenne* v *Belgian State* [1971] ECR 445.
[3] *Bulletin of the EC* 1962 No 1, p 79.

Direct effect

Among the most important, and certainly the best known, of the cases considered by the European Court in relation to equal pay are those brought by Ms Defrenne against Belgium and its national airline, Sabena. Gabrielle Defrenne was an air hostess employed by the state airline, Sabena. According to her contract of employment she was forced to retire at 40. In the first of three cases[4], she applied to the Belgian *Conseil d'Etat* for annulment of a Royal Decree which provided special rules about the entitlement of civil aviation air crews to a pension. Under these rules a female air hostess was required to retire at 40 whereas a male air steward could remain in employment until the normal pension age. In this first action, the *Conseil d'Etat* made use of the Article 177 procedure to refer a number of questions to the European Court, foremost of which was the question of whether the particular pension scheme provided for in this case fell within the definition of pay in Article 119. In answering no to this question the European Court commenced the long and complicated process of interpreting the application of the principle of equal pay to occupational pensions.[5] The Court was not required to rule on the issue of the potential direct effect of this provision but the Advocate General indicated that he considered that at least since 31 December 1964 the Article had created individual rights.

In 1976, Ms Defrenne's situation was again considered by the European Court, this time as a result of a reference from the *Cour du Travail* of Brussels resulting from her application for compensation for loss of salary, severance allowance and pension, on the basis that she had not received equal pay with a man who was engaged as an air steward.[6] Two questions were posed by the national court: first, is Article 119 directly enforceable in the national courts and if so, from what date?: and secondly, has Article 119 become applicable in national law by virtue of European Community measures or does the national legislature alone have competence in this matter?

In the written observations to the Court, the United Kingdom put forward the opinion that, while Article 119 was unconditional, it was insufficiently clear and precise to satisfy the conditions for direct effect developed by the Court. It contained no comprehensive definition of the principle of equal pay for equal work and it was for that very reason that Directive 75/117 had been introduced. The scope for comparison was further unclear, with no indication as to whether or not equal pay must be available within a particular establishment or throughout an entire trade or profession. Confusion and

---

[4] Case 80/70 *Defrenne*, cited in note 2, *supra.*
[5] See chapter 5.
[6] Case 43/75 *Defrenne* v *Sabena (No 2)* [1976] ECR 455.

uncertainty would be created if Article 119 was held to give rise to direct effect, in particular if its direct effect was to operate retrospectively. The UK government concluded that, in any event, in view of the language of the Treaty, the obligation to ensure equal pay was addressed to the Member States and the right to equal pay could not be enforced by one individual against another.

An interesting distinction was raised by the Irish government between Article 119 and the other Articles to which direct effect had already been attributed. The latter were concerned with "the attainment of the 'fundamental freedoms' provided for by the Treaty"[7] whereas Article 119 was "pursuing a social objective which is limited to a specified class of persons". Article 119 could therefore be distinguished from the provisions previously held to have direct effect and on that basis should not be regarded as giving rise to individually enforceable rights.

In his Opinion Advocate General Trabucchi placed Article 119 within the context of ILO Convention 100, which by the date of the hearing had been ratified by all of the Member States, and of the EEC Treaty. The principle of equal pay, in other words, should have been neither a new nor alien concept to any of the Member States. The Advocate General further set the scene by reflecting on the time limits set for implementation by the Member States and on their failure to comply. In this context, the Advocate General considered that while the words of the Article may be regarded as vague and unspecific, the purpose of the provision – the prohibition of discrimination against women with regard to pay – was clear. The fact that the concepts used might require to be interpreted by the national courts did not prevent the Article from being relied upon directly, particularly in view of the availability of the Article 177 reference procedure. Having given a clear opinion in favour of the attribution of direct effects to Article 119, the Advocate General equally firmly rejected the possibility that the Resolution of the Member States of 31 December 1964 could have extended the time limit for the application of the equal pay principle laid down in the Treaty.

In its judgment the European Court confirmed the dual social and economic objectives of Article 119 and followed the lead of the Advocate General in stating the importance of considering the issue within the context of the principle of equal pay and the EC Treaty. The Court then distinguished in the application of Article 119 between:

> "direct and overt discrimination which may be identified solely with the aid of the criteria based on equal work and equal pay referred to by the article in question and, secondly, indirect and disguised discrimination which can only be identified

[7] *Ibid* at p 461.

by reference to more explicit implementing provisions of a Community or national character".

It recognised that, in certain circumstances, further measures would be required at both Community and national level. In the first situation, Article 119 would give rise to individual rights which must be protected by the national courts. This statement by the Court has given rise to much debate as to its meaning, and the apparent distinction between direct or overt discrimination and indirect or disguised discrimination has been subject to further interpretation.

In a reference from the Court of Appeal in *Worringham*, the European Court, in discussing the direct applicability of Article 119, further defined it as operating in relation to discrimination which can be identified solely with the aid of the criteria of equal work and equal pay and "without national or Community measures being required to define them with greater precision in order to permit of their application".[8]

The argument put forward by the UK government to the effect that the term "principle" as used in Article 119 was clear evidence of the vague nature of the provision was rejected and the Court concluded, on the contrary, that the term indicated the fundamental nature of the provision.

The notion of the principle of equal pay as a fundamental provision of the European Community was developed further by the Court in the third case concerning Ms Defrenne.[9] Here the Court confirmed that the elimination of discrimination based on sex as regards conditions of employment of men and women was one of the fundamental personal human rights of Community law.

The European Court in *Defrenne (No 2)*, agreeing with the Advocate General, confirmed that Article 119 took effect from 1962 for the original Member States and from 1973 for the first accession States. Recognising to some extent the concerns raised by the intervening governments and by the Commission as to the confusion and uncertainty which might result from backdating the direct effect of Article 119, the Court placed a temporal limit on its judgment. Individuals could only rely directly upon Article 119 from the date of the decision with the exception of those who had already initiated proceedings. The Court made it clear that this concession was given not in response to the economic concerns raised but in recognition of the need for legal certainty and the fact that certain States and the Commission, by their failure to act, may have created expectations that the Article did not create individual legal rights. The Court confirmed that neither the Resolution of the

---

[8] Case 69/80 *Worringham & Humphreys* v *Lloyds Bank Ltd* [1981] ECR 767 at 792, para 23.
[9] Case 149/77 *Defrenne* v *Sabena (No 3)* [1978] ECR 1365.

Member States of 30 December 1961 nor Directive 75/117 were capable of amending the timetable set out in the Treaty provision itself.

This important decision established the direct effect of Article 119 and set the way clear for individuals to raise actions in the national courts to uphold the right to equal pay. As the Court itself recognised in *Defrenne (No 2)*, Article 119 alone could not eliminate differences in pay between men and women but it was, nonetheless, a very important step forward. Throughout a series of subsequent decisions, the Court has further defined and developed the principle of equal pay.

The Equal Pay Directive – 75/117/EEC

In addition to Article 119, Directive 75/117/EEC[10] was adopted in February 1975, following on from the Social Action Programme of 1974.[11] The Directive defines in more detail the principle of equal pay and sets out the specific steps which the Member States are required to take in order to give effect to the principle.

Article 119, while being based on ILO Convention 100, provided a more restricted right to equal pay for equal work than that set out in the Convention which referred also to work of equal value. Article 1 of Directive 75/117 purports to define the principle in Article 119 and in so doing to include the concept of work of equal value. It states that:

> "The principle of equal pay for men and women outlined in Article 119 of the Treaty ... means, for the same work or for work to which equal value is attributed, the elimination of all discrimination on grounds of sex with regard to all aspects and conditions of remuneration."

The Directive did not specify how individual jobs were to be evaluated but it did specify that any job classification scheme "must be based on the same criteria for both men and women and so drawn up as to exclude any discrimination on grounds of sex".

The remaining provisions of the Directive were concerned with the specific steps to be taken by Member States in order to implement the principle of equal pay. Article 2 requires Member States to introduce into their legal systems whatever measures are necessary to enable individuals to pursue claims for equal pay through the judicial process.

Articles 3 and 4 indicate the scope of the application of the principle of equal pay. Under Article 3, Member States are required to abolish discrimination contrary to the principle of equal pay which results from laws, regulation

---

[10] OJ 1975 L 45/19. For text see Appendix.
[11] OJ 1974 C 13/74.

or administrative processes. Article 4 makes it clear that the principle applies equally to provisions existing in the private sphere of employment. Member States must act in relation to collective agreements, wage scales, wage agreements and individual contracts of employment and they must ensure that any discriminatory provisions are or may be abolished or amended.

Protection against potential victimisation is provided for in Article 5 which requires Member States to take measures to protect workers against dismissal as a result of raising an internal complaint or taking legal action against the employer in relation to an equal pay claim.

Article 6 is a general provision which requires Member States to act to ensure that the principle of equal pay is applied by whatever means are necessary.

There has been debate as to the relationship between Article 119 and the Equal Pay Directive but it seems to be accepted that the Directive is intended to clarify and further define the Treaty provision. The European Court held in *Worringham*[12] that the Directive in no way affected the concept of pay as set out in Article 119 and further, in *Jenkins*,[13] that the Directive "is principally designed to facilitate the practical application of the principle outlined in Article 119 of the Treaty [and] in no way alters the content of that principle". In view of this approach, the Court in subsequent decisions has concentrated on interpretation of the Treaty provision, in most cases regarding interpretation of the Directive itself as unnecessary.

The principle of equal pay – its interpretation by the European Court

What is pay?

One of the most frequently considered aspects of Article 119 has related to its material scope and in particular to the question of "what is pay?" It is defined in Article 119 as:

> "the ordinary basic or minimum wage or salary and any other consideration, whether in cash or in kind, which the worker receives, directly or indirectly, in respect of his employment from his employer."

---

[12] Case 69/80 *Worringham*, cited in note 8, *supra*.
[13] Case 96/80 *Jenkins* v *Kingsgate (Clothing Productions) Ltd* [1981] ECR 911.

Many of the cases referred to the European Court relating to the definition of pay have been concerned with the application of the principle of equal pay to occupational pensions and this issue is considered separately in chapter 5. Questions have also been raised in relation to, for example, redundancy payments, benefits in kind and overtime, and the concept of pay has been interpreted broadly

Travel facilities

The question of whether or not travel facilities provided to former employees after their employment fell within the definition of pay was considered by the European Court in *Garland*.[14] Mrs Garland, a retired employee of British Rail Engineering, sought to establish that the provision of concessionary travel facilities to former male employees and their families where such facilities, while being provided to former female employees, were not provided to their families, constituted discrimination against former female employees contrary to Article 119, Article 1 of the Equal Pay Directive and Article 1 of the Equal Treatment Directive. The House of Lords, in a reference to the European Court, asked whether the provision of different travel facilities to male and female former employees fell within the scope of any of these three EC provisions and, if they did, did Article 119 or either of the Directives give rise to individual rights capable of enforcement in the national court. In its submissions to the Court the UK government argued that such facilities did not fall within Article 119 as they were gratuitous benefits which arose after retirement and to that extent did not fall within the scope of the working relationship. Even if free travel facilities were held to fall within the scope of the definition of pay, they could not be regarded as directly applicable "without the aid of national or Community measures which resolve the questions of how to approach the different retiring ages and life expectations which directly affect the cost of the benefit to the employer and its value to the employee".[15]

In confirming that such facilities constitute pay, the Court referred to the definition of pay which it had earlier given in *Defrenne (No 1)*[16] to the effect that it includes: "any other consideration, whether in cash or in kind, whether immediate or future, provided that the worker receives it, albeit indirectly, in respect of his employment from his employer". Provided that such facilities are made available in respect of the employment it is irrelevant that they do not stem from a contractual obligation or that they are voluntary.

---

[14] Case 12/81 *Garland* v *British Rail Engineering Ltd* [1982] ECR 359.
[15] *Ibid*, p 366.
[16] Case 80/70 *Defrenne (No 1)*, cited in note 2, at p 451.

With regard to the second question raised by the House of Lords, the European Court replied that where the national court is able to establish, on the basis of the equal work and equal pay, that the provision of special travel facilities constitutes discrimination on the grounds of sex, without the need for additional Community or national measures, Article 119 is directly applicable.

Sick pay

The scope of the definition of pay in Article 119 was discussed briefly in the case of *Rinner-Kuhn*[17] in which the European Court considered a provision of German legislation which permitted an employer to exclude part-time employees from sick pay. The Court confirmed the opinion of the national court, that where an employer continued to pay wages to an employee who was absent from work due to illness, such payment fell within the concept of pay in Article 119. Advocate General Darmon set out a number of factors in favour of the inclusion of this sick pay within the definition of pay including the fact that it was the employer who continued to pay the wages, although there was some provision for partial reimbursement from insurance funds, and that the conditions of eligibility for receipt of sick pay had "their genesis in the employment relationship".[18] This decision was also of interest in that it was a statutory provision itself which was held to be discriminatory.[19]

Redundancy and severance payments

The Court issued its opinion on 17 May 1990 in the important decision of *Barber*.[20] This case, which is discussed in detail in chapter 5, concerned benefits paid to Mr Barber on redundancy and its main impact lies in the field of occupational pensions. The decision is also significant, however, in relation to redundancy payments and their inclusion within the scope of Article 119. Advocate General van Gerven, in his Opinion, distinguished between the minimum redundancy payment required by statute and any severance payment in excess of that minimum sum. There was no disagreement between the parties as to the inclusion within the scope of "pay" of any severance payment over and above that required by statute. Since the decision of the European Court in *Garland*[21] it had been clear that pay could continue to be received as

---

[17] Case 171/88 *Rinner-Kuhn v FWW Spezial-Gebaudereiniging GmbH & Co KG* [1989] ECR 2743.
[18] *Ibid*, at p 2751.
[19] The potential for scrutiny of legislation has recently been exploited in the UK by the House of Lords decision in *R v Secretary of State for Employment ex parte EOC* [1994] IRLR 176: see chapter 6.
[20] Case C-262/88 *Barber v Guardian Royal Exchange Assurance Group* [1990] ECR I-1889.
[21] Case 12/81 *Garland*, cited in note 14.

a result of employment even after the termination of that employment. The question at issue was whether or not the minimum statutory redundancy pay fell within the scope of Article 119. The Advocate General disagreed with the submissions of the UK government to the effect that the statutory redundancy payment was a form of social security benefit and therefore fell within Article 118 and stated that simply because pay is required by legislation it does not fall outside the scope of Article 119. Further, an underlying consideration of social security does not remove a payment from the ambit of Article 119. The Court followed closely the Advocate General's Opinion in confirming that a redundancy payment paid by an employer to a worker falls within the scope of Article 119 whether it is "paid under a contract of employment, by virtue of legislative provisions or on a voluntary basis".[22]

In the later case of *Kowalska*,[23] referred to the European Court from the Hamburg Arbeitsgericht, the Court again confirmed that payments do not cease to constitute pay within the scope of Article 119 simply because they are received after the termination of the employment relationship. A collective agreement providing for severance payments to employees excluded part-time workers and was challenged by Ms Kowalska on the basis that it discriminated indirectly against women. The Court stated that such severance payments fell within the scope of Article 119 and should be regarded as a "form of deferred pay" provided, as in *Barber*, to help the former worker to adjust to the new circumstances arising from the termination of employment.

Salary grading

Discrimination in the system operated by an employer for classifying employees in salary grades falls within the scope of Article 119. The European Court in *Nimz*[24] was asked to consider a collective agreement which classified employees in salary grades, taking into account their length of service. Less favourable rules were applied to part-time workers with the effect that Ms Nimz, who worked part-time, was refused classification in a higher salary grade. The Court stated that this scheme came within the scope of pay in Article 119 and confirmed that Article 119 applies not only to the state but also to collective agreements and individual contracts of employment.

Compensation for attending training courses

Ms Botel, a home nurse employed by the Berlin Welfare Department, attended several trade union training courses in 1989 and in order to do so she

---

[22] *Ibid* at p 1950, para 20.
[23] Case C-33/89 *Maria Kowalska v Freie und Hansestadt Hamburg* [1990] ECR I-2591.
[24] Case C-184/89 *Nimz v Freie und Hansestadt Hamburg* [1991] ECR I-297.

was given leave by her employer. Under German law, employees were entitled to time off work to attend such courses without loss of pay. The courses lasted longer than Ms Botel's normal working week of 29.5 hours and while she was paid in respect of her working hours she did not receive any payment in respect of the additional hours which she spent on the training courses. A full-time employee who had attended the same courses would have received pay for the full period, as it was less than the normal working week. A reference was made to the European Court from the Berlin *Landesarbeitsgericht* as to whether the German law in question was contrary to Article 119 and Directive 75/117.[25] The German government argued that the provision was intended to ensure that employees received the pay which they would have received had they not been absent on training courses. It was not intended to compensate employees for time spent on training courses or to represent payment for attending such courses. The Court confirmed that payments of this type do fall within the scope of pay as defined in Article 119 and the Equal Pay Directive. Although the obligation to pay this compensation is not based in the contract of employment it does arise as a result of the employment relationship and the legislative provisions.

Piece work

Paragraph 3(a) of Article 119 expressly refers to the application of the principle of equal pay to work which is remunerated at piece rates, and the inclusion of piece rate pay schemes within the concept of pay has been confirmed by the European Court in a decision involving *Royal Copenhagen*,[26] referred to the Court by the Danish Arbitration Board. Accordingly, the principle of equal pay will apply to pay schemes in which pay depends entirely or in large measure on the individual output of each worker.

Indirect discrimination

Neither Article 119 nor the Equal Pay Directive refer to the way in which discrimination will arise. In particular they do not distinguish between direct and indirect discrimination. The concept of indirect discrimination is one which has been developed by the European Court of Justice, particularly in the context of part time workers.[27] In a reference from the Employment Appeal Tribunal (EAT) in *Jenkins*[28] the Court was asked to consider whether

---

[25] Case C-360/90 *Arbeiterwohlfahrt der Stadt Berlin e V v Botel* [1992] IRLR 423.
[26] Case C-400/93 *Specialarbejderforbundet i Danmark v Dansk Industri, formerly Industriens Arbejdsgivere, acting for Royal Copenhagen A/S* [1995] All ER (EC) 577.
[27] Part-time workers are considered more fully in Chapter 6.
[28] Case 96/80 *Jenkins*, cited in note 13, *supra*.

the principle of equal pay contained in Article 119 and the Equal Pay Directive applied regardless of the number of hours worked. The Court responded to the effect that the payment of different rates of pay depending on hours of work is not in itself contrary to the principle of equal pay. It went on, however, to provide that such differential rates must be attributable to objectively justified factors which are in no way related to discrimination based on sex. The determination of this question was one which should be left to the national courts.

The test of objective justification was considered again by the Court in *Bilka*[29] where further guidance was given on its application. Ms Weber was refused access to her employer's occupational pension scheme on the basis that she worked only part time. She argued that the pension scheme was contrary to Article 119 since it imposed a qualifying condition which placed women at a disadvantage. The employers argued that they had a defence in the form of objectively justified economic grounds. The Court, following *Jenkins*, ruled that the exclusion of part-time workers from the occupational scheme was contrary to Article 119 where a much lower proportion of women than men were engaged on a full-time basis. In this case the employer would then be required to show objective justification not related to discrimination on the grounds of sex. While the question of justification is one to be determined by the national courts, the European Court gave some further guidance as to what is required. In describing what has become the very important "proportionality" test, the Court stated that the employer could exclude part-time workers from the pension scheme where he or she had the objective of minimising the number of part-time employees and where "the means chosen for achieving that objective correspond to a real need on the part of the undertaking [and] are appropriate with a view to achieving the objective in question and are necessary to that end".

In *Rinner-Kuhn*,[30] a case concerning the exclusion of part-time workers from German legislation providing for sick pay, the Court applied the proportionality test defined in *Bilka*. The assumption which seemed to have been accepted in *Bilka* that the discouragement of part-time workers was an acceptable objective was challenged to some extent in *Rinner-Kuhn* where the Court held that measures introduced by the State which had the effect of placing women at a disadvantage would require to be shown as responding to a "necessary goal of social policy".

The operation of indirect discrimination in relation to overtime pay for part-time workers was considered by the European Court in *Angelika Helmig*

---

[29] Case 170/84 *Bilka-Kaufhaus GmbH* v *Weber von Hartz* [1986] ECR 1607.
[30] Case 171/88 *Rinner-Kuhn*, cited in note 17, *supra*.

and five other cases.[31] Collective agreements provided for the payment of an overtime supplement in respect of time worked in addition to the ordinary working hours established by the collective agreements. These provisions were argued to discriminate indirectly against women, who formed the majority of part-time workers and who, while working more than their normal hours, worked less than the ordinary full-time hours and therefore did not qualify for overtime supplements. The Court held that this situation disclosed no element of discrimination.

In practice, in these decisions of indirect discrimination, once a *prima facie* case of discrimination has been established, the burden of showing objective justification for the differential treatment is placed on the employer.

A lack of transparency in a pay system which provided for individual supplements to workers based on a number of criteria was held by the European Court in *Danfoss*[32] to give rise to a *prima facie* case of discrimination where the average pay of a woman was considerably lower than that of a significant group of men engaged on work of equal value. The burden of proof again transferred to the employer to show that the system was not discriminatory.

In these decisions relating to indirect discrimination against part-time workers, the Court can be seen to be applying a test similar to that employed in the UK Sex Discrimination Act 1975 in respect of indirect discrimination: *i.e.* considering a requirement or condition, such as the requirement of full-time work, which is applied to both men and women but which has a greater detrimental effect upon women. In *Enderby*[33] it may be argued that the Court has gone further by accepting the possibility of discrimination in a situation where a group of predominantly female workers is paid at a lower rate than a group of predominantly male workers, where their work is of equal value, even where no requirement or condition has been applied nor any specific obstacle placed in the way of women wishing to join the predominantly male group. The Court has adopted an approach which, as described by Fredman, "focuses on results rather than processes" and which recognises "that job segregation itself raises a strong suspicion of discrimination".[34]

In this case which was referred to the European Court by the Court of Appeal, Pamela Enderby, a speech therapist employed in the National Health Service, sought equal pay with NHS clinical psychologists and pharmacists on the basis that their work was of equal value. Her profession was predominantly

---

[31] Cases C-399/92, C-409/92, C-425/92, C-34/93, C-50/93 and C-78/93, decision of 15 December 1994, [1994] ECR 5727.

[32] Case 109/88 *Handels-og Kontorfunktionaerernes Forbund i Danmark* v *Dansk Arbejdsgiverforening (acting for Danfoss)* [1989] ECR 3199.

[33] Case C-127/92 *Enderby* v *Frenchay Health Authority* [1994] ICR 112.

[34] Fredman, "Equal Pay and Justification" (1994) 23 *Industrial Law Journal* 37, at 39.

female whereas those of her comparators, at her level of seniority, were predominantly male. The first question referred by the Court of Appeal related to the *prima facie* existence of discrimination in this situation. Where there is a difference in pay between two groups of workers engaged in work of equal value, where one group is predominantly female and the other predominantly male, does the principle of equal pay require the employer to justify objectively the difference in pay? The employer and the UK Government argued that there was no indirect discrimination and therefore that the issue of justification should not arise. In order to establish indirect discrimination a condition or requirement must be applied which has a disproportionate and detrimental effect on women. Unlike the decision in *Bilka*, where there was a requirement of full-time work, in the current case no specific requirement had been applied by the employer and no barrier had been placed in the way of entry by women to the higher paid professions. There was, therefore, no *prima facie* case of discrimination. The Court, while recognising that the facts of *Enderby* were different from those of earlier decisions on indirect discrimination, held nonetheless that in the situation where two groups of workers are engaged in work of equal value, and the lower paid group is almost entirely female whereas the higher paid group is predominantly male, there is a *prima facie* case of discrimination. In such a situation, the burden of proof then shifts to the employer to show objective justification for the difference. In this decision, the European Court appears to have taken some account of the underlying social pressures or constraints operating in relation to female employment.[35]

In the recent decision involving *Royal Copenhagen*[36], the Court was asked to decide whether there was a *prima facie* case of discrimination in the operation of a piece work pay scheme simply on the basis that the average pay of a group of predominantly female workers was appreciably lower than the average pay of a group of predominantly male workers, where both groups were engaged on work considered to be of equal value. In such a situation, and provided that the unit of measurement is the same for both groups of workers, the Court held that the simple fact of a difference in average pay does not give rise to a presumption of discrimination. Applying the notion of transparency used in *Danfoss*, however, it may be necessary for the burden of proof to be shifted to the employer to show that the system is not discriminatory. This might arise in a system where an element of the remuneration is based on a fixed unit of pay and another element is variable depending on the individual output of the worker. In that situation, it is for the national court to determine whether the burden of proof should be transferred.

---

[35] See discussion of implementation, pp 32 ff.
[36] Case C-400/93 *Royal Copenhagen*, cited in note 26, *supra*.

Objective justification

The test for objective justification set out in *Bilka* is clear and has now been confirmed on a number of occasions by the European Court. It has been held that it is for the national courts to apply this test in each individual case but the Court has considered and given guidance on factors which may provide objective justification. In *Danfoss*, a pay scheme was challenged which provided for the payment of supplements to individual workers based on criteria including mobility, training and length of service. The lawfulness of each of these criteria was considered by the Court which held that, in relation to mobility and training, while these factors may place female workers at a disadvantage, their use may be justified by the employer by demonstrating their importance for the worker's performance. While recognising that rewarding length of service may also disadvantage female workers whose careers have been interrupted by family responsibilities, the Court held nevertheless that "since length of service goes hand in hand with experience", and that in general a worker's ability to carry out work would be enhanced by experience, it could be used as a criterion for additional reward without specific justification.

The acceptability of specific factors was also considered by the Court in *Enderby*. Here the employer argued that the difference in pay between speech therapists, pharmacists and psychologists was objectively justified by the fact that the rates of pay were negotiated by separate collective bargaining processes which were not internally discriminatory.[37] As the German Government pointed out, to allow an employer to rely on separate bargaining structures as sufficient justification would provide employers with an easy way of avoiding the application of the principle of equal pay and it was rejected by the Court as being sufficient justification.

In some cases there may be doubt as to whether differences between the terms and conditions of two jobs should be considered as preventing them from being considered as of equal value or whether, having decided that the work is of equal value, the differences may be used as factors which justify the difference in pay. In *Royal Copenhagen*, the Court confirmed that such questions are to be determined by the national courts, thus providing little guidance to the UK courts who have been concerned with these issues in a number of decisions.[38]

---

[37] The operation of separate collective agreements had been considered by the EAT to constitute a genuine material difference in *Reed Packaging* v *Boozer* [1988] IRLR 333.

[38] See discussion below of *Hayward* v *Cammell Laird* [1988] IRLR 257 and *Leverton* [1989] IRLR 28.

Market forces

The operation of market forces as an objective justification for indirect discrimination was considered and accepted by the Court in *Enderby*. A complicating factor in this case, however, was the finding by the UK courts that market forces accounted for only part of the difference in pay and the Court of Appeal asked the European Court what approach should be adopted in that situation. Three possibilities were raised: if market forces justified part of the difference in pay, should they be accepted as justifying the whole difference, only that part of the difference or should they be rejected as justification and equal pay required? The Court confirmed that this is a matter for the national courts and held that, in a situation where the national court is able to determine precisely the proportion of the pay difference which is attributable to market forces, only that proportion of the difference is justified. Where no precise determination is possible, the national court must decide whether market forces are sufficiently significant to provide objective justification for all or only part of the difference. Aside from the practical difficulties which these kinds of assessment will present for national courts, this decision also raises the possibility of a remedy other than equal pay – *i.e.* a proportionate increase in the applicant's pay rather than the award of equal pay.

What is equal work?

Article 119 requires equal pay for equal work and, although there is little guidance as to how jobs are to be evaluated, this is a question which has only rarely been considered by the European Court. In *Murphy*,[39] Mary Murphy and 28 other women employed as factory workers by Bord Telecom Eireann claimed equal pay with a male stores labourer engaged in the same factory. Their claim was initially rejected under the Irish equality legislation on the basis that their work was found to be of higher value than that of the male worker who was nonetheless remunerated at a higher rate. The Labour Court referred the question to the European Court of the scope of the concept of equal pay for equal work and in particular whether Article 119 should be interpreted as applying to a case where the chosen comparator's work was of higher value.

The Court, not surprisingly, confirmed that if Article 119 prohibited wage differences in relation to equal work it must certainly prohibit a difference in pay where the claimant's work was considered to be of even greater value.

The Advocate General stressed that there was no suggestion in this case that the applicant was seeking "proportionality between work and pay".[40] This

---

[39] Case 157/86 *Mary Murphy* v *Bord Telecom Eireann* [1988] ECR 673.
[40] *Ibid*, p 683.

clearly demonstrates the limited scope of Article 119 and the Directive which are designed simply to eradicate differences between the pay of men and women carrying out comparable work and not to disturb on a wider scale the system of wages and pay structures. This is an issue which has been considered again in *Enderby*.

Job evaluation

While neither Article 119 nor the Equal Pay Directive dictate how jobs should be evaluated, Article 1(2) of the Directive does require that where a job classification system is employed it must not discriminate on grounds of sex, and the same criteria must be applied to both men and women. This provision was considered in *Rummler*[41] which concerned the compatibility of a scheme involving criteria related to physical strength with the Directive. The Court held that the use of the criterion of muscular effort or heaviness of work is not prohibited where it is relevant to the nature of the work involved and where the system as a whole is not discriminatory. Where appropriate, the use of a criterion which is commonly associated with the attributes of one sex is not outlawed provided that the system as a whole is fairly balanced and takes into account criteria which reflect the strengths of members of the opposite sex. Where possible, the job evaluation scheme should take into account factors for which workers of each sex may show particular aptitude. In all situations, the criteria used must clearly reflect the nature of the work involved. The compatibility of the system used with the Directive is a matter for the national courts.

Comparators

Article 119 and the Directive require the provision of equal pay for equal work and this test implies the need for comparison between two jobs. The nature of this comparison and in particular the need for a comparator was considered by the European Court in *Macarthy v Smith*.[42] Wendy Smith, a stockroom manager with Macarthy's, sought equal pay with her male predecessor who had been paid at a higher weekly rate. On appeal to the Court of Appeal by Macarthy's, a number of questions concerning the scope of the concept of equal pay were referred to the European Court. The principal question related to whether equal pay for equal work, as defined in Article 119 and the Directive, required comparison with a male employee who was engaged contemporaneously with the female claimant.

---

[41] Case 237/85 *Gisela Rummler v Dato-Druck GmbH* [1986] ECR 2101.
[42] Case 129/79 *Macarthys Ltd v Smith* [1980] ECR 1275.

Mrs Smith argued that the economic and social aims of Article 119 required that the principle of equal pay should apply to workers who were unable to compare themselves to workers of the opposite sex. Otherwise the aims would be frustrated and the segregation of workers would be encouraged. Article 119 referred to "the same work" and "the same job" as forming the basis for comparison with no restriction to workers engaged at the same time. The Court held that the concept of equal work "is entirely qualitative in character and that it is exclusively concerned with the nature of the services in question"[43] and it cannot be restricted by a requirement of contemporaneity.

More ambitiously, Mrs Smith sought to introduce the concept of the hypothetical comparator into the test for equal pay. The use of this concept, however, was described by the Court as "indirect and disguised discrimination" as defined in *Defrenne* and as such it fell outside the scope of the directly effective principle of equal pay. Comparisons within Article 119 "are confined to parallels which may be drawn on the basis of concrete appraisals of the work actually performed by employees of different sex within the same establishment or service."[44]

In *Royal Copenhagen*, the Court was asked for guidance as to the composition of groups of workers used as comparators. The facts of the case were complicated with three groups of workers: turners, painters and unskilled machine operators and further subdivisions of these groups. The guidance given by the Court was very general in nature and placed the onus of assessing the appropriateness of the groups to be compared on the national court. Each group to be compared must include all of the workers who, in terms of certain factors such as type of work, working conditions and training requirements, can be considered to be in a comparable situation. The groups must comprise a relatively large number of workers and efforts must be made to ensure that "the differences are not due to purely fortuitous or short-term factors or to differences in the individual output of the workers concerned". Comparisons cannot be made between groups which are formed in an arbitrary way.

Implementation in the UK

The principle of equal pay is given effect in the UK by the Equal Pay Act 1970 which came into force on 29 December 1975, together with the Sex Discrimination Act 1975. While entry of the UK into the European Community was the immediate impetus for the introduction of legislation on equal pay, it has a much longer history. Equal pay for women had first been called for by

[43] *Ibid*, p 1288.
[44] *Ibid*, p 1289.

the TUC in 1888 and the campaign grew during the 1950s and 1960s with the TUC calling for ratification of ILO Convention 100 on equal pay in 1961. When the Labour Party came to power in 1964, it had a commitment to the principle of equal pay and, from that time, the pressure for the introduction of equal pay increased. In 1969 Barbara Castle announced that she would introduce equal pay legislation in the next session of Parliament and in May 1970 the Equal Pay Act received Royal Assent.

While the Equal Pay Act 1970 was intended to bring UK law into line with EC law, it was not introduced directly in response to Article 119 and therefore the wording and form of the Act differ in some ways from the Treaty provision. There was considerable Parliamentary debate as to the definitions to be used to give effect to the concept of equal pay for equal work. Mrs Castle stated that the Government had rejected the notion of equal value as being too vague, aiming instead to "eradicate discrimination in pay in specific identifiable situations by prescribing equally specific remedies".[45] The Act in its original form provided for equal pay in two situations: first, where a woman was engaged on like work with that of a man and, secondly, where the woman's job had been rated as equivalent under a job evaluation scheme with that of a man. The operation of this second test was dependent on the willingness of the employer to carry out such a job evaluation scheme. The Act therefore had little effect on women employed in areas of work where there were few or no men.

Doubts were raised as to the adequacy of the UK's implementation of Article 119 which required equal pay for equal work and following the further definition of the principle in Directive 75/117 and the confirmation that equal work included the concept of work of equal value, it became clear that the UK provision for equal pay was too restricted. In 1980 the Commission commenced infringement proceedings against the UK resulting in the decision of the European Court in *EC Commission* v *United Kingdom*.[46] The Commission argued that the Equal Pay Act did not implement Community law as a woman could not obtain equal pay for work of equal value unless a job evaluation scheme had been carried out by the employer. The Court confirmed that the UK had not properly implemented the principle of equal pay, in particular as women had no independent means of establishing equal value. As a result of this decision, the Equal Pay Act 1970 was amended by the Equal Pay (Amendment) Regulations 1983 which introduced the third test of "equal value".[47]

---

[45] Hansard, "Equal Pay (No 2) Bill", 2nd reading, 9 February 1970, p 917.
[46] Case 61/81 *EC Commission* v *UK* [1982] ECR 2601.
[47] Equal Pay Act 1970, s.1(2)(c).

Although the most obvious inconsistency between the UK legislation and the EC measures appeared to have been removed, a number of difficulties and uncertainties have continued to affect the interpretation of the UK legislation.

Market forces

Section 1(3) of the Equal Pay Act 1970 provides a defence to employers in equal pay claims where they can show that the variation in pay "is genuinely due to a material factor which is not the difference of sex". This defence may be raised by the employer at the initial hearing of the tribunal and, if accepted, the complaint will not proceed.

In the earlier decisions under the Equal Pay Act, it appeared that such a material factor required to be personal to the claimant and the comparator and could not include extrinsic and economic factors. The Court of Appeal in *Clay Cross*[48] held that an employer could not rely on market forces to provide objective justification of a pay differential. The House of Lords in *Rainey*[49], however, opened the way to the defence of market forces.

Mrs Rainey, a National Health service prosthetist sought equal pay with Mr Crumlin, a prosthetist who had transferred into the NHS from the private sector at a higher salary than that of Rainey. On appeal to the House of Lords by Mrs Rainey, it was held that the difference in pay was due to a genuine material difference within section 1(3) which was that the higher rate of pay was the result of a shortage of suitably qualified candidates within the NHS and the need to attract candidates from the private sector: *i.e.* market forces. The previous approach, as adopted in *Clay Cross*, that an employer could not rely on market forces to provide objective justification of a pay differential, was rejected as being too restricted.

Considerable concern was expressed at the introduction of market forces, particularly in view of the traditional undervaluation of women and women's work. The European Court has subsequently confirmed that economic justifications and market forces can be relied upon by an employer provided that he or she satisfies the proportionality test set out in *Bilka*. In *Enderby* the Court has gone further by stating that, where possible, the effect of market forces must be subject to close scrutiny in order to determine the extent to which market forces require a difference in pay. While the practical implementation of the Court's decision would pose difficulties for national courts and tribunals, it is an important ruling against the acceptance of market forces as a blanket defence. The Court has not, however, questioned the operation of market

---

[48] *Clay Cross (Quarry Services) Ltd* v *Fletcher* [1978] IRLR 361.
[49] *Rainey* v *Greater Glasgow Health Board Eastern District* [1987] 1 All ER 65.

forces and the possibility that they may be inherently discriminatory and may simply allow the perpetuation of discriminatory stereotypes.

Equal pay?

Following on from the European Court's decision in *Enderby* the question has been raised of proportional pay: can a successful applicant be awarded higher pay although she is not entitled to equal pay. From the point of literal interpretation of both the European measures and the UK legislation, it appears that only equal pay can be awarded.

There is considerable opposition to the notion of the equal pay principle being used to upset pay structures on a wider scale, and the European Court itself in *Murphy* confirmed the restricted scope of the principle by stating that Article 119 requires equal pay "solely in the case of equal work or ... in the case of work of equal value, and not in the case of work of unequal value."[50] Concern was raised in both *Kowalska* and *Nimz*, which concerned discrim- inatory provisions in collective agreements, as to the effect of the Court's finding that they were contrary to the principle of equal pay. The requirement that these provisions be equalised by the decision of the national court was feared on the basis that it would interfere with the principle of free collective bargaining. Similar concerns were raised by Wood J in the EAT in *Enderby* where he said that to engage in assessment of the precise impact of market forces on a pay difference would involve "an industrial tribunal in a wage fixing role, which was never intended and is undesirable".[51] If the European Court continues with the line of reasoning employed in *Enderby* it appears that these issues and in particular the possibility of proportionate increases in pay will have to be considered.

What is pay?

An important decision in the development of the concept of equal pay for equal value in the UK was that of the House of Lords in *Hayward*.[52] Ms Hayward established that her work as a cook was of equal value to that of a number of male tradesmen employed in the same enterprise. The industrial tribunal, EAT and Court of Appeal, however, found that she was not entitled to equal pay on the basis that her contract, as a whole, was not less favourable than the contracts of the male comparators. Although her basic rate of pay was lower, she received other contractual benefits. The House of Lords

---

[50] Case 157/86 *Murphy*, cited in note 39, *supra* at p 689.
[51] *Enderby* v *Frenchay Health Authority* [1991] ICR 392 at p 423.
[52] *Hayward* v *Cammell Laird* [1988] IRLR 257.

rejected the argument that the contract should be looked at as a remuneration package and held instead that each term of the woman's contract must be compared and equalised with that of the men. This decision gave rise to fears that the men could now seek equal terms with Ms Hayward – the process of "leap-frogging".

In *Hayward*, the possibility of a genuine material factor defence under s.1(3) was not raised but in the later case of *Leverton*[53] the House of Lords upheld the decision of the industrial tribunal that a difference in hours and holiday entitlement between the female applicant and her male comparator constituted a genuine material factor which justified the difference in pay. This decision casts doubt on the earlier decision in *Hayward* and seems to lay to rest fears of leap-frogging. The same factors are capable of use at different stages in a complaint. An increasing emphasis by employers on the provision of an "attractive remuneration package" which may include fringe benefits such as flexitime or child care vouchers may be used to justify a lower basic rate of pay.

In *Barber*, the European Court confirmed that the principle of equal pay should be applied to each element of remuneration and that remuneration should not be regarded as a package.[54] This is required from the point of view of transparency. The Court in *Royal Copenhagen* has considered the use of different terms in relation to both equal value and justification and has stated that it is for the national court to decide whether differences between two jobs should be considered as preventing the jobs from being of equal value or as factors which can provide objective justification for pay differentials.

Indirect discrimination

Neither the European measures nor the Equal Pay Act 1970 provide specifically for indirect discrimination in relation to pay. This concept was introduced into Article 119 by the European Court in *Jenkins* and developed in *Bilka* and accordingly UK courts must now attempt to interpret the domestic legislation in line with these decisions. There remains some doubt, however, as to the precise form of the test for indirect discrimination and the extent to which the domestic courts have adopted the *Bilka* approach to justification of indirect discrimination.

The concept of indirect discrimination does exist in the UK as part of the Sex Discrimination Act 1975.[55] In that context the test is that a condition or requirement must be applied equally to men and women but it is such that a

---

[53] *Leverton* v *Clwyd County Council* [1989] IRLR 28.
[54] Case C-262/88 cited in note 15, *supra*.
[55] s 1(1)(b).

substantially smaller proportion of women can comply and it is to the woman's detriment that she cannot comply. The onus of proof then shifts to the employer to show that the condition or requirement is justifiable. Should this test equally be applied to equal pay? As an effective means of eliminating practical discrimination, the test for indirect discrimination set out in the Sex Discrimination Act seems likely to prove inadequate as it is dependent on the employer having applied "a requirement or condition". It is argued that much discrimination is the result not of the practices and policies of individual employers but of structural inequalities in the labour market and in society.[56] The European Court in *Enderby* has moved away from the application of a test based on a specific requirement or obstacle but to what extent has this approach been followed in the UK courts?

The industrial tribunal in *Staffordshire County Council* v *Black*[57] applied different tests for indirect discrimination in relation to complaints raised by part-time teachers under both the Sex Discrimination Act and Article 119. On appeal, the EAT held that the test for indirect discrimination under Article 119 is the same as that under the 1975 legislation. The recent decision of the House of Lords in *Ratcliffe* v *North Yorkshire County Council*[58] seems to have made it clear that indirect discrimination in equal pay should not be based on the test in the Sex Discrimination Act. Lord Slynn of Hadley stated that the Equal Pay Act should be interpreted without a distinction between "so-called 'direct' and 'indirect' discrimination".[59] It may be argued that he was rejecting the need for a formal test of indirect discrimination as used in the 1975 Act rather than rejecting the possibility that discrimination in pay may result from the operation of an apparently gender-neutral factor. If that interpretation is correct it would bring the UK closer into line with the reasoning of the European Court in *Enderby*.

Indirect discrimination under the Sex Discrimination Act allows the employer to show that the discriminatory requirement or condition is "justifiable". There is evidence that the UK courts, while purporting on a number of occasions to be following *Bilka*, in fact interpret the notion of "justified" much less stringently than the European Court. In *Rainey*, for example, the test seemed to be closer to the notion of "sound . . . administrative reasons" than necessity, while in *Hampson* it was held that "the correct test is one which requires an objective balance to be struck between the discriminatory effect of

---

[56] For an interesting analysis of indirect discrimination see von Prondzynski and Richards, "Equal Opportunities in the Labour Market: Tackling Indirect Sex Discrimination" (1995) 1 *European Public Law* 117.

[57] *Staffordshire County Council* v *Black* [1995] IRLR 234.

[58] *Ratcliffe* v *North Yorkshire County Council* [1995] IRLR 439.

[59] *Ibid*, p 442.

the requirement or condition and the reasonable needs of the person who applies it".[60]

In 1993 both the TUC and the Equal Opportunities Commission (EOC) submitted formal complaints to the European Commission in relation to alleged breaches by the UK of Article 119 and the Equal Pay Directive. Two of the issues raised by both complaints related to access to judicial protection and remedies and the UK's failure to ensure or maintain equal pay.

Access to justice

Article 2 of the Equal Pay Directive requires Member States to introduce "such measures as are necessary to enable all employees who consider themselves wronged by failure to apply the principle of equal pay to pursue their claims by judicial process after possible recourse to other competent authorities". Both the TUC and the EOC have argued consistently that the UK has failed to provide adequate access as a result of the inordinate complexity of the legislation,[61] the delays involved particularly in relation to equal value claims, the lack of legal aid provision for industrial tribunals and the failure to provide for class actions.[62] The EOC also presented to the Government a list of specific recommendations aimed at dealing with some of these issues.[63] These recommendations included the appointment of permanent independent experts to deal with equal value claims, the provision that the EAT should become the court of first instance for cases raising important or complex questions, and a number of procedural changes which would have the result of reducing delays. Most of the recommendations were rejected although some limited amendments have now been made[64] including the requirement that an independent expert, within 14 days of being asked to report on an equal value claim, give written notice of the expected date of

---

[60] *Hampson* v *Department of Education and Science* [1989] ICR 179, per Nourse LJ at p196.

[61] The EOC has issued a draft code of practice aimed at providing practical guidance on the operation of the law relating to equal pay and on good practice: "Draft Code of Practice on equal pay – a consultative draft on practical guidance and good practice for those concerned with pay arrangements".

[62] "Request to the Commission of the European Communities by the Equal Opportunities Commission of Great Britain in relation to the implementation of the principle of equal pay". TUC Complaint 89/C26/07 (TUC, 1993). For discussion of these complaints, see "UK Equal Pay breach complaint to Europe" (1993) 51 EOR 2; "EOC looks to Europe for action over UK equal pay laws" (1993) 52 EOR 20.

[63] See "Equal pay for men and women – strengthening the Acts" (Equal Opportunities Commission, 1991).

[64] See Equal Pay Act 1970, s 2A and Complementary Rules of Procedure in Schedule 2 to the Industrial Tribunal (Constitution and Rules of Procedure) Regulations 1993 (SI 1993 No 2687); Industrial Tribunals (Constitution and Rules of Procedure) (Amendment) Regulations 1994 (SI 1994 No 536).

submission to the tribunal of this report. Expected delays must be reported, the tribunal can demand a progress report and, if necessary, the tribunal can appoint an alternative independent expert. The Government has also consulted on other procedural changes including the employment of full-time experts, the abolition of the independent expert system and the provision of bonus payments to experts who produce their reports on time.

The lack of legal aid for industrial tribunal claims is likely to place women seeking to claim equal pay at an increasing disadvantage. Their position is aggravated by the traditionally low proportion of women who are trade union members. The need for specialised representation is increased by the growing complexity of the law relating to equal pay and by the potentially significant amounts of money which may be involved following the removal of the limit on awards resulting from the decision of the European Court in *Marshall*[65] and the Sex Discrimination and Equal Pay (Remedies) Regulations.[66]

Failure to ensure equal pay

The second issue of complaint raised by both the TUC and the EOC relates to the failure of the Government to ensure and maintain equal pay as required by Article 119 and Article 6 of the Equal Pay Directive. These provisions require Member States to take measures to ensure and subsequently maintain the principle of equal pay. General evidence of this failure is provided by the continuing disparity between the pay of men and women in the UK. Statistics have consistently shown average female earnings to be approximately 75% of those of men. More specifically, the Government has been criticised for the abolition of wages councils which previously set minimum hourly rates in a number of industries.[67] In addition to setting minimum wage rates in many female dominated areas of industry, the wages councils also had the task of ensuring that the principle of equal pay was observed and both the TUC and the EOC have argued that, by their abolition, the UK Government has breached its obligations to ensure and maintain pay equality. Due to the segregation of the workforce, and the concentration of women in trades and industries previously regulated by wages councils, their abolition is likely to have a disproportionate impact on female workers and, in particular, the lowest paid.

---

[65] Case C-271/91 *Marshall* v *Southampton and South West Hants Area Health Authority (No 2)* ECR-I 4367.
[66] SI 1993 No 2798.
[67] The process of abolition was completed in 1993 as a result of s.35 of the Trade Union Reform and Employment Rights Act 1993.

Conclusions

While considerable progress has been made in legal terms since the introduction of Article 119 and all that has followed, in practice neither the legislation nor the decisions of the courts have secured equal pay for women. The Commission, in its Memorandum on Equal Pay for Work of Equal Value in 1994,[68] highlighted the need for action in a number of related areas including the improvement of data concerning female employment and pay, encouragement of dissemination of information and the provision of better training in relation to the implementation of equal pay. They also proposed the introduction of a Code of Practice. While such developments may assist in the promotion of equal pay, they will do little to change the structure of the labour market, the segregation of male and female workers and the division of labour within society.

A further area of uncertainty, and one which is likely to require interpretation and clarification by the European Court, relates to the commitment to equal pay – shown in Social Protocol to the Treaty on European Union and the annexed Agreement on social policy – by the Member States with the exception of the UK and Northern Ireland. Article 6, which reiterated the principle of equal pay, included an additional provision in paragraph 3 which provides that:

> "This Article shall not prevent any Member State from maintaining or adopting measures providing for specific advantages in order to make it easier for women to pursue a vocational activity or to prevent or compensate for disadvantages in their professional careers".

It would seem that the drafters of this provision may have had in mind some form of positive or affirmative action. Following the decision of the ECJ in *Kalanke*[69] it is clear that positive discrimination is unlawful within the Equal Treatment Directive and this decision would seem to cast doubt on the scope for development of Article 6(3) and raises questions as to the legal relationship between the Treaty, the Protocol and the Agreement.[70]

---

[68] Com (94) 6 final, 23 June 1994.
[69] Case C-450/93 *Kalanke* [1995] IRLR 660.
[70] See further discussion of *Kalanke* in chapter 3 and of the Social Protocol and Agreement in chapter 13.

Questions

1. To what extent has the ECJ accepted 'market forces' as a possible justification for pay differentials between men and women?

2. Has the ECJ now opened the door to proportionate pay increases as opposed to equal pay?

3. Is there a clear test for indirect discrimination in the context of equal pay? Is the test applied consistently by the ECJ and the national courts?

Contents of Chapter 3

EQUAL TREATMENT IN WORKING CONDITIONS

Chapter 3

EQUAL TREATMENT IN WORKING CONDITIONS

This chapter addresses the issue of equal treatment for men and women in working conditions. The main legal instrument in this area is Directive 76/207/EC which provides for equal treatment as regards access to employment, vocational training and promotion, and working conditions.[1] However, a further directive has been adopted in the area of equal treatment. Directive 86/613/EC applies the principle of equal treatment to those engaged in an activity, including agriculture, in a self-employed capacity, and on the protection of self-employed women during pregnancy and maternity.[2] In addition to these legislative instruments, which might be described as "hard law", there are a number of recommendations which also deal with equal treatment issues, the most significant being the recommendation in relation to sexual harassment at work.[3]

Background

The Equal Treatment Directive was first foreseen in the Resolution of the Council concerning a Social Action Programme of 1974.[4] That Resolution was one of the first responses of the European Community to the impact on

---

[1] OJ 1976 L39/40. For the text see Appendix.
[2] OJ 1986 L395/56. For the text see Appendix.
[3] OJ 1992 C27/4. For the text see Appendix.
[4] Council Resolution of 21 January 1974 concerning a social action programme OJ 1974 C13/1.

individuals of the recession induced by the oil crisis. Full and better employment was the goal set by the Council and this was to be achieved in part by achieving equality as regards "access to employment and vocational training and advancement and as regards working conditions". The Resolution was translated into an action programme in the course of 1974 by the creation of a Community documentation centre on women's problems as well as a permanent working group on women's employment problems. Significantly the Commission also decided to prepare a contribution to the International Women's Year (1975) which had been declared by the United Nations.[5]

The contribution of the Commission turned out to be a legislative programme which was designed to run parallel to the equal pay provisions which are discussed in the previous chapter. However, by January 1975, the Commission was unable to report to the European Parliament that any progress had been made on the draft.[6] The proposed legislation was clearly a priority for the Commission so that by February of the same year it was able to present a first draft.[7] Both the Commission's background paper and the debates in the European Parliament at the time show that the European Community wanted to be seen to make a substantial contribution to the success of International Women's Year but they make interesting reading 20 years later in that they display an almost complete shift in emphasis to the response to economic crisis and recession to that displayed in 1995. Whereas today the emphasis is on deregulation and flexibilisation of the labour market, in 1975 the emphasis was on the creation of legal norms which would facilitate the entry of women into the labour market as full time, permanent and secure employees. To the reader in 1995 it is surprising to see the views of Mr Dykes (Conservative) comparing the situation in the People's Republic of China in the provision of child care with that in the United Kingdom and concluding that urgent action is necessary to bring European standards up to those which he had witnessed on his tour to China.

The European Parliament by and large supported the Commission's draft although two issues were raised. The first related to the need for strengthened control mechanisms and the second related to social security measures. The original Commission proposal called for equal treatment in respect of working conditions which was to include social security provisions. The Parliament amended this to exclude maternity benefits, the reason being given that a full-

---

[5] See Bulletin of the European Communities, Supplement 2/74 on the Social Action Programme (1974).
[6] See the answer of Mr Clinton to Mrs Carettoni Romagnoli in EP Debates OJ(Annex) 1975 185/117 at 118.
[7] *Equality of treatment between men and women workers* COM (75) 36 final, Brussels, 12 February 1975.

scale review would be needed if these provisions were to be harmonised in the Member States.[8].

The response of the Economic and Social Council (ECOSOC) to the proposal was more radical than that of the European Parliament. ECOSOC noted the absence of provisions in relation to self employed women or women who were employed in family businesses, and hoped that these women could be covered by the Directive.[9] In the event, this suggestion was not taken up but it seems to be the origin of Directive 86/613 which was adopted ten years after this initial proposal.

Like the European Parliament, ECOSOC was concerned that the Commission's proposal omitted any reference to family policy, noting that the roles of men and women within the family were undergoing significant change, with wives and mothers increasingly taking up employment outside the home. The significance of this discussion becomes apparent in the cases brought by men in relation to paternity leave which are discussed below. From the background documentation it is clear that the Commission realised that matters of family policy did not fall within the ambit of the EC. Two other omissions were noted by ECOSOC; the absence of any reference to tax matters and of any reference to a right to work of both men and women. Personal taxation is not, of course, a matter of Community law and yet ECOSOC was quite correct to argue that taxation systems are often discriminatory in their impact. This is, however, a matter for national law. Finally, ECOSOC argued for a reversal of the burden of proof in relation to sex discrimination cases. Again this was not taken up by the Commission but a later proposal for a directive was published in 1988.[10].

Certain changes were made to the Directive before it was finally adopted in February 1976.[11] The most important changes were in relation to exclusions. Social security was withdrawn from the ambit of the Directive and was to become the object of further legislation at a later stage. The final text also allows a Member State to exclude from its field of application those jobs where sex is a determining factor and provisions relating to maternity. The Directive also allows Member States to adopt some forms of positive action and explicitly states that the principle of equal treatment applies to both direct and

---

[8] See *Report on the proposal from the Commission of the European Communities to the Council (Doc 520/74) for a directive on equality of treatment between men and women workers*, European Parliament Working Documents 1975-1976, DOCUMENT 24/75.For Parliament's Resolution and amendments see OJ 1975 C111/14.

[9] OJ 1975 C 286/8.

[10] The proposal for a Directive on the reversal of the burden of proof is to be found in OJ 1988 C176/88.

[11] The Council adopted the proposal in principle in December 1975 but did not accept the Commission's draft in full. See Bulletin of the EC, December 1975.

indirect discrimination. Two further changes oblige Member States to review any legislation in relation to excluded areas such as protective legislation in the light of changed circumstances and Member States were given slightly longer to implement the Directive – 30 months instead of 12.

Directive 76/207 and its interpretation by the European Court

The legal base for the equal treatment Directive is Article 235/EC which allows the Council to take appropriate measures, after consulting the European Parliament and acting on a proposal from the Commission, where action is needed to attain one of the objectives of the Community but where the Treaty does not provide the necessary powers. The choice of the legal base is significant as it demonstrates that the attainment of equal treatment is one of the objectives of the Community and that it is a new development in Community legislation and not merely an extension of the principle of equal pay.

The purpose of the Directive is set out in Article 1 which provides that the equal treatment principle is to be put into effect in the Member States as regards access to employment, including promotion, and to vocational training and as regards working conditions and in social security. In the case of equal treatment in social security, however, paragraph 2 states that the Council will determine the substance, scope and arrangements for its application.

Article 2 defines the principle of equal treatment as meaning that there is to be no direct or indirect discrimination on grounds of sex by reference in particular to marital or family status. Member States may define certain occupational activities and exclude them from the scope of the Directive where the sex of the worker is a determining factor. A further exception to the principle of equal treatment allows Member States to maintain in force provisions concerning the protection of women, particularly as regards pregnancy and maternity. Measures to promote equal opportunities, in particular those which remove existing inequalities, are unaffected by the principle of equal treatment in the areas covered in Article 1.

Article 3 provides for the application of the principle of equal treatment in the conditions, including selection criteria, for access to all jobs or posts, irrespective of the economic sector concerned and to all levels in the occupational hierarchy. Member States must abolish legislation or practices which are contrary to the principle of equal treatment, they must ensure that provisions in collective agreements, contracts of employment, internal rules of undertakings and the rules governing professional bodies comply with the equal treatment principle and they must revise those laws which were originally designed to protect women but which may no longer be required with a view to repeal.

Article 4 lays the same obligations on the Member States in regard to access to all types and levels of vocational guidance and vocational training and retraining.

Article 5 applies the principle of equal treatment to working conditions, including the conditions governing dismissal. This article requires that the same conditions be applied to men and women. Member States are to fulfill their obligations in respect of working conditions in the same way as for other aspects of the Directive.

Article 6 requires Member States to introduce into their national legal systems measures which allow claimants under the terms of Articles 3, 4, and 5 to pursue their claims in courts of law after possible recourse to other competent authorities.

Article 7 requires Member States to provide protection for employees against dismissal by an employer in reaction to a complaint or to legal proceedings brought against the employer.

Article 8 requires Member States to inform employees of their rights arising under the Directive and any relevant national legislation.

Article 9 gave Member States 30 months to transpose its provisions into national law (by August 1978). Within four years of its notification Member States were obliged to carry out a detailed study of protective legislation to ensure that it was necessary in the light of changing social conditions and they were further obliged to assess periodically the justification for maintaining exclusions under Article 2.

Interpretation of Directive 76/207 by the European Court – the issues

The direct effect of the Directive

The question of whether provisions of Directive 76/207 (in this case Article 5) were sufficiently clear, precise and unconditional to enable individuals to rely on these provisions in their actions before the national courts had been raised several times before the case of *Marshall* where it was finally determined that the Directive could create directly enforceable Community rights.[12] However, the Court of Justice had been able to decide these cases on the basis of the equal pay provisions. In *Marshall,* the Court was asked to decide whether an employer's policy of requiring women to retire at an earlier age than men was contrary to the equal treatment Directive and, if so, whether Ms Marshall could rely on the terms of the Directive as against her health board employer. The Court held that such a policy did contravene the Directive since Article 5 governed the question of dismissal and compulsory retirement was dismissal. The Court also held that the Directive did create direct effects and that Ms Marshall could rely on it as against her employer since that employer was part of the State. The justification for this is that the State cannot rely on its own failure to transpose directives into national law in order to avoid its obligations. This justification could not, however, apply to employers who were not part of the State and, therefore, the Court held that Directive 76/207 did not create obligations for a private sector employer.

The distinction drawn by the Court in this case is applicable to all directives and so *Marshall* is not only a case of relevance to the equal treatment Directive but is of fundamental importance to the Community legal order. The distinction has come to be known as the distinction between the horizontal and vertical direct effect of directives. Directives are only capable of creating obligations for Member States (vertical direct effect) whereas Treaty provisions, such as Article 119, create obligations for both the state and individuals (horizontal direct effects). In employment matters this distinction means that where an individual is employed by the State he/she can rely directly on those provisions in directives which are clear, precise and unconditional as against his/her employer but an individual employed in the private sector cannot. The fact that this creates an anomaly is not a fault inherent in Community law, according to the Court, but is attributable to the fact that the Member State has failed to implement Community law. The solution is correct implementation.

In *Marshall,* the Court stated that it was the task of the national court to apply its considerations to the cases which come before it to determine whether or not an individual can rely on a directive against a particular employer. Whether such an employer is part of the State is a question of fact.

The compulsory retirement of women was also in issue in *Foster* in which the English court sought guidance as to how to make the determination of whether or not a particular employer can be categorised as being part of the

---

[12] Case 152/84 *Marshall* v *Southampton and South West Area Health Authority (Teaching)* [1986] ECR 723. In case 222/84 *Marguerite Johnston* v *Chief Constable of the RUC* [1986] ECR 1651 the Court held that the provisions in Articles 3 and 4 were also capable of creating direct effects.

State for the purposes of the direct effect of directives.[13] Ms Foster had been employed in a nationalised industry, British Gas, which had subsequently been privatised. Could she rely on the direct effect of Article 5? The UK government argued that the national court should determine the categories of persons against whom an individual could plead the direct effects of directives. The European Court disagreed and held that the determination of such categories was a question of interpretation of the Treaty, therefore a matter within its jurisdiction. The function of the national court is to decide whether a particular body falls within such categories.

The Court held that a body, irrespective of its legal form which (a) has been made responsible, pursuant to a measure adopted by the State, for providing a public service under the control of the State and (b) has special powers beyond those normally applicable in relations between individuals, is among those bodies against which the provisions of a directive may be relied upon.

Indirect effects

The interpretation of Directive 76/207 gave the European Court its opportunity to lay down the important guiding principle to the courts of the Member States as to how they should interpret national law in the face of a provision of a Directive which was not sufficiently precise to allow for direct effect.

The Court was asked whether Article 6 of the Directive which requires the Member States to introduce into national law measures which are necessary to ensure that individuals who claim a breach of the Directive, can create direct effects.[14] In *von Colson*, the Court was asked whether the refusal to hire two female candidates for a post in a prison was contrary to the equal treatment Directive and whether the German law which provided that individuals could be compensated only to the extent of their actual losses incurred was contrary to Article 6. The Court was also asked to determine whether Article 6 could create direct effects. The Court held that the Directive did not require that specific sanctions should be adopted by the Member States but that the choice of sanctions was within their discretion. However, any sanction must be such as to guarantee real and effective judicial protection. If compensation is the chosen sanction, then that compensation must be "adequate" in relation to the damage sustained. It is for the national court and all the national authorities to interpret the provisions of national law to ensure fulfilment of the obligation in Article 6. Therefore, even although Article 6 does not create

---

[13] Case C-188/89 *Foster* v *British Gas* [1990] I ECR 3313.
[14] Cases 14/83 *Sabine von Colson and Elisabeth Kamann* v *Land Nordrhein-Westfalen* [1984] ECR 1891 and 79/83 *Dorit Harz* v *Deutche Tradax GmbH* [1984] ECR 1921.

direct effects in the sense of demanding specific remedies, the national court must interpret the relevant national legislation in the "light of the wording and purpose of the Directive in order to achieve" its binding effects.[15]. In doing so the national court must bear in mind that where compensation is the method chosen to penalise breaches of the principle of equal treatment then compensation must be at such a level to ensure that it has a deterrent effect and it is effective to achieve the aims of the Directive.

National remedies

It is clear from *von Colson* that national remedies lie within the discretion of the Member States subject to the proviso that any such remedies must be effective and have a deterrent effect. The question of effectiveness was raised by Ms Marshall after her successful challenge to her employer's decision to retire her at the age of 63. Ms Marshall challenged the statutory limits for compensation laid down in the UK Sex Discrimination Act.[16] The Court examined the available options which could be followed to restore equality in the event of a discriminatory dismissal contrary to Article 5(1). This could either be done, said the Court, by re-instating the victim or by granting financial compensation for the loss and damage suffered. A statutory limitation, by definition, could not achieve this equality of opportunity. Only adequate compensation, including the award of interest where relevant, could meet this test. Furthermore, the provisions of Articles 5 and 6 together were sufficient to give a right to an individual to adequate compensation for dismissal in an action against an employer which is part of the State.[17]

Substantive issues

Scope

Directive 76/207 introduces the principle of equal treatment for men and women. The European Court has not had occasion to determine whether it applies to discrimination against individuals on the basis of their sexual

---

[15] The wording of the Court was repeated in case 222/84 *Johnston* cited in note 12 *supra*.

[16] Case C-271/91 *Marshall* v *Southampton and South West Area health Authority* [1993] CMLR 293.

[17] Following this case the UK amended its legislation in respect of compensation for breaches of the Sex Discrimination Act in the Sex Discrimination and Equal Pay (Remedies) Regulations 1993, SI 1993/2798.

preference,[18] although it has been recently asked whether the Directive prohibits discrimination against a transsexual.[19]

Both direct and indirect discrimination are prohibited under the terms of the Directive although the terms are not defined. The two major issues which have arisen in respect of the distinction between direct and indirect discrimination relate to the rights of part-time workers and pregnant workers. These issues are dealt with in separate chapters in this book.[20]

Exclusion of social security (Article 1)

As noted above, the Commission's original proposal for a Directive on equal treatment included a reference to equal treatment in matters of social security. The Council, however, rejected this proposal and instead included social security subject to the proviso that it would, acting on a future proposal from the Commission, adopt provisions defining its scope and substance.[21] In a series of cases, the Court held that Directive 76/207 was not intended to apply to social security but in a recent case the Court has changed this approach.[22] In *Meyers*, the Court held that the conditions for the award of family credit in the UK are covered by Article 5 of Directive 76/207 in so far as family credit is intended to encourage individuals to take up low paid jobs without lowering their standard of living.[23] Article 1 did not exclude family credit from the ambit of the equal treatment principle. As such, Member States are obliged to ensure that the equal treatment principle applies to the regulations governing access to family credit. In interpreting Article 1 in this way, the Court insisted that exceptions and derogations to the principle of equal treatment must be construed narrowly as this principle is a fundamental principle of Community law. This approach is similar to that taken by the Court in interpreting the exceptions in Article 2.

---

[18] Although the English courts have held that the Directive does not apply in such cases. In *R* v *Minister of Defence ex parte Smith and others* the English High Court (per Simon Brown LJ) said that the Directive "is an instrument which says everything about gender discrimination . . . nothing about orientation discrimination". In this judgment Jacques Delors is quoted as saying that "The Community has no power to intervene in respect of possible discrimination by the Member States against sexual minorities". The case is discussed in 524 Industrial Relations Law Bulletin (1995) 9. In November 1995, the Court of Appeal upheld the decision of the High Court.

[19] Case *P and S* v *Cornwall* (not yet decided). The Court has been asked whether the dismissal of a transsexual for a reason related to gender reassignment constitutes a breach of the Directive and whether Article 3 prohibits unequal treatment of an employee on grounds of that employee's transsexual state. Discussed in EOR *Discrimination Case Law Digest* No 21 (1994).

[20] See chapters 6 and 7 *infra*.

[21] This legislation is the subject of chapters 4 and 5 *infra*.

[22] See Chapter 4 for a discussion of the Court's approach.

[23] Case C-116/94 *Meyers* v *Chief Adjudication Officer* [1995] IRLR 498.

Derogations from the equal treatment principle – sex as a determining factor Article 2(2)

The Commission brought an action against the UK alleging that the limitation on the training of male midwives in Schedule 4 of the Sex Discrimination Act was contrary to Article 2 of the Directive.[24] The UK argued that Article 2 allowed an exception to the principle of equal treatment and this exception allowed the Member States to take into consideration respect for the sensitivities of certain female patients. The UK recognised the necessity to keep such provisions under review in order to decide whether social developments required them. The Court accepted the argument of the UK and held that in this respect the UK had not failed to comply with the requirements of the Directive. In this same case, the Commission complained of the exclusion within the Sex Discrimination Act of the prohibition of discrimination in the case of employment in a private household or in undertakings which employ less than five people. The Court accepted that certain occupations within a private household may be reserved to one sex only but objected to the generality of the UK provision. In respect of small undertakings, the Court observed that the UK had failed to provide any justification for this exclusion. Consequently, section 6(3) of the Sex Discrimination Act was held to be incompatible with the equal treatment Directive.

This case does not sit well with a later case referred to the European Court on whether German law which exempts small businesses from the legislation on unfair dismissal was contrary to Article 2 of the Directive.[25] For the purpose of defining what is a small business, employees who work less than ten hours per week are excluded from the calculation. The European Court accepted that national law involves indirect discrimination where, although the law is formulated in a neutral way, it disadvantages a much higher percentage of women than men, unless that difference can be objectively justified. However, it rejected the view that failing to take account of part-time workers in the determination of what is a small business could be shown to disadvantage a higher percentage of women since it had not been established that a higher percentage of women than men worked in small businesses. The Court held that indirect discrimination could only be shown "if it were established that small businesses employ a considerably greater number of women than men". This generous approach of the European Court to small businesses is explained by its acceptance that the rationale behind the legislation was "to alleviate the constraints on small businesses, which play an

---

[24] Case 165/82 *Commission v United Kingdom* [1983] ECR 3431.
[25] Case C-189/91 *Kirshammer-Hack v SIDAL* [1994] IRLR 185.

essential role in economic development and job-creation within the Community". However, if it were demonstrated that the national provisions did indeed discriminate against women (the Advocate General pointed to the inadequacy of the statistical data) then such a rationale must give way to the principle of equal treatment since this is recognised as being a fundamental principle of Community law.

Germany was however found to have breached Article 2 as a result of an action brought by the Commission.[26] In this case the Court held that Article 2 of the Directive permits Member States to exclude some occupational activities from the scope of the equal treatment principle and that such exclusions are within the discretion of each Member State. However, Article 2 must be read in conjunction with Article 9 of the Directive and that Article requires the Member States to re-assess all exclusions periodically and to justify them to the satisfaction of the Commission. In order to do this Member States must compile a list of exclusions and submit this list to the Commission. Germany had never done this and had therefore prevented the Commission from exercising effective supervision and was therefore in breach of its Community law obligations.

France maintained that its system of recruitment to certain posts in the civil service was not contrary to Article 2 of the Directive. However, the Commission disagreed and brought an action against France arguing that the exclusion of certain posts in the prison and police service was contrary to Article 2.[27] The Court upheld the complaint of the Commission holding that Article 2 requires that the exceptions provided for in that Article must be for specified functions rather than for categories of staff, that all exceptions must be transparent so as to allow the Commission to exercise its supervisory function and also that all exceptions must be capable of being adapted to changing social conditions. The French system of recruitment into "corps" and then subjecting such "corps" to sexual quotas did not meet the requirements of the Directive.

Derogations – protection as regards pregnancy Article 2(3)

Article 2(3) of the Directive provides that the equal treatment principle is without prejudice to protection of women, particularly as regards pregnancy and maternity. The Court has held that this derogation must be construed strictly. In *Johnston*[28] the Court was asked whether the derogations in Article 2

---

[26] Case 248/83 *Commission* v *Germany* [1985] ECR 1459.
[27] Case 318/86 *Commission* v *France* [1988] ECR 3559.
[28] Case 222/84 *Johnston* cited in note 12 supra.

allowed the Chief Constable of the RUC to decide not to renew the contracts of female members of the RUC full-time reserve on the grounds that women police officers did not carry firearms. They were not trained to carry firearms because of the desire to protect women against the risks of assassination. The Court held first of all that there is no general derogation available to Member States to enable them to introduce measures for the protection of women on grounds of public security. However, in the context of policing in Northern Ireland the Court held that the UK was permitted to consider the sex of the officer as a determining factor for a particular post. The exercise of this discretion was, however, tempered by Article 9 of the Directive which requires the Member States to assess periodically the activity concerned in order to decide whether the derogation from the general scheme is permissible. Such derogations must, however, be subject to the general principle of proportionality and it is for the national court to determine whether the reasons behind the policy are well founded.

The concern for protection which is covered by Article 2 (3) was also discussed by the Court. Mrs Johnston argued that this provision was solely related to pregnancy and maternity. The Court agreed that this provision must be interpreted strictly stating that the Directive is "intended to protect a woman's biological condition and the special relationship which exists between a woman and her child". In the present case the derogation could not apply. This formula in relation to Article 2 (3) has been repeated several times by the Court so it is clear that other aspects of protective legislation would fall under Articles 3 to 5.[29]

Derogations – positive action Article 2 (4)

The French system of special rights for women was also subject to scrutiny by the European Court.[30] Under the French system, collective agreements could contain provisions, such as additional days leave for mothers, time off on Mothers Day, shorter working hours for women over 59 or obtaining leave when a child was ill. The Commission argued that some of these terms may be justified under the Directive but the generality of the Law in question which allowed for "special rights for women" to remain in force was contrary to

---

[29] See, for example, the discussion on night work below. The UK government introduced Regulations in February 1995 amending the general ban on the employment of women in the armed forces which is contained in the Sex Discrimination Act 1975. The new Regulations bar women "for the purpose of ensuring the combat effectiveness of the naval, military or air forces of the Crown". The government has been warned by both the Equal Opportunities Commission and the Joint Lords and Commons Committee on Statutory Instruments that these regulations go beyond what is possible in terms of the derogations in Article 2 of the Directive. See *The Observer* 1 October 1995.

[30] Case 312/86 *Commission* v *France* [1988] ECR 6315.

Article 2 of the Directive and the Court agreed. Furthermore, the Court did not accept the view offered by the French government that, as the provisions in question were governed by collective agreements rather than legislation, that the most appropriate method of achieving equality was to leave the matter to both sides of industry to negotiate out special rights. France was, therefore, found to be in breach of Community law.

Most recently, the Court has been asked to decide whether a "tie-break" rule is contrary to Article 2(4) which provides that priority has to be given to a female candidate where two candidates are equally qualified for the post but where women make up less than 50% of a particular category of employment. In *Kalanke* the Court held that Article 2(4) did not justify a rule which guaranteed absolute and unconditional priority to females, even where the female candidate in question was equally well qualified as the male and women were under-represented in management positions. The Court held that the Directive has only a precise and limited aim and only authorises national measures which favour women in the sense of improving their ability to compete in the labour market. Following this decision, the Commission has indicated that it will issue a Communication on positive action which will stress that only rigid quotas were outlawed by this ruling and that the Commission would seek an amendment to Directive 76/207 to reflect the need for positive action in favour of women.[31]

Equal treatment in access to vocational training, guidance and retraining (Article 4)

The provision in Article 4 of the Directive which requires Member States to ensure that collective agreements comply with the principle of equal treatment (and *mutatis mutandis* the decision of the Court would apply to Articles 3 and 5) was raised in the case brought against the UK which is discussed above.[32] The Commission alleged that by failing to ensure that collective agreements complied with the equal treatment principle, the UK had failed to fulfill its obligation to transpose the Directive into UK law. The UK argued that collective agreements were not legally binding in the UK legal order and therefore that there had been no failure on its part. The Court rejected this view. It held that the Directive applies to all collective agreements without distinction as to their legal effects since collective agreements have important *de facto* effects on the parties concerned.

---

[31] Case C-450/93 *Kalanke* v *Freie Hansestadt Bremen*, Decision of the Court of 17 October 1995. The reaction of Commissioner Padraig Flynn is noted in Reuters News Service, 24 November 1995.
[32] Case 165/82 cited in note 24 *supra*.

Working conditions – maternity/paternity leave

Directive 76/207 is not intended to settle questions about the organisation of the family or to alter the division of responsibilities within it. In *Hofmann* the Court held, therefore, that Member States may offer maternity leave to women where paternity leave is not offered to men.[33] The basis for this argument of the Court was that there is a natural bonding process between a woman and her child and Member States may take steps to allow for this process even after the woman has recovered from the effects of childbirth.

Working conditions – dismissal

The fixing of different pensionable ages in the UK and the exclusion of provisions relating to death and retirement from the ambit of the Sex Discrimination Act led to cases being brought to the European Court from several UK courts. In *Burton*[34] the Court was asked whether the same conditions of access to voluntary redundancy should be available to men and women. In this case access to voluntary redundancy was only available within five years of the employee attaining the pensionable age which was different for men and women. The Court held that Article 5 applies to such conditions of access but that Community law does not prohibit the determination of different pensionable ages. Fixing access to voluntary redundancy to the pensionable age was not, therefore, contary to Article 5.

In *Roberts*[35] the Court was asked whether Article 5 would apply in the circumstances of a scheme of mass redundancy in which early access to the ocupational pension scheme was provided for. Mrs Roberts was dismissed at 53 and she would normally have access to her occupational pension at 60, i.e. seven years later. A man of 53 would normally gain access to the benefits under the scheme at 65, i.e. 12 years later. Mrs Roberts argued that the men were advantaged by gaining their pension earlier. The Court held that conditions as regards redundancy, even where these related to occupational pensions, fell under the terms of Article 5 of Directive 76/207 and not under Directive 79/7 relating to equal treatment in social security since redundancy was dismissal. However, a redundancy scheme which lays down a single age for redundancy for men and women does not violate Article 5 even though this may have implications for the date of access to pensions.

---

[33] Cases 163/82 *Commission* v *Italian Republic* [1983] ECR 3273; 184/33 *Ulrich Hofmann* v *Barmer Ersatzkasse* [1984] ECR 3047. The Commission has proposed that a Directive be adopted on leave for family reasons.
[34] Case 19/81 *Burton* v *British Railways Board* [1982] ECR 555.
[35] Case 151/84 *Joan Roberts* v *Tate and Lyle Industries Ltd* [1986] ECR 703.

In *Marshall*[36] the Court held that a differential compulsory retirement age for men and women amounted to discrimination within the meaning of Article 5 since this was a condition in respect of dismissal. This is so, said the Court, even where the dismissal brings with it the grant of an occupational pension and despite the fact that national legislation provides an exception to provisions relating to death or retirement. In this case the Directive could be used by Ms Marshall in challenging her compulsory retirement since her employer was part of the British State and the European Court held that under these circumstances the Directive created direct effect. Such an action could not be brought by an employee against an employer in the private sector.

Working conditions – night work

One problem which has come to light in the interpretations given by the Court on the meaning of Article 5 has been that of the relationship between this Article and provisions of international treaties to which the Member States may be parties. Three cases brought the attention of the Court to a potential conflict of rules to be applied by a Member State when legislating in the area of night-work for women.[37] These cases involved the Court in interpreting the derogation in Article 2(3) in favour of protective legislation, particularly as regards pregnancy and motherhood and Article 5 which relates to equal treatment in working conditions. As noted above, the Court had already held that Article 5 was capable of creating direct effects.

In *Stoeckel* the question at issue was French legislation which prohibited night-work for women with certain exceptions to this prohibition defined by law or set out in collective agreements. The law in question had been adopted to bring French law into conformity with Convention No. 89 of the International Labour Office (ILO) which had been opened for ratification in 1948. The French law had been adopted in September 1953 prior to the Treaty of Rome (1957) which established the EEC and certainly prior to the adoption of Directive 76/207. At the material date in this case France had not denounced the ILO Convention.[38]

Mr Stoeckel was prosecuted under French law for employing women in his audio cassette packing factory at 12.30 a.m. contrary to the *Code de Travail*. He argued that the provisions of the *Code de Travail* were contrary to Article 5 of the Directive and the *Tribunal de Police* referred a question to the Court asking

---

[36] Case 152/84 *Marshall* cited in note 12 *supra*.
[37] Cases C-345/89 France v *Stoeckel [1993] ECR 3* ; *C-158/91 Ministere Public et Direction du Travail et de l'Emploi* v *Levy* [1994] IRLR 138; C-13/93 *Office National de l'Emploi* v *Madeleine Minne* [1994] ECR I-371.
[38] France denounced this Convention on 26 February 1992.

whether Article 5 imposes an obligation on a State not to lay down in its legislation the principle that night-work for women is prohibited. The Court held that protective legislation is valid only if there is a justified need for a difference in treatment between men and women. The justifications offered by the French government that women could be attacked at night or that they had family responsibilities were not sufficient to maintain in force a blanket prohibition. The fact that there could be exceptions did not bring French law into line with Article 5 of the Directive. Article 5, therefore, required Member States not to lay down such legislation. Anyone reading this case would, therefore, assume that Mr Stoeckel and other employers in his situation would have a valid Euro-defence to a criminal conviction.

Mr Levy was such an employer. He was prosecuted under French law for employing women in his pork manufacturing business. He argued that he had a valid Euro-defence based on Article 5. The Police Court was not so sure and it referred a question to the European Court which specifically asked what account France should take of ILO Convention No. 89. The Court reaffirmed what it had said in *Stoeckel* that Article 5 in principle prohibits a Member State from legislating to prohibit night work for women where it does not do so for men and it follows from this that the national judge must refuse to apply any conflicting national provision. Whether the judge must do so where there is a conflict between Article 5 and a prior obligation assumed by the State under an international Treaty is, however, a different matter.

Here the Court turned to Article 234/EC which provides that rights and obligations arising from agreements concluded by Member States before the entry into force of the EEC Treaty shall not be affected by the provisions of the latter. However, Article 234 (2) obliges the Member States to take all appropriate steps to eliminate the incompatibilities established between an agreement and the Treaty. Member States are, therefore, obliged to respect the rights of third parties arising out of an earlier obligation. In the case of the ILO Convention, third states could expect France not to lower its protective standards as this might create a comparative advantage for France as against third states. Under these circumstances, the obligation on the national judge is to give full effect to Article 5 of the Directive and not apply any contrary rule of national law unless the application of such a rule is "necessary" in order to ensure that the Member State concerned fulfils its obligations arising out of an agreement concluded with a non-member country before the entry into force of the EEC Treaty. Did Mr Levy have a Euro-defence?

The Court left this decision to the national judge who was to determine to what extent Convention No. 89 required the type of legislation adopted in France. The choice of the word "necessary" by the Court does imply a fairly stringent test. Presumably, if the national judge decided that the legislation was not necessary, for example, there may be alternative ways of achieving equality and prohibiting night work such as a total ban, then he or she must apply Article 5. Mr Levy's Euro-defence was, however, not guaranteed.

The ILO Convention had been raised as an issue in *Stoeckel* but the Court had not taken the arguments into consideration. The Advocate General had suggested that Article 234 could not be used in such a way as to allow a Member State to evade its obligation to ensure the principle of equal treatment. He had argued that Community law does not require Member States to allow women to work at night, it only prevents discrimination. The answer for France would be to prohibit night work for all or to denounce the Convention. In fact, France later denounced the Convention.

The *Levy* approach was also taken by the Court in the Belgian case of *Minne*. Mrs Minne, who was unemployed, refused to accept catering work offered to her on the grounds that she would have to work at night and could not do so for family reasons. The authorities said that she had refused suitable employment and excluded her from unemployment benefits. She brought an action to have that decision set aside and was successful on the grounds that Belgian law prohibited night work. At the relevant time, Belgian law prohibited night work for men and women but there were numerous exceptions which were more "generous" to men in that there was a wider range of exceptions for them. There was a prohibition on women, but not men, on working at night in hotel and catering. The national legislation was adopted by Belgium to comply with the ILO Convention. The Court was asked whether discrimination in the range of derogations was prohibited by Article 5.

The Court held that the maintenance in force of more restrictive conditions for women than men in the derogations from the prohibition of night work did indeed infringe Article 5, where these derogations could not be justified on the need to ensure protection of the woman's biological condition in pregnancy or by the special relationship between a mother and her child. However, Article 5 cannot apply to the extent that national provisions were intended to ensure performance by a Member State of its obligations entered into before the entry into force of the EEC Treaty. It is the national court which must ascertain the extent of those international obligations. Belgium, in fact, had denounced the Convention in order to comply with its Community obligations but that denunciation only took effect in February 1993 after the material time in this case.

These cases demonstrate that the national judge is faced with a difficult task in applying Community provisions where there is a conflict with an existing prior obligation entered into with third states. The national judge must choose between two conflicting rules (at least two – if French or Belgian law had incorrectly implemented the ILO Convention there would be three) and apply the law to the facts before him or her. What the European Court has said is that prior international obligations take precedence over directly effective

Community provisions. National legislation implementing such obligations is not, therefore, subject to the rule of supremacy of Community law.[39]

Implementation in the United Kingdom

Implementation of the equal treatment Directive has not been without its problems in the UK. In 1975, the year before the equal treatment Directive was adopted, the UK Sex Discrimination Act came into force.[40] That legislation was intended to pursue the same type of objectives as those covered in the Directive but, in fact, there were significant differences in the UK and the European approach. These differences gradually came to light. However, it was the view of the UK that no new legislation or amendments to existing legislation were required in order to implement the Directive.

In 1981, the Commission drew up a report on the principle of equal treatment within all the existing Member States of the Community and this report highlighted those areas where UK law and European law diverged.[41] The most significant differences lay in the definition of equal treatment and of indirect discrimination, the absence of a reference to marital or family status in UK legislation, the extent of UK exclusions and the failure of the national legislation to cover collective agreements.

UK legislation does not use the definition of discrimination contained in the Directive. Instead, the Sex Discrimination Act Section 1(1) and the corresponding provision of the Northern Ireland Order (Section 3 (1)) draw a distinction between direct and indirect discrimination. Direct discrimination occurs where a person of one sex is treated less favourably than a person of the other sex in areas covered by the Act and Order whereas indirect discrimination occurs where a requirement or condition is applied to both sexes but the effect of the requirement or condition is to disadvantage one sex and is not justifiable. In both cases UK law requires a comparison between the relevant circumstances. Direct discrimination is outlawed but indirect discrimination may be justifiable. The legislation does not specify the tests to be applied to

[39] The Member State will, however, be in breach of its Community obligations if it fails to take all the necessary action to comply with the Community rule i.e. Member States should denounce the ILO Convention if their legislation results in discrimination. At the time of writing, Greece and Italy appear not to have denounced the ILO Convention.
[40] In Northern Ireland the Sex Discrimination (Northern Ireland) Order came into effect in July 1976.
[41] *Report from the Commission to the Council on the situation at 12 August 1981 with regard to the implementation of the principle of equal treatment for men and women*, COM(80) 832 final, Brussels, 11 February 1981.

determine what is or is not justifiable, leaving this to be determined by the courts. Furthermore, UK legislation contains no reference to family status and the EOC reported that UK courts do not automatically include direct or indirect sex discrimination by reference to marital or family status as being within the scope of the legislation.

In fact, the Commission did not raise infringement proceedings against the UK for failing to reconcile the definitions within the UK legislation with that of the Directive, effectively leaving the UK courts to reconcile the differences in approach. This has led the UK courts in the past to come to conclusions in relation to questions of discrimination opposite to those arrived at by the European Court of Justice when it has been asked to interpret provisions of the Directive, leaving the UK courts to backtrack. The clearest example of this is in relation to pregnancy dismissal.[42]

Ellis has argued that the approach of the European Court to the concepts of direct and indirect discrimination demonstrates a better understanding than that of UK courts as to what sex equality law is trying to do.[43] However, it can be argued against this position that the difference in approach is the result of different definitions being provided within the Act and the Directive and it is only with the benefit of European Court interpretations of the Directive that UK courts can now attempt a rather more sophisticated approach to concepts of discrimination than that provided in the legislation itself.

An example of the way in which the UK courts and tribunals have been able successfully to interpret the provisions in the Sex Discrimination Act in the light of the rulings of the European Court on objective justification in cases relating to indirect discrimination is the case of *Meade-Hill*.[44] Here the Court of Appeal was asked to make a declaration that a mobility clause in a woman's contract which required an employee to serve in such parts of the UK as the employer requires was unenforceable on the grounds of sex discrimination. The Court of Appeal was asked to interpret section 77(2) of the Sex Discrimination Act in the light of the Equal Treatment Directive and the Court did so making reference to the Directive and the interpretations given by the European Court on the concept of indirect discrimination.[45] The simplest

---

[42] For a full discussion see Chapter 7 *infra*.

[43] Ellis "Discrimination in European Community Sex Equality Law" 19 *European Law Review* (1994) 563.

[44] *Meade-Hill and National Union of Civil and Public Servants* v *British Council* [1995] IRLR 478.

[45] However, compare this case with that of *Bhudi and others* v *IMI Refiners Ltd* [1994] IRLR 204 where the EAT stated that the equal treatment Directive did not require a UK court to construe the Sex Discrimination Act so as to disregard the provision in section 1(1)(b) relating to proof of a requirement or condition. See the comment on this case by Rubenstein in the case reports.

solution to this problem is to bring UK law into line with the Directive and to use the same concept of direct and indirect discrimination. No legislative proposals have been put forward on this matter despite calls from the EOC.[46]

The Sex Discrimination Act was amended, however, in 1986 following the case brought against the UK and the cases involving Ms Marshall. The Sex Discrimination Act 1986 repealed those sections of the 1975 Act which excluded small undertakings and private households except where there was a genuine occupational qualification in terms of the degree of physical intimacy or social contact.[47] It also repealed the provisions of the 1975 Act in terms of the exclusion of partnerships of six partners or less. The 1986 Act also amended the provisions relating to retirement, and in particular, discrimination in relation to retirement age which was raised to 65 in so far as employees were concerned. The Act did not, however, equalise the normal pensionable age for the purposes of receiving the old age pension. This has now been done by way of the 1995 Pensions Act.[48] The 1986 Act also addressed the problem of discriminaion in collective agreements by making it illegal to include in a collective agreeent any provision which would operate against the principle of equal treatment. Finally the Act repealed provisions in earlier legislation which had been aimed at the protection of female workers in relation to hours of work, employment in bakeries, in mines and quarries and in factories. This amendment was in line with the obligation on the UK to review its provisions relating to protective legislation in the light of social trends to determine whether it was necessary. By 1986, the UK had no special legislation protecting women as a group.

One final issue remained to be determined in the UK and that was the question of availablity and adequacy of national remedies for breach of the sex discrimination provisions. Ms Marshall had successfully challenged the provisions in the Equal Pay and Sex Discrimination Acts which placed a statutory limitation on the amount of available compensation. The European Court had held in *Marshall II* that such a limitation by definition could not meet the requirements of Community law that national remedies must have a deterrent effect and, in cases of dismissal, must provide for re-instatement or compensation. The UK accordingly amended its legislation to remove the statutory limitations leaving the tribunal to determine the level of compensation to be

---

[46] For example in the EOC reports *Equal treatment for men and women; strengthening the acts* (1988) and *Legislating for change* (1986).

[47] The Sex Discrimination Act 1986 chapter 59.

[48] The Pensions Act 1995 chapter 26. This issue is discussed in chapters 4 and 5 *infra*.

awarded in any particular case.[49] In the UK some very high awards have been made to servicewomen who were dismissed on becoming pregnant.[50]

The equal treatment Directive has, therefore, had a major impact on the sex discrimination laws in the UK. It has led to significant legislative amendments and the decisions of the European Court have proved to be very influential in the way in which UK courts approach concepts of indirect discrimination and in the interpretation of UK legislation. What is still needed in the UK is a rationalisation of the legislation to bring it fully into line with European law in the interests of clarity and certainty on the part of employees, employers and tribunals.

The self-employed Directive (86/613/EC)

Directive 86/613/EC on the application of the principle of equal treatment between men and women engaged in an activity, including agriculture, in a self-employed capacity, and on the protection of self-employed women during pregnancy and motherhood was adopted on the basis of Articles 100 and 235/EC. The Directive is intended to complement Directive 76/207 and to extend the principle of equal treatment to the self-employed. However, the Directive also provides a framework in which the Member States can develop legislation by recognising the needs of a particular category of persons who have not hitherto been able to claim employment related rights. The Directive provides for those women who work in family firms such as shops, farms or small businesses. Such women often receive little pay and very often little recognition for their efforts.[51] The preamble to the Directive demonstrates that it is intended to cover specific groups of people who are not covered by Directive 76/207 (i.e. are not employees) and those members of the working population not covered by Directive 79/7 on equal treatment in social security.

The personal scope of the Directive extends to all self-employed persons, a term which is defined to include those who pursue a gainful activity for their own account, including farmers and members of the liberal professions. It also includes their spouses, except employees or partners, where they participate in

---

[49] The Regulations are cited in note 17 *supra*.
[50] These cases are discussed in chapter 7 *infra* and in Arnull "EC law and the dismissal of pregnant servicewomen" (1995) *Industrial Law Journal* 215. The Regulations entered into force on 22 November 1993 but the EAT has held that they apply to awards made by tribunals from that date even though the dismissal took place before the Regulations were adopted see *Harvey* v *Institute of the Motor Industry* (No 2) 525 *Industrial Relations Law Bulletin* (1995) 14.
[51] In the UK, for example, women who work in family businesses do not appear in the government statistical returns on the workforce.

the activities of the self-employed partner and perform the same or ancillary tasks – the farmer and his/her spouse, for example, when the spouse works on the farm. The term applied by the Commission is "assisting spouses" for this category of persons.[52]

Article 4 of the Directive requires Member States to ensure the elimination of discrimination in respect of the establishment, equipment or extension of a business and in its financing. This Article would, for example, outlaw the restriction of lending facilities to a person on the basis of their sex or their marital status.

Article 5 requires Member States to abolish the prohibition on spouses being partners in a company so that the same conditions must apply to married couples as apply to other partnerships. The Commission's explanatory memorandum on this Directive shows that this provision is designed to encourage family businesses to be run as partnerships so as to recognise the contribution of both spouses.[53] This provision also provides protection for spouses on dissolution of marriage due to divorce. Very often, women who had no assets in a family business would find themselves in a difficult financial position when they divorced. The pooling of resources in the family business would put them onto an equal footing in the event of divorce.

Article 6 provides that Member States must provide a mechanism for the spouses of self-employed persons to have access to any contributory social security scheme where they are not already covered by the protection offered by the scheme to which their spouse is a party.

Article 7 obliges Member States to attempt to find ways in which to recognise the contribution of the work of spouses of self-employed persons. This Article can only be explained in the light of the Commission's explanatory memorandum on the Directive which set out the original proposal. Four areas of action were recommended: recognition of the consideration in respect of work performed; the right to build up entitlements in respect of social security; the right to be enrolled in relevant professional organisations, and the right to vote and stand for election in such organisations. As it stands, however, the Directive on this point is so vague as to be meaningless in any attempt to translate it into national law.

Article 8 requires Member States to examine whether and how women, self-employed workers and wives of self-employed workers should have access to services supplying temporary replacements or national social services and to

---

[52] *Report from the Commission on the implementation of Council Directive . . . 86/613/EEC* COM (94) 163 final of 15 September 1994.

[53] *Proposal for a Council Directive on the principle of equal treatment for men and women in self-employed occupations, including agriculture, and on protection during pregnancy and maternity*, COM (84) 57 final of 13 March 1984.

entitlements to cash benefits under social security and social protection schemes.

The general provisions of the Directive require the Member States to ensure that recourse to a judicial remedy is available to any person who believes that the provisions have been violated. The measures taken to implement the Directive are to be brought to the attention of bodies representing self-employed workers and vocational training centres. The Directive was to be reviewed by the Commission by 1 July 1993.[54] Two separate dates were given for the transposition of the Directive into national law. Where amendments were required to existing matrimonial law, the date of transposition was June 1991. In all other cases, the date of transposition was June 1989. This difference of dates was in recognition of the difficulties inherent in making changes to fundamental areas of private law in the Member States.

Directive 86/613 has not, to date, been the subject of any actions before the European Court of Justice. The interpretation of its provisions is still to be determined. However, given the wide sweep of some of the provisions, it is probably true to state that Member States have a great deal of flexibility in the way in which the Directive is to be implemented.

Implementation in the United Kingdom

In its report on the implementation of Directive 86/613, the Commission finds that the letter of the law is complied with in most of the Member States. However, the practical result is far from satisfactory since there appears to have been little overall policy on the position of assisting spouses. The reasons for such an absence of policy appear to be due to several factors. There is the problem of defining the relevant category of persons. The self-employed are not a homogeneous group and they are covered, particularly in social security schemes, by a wide variety of arrangements. The second problem is in the vague character of the Directive itself. Many of the specific proposals in the Commission's draft were withdrawn before the adoption of the Directive which calls on Member States to consider strategies for improving the situation of assisting spouses. This has led to what the Commission defines as being minimal response. The Commission concludes that a great deal more work will need to be completed in this area.

In the UK certain aspects of the Directive are fully implemented. The Sex Discrimination Act and the Equal Pay Act prohibit discrimination on grounds

---

[54] It was in fact reviewed in 1994 see *Report from the Commission on the implementation of Council Directive . . . 86/613/EEC* cited in note 52 *supra*.

of sex for each self-employed category in access to the professions, vocational and in-service training, vocational guidance and retraining. There is equal treatment as regards setting up business and government advice and assistance is available to all regardless of sex. The Partnership Act of 1890 places no obstacles to the provision of equal rights but provides that the rights and duties of partners are determined by the partnership agreement. Companies may be set up by married persons on an equal footing and the funds can be used as common property. The relevant legislation, the 1985 Companies Act does not create any barriers to the attainment of equal treatment. Neither are there provisions in national legislation which prevent a company from continuing its business on the death or divorce of one of the participating spouses.

In matters of social security, however, the UK has implemented the Directive in only a minimal way. The contributory social security scheme covers sickness, retirement and death and provides benefits for assisting spouses (indeed for all spouses). Maternity allowance is available for those who meet the qualifying conditions but there is no entitlement to maternity leave and no maternity allowance is available for the spouses of self employed husbands or partners as of right.[55]

The obligation on the part of Member States to undertake to encourage the recognition of the work of assisting spouses has elicited the response from the UK that initiatives in the area are not necessary. This is presumably because of the government's desire to restrict the impact of regulation on small business but it does mean that there is no clear policy in the UK as compared, for example, to Denmark. If the Commission does intend to develop clearer European guidelines in this area then the UK does need to think through what its approach should be. Further study is clearly essential to develop such policies.

Community recommendations

The Social Action Programme shows that the Commission is contemplating moving towards the development of social law more and more with the adoption of "soft-law" measures. These are measures which are not legal instruments as such but which provide the framework for co-ordinated development of the law and practice of the Member States. In the area of equal treatment, the most important development in the use of soft-law has been in relation to sexual harassment. The Commission adopted a Recommendation on the protection of the dignity of men and women at work in 1992 and annexed to the Recommendation is a Code of Practice.[56] The

[55] See Chapter 7 for a discussion of the maternity provisions in the UK.
[56] Cited in note 3 *supra*.

Commission's approach to sexual harassment is that it constitutes sex discrimination and may fall within the terms of Directive 76/207 although this has not, as yet, been tested at the level of European law.[57] The Recommendation, therefore, supplements the provisions of the Directive.

The Recommendation states that unwanted conduct of a sexual nature is unacceptable and may, in certain circumstances, be contrary to the equal treatment Directive. It is recommended that Member States take action to promote awareness of the problem and take action in the public sector to implement the Code of Practice as an example to the private sector. Employers and employees are encouraged to implement the Code and, finally, Member States will report to the Commission on steps which they have taken in this respect.

The Code of Practice is intended to provide practical guidance for employers, employees and trade unions. The Code defines sexual harassment as being "unwanted conduct of a sexual nature, or other conduct based on sex affecting the dignity of women and men at work". It is recognised that sexual harassment may have implications for other areas of law but the Code specifically places the issue in the context of equal opportunities rather than say, health and safety or criminal law. The aim of the Code is to change behaviour and attitudes.

In order to prevent sexual harassment, it is recommended that employers develop a policy statement to define what is unwanted behaviour and the procedures to be followed in the event of an incident of sexual harassment arising. The policy should be communicated to employees, and employers must demonstrate a serious commitment to the elimination of sexual harassment at work, for example, by providing training. Clear and effective procedures should be set up to deal with sexual harassment and, in particular, an individual should be nominated to whom an employee can go to seek effective advice, preferably, in the first instance, a person of the same sex as the person making the complaint. Where informal attempts to solve a problem fail then the employer should set up a formal complaints procedure. Breaches of the Code should be seen as a disciplinary offence and, where transfers are to be made as a result of a complaint, it is the complainant who should be given the first choice as to any transfer.

Trade unions are urged to consider including measures aimed at protecting the dignity of workers in collective agreements. They should also develop policy statements in respect of sexual harassment in order to raise awareness and to encourage employers to implement the Code. According to the Code,

---

[57] It has been argued that sexual harassment should not necessarily be treated as an issue of discrimination but as delictual or criminal see Dine and Watt "Sexual Harassment: Moving Away from Discrimination" 58 *Modern Law Review* (1995) 343.

employees have a responsibility to raise awareness about the problem and to support colleagues who are, or who have been, victims of a violation.

The legal status of such recommendations has been addressed by the Court of Justice. Although they are not legally binding instruments, the Court has said that Recommendations have legal significance in that national courts are bound to take them into consideration in disputes submitted to them, particularly where national measures are designed to implement Community provisions.[58]

Implementation in the United Kingdom

In the United Kingdom sexual harassment has been held to fall within the definition of discrimination in section 1(1) of the Sex Discrimination Act which defines discrimination in terms of the less favourable treatment accorded to a woman than that which would be accorded to a man. Section 6(2)(b) of the Act makes it unlawful for a person, in the case of a woman employed by him, to discriminate against her by . . . subjecting her to any . . . other detriment. In *Porcelli* the Court of Session in Scotland equated sexual harassment with discrimination where a woman lab technician had been subjected to a variety of forms of unacceptable behaviour.[59] This case was decided before the adoption of the Recommendation but the reasoning of the Court is similar to that contained in the Recommendation. In cases heard following the adoption of the Recommendation it seems that tribunals in the UK are willing to consider its implications without, however, making it easier for women to succeed in their claims.[60]

Proposed new legislation[61] would give industrial tribunals the power to restrict publicity in cases alleging sexual misconduct by issuing a restricted reporting order having effect until the promulgation of the decision. A breach of such an order by a newspaper, periodical or programme maker would be an offence. In the context of the Bill, the term sexual misconduct means, amongst other things, sexual harassment. The provision is designed to protect the character of the parties in this type of dispute from the prurient interest of the media. This Bill explicitly recognises sexual harassment as misconduct within the workplace.

---

[58] Case C-322/88 *Grimaldi v Fonds des Maladies Professionelles* [1989] ECR 4407.
[59] *Porcelli v Strathclyde Regional Council* [1986] ICR 564.
[60] *Wadham v Carpenter Farrer Partnership* [1993] IRLR 374; *Stewart v Cleveland Guest (Engineering) Ltd* [1994] IRLR 440.
[61] Industrial Tribunals Bill [H.L.] HL Bill 95 which received its second reading on 5 June 1995.

Concluding remarks

It can be seen that the equal treatment Directive, in particular, has had a significant impact on the law of sex discrimination in the UK. However the two sources of sex discrimination law have provided a series of problems for the UK courts which should be rectified by amendment or restructuring of existing UK law in order to satisfy European requirements.

Questions

1. How far can a Member State go in introducing positive action programmes for women?

2. To what extent do you support the view of the ECJ in *Hofmann* that Directive 76/207 is not intended to settle questions about the organisation of the family or the domestic division of labour?

3. What approach should national courts adopt when faced with a conflict between Community provisions and an existing prior obligation entered into with third states, for example, an ILO Convention.

4. What is the legal status of the Recommendation on the protection of the dignity of men and women at work?

Contents of Chapter 4

EQUAL TREATMENT FOR MEN AND WOMEN IN SOCIAL SECURITY

Chapter 4

EQUAL TREATMENT FOR MEN AND WOMEN IN SOCIAL SECURITY

Background to the Directive

Directive 79/7/EEC on the progressive implementation of the principle of equal treatment for men and women in matters of social security is the third of the equal treatment directives to be adopted by the European Community.[1] As was noted in Chapter 3, the Equal Treatment Directive 76/207 stated that the principle of equal treatment should apply in the field of social security but it also provided that further legislation would be required to define the scope, substance and the arrangements for the application of that principle in matters of social security.[2] In the first draft of Directive 26/207 the Commission had included social security schemes since such schemes tended to see the typical family unit in Europe as being based on a model of dependent, non-working, traditionally female spouse, supported by a male breadwinner.[3] Introducing equal treatment into employment-related social security benefits was seen as part and parcel of attempts to change the legal structures in order to accord with the realities of the employment market of dual income families, families where the female was the breadwinner, or single parent families, predominantly headed in Europe by females.

---

[1] OJ 1979 L6/24 for the text see Appendix. Generally see McCrudden *Equality of Treatment Between Women and Men in Social Security*, (Butterworths, 1994).
[2] See Chapter 3 for a discussion of how the European Court has interpreted this provision of Directive 76/207.
[3] The legislative and negotiating history of the Social Security Directive is discussed in Hoskyns and Luckhaus "The European Community Directive on Equal Treatment in Social Security" 17 *Policy and Politics* (1989) 321.

At the time of the negotiation of Directive 76/207, the debate had hardly begun on the implications of introducing the equal treatment principle in matters of social security and it is probably true to say that the debate has still not properly resolved itself in the Member States.[4] At least two approaches could have been taken by the Commission in the preparation of the draft. The first of individualisation of benefits would have treated men and women as entirely equal and separate even if they were part of a unit and living together with children. This radical step was rejected partly on ideological grounds as it might be seen to threaten the stability of, and government support for, the family – a policy even more strongly supported by several governments of Europe today – and partly for financial considerations. The family unit is the cheapest way of providing support for dependants, whether they be children, spouses or elderly parents.[5] A more conservative approach was chosen which was to attempt to remove inequalities in a number of areas without fundamentally rejigging the social security systems in Europe. This approach meant that further legislation would need to be adopted to provide for equal treatment in excluded areas, such as occupational pension schemes[6] and in other statutory schemes.[7]

It is also clear from the wording of the Directive and from its interpretation by the Court in *Grau-Hupka* that the Directive does not confer an obligation on the Member States to introduce any new social security scheme which might confer advantages on women and change the nature of social security systems.[8] In *Grau-Hupka,* for example, the Court held that the Directive "in no way obliges the Member States to grant advantages in respect of old-age pension schemes to persons who have brought up children".

Description of the measure and its interpretation by the European Court

Directive 79/7/EEC relates to the progressive implementation of the principle of equal treatment in matters of social security and certain elements of

[4] For a discussion of the sometimes confused debate on equality issues in social security matters, see Luckhaus "Changing Rules, Enduring Structures" 53 *Modern Law Review* (1990) 655. Luckhaus takes the view that "quality" implementation of the Social Security Directive would require a Member State to establish a social security system which gave women the right to claim for themselves irrespective of her status within a family or in a cohabiting relationship. Her discussion is in the context of changes brought about in the social security legislation occasioned by the need to implement the social security Directive.

[5] For a discussion of individualisation see McCrudden in note 1 *supra* chapter 6.

[6] See chapter 5 *infra.*

[7] The proposed Directive was not adopted. For the most recent version see COM(87) 494 final of 23 October 1987. The Directive is still pending as it has not been withdrawn.

[8] Case C-297/93 *Rita Grau-Hupka v Stadtgemeinde Bremen* [1994] ECR I-5535.

social protection as laid out in it. "Progressive" in this context means that the Directive is intended to be part of a scheme of legislation on statutory and occupational social security. The terms "social security" and "social protection" are not defined within the Directive itself but a broad distinction might be drawn between measures of social security, whether contributory or non-contributory, which are intended to insure the individual against risks related to employment or unemployment, and measures of social assistance which are intended to supplement social security provisions.

The personal scope of the Directive is outlined in Article 2. The Directive applies to the "working population". Again this term is not given a strict definition but it is clear from the illustrative list given in Article 2 that the Directive is not intended to cover all aspects of social welfare policies. Included in the illustrative list are workers and self-employed persons whose activity is disrupted by illness, accident or involuntary unemployment; persons seeking employment; retired and invalided workers; and self-employed persons. Although the Court of Justice has helped to clarify the personal scope of the Directive it remains true to say that a large number of females, particularly married or cohabiting women who gave up their careers to bring up children, are not included in this Directive.

The material scope of the Directive is given in Article 3. It applies to statutory schemes providing protection against sickness, invalidity, old age, accidents at work and occupational diseases and unemployment. These are social security measures. In addition, the Directive applies to social assistance in so far as it is designed to supplement or replace the above schemes. Article 3(2) excludes from the scope of the Directive provisions concerning survivors benefits and family benefits except, in the latter case, for those benefits granted by way of increases due to the risks outlined above. As far as the principle of equal treatment in occupational schemes is concerned, Article 3(3) provides that the Council will adopt provisions concerning its substance, its scope and the arrangements for its application.

Article 4 defines the principle of equal treatment as meaning that there should be no discrimination on the ground of sex (either directly or indirectly) by reference, in particular, to marital or family status as concerns the scope of schemes and the conditions of access; the obligation to contribute and the calculation of contributions; the calculation of benefits (including increases due in respect of a spouse and for dependants), and the conditions governing the duration and retention of entitlement to benefits. Article 4 excludes from the principle of equal treatment provisions relating to the protection of women on the grounds of maternity. The definition of equal treatment in social security matters is the same as that for equal treatment in matters of access to employment set out in Directive 76/207/EC.

Article 5 provides that Member States shall take the necessary measures to ensure that any existing national measures which violate the principle of equal treatment are abolished.

Article 6 requires Member States to ensure that effective recourse to judicial remedies is available to individuals who consider their rights to have been violated, possibly after recourse to other competent national authorities.

Article 7 permits Member States to exclude from the scope of the Directive the determination of pensionable age for the purpose of granting old-age and retirement pensions and the possible consequences for the calculation of other benefits; advantages in old age pensions to individuals who have brought up children and the acquisition of benefit entitlements following work breaks to bring up children; the granting of old age or invalidity benefits by virtue of a wife's derived entitlements; the granting of long-term invalidity, old age, accidents at work and occupational disease benefits for a dependent wife; and the consequences of the exercise, prior to the adoption of the Directive, of a right of option not to acquire rights or incur obligations under a statutory scheme. In all these areas, which are primarily matters of support for dependent wives of working husbands, Member States are obliged to review periodically their legislation, in the light of social developments, in order to determine whether the measure remains justifiable.

Article 8 gives to the Member States six years to comply with the Directive.[9] Six years is an unusually long implementation period and reflects the level of complexity in introducing the principle of equal treatment in social security. Member States are required to furnish the Commission with copies of relevant national legislation and to justify to the Commission any measures adopted by them under the terms of Article 7. After seven years the Member States are required to provide information to the Commission to enable it to report on any further measures which need to be taken to implement the principle of equal treatment.

The important issues to be noted about the Directive are (i) it does not apply to the whole field of social security – it is limited to cover employment-related social security and social assistance benefits; (ii) the personal scope of the Directive is limited to the working population; (iii) the Directive applies only to the benefits listed in it; (iv) it applies to direct and indirect discrimination; (v) it requires adequate implementation by the Member States both in terms of substantive law and procedures; and (vi) certain aspects of employment-related social security benefits are excluded from its scope, but these areas must be kept under review by the Member States. All of these issues are discussed below in the light of the jurisprudence of the European Court.

[9] The Directive was to have been implemented by December 1984.

Interpretation of the Directive by the European Court – the issues

The question of direct effect and national remedies

One of the key issues in relation to any Directive must of course be the question of whether it can confer rights on individuals so that they may raise an action in a national court, that is, the question of its direct effects. The distinction between the horizontal and vertical direct effects of Directives which is discussed elsewhere in this book[10] would normally also be of importance. In the case of the Social Security Directive, however, the latter distinction is irrelevant since, by definition, statutory social security schemes could only create rights as far as a claim against the state is concerned.

The European Court of Justice first addressed the issue of the direct effect of the Social Security Directive in a case referred to it from the Netherlands (*FNV*).[11] A Dutch trade union brought an action for wrongful legislation when the Dutch government failed to amend existing legislation which disqualified certain married women from unemployment benefit. The Dutch government did not oppose the view that the legislation was discriminatory but argued that it was unable to adopt the relevant amending legislation in time. The FNV, a Dutch trade union one of whose statutory duties included the duty to safeguard the rights of workers and their families, asked the Court to grant an order requiring the state to suspend the offending legislation. The Dutch court referred the question of the direct effects of the Directive to the European Court asking whether, if the Directive does create direct effects, this would mean that the Dutch legislation was inapplicable. The Court held that Article 4(1) gives practical expression to the principle of equal treatment in social security matters and that it "generally and unequivocally" precludes all discrimination. It is therefore capable of creating direct effects. The existence of Article 7 giving discretion to the Member States in respect of exceptions to the principle of equal treatment and the existence of Article 5 which leaves the choice of methods of implementation to the Member States did not mean that the obligation in Article 4 was equivocal. The date from which the Directive could create rights in the national courts was set by the European Court as that of 23 December 1984 and, as from this date, Article 4(1) precluded the application of the offending Dutch legislation.

The European Court applied this decision in *McDermott and Cotter*, a case referred from the High Court in Dublin in which it held that until national

---

[10] See chapter 3 *supra*.
[11] Case 71/85 *The Netherlands v FNV* [1986] ECR 3855.

implementing measures had been adopted which eliminated discrimination in national social security systems, then women could rely, as of 23 December 1984, on the provisions of Article 4. In this case the issue was the lower unemployment benefits received by married women and the shorter period of pay-related unemployment benefits for them.[12]

Following this decision, the Irish government amended its legislation so that, as from November 1986, both husbands and wives could claim additional social security benefits in respect of a spouse. Prior to this, husbands could automatically make such a claim but wives had to show that their husbands were dependent on them. Transitional rules were introduced, however, to compensate those husbands whose wives were not in fact dependent on them (because, for example, the wife was employed) and who would not, therefore, continue to receive the automatic increase. Mrs Cotter and Mrs McDermott again raised an action in the Irish High Court[13] arguing that wives were entitled to the same compensatory payments as husbands even if their husbands were not dependent upon them. The Irish Court referred the question of whether the principle of Irish law which prohibits unjust enrichment and which constitutes a ground for an Irish court to restrict or refuse relief in certain circumstances was compatible with Article 4(1) of the Social Security Directive.[14] The European Court held that men and women were entitled to have the same rules applied to them and that the Directive did not require proof of dependency so an automatic increase paid to a husband implied that an automatic increase should be paid to a wife in respect of both her spouse and her children. The Irish Government pointed out that this would lead to the situation where in some families automatic increases could be paid twice, hence the issue of unjust enrichment. The European Court held, in response, that the Irish State could not rely on such an argument since this would allow it to rely on its own unlawful conduct in failing to implement the Directive on time as a means of depriving Article 4 of its full effect.

The European Court has had to turn its attention to other questions of national remedies and has strengthened the means by which individuals might enforce effective compliance with the terms of the Directive against their own Member State which has failed adequately to transpose the Directive into

---

[12] Case 286/85 *McDermott and Cotter v Minister for Social Welfare and the Attorney General* [1987] ECR 1453. The European Court reiterated this view in Case 384/85 *Borrie Clarke v Chief Adjudication Officer* [1987] ECR 2865 where it held that individuals could rely on the Social Security Directive from the date of expiry of the implementation period to the date that national implementing measures were adopted. Article 4 prevents the continued application of pre-existing discriminatory measures.

[13] *Cotter v Minister for Social Welfare and the Attorney General*, Irish High Court [1990] 2 CMLR 141 and *McDermott v Minister for Social Welfare and the Attorney General*, Irish High Court, [1990] 2 CMLR 94.

[14] Case C-377/89 *Cotter and McDermott v Minister for Social Welfare and Another* [1991] ECR 1155.

national law. Two issues in particular have arisen which relate to time limits. The first issue arose in *Dik* and related to the question of whether the direct effects of Article 4 could be relied on retro-actively.[15] In this case women workers who were married could not be described as "wage earners" for the purposes of Dutch law relating to unemployment benefit. The Dutch Government repealed this legislation in order to comply with the social security Directive but the Dutch law was adopted after the period of implementation laid down in the Directive had expired. The new Dutch legislation, however, continued to discriminate against women whose claim for unemployment benefit accrued prior to the date for implementation given in the Directive and therefore who continued to be discriminated against even after the date of its full implementation. The European Court held such legislation to be contrary to the Directive and , whilst agreeing that retro-active implementation was lawful, it held that women who derived rights from Article 4 must have those rights guaranteed as from December 1984.

This issue of retro-activity was accepted, amongst others, by the Irish courts[16] although this created a further problem of the relationship between domestic rules on limitations of actions and the direct effects of a Community provision . In *Emmott*, the Irish Government had maintained in force the discriminatory transitional measures which had been declared illegal in the second *Cotter and McDermott* case.[17] By way of judicial review Mrs Emmott challenged the Minister's refusal to grant her an increase, which would have been granted to a man, in her disability benefit in respect of additional benefits for her two children. However national rules would have precluded Mrs Emmott from bringing this action since a claim must be made within three months from the date at which the grounds for the claim arose. The Irish High Court, therefore, applied to the European Court for a preliminary reference on the validity of this national rule. The Court held that it is for national law to determine the procedural conditions governing actions which can be brought by individuals to protect their Community law rights, provided such national measures satisfy two tests. The first is that they are not less favourable than rules applying to purely domestic matters and that they do not make the exercise of Community rights virtually impossible. The Court added that due to the particular nature of directives, which had to be transformed into national law and which could only create direct effect in the absence of adequate national implementation measures, there was the additional element

---

[15] Case 80/87 *Dik and Others v College Van Burgemeester en Wethouders* [1988] ECR 1601.
[16] *Carberry v Minister for Social Welfare and the Attorney General* [1990] 1. CMLR 29 in which the Irish High Court held that unless the European Court had made its ruling in 286/85 prospective then the date at which claimants became entitled to rely on the Directive was December 1984. The European Court had not, in fact, placed any temporal limitation.
[17] Case C-208/90 *Emmott v Minister for Social Welfare and another* [1991] ECR 4269.

for an individual of uncertainty as to his or her rights. Legal certainty for an individual can only be created by adequate implementation by Member States and, therefore, in the absence of adequate implementation, a State cannot rely on national limitation measures to prevent the bringing of an action against itself. Such limitation periods can, therefore, only begin to run as from the date of effective implementation of a directive.

It has been established that, following *Emmott*, the Irish government paid out over IR£60 million in backdated payments.[18] It may be that the sheer size of such payments led the European Court to rethink the issue of national limits and to reconsider the implications of its own case law. Certainly, in *Steenhorst-Neerings*, when a Dutch court asked the European Court whether Community law precluded the application of a national rule according to which benefits for incapacity to work can only be backdated to one year before the lodging of claim, where an individual sought to rely on directly enforceable Community rights as from 23 December 1984 and where, at the date of the claim, the Member State concerned had not properly transposed the Directive, the European Court appeared to retreat somewhat from the *Emmott* position.[19] The Court distinguished the situation in the Dutch case from that pertaining in *Emmott*. In the latter case, the national provision was such as to preclude an individual from bringing an action against the state to ascertain the full extent of his or her Community rights. In the Dutch case, the national provision was no less favourable than the provisions relating to similar domestic actions (it was the same rule) and it was not framed in such a way as to render virtually impossible the exercise of the rights conferred by Community law. The Dutch rule was, therefore, compatible with Community law.

National procedural time limits were raised in the second of Mrs Johnson's cases to come before the European Court.[20] Mrs Johnson had been able to rely on the social security Directive in relation to her claim for severe disablement allowance which the Social Security Commissioners in the UK granted for the period of 12 months prior to her claim. The Court of Appeal questioned whether *Emmott* set a precedent in Mrs Johnson's case. The European Court applied the same approach as it had taken in the Dutch case on the test of comparability with similar domestic actions and the "virtual impossibility" test and distinguished *Emmott*.

---

[18] See Cousens "Equal Treatment and Social Security" 19 *European Law Review* (1994) 123. A case pending before the Court will determine whether a benefit granted with retroactive effect should be awarded with interest. Case C-66/95 *R ex parte Eunice Sutton v Secretary of State for Social Security*.

[19] Case C-338/91 *Steenhorst-Neerings v Bestuur Van de Bedrijfsvereniging voor Detailhandel, Ambachten en Huisvrouwen* [1994] IRLR 244.

[20] Case C-410/92 *Elsie Rita Johnson v Chief Adjudication Officer*, [1994] ECR-I 5483. The first Johnson case is discussed below under the discussion of the personal scope of the Directive.

The final issue in relation to national remedies is the question of what rules to apply in the case of incorrect implementation of a Directive and the absence of national rules creating an effective remedy. In *Ruzius* the Court has held that claimants who have been discriminated against should have the same national rules applied to them as to other claimants.[21]

The personal scope of the Directive

Article 2 sets out the personal scope of the Directive which applies to the "working population". The Court of Justice has needed to define this concept on a number of occasions. Jacqueline Drake argued that the social security Directive should apply to her and that she should be entitled to an invalid care allowance since she gave up work to look after her severely disabled mother (*Drake*).[22] However, the UK Social Security Act 1975 provided, at the relevant time, that such an allowance was not available for any woman who lived with her husband. Such a restriction, Mrs Drake argued, was contrary to the social security Directive. The Court agreed that Mrs Drake was part of the working population since Article 2 is based on the idea that a person who gives up work because of one of the risks outlined in the Directive is part of the working population. Mrs Drake had given up work because of one of these risks, namely invalidity, albeit the invalidity of her mother.

Mrs Drake had given up work to look after her mother. In the case of *Achterberg Te Riele* a group of Dutch women who had not had an occupation and who were not seeking work and others who had had an occupation and who had voluntarily given up work to become housewives claimed that they too fell within the personal scope of the Directive.[23] They wished to challenge a Dutch law on old age pensions, calculated on the basis of contributions paid by husbands employed in the Netherlands. The Court refused to accept that housewives who had never been available for employment or who had given up their employment for reasons other than those set out in the Directive could be described as being part of the working population. The Court explained its position on the basis that Community law in respect of equal treatment applied only to women in their capacity as workers and not as women *per se*. In Community law, therefore, housewives are not workers since they are not paid by an employer for their labour but are supported by their husbands.

[21] Case C-102/88 *Ruzius-Wilbrink v BestuurVan de Bedrijfsvereniging Voor Overheidsdiensten* [1989] ECR 4311.
[22] Case 150/85 *Drake v The Chief Adjudication Officer* [1986] ECR 1995.
[23] Joined cases 48/88, 106-107/88 *Achterberg Te Riele and Others v Sociale Verzekeringsbank* [1989] ECR 1963.

The Court has insisted that decisions as to the personal and material scope of the Directive are distinct (*Verholen*).[24] This means that, although a person may be affected by national rules referred to by Article 3 of the Directive, the national court cannot alter the personal scope of the Directive to persons not covered by it. An individual must, therefore, satisfy the requirements of both the personal and the material scope of the Directive. In *Verholen*, however, the Court extended the group of individuals who might rely on the provisions of the Directive to those "who may have a direct interest in ensuring that the principle of non-discrimination is respected as regards persons who are protected". It is for national law to determine who may have such a direct interest but any national provision should not undermine the Community right to effective judicial protection. An individual who bears the effects of a discriminatory national provision, such as a husband whose wife is the victim of the discrimination and who herself comes within the scope of the Directive but is not party to the proceedings, is able to rely on the Directive in the national court.

In its most recent jurisprudence in relation to the personal scope of the Directive, the Court has re-emphasised the relationship between the element of employment and of risk.[25] Mrs Johnson gave up work to look after her child. She wished to resume work but was unable to do so as she had damaged her back during the time in which she had been occupied with child care. She was awarded a non-contributory invalidity pension which was stopped when she began cohabiting with a man because she could not show that she was incapable of performing normal household duties as was required at that time of married and cohabiting women. The non-contributory invalidity pension was abolished in 1984 and replaced with the severe disablement allowance, open to both sexes on the same conditions. Persons eligible for the old invalidity pension automatically became entitled to the new allowance. Mrs Johnson argued that she would be in this position but for the additional discriminatory household duties test. She wished to rely on the social security Directive and the matter was referred to the European Court on the question of whether she fell within its personal scope.

The European Court reiterated its position that the Directive applied only to those who are available on the labour market or who have ceased to be so because of one of the risks outlined in Article 3. A person who gives up work to look after a child is not covered by the Directive. However, a person who is

---

[24] Joined cases C-87/90, C-88/90 and C-89/90 *Verholen and Others v Sociale Verzekeringsbank* [1991] ECR-I 3757. In a case pending before the Court, the carer of a handicapped spouse claims to fall within the personal scope of the Directive. Case C-77/95 *Bruna-Alessandra Zuchner v Handelskrankenkasse, Bremen*.

[25] Case C-31/90 *Elsie Rita Johnson v Chief Adjudication Officer* [1991] ECR-I 3723.

seeking employment but whose search is stymied because of the materialisation of one of the risks in Article 3 may be covered by the Directive. The reason why the person gave up work in the first place is irrelevant provided that he or she can prove to the satisfaction of the national court that he or she was genuinely seeking employment when the incapacity occurred. Such proof could be constituted by examining whether a person had registered with an employment agency or whether they had applied for jobs or attended interviews.

The early fairly liberal approach of the Court in *Drake* appears to have been more restrictive in *Johnson*, although in the case of the particular individual she was able to meet the "seeking employment" test. It is clear however that the definition of working population will not be greatly extended by the Court and will not be applied to housewives and other carers. This means , given the lower rates of participation of women in the economically active labour force within Europe, that the impact of the Directive will only be felt by limited groups. It does not have an overall impact on the status of women as a whole.

The material scope of the Directive

Article 3 sets out the schemes to which the social security Directive shall apply. However, given the multiplicity of social security schemes within the European Community, it is not surprising that the European Court has had occasion to interpret Article 3. In the first case relating to the material scope of the Directive, *Drake*, the Court adopted a liberal interpretation leading many commentators to hope for a very liberal interpretation of the Directive as a whole.[26] Mrs Drake gave up employment to look after her elderly mother. The European Court was asked to determine whether the right to a payment of a benefit to a person who cares for a disabled person constitutes part of a statutory scheme providing against the risk of invalidity as provided in Article 3 of the Directive. The Court held that in order to fall within the scope of Article 3, a benefit must constitute "the whole or part of a statutory scheme providing protection against one of the specified risks or a form of social assistance having the same objective". The Court then added that a benefit given to a carer depends on the existence of a situation of invalidity. The fact that the carer's benefit is paid directly to him or her does not place it outside the scope of the Directive.

[26] Case 150/85 *Drake* cited in note 22 *supra*.

The broad interpretation of the Court in *Drake* can be contrasted to its narrow approach in the later case of *Smithson*.[27] The case relates to a refusal to pay housing benefit to a woman in receipt of an old age pension at the age of 67 who was not in recept of an invalidity pension. The criteria for the award of the housing benefit was that a person must be in receipt of such an invalidity pension. Prior to her being awarded an old age pension at the age of 60, Mrs Smithson had been in recept of an invalidity pension. A man in these same circumstance could have opted to exchange his pension for an invalidity pension but that option was not open to women since the option only lasted for five years after achieving pensionable age. The Court was asked whether the payment of housing benefit, in the form of a supplement to the pension, fell within the scope of Article 3.

The Court held that the housing benefit was merely part of a benefit and was not an autonomous scheme providing protection against the risks provided in Article 3. This was so even though the calculation of the benefit took into consideration the criteria outlined in Article 3. It is not easy to see how the Court reached this decision as the reasoning of the Court is so thin.[28] However, it does indicate a certain narrowness of view in respect of the interpretation of the social security Directive.

The case of *Jackson* is another example of this narrow approach taken by the Court. In this case the Court held that benefits (such as supplementary allowance or income support), which are granted to individuals in a variety of circumstances to enable them to attain a certain level of income, do not fall within the scope of the Directive, even though the persons who are in receipt of the benefit are suffering from one of the risks laid down in Article 3 (in this case unemployment).

Although few in number, the cases which have come before the Court to determine the material scope of the Directive, again indicate a certain narrowing by the Court in comparison to the early case of *Drake*. It seems the Court will apply a test which is a measure of the directness or otherwise of the link between the benefit and the risks outlined in Article 3. "Indirect benefits" will not, therefore, fall within the scope of the Directive. It is not clear why this should be the case.

---

[27] Case C-243/90 *Regina v Secretary of State for Social Security ex parte Smithson* [1992] ECR-I 467.
[28] Advocate General Van Gerven in the later case of *Jackson* attempted to explain the *Smithson* rationale. It is worth quoting him in full. "In *Smithson* the relationship between the risks referred to in Directive 79/7 and housing benefit was in fact only indirect: invalidity is the only criterion for the grant of an invalidity pension, the grant of which is a precondition for receipt of a higher pension premium; in turn the latter is taken into account (along with other factors) in order to calculate the notional income of the person claiming housing benefit" (para 13 of his opinion). The Advocate General here stresses the indirect link as being the rationale of the Court. Joined cases C-63/91 and C-64/91 *Jackson v Chief Adjudication Officer* [1992] ECR-I 4737.

The principle of equal treatment

The principle of equal treatment is laid out in Article 4 of the Directive and it is this Article that the Court has determined is such as to create direct effects. Both direct and indirect discrimination are prohibited under the terms of the Directive and the Court has been asked on a number of occasions to state whether Article 4 applies in particular factual situations.

Direct discrimination

The first two cases relating to Article 4 both involved discriminatory provisions contained in transitional measures as the UK and the Netherlands moved from discriminatory to non-discriminatory legislation whist implementing the Directive itself. In the UK an additional requirement for access to severe disablement allowance was still applied to women whose claims were made before December 1984 and this transitional arrangement was held, in *Borrie Clarke*, to infringe Article 4.[29] An additional requirement was similarly part of the Dutch rules for access to unemployment benefit and this was also declared contrary to Article 4 in *Dik*.[30] *McDermott and Cotter* was similarly a question of discriminatory transitional rules.[31]

Dutch legislation withdraws incapacity benefits from women who become entitled to a widow's pension. Mr Gemert-Derks died and his widow had her incapacity benefit withdrawn and substituted by a widow's pension. Her income dropped considerably. The Dutch court asked whether such a withdrawal was contrary to the Directive.[32] The Court held that this was direct discrimination since it deprived women, but not men, of choice. It was, therefore, contrary to the Directive. If widows were to be given a choice between benefits, and full information was given to them, then this would not constitute discrimination.

Another Dutch court referred three questions to the European Court as a result of the Dutch legislation on incapacity. Two of these questions relate to direct discrimination and one to indirect discrimination.[33] In *Roks*, the first

---

[29] Case 384/85 *Borrie Clarke* cited in note 12 *supra*.
[30] Case 80/87 *Dik and others* cited in note 15 *supra*.
[31] Case 286/85 *McDermott and Cotter* cited in note 12 *supra*.
[32] Case C-337/91 *van Gemert-Derks v Bestuur van de Nieuwe Industriele Bedrijfsvereniging* Decision of the Court of 27 October 1993 n.y.r.
[33] Case C-343/92 *MA Roks and others v Bestuur van de Bedrijfsvereniging voor de Gezondheid, Geestelijke en Maatschappelijke Belangen*, [1994] ECR 571.

question related to a provision of Dutch law which imposed a condition for entitlement for women which was not imposed on men. The question arose because Dutch law had had to be amended with retrospective effect in order to comply with the Directive. The new law imposed the same conditions on men and women but did so belatedly. This meant that men who claimed the benefit prior to the new legislation were better off than women who were unable to claim the benefit. The European Court held that this infringed Article 4. The effect of the Dutch legislation was to level down the benefit for everyone as the new legislation was now more restrictive. The European Court held that this was permissible since Directive 79/7 leaves intact the powers of Member States to define their social policy, subject to the duty to act in co-operation with the Commission. The final point raised in this case was whether a benefit which required the claimant to have earned a certain level of wages in the year preceding the award of the benefit was indirectly discriminatory since women's wages were, typically, lower than men's. The Court held this to be an instance of indirect discrimination since the justification offered by the Netherlands was purely budgetary, i.e. the rule made it cheaper to operate the benefit as it restricted the number of applicants and this was not an objective justification. Budgetary considerations alone were not sufficient objective justification.

Indirect discrimination

Teuling was the first case which related to indirect discrimination and it arose out of a Dutch system of incapacity benefits which paid supplements determined partly on the basis of marital or family status, taking into account the salary of the spouse. Mrs Teuling challenged the system because her husband's income took her out of the range of beneficiaries under this scheme.[34] She claimed that this was indirect discrimination since husbands, in general, had higher wages than wives so that in the category of person who could claim the supplement there was a higher proportion of men. The Court held that such a system which relies on marital or family status and under which a considerably smaller proportion of women can claim is contrary to Article 4 unless it can be objectively justified. The Court examined the aid of the benefit which was to guarantee a minimum subsistence level and held that if the benefit was to guarantee this level of benefit to those who bear the burden of dependants then they may be justified under the Directive. It is the national court who should make such an assessment. Furthermore, the Court added,

---

[34] Case 30/85 *Teuling v Bedrijfsvereniging voor de Chemische Industrie* [1987] ECR 2497.

Community law does not prevent a Member State, in controlling expenditure, from taking these additional burdens into consideration in determining the levels of benefit.[35]

The Dutch system relating to incapacity benefits was challenged on the ground that it excluded part-time workers from its scope.[36] In *Ruzius*, the Court held that indirect discrimination arose because a greater percentage of part-time workers are female. The Court rejected the justification that to allow them the allowance would raise their income higher than it would have been for their part-time work. The part-timers, therefore, should have the same rule applied to them as the full-timers.

In one of the few cases brought in this area by the Commission against a Member State, the Court further clarified the concept of indirect discrimination.[37] The Commission argued that Belgian unemployment legislation which granted preferential treatment to unemployed heads of households with a dependent spouse, cohabitee or child constituted indirect discrimination since the category of persons to whom this rule applies is made up predominantly of men. The effect of the rule is, therefore, to discriminate against women. The Court agreed that Article 4 prohibits indirect discrimination unless it can be objectively justified using factors unrelated to discrimination based on sex. It repeated its decision in *Teuling* that a social security scheme which takes account of marital and family status and which is paid to a smaller proportion of women than men is contrary to Article 4 unless there is an objective justification. Therefore, the Court turned to the justification offered by Belgium. Belgium argued that there were fewer women than men in the economically active population which explains why fewer women had dependants. The Court rejected this approach. Instead it applied a kind of proportionality test. If Belgium could demonstrate that the system met a necessary aim of its social policy and the measures are requisite and suitable to attain that aid, the mere fact that the system favours more males than females would not lead to an infringement of the principle of equal treatment. The aim of the Belgian system was to meet differing needs of different categories of persons, and it forms part of a social policy most aspects of which are still matters of national law. The Court added that Member States retain "a

---

[35] The rationale in Teuling was applied in the most recent case in respect of indirect discrimination. In case C-226/91 *Molenbroek v Bestuur van de Sociale Verzekeringsbank* [1992] ECR-I 5943. Here the issue was again whether the occupational income of a spouse should be taken into account in the calculation of the old age pension. The Court accepted the justification of the Dutch government that the system was to provide minimum levels of subsistence and was part of an overall social policy.

[36] Case C-102/88 *Ruzius Wilbrink* cited in note 21 *supra*.

[37] Case C-229/89 *Re Unemployed Heads of Household: Commission v Belgium* [1991] ECR 2205.

reasonable margin of discretion" as regards protective measures of this kind. For these reasons, the Court rejected the Commission's claim.[38]

It is clear that both direct and indirect discrimination are covered by the Directive. However the Court has held that the justification offered by a Member State in relation to indirect discrimination is not the more stringent test of proportionality which is used elsewhere in equal treatment matters since the Court has acknowledged that there exists a margin of discretion to the state in determining overall social policy. The justification test in this area is that a measure must be necessary, requisite and suitable to meet the needs of a states' social policy, the goals of which fail to be determined by the state itself. Indirect discrimination may be justified, therefore, if the benefits system as a whole attempts to set minimum levels of income even if, within the system, women are the victims of discrimination. In coming to this decision the Court has realised the limitations to the principle of equal treatment and it is now up to the Member States to overhaul their benefits system so that social goals are set within a non-discriminatory framework if they wish to achieve real equality for women.

National exclusions

Article 7 allows (but does not require) Member States to exclude from its ambit a variety of social security matters including the right to maintain differential pensionable ages and a number of specific benefits which are granted to dependent wives of working husbands. The effect of these exclusions is to allow Member States to retain control of policy in these areas. However, Member States are obliged to reassess such policies in the light of social developments.

The Court of Justice has examined the issue of the determination of pensionable ages and the consequences of maintaining different ages on a number of occasions. In three early cases, the European Court developed a form of words which was used to distinguish the consequences of maintaining different pension ages in terms of the knock-on effect for other related working conditions, such as redundancy schemes, which were covered by the Directive 76/207, and the consequences for social security, covered by Directive 79/7/EEC.[39] In these cases the Court held that Article 7 (1) (a) "applies only

---

[38] Cases pending on questions of indirect discrimination are: C-317/93 *Inge Nolte v Landesversicherungsanstalt Hannover*; C-444/93 *U. Megher and Another v Inningskrankenkasse Vordepfalz*; C-8/94 *C. B. Laperre v Bestuurcommissie Beroepszaken in de Provincie Zuid Holland*; C-280/94 *Y.M.Posthuma, van Damme and others v Bedrijfsvereniging voor Detailhandel, Ambachten en Huisvrouw and others*.
[39] Cases 262/84 *Beets-Proper v Van Lanschot Bankiers NV* [1986] ECR 773 (para 38); 151/84 *Joan Roberts v Tate and Lyle Industries Ltd* [1986] ECR 703 (para 35); 152/84 *Marshall v Southampton and South-West Hampshire Area Health Authority* [1986] ECR 723 (para 36–37).

to the determination of the pensionable age for the purpose of granting old-age and retirement pensions and the consequences thereof for other social security benefits". The Court also stated that the derogation must be interpreted strictly. This wording is almost lifted from the Directive itself except that the Court has replaced the words "other benefits" with the words "social security" benefits. It is unlikely however that the Court really intended to distinguish between social security and other social assistance benefits although, if the Court had so intended, then the scope of the exception would have been more limited.

In 1992, the European Court was asked to give an interpretation of Article 7(1) (a) in the context of a preliminary ruling from the English High Court.[40] The Equal Opportunities Commission (EOC) had challenged the legality of maintaining in force the obligation to contribute towards pension entitlement from the age of 16 for both men and women, thereby requiring men to contribute for five additional years. The European Court was asked to determine not whether different pension ages were illegal – they clearly fell under the exception in the Directive – but whether the contribution arrangements were illegal. It held that the contribution arrangements only fell within the scope of the derogation if they are "necessary in order to achieve the objectives the directive is intended to pursue". The Court noted the absence within the Directive itself of any rationale for maintaining the exceptions in Article 7 and, therefore, deduced that they existed to give time to Member States to adjust their social security systems "without disrupting the complex financial equilibrium" of those systems. If the Court were to accept the views of the EOC that the contribution system was illegal but not differential pension arrangements then the derogation would be rendered nugatory since the consequence would have been to require Member States to have the same pensionable age. In these circumstances, therefore, the necessary link between pensionable age and contribution record had been established. One was consequential on the other.

The Court was asked to decide in *van Cant* whether the calculation of statutory pension benefits in Belgium, which were calculated over a period of 45 years for men and 40 years for women, was permitted under the terms of the Article 7(1)(a) derogation.[41] The difference between this case and that

---

[40] Case C-9/91 *Regina v Secretary of State for Social Security ex parte the Equal Opportunities Commission* [1992] ECR-I 4297. This case is discussed by Hervey in 30 *Common Market Law Review* (1993) 653-665. Hervey criticises the Court for failing to understand that the derogation which allows different pension ages was intended to provide a benefit for women to reward them for having a double burden of work and care responsibilities rather than a financial benefit to Member States. She argues that the Court should have applied a proportionality test which would have led to a different result but that the Court was influenced by the costs arguments put by the UK in its submissions. Hervey's argument is interesting but ultimately not totally convincing.
[41] Case C-154/92 *van Cant v Rijksdienst voor Pensioenen*, decision of the Court of 1 July 1993 n.y.r.

brought by the EOC was that Belgium had equalised its pension age with the introduction of a minimum pension age of 60 for both men and women. The Court held that in these circumstances the differential calculation rates could not be justified.

In *Thomas*, the European Court examined the gearing of the award of non-contributory benefits (severe disablement allowance and invalid care allowance) to the normal pensionable age in the UK.[42] The Court asked whether the linkage between the award of non-contributory benefits and the pension age is "objectively necessary in order to avoid disrupting the complex financial equilibrium" of the social security system and other benefits. The Court then held that non-contributory benefits of the kind in question have no such influence on the financial equilibrium of the contributory pension scheme. This is even more so when the national system contains rules which prevent an individual receiving overlapping benefits such as allowances and pensions.

UK legislation relating to increases in pensions for dependent spouses is governed by the Health and Social Security Act 1984. Before this Act was adopted, only male pensioners were entitled to such increases. However conditions were attached to the right to bring a claim, namely that the female claimant's retirement pension began immediately upon the termination of a period for which she was entitled to an increase in unemployment benefit, sickness benefit or invalidity pension in respect of adult dependants. This same requirement was not applied to males. These rules were challenged in the case of *Bramhill*.[43] It was not disputed that the rules discriminated against women but the UK argued that increases in relation to retirement benefits were governed by the exclusions in Article 7 and the Court agreed. The discrimination was, therefore, allowed to remain. The argument in this case turned on the interpretation of Article 4(1) which prohibits discrimination in respect of "the calculation of benefits including increases due in respect of a spouse". The Court pointed out, however, that the UK legislation was intended to reduce the inequality in the previous regime and that increases in respect of dependent wives fell within the terms of the Article 7 exceptions. It is difficult to justify this case or, indeed, to explain it. The case must turn on the Court's interpretation of the progressive nature of the Directive in that the Member State is given the benefit of the doubt where new legislation is introduced which reduces but does not eliminate inequality and discrimination.

The Court also applied a very broad interpretation of Article 7 in *Graham*.[44] Mrs Graham had her invalidity benefit cut on reaching the state pensionable age. She argued that this drop in income discriminated against women since

---

[42] Case C-328/91 *Secretary of State for Social Security v Thomas and others* [1993] CMLR 880.
[43] Case C-420/92 *Bramhill v Chief Adjudication Officer* [1994] ECR I-3191.
[44] Case C-92/94 *Secretary of State for Social Security v Rose Graham and others*, decision of the Court of 11 August 1995 n.y.r. see The Times 12 August 1995.

men retired five years later than women and, therefore, that the cut in benefit was contrary to the Directive. The Court rejected her claim on the ground that the payment of benefit was tied to the pensionable age which was an exception to the principle of equal treatment permitted under Article 7. In contrast, in *Richardson*, the Court held that providing free prescriptions to men at age 65 and to women at 60 was contrary to the Directive as the award of this benefit was not "necessarily and objectively" tied to the state pension age.[45]

Limitations of the Directive

Directive 79/7 is an imperfect legislative instrument in that it is limited both in its scope of benefits covered and in the range of individuals who are able to claim under it. The Directive is designed as an exception to the rule that there shall be equal treatment in working conditions and access to employment (Directive 76/207). It is, therefore, a measure which is designed to apply to the working population of the EC and not a measure of general harmonisation of social security law. This explains the limitation as to the material scope of the Directive which is to cover risks to the working population against evils which befall them before entry into the workforce, during their working lives and, to a limited extent, after their exit from the workforce due to contingencies such as occupational diseases, accidents or invalidity.

The Court can be criticised for its failure to interpret the Directive more generously to cover a greater number of individuals, such as housewives or carers, or to cover a wider range of benefits. However the limitations are in the legislation itself. The Directive does provide for equal treatment for those women who conform to the male model of steady and continuous employment but it does not assist those who take career breaks, for example to take on a caring role. Neither does the Directive tackle the problems inherent in gearing a system to a traditional family model of breadwinner and dependants which does not accord with the realities of the lives of many women. The Directive does not address itself, for example, to the existence of a two-tier system of benefits, contributory and non-contributory with, for the most part, women being dependent on the latter and men on the former. The form which a social security system takes is left within the hands of the Member States.

---

[45] Case C-137/94 *R (ex parte Cyril Richardson) v Secretary of State for Health*, decision of the Court of October 20 1995 n.y.r. Yet to be decided is Case C-228/94 *Atkins v Wrekin District Council and others* re reduction of public transport tarriffs.

Another problem is that, in allowing for national exclusions, the Directive, particularly as interpreted by the Court, allows consequential discrimination to continue. The most notable area is apparent from the cases coming from the UK where the tardy implementation of equal pension ages in state pensions has allowed avowedly discriminatory measures to continue. Furthermore, the legislation which will equal pension ages in the UK is only one illustration of the fact that Member States are free to level down social security systems to accord with the principle of equal treatment, a solution which hits hardest at those most in need of support.

The implementation of the Directive in the UK

The equalisation of the state pension age is the most striking example of how UK legislation has been amended as a result of EC influence. This is despite the fact that Directive 79/7 specifically excludes the setting of the pension age from its ambit. The impact of cases being brought in respect of dismissal at the state pension age (*Marshall*) and the European Court's decisions in respect of occupational pension schemes has convinced the UK that the anomaly of maintaining a five year difference in the normal pension age must be removed.[46] The Pensions Act 1995[47] levels up the normal pension age to 65 for men and women. The full effect of these provisions will be felt by the year 2020 as there is to be a gradual phasing in of the equalised age. Starting in the year 2010, two months will be added to the normal pension age so that, for example, a woman whose birthday falls before 6 April 1950 will attain the normal pension age when she attains the age of 60, a woman born in April 1953 will attain the normal pension age at the age of 63 years and 1 month, and a woman born after 5 April 1955 will attain pensionable age when she is 65. There are no changes as far as men are concerned.

The impact of these changes as far as gearing of benefits is concerned will be a gradual elimination of discrimination. A woman in the situation of Mrs Graham, for example, will be treated in the same way as a man in the year 2020 according to this plan. Equalisation of the pensionable age has not, however, been universally welcomed, at least not in the way it has been

---

[46] The government's plans for the equalisation of the state pension age were set out in the White Paper *Equality in State Pension Ages* Cmnd.2420 (1993). This was published following consultation on *Options for Equality in the State Pension Age*, in which the different options were laid out ranging from flexibility in the pension age, levelling up to 65, levelling down to 60 and taking the average of 63.

[47] The Pensions Act 1995 Chapter 26. Schedule 4 sets out the arrangements for equalisation.

implemented in the UK. One study has shown that women will end up with lower pensions in real terms once the Act is fully implemented.[48]

There has been no study to date of how the principle of equal treatment has influenced the social security system as a whole. However some studies have been completed on aspects of the social security system. Luckhaus has studied the implementation of the Directive in the area of supplementary benefit.[49] She believes that the UK Government acted promptly to implement the provisions of the Directive. Most of this legislation, including the detailed delegated legislation, was in place by 1983. Luckhaus points out that the rules on supplementary benefit (now income support), family income supplement (now credit) and dependency allowances were amended. Slightly later, invalidity benefit was replaced by severe disablement allowance. However, timeous implementation in the sense of the bringing of national rules into line with the Directive has had little impact, she argues, on the way in which the rules operate. Rather than reform there was a "reshuffle" of rules which "ingeniously reproduced the effect existing prior to the rule change". The effect was to replace direct discrimination with indirect and to continue to prevent women from claiming benefits independently of their husbands or partners. She argues that this cannot be quality implementation since it does not improve the situation of women claimants. In respect of supplementary benefit (income support) she admits, however, that the picture is incomplete since there is insufficient research in the area.

Luckhaus has also demonstrated how one benefit, non-contributory invalidity pension, was replaced by severe disablement allowance thereby replacing direct with indirect discrimination[50] Directive 79/7 has, therefore, begun to have an impact on the UK social security system. Changes in legislation have been introduced although these are not always to the benefit of claimants. The Directive itself provided for a six year implementation period which, at the time, was considered to be a long lead-in period. However, the cases which have been brought before the Court display the complexity of the issues and the need for careful planning where changes to benefits are to be introduced. On the issue of the pension age, for example, full

[48] This is because the SERPS element of the pension will be calculated on a woman's earnings including the years between 60 and 65. Women will need to secure well-paid work in the last five years of earning to give them the current rate of pension. See 60 *Equal Opportunities Review* (1995) 6.

[49] Luckhaus "Changing Rules . . ." cited in note 4 *supra*. See also Millar "Social Security, Equality and Women in the UK" 17 *Policy and Politics*. Millar's article argues that the equal treatment principle fails to address the issue of the feminisation of poverty, it benefits only those women who follow a "male pattern" of employment since implementation measures have been merely added on to existing schemes which were designed with the breadwinner/dependant model in mind and, therefore, that further legislative change is needed.

[50] Luckhaus "Severe Disablement Allowance: the old dressed up as new" (1986) *Journal of Social Welfare Law* 153.

equalisation will occur 41 years after the date of adoption of the Directive and its full impact in the UK may not be felt until that time. Gearing of benefits to the pension age seems to be in accordance with Community law if to do otherwise would jeopardise the complex financial equilibrium of the system, and Member States appear to have a fairly wide discretion in deciding on this point. This is one area where the European Court appears to be afraid of pushing forward the principle of equal treatment for fear of the financial consequences on Member States. With this in mind, it is difficult to make a full assessment of how equal treatment operates and how it should operate (in terms of European law) within the UK. This is clearly one area where there will be many more developments.

Questions

1. What approach has the ECJ adopted to a definition of the "working population"? Can the Court be criticised for its interpretation of the Directive?

2. To what extent do the provisions for national exclusions weaken the impact of Directive 79/7?

3. Has the jurisprudence of the ECJ disturbed the existing rules relating to temporal limitations in national courts?

Contents of Chapter 5

EQUAL TREATMENT IN OCCUPATIONAL SOCIAL SECURITY

Chapter 5

EQUAL TREATMENT IN OCCUPATIONAL SOCIAL SECURITY

Background to the Directive

This chapter examines the issues arising out of the adoption of Directive 86/378/EEC on the implementation of the principle of equal treatment in occupational social security schemes.[1] As noted in Chapter 3, Directive 76/207/EEC on equal treatment in working conditions incorporated an exception to the principle of equal treatment for matters relating to social security. The Council would adopt further legislation in this field. For matters of employment related state social security this was done in Directive 79/7/EEC. That Directive specifically excepted occupational social security from its ambit, again with the proviso that the Council would subsequently adopt legislation relating to occupational schemes. That legislation, Directive 86/378/EEC, is the subject of this chapter.

In parallel with this legislative activity, the Court of Justice was turning its attention to the relationship between Article 119 on equal pay and aspects of occupational social security, most notably pensions. The Court had been asked whether occupational pensions schemes were covered by the equal pay provisions of the Treaty and had held that certain aspects of occupational schemes did constitute pay. The case law of the Court inevitably led to the conclusion that Directive 86/378/EEC was, in some respects, *ultra vires*. To add to the confusion, the Member States, fearful of the implications of some of the Court's decisions, sought to set limitations on it by the addition of a Protocol to the Treaty on European Union.[2] A process of amendment has also

---

[1] OJ 1986 L225/40 and 1986 L283/27. For the text see Appendix.
[2] For the text of the Protocol see Appendix.

begun to bring the Directive itself into line with the Court's decisions and the Protocol.[3]

This chapter will deal first with the case law of the Court in relation to Article 119. It will then examine Directive 86/378/EEC and the proposed amendments to it. Finally it will examine the implementation of equal treatment in occupational social security in the UK.

Article 119 and occupational pensions

It was the pioneering Ms Defrenne who first raised the question of whether the contributions which her employer made to a statutory scheme which provided occupational pensions for air crews could be categorised as pay for the purposes of article 119.[4] In this case, Ms Defrenne argued that pay could be made up of different elements – the direct salary and the social salary – and that Article 119 applied to both elements, including the retirement pension. In her case, women were required to retire at the age of 40 and therefore her pension entitlement was much lower than that of male colleagues. The Court did not dispute that certain considerations in the nature of social security benefits could be seen to fall within the concept of pay but the particular scheme in question could not. Its distinguishing features were that it was a scheme directly governed by legislation, displaying no element of agreement between employers and workers and it was generally applicable to categories of workers. Contributions to such schemes may come from workers, employers and the state but they were essentially legal schemes governed by questions of social policy rather than reflective of the employment relationship.

The Court had not thrown out the possibility that occupational pension schemes could be covered by Article 119. The problem was to determine which schemes and what aspects of them could be categorised as pay. The English courts referred a question to the European Court in relation to a scheme operated by a bank which effectively created two pension schemes, one for men and one for women.[5] Men were required to join the pension scheme from the date of their joining the company whereas women were only required to do so from the age of 25. To compensate men for the additional contributions which they were required to make, a supplement of 5% was added to their gross pay. That 5%, however, was immediately deducted and paid into the pension fund. A man who left the company before reaching the

[3] For the proposed amendments see COM(95) 186 final, 16 May 1995 and OJ 1995 C218/5.
[4] Case 80/70 *Defrenne* v *Belgian State* (the first Defrenne case) [1971] ECR 445.
[5] Case 69/80 *Worringham and Humphreys* v *Lloyds Bank Ltd* [1981] ECR 767.

age of 25 was entitled to a refund of his contributions. The women argued that the award of higher gross pay to men was contrary to Article 119 since gross pay was used to calculate other benefits, such as social security, credit facilities, and so on.

To determine the outcome of this case, the Court did not examine the nature of the scheme along the lines of the test developed in *Defrenne I*. Instead it held that the payments in question did fall under Article 119 since they were calculated as part of the gross pay of the employee by the employer and were linked to other advantages as a result. The possibility of a refund was, for the Court, an additional argument to support this view. In somewhat obscure wording, the Court rejected the view of the British Government that the nature of the obligation to contribute should be taken into consideration.

The "gross pay" test was also adopted by the Court in *Liefting*, a Dutch case relating to a social security scheme for civil servants which was attacked as being contrary to Article 119.[6] In this case the scheme was a statutory scheme into which the employer paid contributions calculated on the basis of the employee's salary, subject to a defined limit. Where two civil servants were married, they were treated as one person and the contribution paid by their employers was calculated on their joint income, again within a defined limit. The contribution on behalf of the woman was, however, only payable in so far as her husband's contribution fell short of the upper limit. Her gross salary, therefore, including her pay and the employer's contribution to the pension scheme, was lower than a man's with a knock-on effect for other pay-related benefits. Under these circumstances, the Court held that the contribution to the statutory scheme, in so far as it was included in the calculation of the gross salary, was pay within the meaning of Article 119.

Mr Newstead was a civil servant in the UK.[7] He was single. His occupational pension scheme was funded partly by contributions from employees. In particular, a 1.5% deduction was made from his gross pay to fund a widows' pension scheme. This deduction was not made from the gross pay of women. Should a man leave the civil service who had at all times been unmarried, he would receive a refund of his contributions plus interest. He claimed he was denied immediate access to part of his salary and that this was contrary to Article 119. The Court distinguished this case from *Worringham* and *Liefting* on the basis that in those cases the gross pay of the employee was affected with implications for other benefits. This was not the case here. Mr Newstead's gross pay was not affected by the deduction. What was in issue was his net pay. Article 119 did not apply. In this case the scheme in question was a substitute

---

[6] Case 23/83 *Liefting and others* v *Directie van het Academisch Ziekenhuis bij de Universiteit van Amsterdam* [1984] ECR 3225.
[7] Case 192/85 *Newstead* v *Department of Transport and H.M. Treasury* [1987] ECR 4753.

for a statutory scheme but this did not affect the outcome of the case; the nature of the scheme was not an issue for the Court.

The nature of the scheme was raised as an issue in *Bilka*.[8] Here a pension scheme which paid supplementary retirement benefits to full-time but not part-time workers was challenged as being an example of indirect discrimination contrary to Article 119. The Court returned to its *Defrenne I* test to determine whether the scheme was governed by Article 119. It held that in a scheme established under German legislation by a collective agreement and financed by an employer, where there was an agreement with the staff committee and the scheme formed an integral part of the terms and conditions of service, the benefits payable to employees were pay within the meaning of Article 119.

Following *Bilka*, the Court was asked whether redundancy benefits paid by an employer to an employee and a retirement pension paid under a contracted out private occupational scheme fall within the scope of Article 119, particularly where the pension is awarded in connection with compulsory redundancy.[9] In *Barber*, the Court had no difficulty in determining that redundancy payments paid by an employer to an employee were pay. Turning its attention to the nature of private occupational pension schemes, the Court applied the *Defrenne I* test. The Court said that such schemes were either the result of agreements between employers and employees or imposed unilaterally by employers and they were financed entirely by contributions from employers or by employers and employees jointly without any state contribution. The employer's contribution, therefore, forms part of the consideration paid to the employee. Secondly, the Court argued that such schemes are not available to general categories of workers but only to those employed in certain undertakings. They arise because of the employment relationship. Neither did the Court accept the argument that the fact that legislation laid down the parameters under which such schemes operate altered their nature. Contracted out schemes, the Court said, are governed by their own rules. Finally the fact that they substitute for a statutory scheme does not take them outside the sphere of Article 119. Often contracted out schemes provide for additional benefits which are unavailable under statutory schemes and benefits awarded under such schemes are therefore pay. The fact that funds are administered by trustees and not paid directly by an employer could not take the scheme out of the scope of Article 119 since that article covers consideration received indirectly from the employer. This decision means that all benefits paid under an occupational pension scheme must be non-discriminatory.

[8] Case 170/84 *Bilka Kaufhaus GmbH* v *Karin Weber Von Hartz* [1986] ECR 1607.
[9] Case C-262/88 *Barber* v *Guardian Royal Exchange Group* [1990] ECR-I 1889.

The decision of the Court came as a bombshell to the pensions industry since many occupational pension schemes contain discriminatory provisions. The industry believed that by adopting legislation in 1986 which seemed to exclude occupational social security from Article 119 the Commission and the Council had misled it, thereby causing massive damage to the industry. Eastern Electricity plc attempted to raise proceedings against the Council and Commission in the European Court seeking damages.[10] They alleged a series of faults in relation to the adoption of Directives 79/7 and 86/378 which had misled them.[11]

One of the main worries for the pension industry was the cost of compliance with the Court's decision and another was the extent of the Court's judgment as regards the spread of benefits to which it might apply. A flurry of cases came to the Court seeking further explanation.[12]

Retroactivity of the Court's decision

The Court had been aware of the potential costs to the pensions industry when deciding *Barber*. It acknowledged that Directive 79/7 had authorised the Member States to defer implementation of the principle of equal treatment with regard to the determination of the pensionable age. That exception was then incorporated into Directive 86/378 on occupational social security schemes. In the light of this, the Court held that the parties concerned and the Member States were reasonably entitled to believe that Article 119 did not apply to contracted out schemes and that derogations from the principle of equal treatment were still permissible. Legal certainty required the Court to limit the temporal effects of its judgment except for those individuals who had taken action in good time to safeguard their rights. The Court held, therefore, that the direct effect of Article 119 in this area could not be relied on "with effect from a date prior to that of this judgment, except in the case of workers or those claiming under them who have before that date initiated proceedings or raised an equivalent claim under the applicable national law".[13]

---

[10] Case C-324/91 OJ 1992 C57/6.

[11] See 89 Law Society's Gazette (1992) 40.

[12] For a review of most of these cases see Moore "Justice Doesn't mean a Free Lunch: The Application of the Principle of Equal Pay to Occupational Pension Schemes" 20 *European Law Review* (1995) 159. Several of the cases were joined and Advocate General Van Gerven gave his opinion for these cases together. It is reported in case C-152/91 *Neath v Hugh Steeper Ltd* [1994] 1 All ER 929 at 945. The Advocate General's opinion is the clearest explanation of the relationship between Article 119 and occupational social security as well as of the issues arising in the cases referred to the European Court.

[13] Para 45.

Several commentators pointed to the ambiguity in this statement and suggested four possible meanings[14] on the question of time limits. The most restrictive meaning could be that only workers who entered into an occupational pension scheme after the Barber judgment could rely on the direct effect of Article 119. A second interpretation would be that benefits payable in respect of periods of service after the *Barber* decision should be equalised. A third interpretation would mean that benefits paid or payable after the date of the Barber decision should be equalised. Finally, equal treatment could be applied to all pension payments or benefits after the date of the decision and including all backdated payments. Advocate General Van Gerven pointed to the nature of pension schemes which are usually based on payments made over time leading to an accrual of rights to payment. He distinguished between the process of accrual and the due date for payment and explained that the wording of the Court in Barber must mean that the Court recognised this distinction. The Court had used the phrase "the acquisition of entitlement to a pension as from the date of this judgment". He proposed that the Court should hold that Article 119 could not be relied upon to claim entitlement to a pension for periods of service prior to the *Barber* judgment, in other words, the second interpretation. This, he argued, met the demands of good faith of the Member States and the pension industry. It was also a commonsense approach as it would not significantly alter the balance of the pension funds. He also added that his approach was in accordance with the text of the *Barber* Protocol attached to the Treaty on European Union.

Following the decision in *Barber*, and pending the decisions of the Court in the cases which had been brought to clarify the meaning of the Court as to its temporal limitation, the Member States had decided to legislate in order to ensure that the direct effects of Article 119 could not be backdated to the date of *Defrenne II* in which the Court had first declared that Article 119 could create direct effects. Their solution was the addition of a Protocol to the Treaty on European Union which defined the term "remuneration", for the purposes of Article 119, by excluding "benefits under occupational social security schemes . . . if and in so far as they are attributable to periods of employment prior to 17 May 1990". The Protocol excepted from this definition those workers or those claiming under them who had initiated proceedings before that date. The Protocol also adopted the second interpretation of the Barber decision.

The European Court accepted the advice of the Advocate General. In a series of judgments the Court held that the direct effect of Article 119 may be relied upon, for the purposes of claiming equal treatment in matters of occupational pensions, only in relation to benefits payable in respect of periods

---

[14] These are set out in the opinion of the Advocate General cited in note 12 *supra*.

of service subsequent to 17 May 1990 (the date of the *Barber* judgment), except in the case of workers or those claiming under them who had, by that date, initiated legal proceedings or raised equivalent claims in the national court.[15] This time limit was held to apply to claims made by survivors for pension benefits.[16]

The limitation of the effects of time in *Barber* was raised in two cases relating to the right to join an occupational pension scheme. In *Vroege* the Court was asked to explain the consequences of *Barber* for female members of a supplementary occupational scheme who worked on a part-time basis and who had been excluded from membership of the scheme.[17] The Court was also asked to determine whether the Protocol attached to the Treaty on European Union limited in time the right to join an occupational pension scheme. In *Fisscher* the Court was asked similar questions in relation to a scheme which excluded married women from membership.[18]

The Court held in *Vroege* that the right to join an occupational pension scheme falls within the scope of Article 119 and that the exclusion of married women is direct discrimination contrary to Article 119. The exclusion of part-time workers is contrary to Article 119 "only if the exclusion affects a much greater number of women than men, unless the employer shows that it may be explained by objectively justified factors unrelated to any discrimination on grounds of sex".[19] In this case the Court upheld its earlier decision in *Bilka*[20] and went on to state that it had declared that it was a breach of the principle of equal treatment not to recognise the right to join an occupational pension scheme in *Bilka*. Therefore, there was no reason to suppose that the pensions industry could have been mistaken about the applicability of Article 119 . In *Bilka*, the Court had not imposed a temporal limitation and, therefore, the right to join an occupational pension scheme arose as from 8 April 1976, the date on which the Court had declared the direct effects of Article 119 in *Defrenne*. It further held that the Protocol attached to the Treaty on European Union, and which by virtue of Article 239/EEC is an integral part of the Treaty, is concerned only with benefits payable under an occupational scheme and does not apply to the right to join such a scheme. However the Court did

---

[15] Cases C-109/91 *Ten Oever* v *Stichting Bedrijfspensioenfonds voor Let Glazenwassers-en Schoonmaakbedrijf* [1993] IRLR 601; [1995] ICR 74; C-110/91 *Moroni* v *Firma Collo GmbH* [1994] IRLR 130; [1995] ICR 137; C-152/91 *Neath* v *Hugh Steeper Ltd* [1994] 1 All ER 929; C-200/91 *Coloroll Pension Trustees Ltd* v *James Richard Russell and Others* [1994] ECR I-4389.

[16] Cases C-109/91 *Ten Oever* and C-200/91 *Coloroll* cited in note 15 *supra*.

[17] Case C-57/93 *Anna Adriaantje Vroege* v *NCIV Instituut voor Volkshuisvesting BV and Stichting Pensioenfonds NCIV* [1994] ECR I-4541.

[18] Case C-128/93 *Geertruida Catherina Fisscher* v *Voorhuis Hengelo BV and Stichting Bedrijfspensioenfonds voor de Detailhandel* [1994] ECR I-4583.

[19] *Ibid* para 17.

[20] Case 170/84 *Bilka* cited in note 8 *supra*.

not wish to place individuals who had been excluded from a scheme in a more favourable position than those who had been included. So, in *Fisscher*, the Court held that the excluded worker could not avoid paying the contributions relating to the period of membership concerned.

National time limits were also an issue in this case. The Court held that national rules relating to time limits for bringing actions are also applicable to actions based on Community law, provided that they do not render the exercise of Community rights impossible in practice and that the actions concerned are not less favourable than for similar domestic actions.[21]

Range of schemes covered

Prior to it's decision in *Barber*, the Court had developed criteria for assessing which elements of occupational social security schemes came within the ambit of Article 119. The *Defrenne I* test used four criteria; whether the scheme was directly governed by legislation; whether there was an element of agreement between employers and workers; whether the scheme was generally applicable to categories of workers; and whether the scheme was financed from contributions by employers and employees without state intervention. In *Worringham and Humphreys*, *Liefting* and *Newstead* the Court had not examined the nature of the schemes but implicit in these judgments must be that the Court accepted that they did fall within the ambit of Article 119. The *Defrenne I* test was resurrected by the Court in *Bilka* to hold that contributions to a supplementary scheme could constitute pay for the purposes of Article 119.

The *Defrenne I* test was applied in *Barber* to bring a contracted out pension scheme within the ambit of Article 119. These schemes are the result of agreement between employers and employees or unilaterally imposed by employers, they are financed by contributions from employers and employees and not by the State, they are not applicable to general categories of workers but arise out of the particular employment relationship and, although they are governed by legislation, they are governed by their own rules and often provide wider benefits than the State schemes.

The Court recognised in *Ten Oever*, *Moroni* and *Coloroll* that it had developed a range of criteria but in these cases it failed to state which criterion was the determining factor in its decision that survivors' benefits and supplementary occupational schemes were covered by Article 119.[22] It is in the case of *Beune* that the Court has, at last, stated that the "only possible decisive criterion is whether or not the pension is paid to the worker by reason of the employment

---

[21] The issue of time limits for bringing actions is still to be decided see chapter 6 *infra*.
[22] These cases are cited in note 15 *supra*.

relationship between him and his former employer".[23] This case relates to a claim that the Dutch civil service pension paid by ABP, a statutory legal person governed by public law, falls within the ambit of Article 119. The civil service pension in question is essentially a top-up pension to bring the state old age pension up to a suitable level, i.e. the old age pension is incorporated into the civil service pension.

The difficulty surrounding the classification of schemes is highlighted in this case. Mr Beune claimed that his pension should fall within the ambit of Directive 79/7/EEC which relates to state social security.[24] The ABP and the Dutch government claimed that the pension fell under Directive 86/378/EEC on occupational pensions. The UK government and the Commission claimed that it fell under Article 119 and the Court agreed. To reach this conclusion the Court analysed the criteria which it itself had laid down. First, this scheme was governed by statute and this is for the Court a strong indication that the benefits payable are social security benefits and, on that basis, should be covered by 79/7. The Court did not confine itself to determining whether the scheme was statutory in origin. It gave precedence to whether there was an agreement. Previous case law indicated that negotiations between employers and employees should result in a formal agreement which may then be subject to legislation or incorporated into a collective agreement. The Court said that in most Member States some form of consultation took place, taking different forms and not necessarily leading to formal agreements. In the present case staff representatives were involved in management of the scheme and in practice there were consultations but the scheme was not the result of agreement between employers and employees. Despite this fact the Court did not discount that it could fall under the ambit of Article 119. The Court then said that the fact that the scheme was linked to a social security scheme was not decisive. The application of Article 119 is not conditional upon a scheme being supplementary. Schemes which replace social security schemes can fall under Article 119. Neither, the Court insisted, do the criteria for funding and managing the scheme make it possible to decide whether the scheme falls under Article 119. Schemes governed by Directive 79/7 might

---

[23] Case C-7/93 *Bestuur van het Algemeen Burgerlijk Pensioenfonds* v *G.A. Beune* [1994] ECR I-4471 at para 45. See also paras 44 to 46 for an apparent disavowal of the need to examine the purpose of the scheme "considerations of social policy, of State organisation, or of ethics or even budgetary preoccupations which influenced, or may have influenced, the establishment by the national legislature of a scheme such as the scheme at issue cannot prevail if the pension concerns only a particular category of workers, it is directly related to the period of service and if its amount is calculated by reference to the civil servant's last salary". If the Court applies this same test to section 17 (2)(c) of the Sex Discrimination Act which makes it lawful to discriminate against men and women in matters of pensions then case C-403/93 *Evans* v *Metropolitan Police Authority* will result in a finding that the Police Pensions Regulations of 1973 are unlawful.

[24] For a discussion of the scope of this Directive see chapter 4 *supra*.

also be financed by contributions from employers and employees. The fact that this scheme might be topped up if need be from the State was not decisive. Finally the Court held that civil servants could not be defined as coming within the definition of a general category of worker. Civil servants are a specific group. It was at this stage that the Court referred to the crucial criteria of the employment relationship.

Beune is very helpful in determining just how to see whether benefits under a scheme are social security or are pay. The link to the employment relationship must be the crucial factor as this is exactly the definition given in Article 119 itself.[25] It also answers some of the critics of the Court who suggested that the criteria laid down in *Defrenne* were somewhat artificial.[26] Indeed in the light of *Beune, Defrenne I* would now be decided differently. Finally the extended definition of the ambit of Article 119 has the merit of drawing a whole range of issues out of the scope of Directive 86/378 thereby avoiding the implications of the horizontal and vertical direct effects of directives debate and also ensuring that Member States cannot interfere with the operation of the principle of equal treatment, which the Court sees as a fundamental principle of Community law in this important area, without resorting to an amendment of the Treaty.

Equalising up or down?

The manner in which equality is to be achieved was raised in two cases decided by the European Court in 1994. In *Smith* the Court was asked whether the adoption of a common pension age of 65 for men and women was consistent with Article 119 where a scheme had previously had different pension ages for men and women.[27] Mrs Smith was a member of a contracted out occupational pension scheme which provided that the normal pensionable age for men was 65 and for women 60. On 1 July 1991, the scheme was amended to provide a common pensionable age of 65 for men and women. The change of age was applied to benefits earned in respect of periods of employment before and after 1 July 1995. It was argued that the change in pensionable age had adverse consequences for a number of women in the level of benefits payable.

The Court was asked to decide whether, in achieving equality in this way, there had been a breach of Article 119. The Court held that prior to 17 May 1990 (the date of the *Barber* judgment) benefits payable under an occupational

---

[25] See chapter 2 *supra*.
[26] For example see Prechal and Burrows *The Gender Discrimination Law of the EC* (Dartmouth, 1990) chapters 3 and 5.
[27] Case C-408/92 *Constance Christina Ellen Smith and others* v *Advel Systems Limited* [1994] ECR I-4435. This case reiterates the same principle enunciated in *Coloroll* at paras 32 to 35.

social security scheme were excluded from the application of Article 119. Up to this date employers and trustees were not required to ensure equal treatment. From 17 May 1990 until 1 July 1991 the pension rights for men must be calculated on the basis of the same retirement age as that for women. The reasoning behind this is that Community law requires, until such time as equality has been introduced, that the disadvantaged group be treated on the same basis as other workers. However when equality is introduced, in this case on 1 July 1991, Community law does not preclude measures which achieve equality by reducing the advantages of persons previously favoured. Furthermore, once equality has been achieved, an employer cannot maintain in force transitional measures which are designed to limit the adverse consequences of such changes for the disadvantaged group.[28]

A similar amendment was made to the pension scheme operated by Shell.[29] A common retirement age of 60 was introduced as from 1 January 1985. However women who had been in the scheme prior to that date could elect to retire at the age of 55, the previous pensionable age for women. Following the Court's decision in *Barber*, the scheme was amended with the result that women lost out financially. Again the Court divided the time scale into three. Prior to *Barber* there was no need to have equal treatment. In the period between *Barber* and the introduction of equality men and women were to be treated alike, with the disadvantaged group being granted the same level of benefits as the advantaged group. Once equality had been introduced into the scheme levelling down could take place. Employees could not be given the option of maintaining in force discriminatory provisions by electing to maintain different pensionable ages.

One question which does potentially remain as a problem is whether pension schemes which are amended to take into consideration the *Barber* decision will substantially disadvantage women by introducing changes which predate the decision. This is an issue to be determined by national law and, in particular, whether national employment law would allow a variation in the terms and conditions of employment (pay) retrospectively. All that the European Court has said in this respect is that Community law "places no obligation which would justify retroactive reduction of the advantages which women enjoyed" prior to *Barber*.[30]

---

[28] It is difficult to reconcile this judgment with the decision of the European Court in case 43/75 *Defrenne* v *Sabena* where the Court ruled, in view of the connection between Article 119 and the harmonization of working conditions while maintaining improvement, against the argument that compliance with Article 119 could be achieved otherwise than by raising the lowest salaries. This extract is quoted in *Smith* as part of the Court's reasoning.

[29] Case C-28/93 *Maria Neleke Gerda van den Akker and Others* v *Stichting Shell Pensioenfonds* [1994] ECR I-4527.

[30] Case C-408/92 *Smith* quoted in note 27 *supra* para 22. In the UK employees can presumably stand on their contractual rights.

Survivors' benefits

The two earliest cases in relation to survivors' benefits seem to indicate that the Court believed that benefits payable to a survivor could not come under the scope of Article 119. In *Newstead*[31] the Court held that, in the absence of specific directives extending the application of the principle of equal treatment to benefits for surviving spouses (whether occupational or statutory schemes), the discrimination suffered by Mr Newstead must come within the exception in Article 1(2) of Directive 76/207.[32] This approach of the Court seemed to be reinforced in the staff case of *Razzouk and Beydoun* where the Court held that Staff Regulations for Commission officials which established two different survivors' pension schemes 'according to whether the deceased official was male or female' were contrary to the principle of equal treatment.[33] In this case the Court held that the equal treatment principle was not limited by Article 119 for staff. Almost implicit in this case is that survivors' benefits do not form pay within the meaning of Article 119.

This impression is reinforced by the exception provided in Article 9(b) of Directive 86/378 which stipulates that Member States may defer the application of the principle of equal treatment in respect of survivors' pensions until such time as a Directive on equal treatment in statutory social security schemes in that regard is adopted. As will be seen, this Article is contrary to Article 119.

The Court returned to the issue of survivors' benefits in the case of *Ten Oever*.[34] Mr Ten Oever claimed a widower's pension following the decision of the Court in *Barber* which had said that no discrimination between men and women was permissible in occupational pension schemes. The pension fund had refused him a pension on the grounds that Mrs Ten Oever had died before the decision of the Court in *Barber*. The Dutch Court asked the European Court whether Article 119 must be understood as covering the payment of non-statutory benefits to surviving relations. The European Court held that the fact that certain benefits are paid after the end of the employment relationship does not preclude the application of Article 119. This is so, said the Court, despite the fact that the benefit is not paid directly to the former employee but to his/her survivor. "Entitlement to such a benefit is a consideration deriving from the survivor's spouse's membership of the scheme, the pension being vested in the survivor by reason of the employment relationship between the employer and the survivor's spouse and being paid to

---

[31] Case 192/95 Newstead cited in note 7 *supra*.
[32] The scope of this Directive is discussed in Chapter 3 *supra*.
[33] Joined cases 75 and 117/82 C. *Razzouk and A. Beydoun* v *Commission* [1984] ECR 1509.
[34] Case C-109/91 Ten Oever cited in note 15 *supra*.

him or her by reason of the spouse's employment".[35] Mr Ten Oever could not, however, rely on the direct effect of Article 119 since Article 119 could only be relied on in relation to benefits payable in respect of employment subsequent to 17 May 1990.

The Court used the same line of argument in respect of survivors' benefits in *Coloroll*, adding that a denial of the right to assert payment of a survivor's pension to the survivor would deprive Article 119 of its effectiveness as far as survivors' pensions are concerned.[36] Accordingly it is now clear that benefits paid to a survivor under the terms of an occupational pension scheme are pay within the meaning of Article 119.

The use of actuarial factors in computing benefits

The European Court was asked whether the use of actuarial factors in determining pensionable benefits is compatible with Article 119 in the case of *Neath*.[37] Mr Neath was employed by Hugh Steeper until June 1990 when he was made redundant at the age of 54 years and 11 months. During his employment, he was a member of two occupational pension schemes transferring into a contracted-out occupational pension scheme in January 1979. The contributions made by the employee in this scheme were the same for men and women but women could retire on full pension at 60 whereas a man had to wait until he was 65. Early retirement was possible any time after the age of 50 but such early retirement required the consent of the employer and the trustees of the pension fund. Mr Neath was denied this possibility but was offered the choice of a deferred pension or a transfer payment of £30,672.59 to another scheme. This sum was calculated on the assumption of a retiral age of 65 except for periods of service after 17 May 1990 (date of *Barber*) when the retirement age was deemed to be 60. It was also based on actuarial assumptions about the longer life expectancy of women. If the actuary had calculated Mr Neath's transfer value assuming an age of 60 for retirement and using male actuarial assumptions it would have amounted to £39,934.36. With the same retirement age and female actuarial assumptions, the transfer value would have been £41,486.25. Mr Neath brought his case before an industrial tribunal.

Advocate General Van Gerven argued strongly against the use of actuarial factors based on the shorter life expectancy of men as a group.[38] However, the

---

[35] *Ibid* para 13.

[36] Case 200/91 *Coloroll* cited in note 15 *supra* at para 19.

[37] Case C152/91 *Neath* cited in note 15 above. The facts are summarised by Advocate General Van Gerven at p.950.

[38] *Ibid* p 962. This section of his Opinion is essential reading to understand the arguments before the Court. See also Hervey's case-note in 31 *Common Market Law Review* (1994) 1387.

Court disagreed. The wording of the judgment and the argumentation is rather obscure but what the Court did was to distinguish defined-benefit occupational pension schemes from contributory schemes. In the case of the former, the contribution made by the employer constituted pay within the meaning of Article 119 but that commitment to pay can be separated from the funding arrangements. Funding arrangements fall outside the scope of Article 119. They presumably fall under the scope of Directive 86/378 although the Court did not say so. In contributory schemes, the employee's contribution is an element of pay and must be the same for men and women. However, the employer's contribution to such schemes is not pay since these contributions are designed to provide a sufficiency of funds to cover the cost of pensions. Therefore the Court held that inequality of employer's contribution paid under funded defined-benefit schemes, which is due to actuarial factors according to sex, is not struck at by Article 119. The Court then said that the conversion of part of a pension into a lump sum and the transfer of pension rights are also matters which are not covered by Article 119.

It is almost impossible to penetrate the meaning of the operative part of the judgment in *Neath*. The Court seems to approve of the use of sex-based actuarial factors in determining the level of overall benefits available under a scheme. It does not seem to approve their use in determining the level of payment to be made in periodic pension payments. However, these issues will need to be determined in the future.

Bridging pensions

The relationship between occupational pension schemes and state schemes was raised in *Birds Eye Walls Ltd,* a case referred to the European Court from the English Court of Appeal.[39] Mrs Roberts retired at 57 due to ill health. She received an occupational pension plus a sum of money which was aimed to bring her pension income up to the level of the state pension. When she reached the age of 60, this bridging pension was reduced to take into consideration her entitlement to the state old age pension. She argued that this was discrimination since a man would have been entitled to continue to receive the bridging pension until the age of 65.

The Court held that it was not contrary to Article 119 to reduce the bridging pension in this way since men and women are not in the same situation between the ages of 60 to 65. It is not discrimination, therefore, to treat them differently. The case was further complicated by the fact that Mrs Roberts did not, in fact, receive the state pension since she had opted not to pay full contributions as she had been entitled to do as a married woman.

[39] Case C-132/92 *Birds Eye Walls Ltd* v *Roberts* [1994] IRLR 29.

Instead she received a widow's pension. The Court rejected the argument that Mrs Roberts had suffered discrimination and should have been entitled to the full bridging pension plus her widow's pension arguing that this would create unequal treatment by giving her a two-fold benefit.[40]

Additional voluntary contributions

Article 119 does not apply in the case of additional voluntary contributions which are paid by employees to secure additional benefits.[41] The type of benefits envisaged by the Court are lump sum payments on death or additional fixed pensions. The Court argued that these benefits are calculated separately and are credited to a special fund and managed by trustees as a distinct fund separate from the normal occupational scheme. In the UK the Social Security Act 1986 section 12 had required occupational schemes to provide the framework whereby individuals could claim benefits additional to those to which they would be entitled by reason of their employment. For these reasons the Court excluded them from the ambit of Article 119.

The role of trustees

Article 119 applies to remuneration which is paid directly or indirectly to employees. Thus, an employer cannot evade the obligations imposed by Community law by setting up a trust fund to administer a pension scheme which is discriminatory.[42] Neither can trustees evade the obligation to ensure the principle of equal pay by arguing that their trust deeds prevent them from doing so. If necessary they must resort to the national courts to alter the terms of such deeds. In their turn, national courts are bound to interpret and apply domestic provisions in conformity with Community law. If such interpretation is impossible then the national court must disapply incompatible national provisions. In *Coloroll* this meant that where pension rights were transferred

---

[40] This case has been criticised as tending to introduce an objective justification test into matters of direct discrimination. However the Court did not do this. It held that no discrimination existed. See the editorial in [1994] IRLR 1. The Court is perhaps confusing the gearing of state benefits to the state pension age (which it is has held to be permissible provided that the financial equilibrium of the system depends on such a gearing under the terms of the social security Directive discussed in Chapter 4 *supra*) with private pension entitlements. If bridging pensions are pay and if there is discrimination between men and women then the Court should recognise this. The response cannot be to rely on a difference in the state pension age, which is in itself inherently discriminatory although permitted under European law as it stands.

[41] Case C200/91 *Coloroll* cited in note 15 *supra* at para 90.

[42] *Ibid.*

due to a change of job the second scheme was obliged, when the worker reached retirement age, to increase the benefits it undertook to pay when accepting the transfer so as to eliminate the effects, contrary to Article 119, suffered by the worker due to the inadequacy of capital transferred from one scheme to another due to the inherent discrimination in the first scheme. The question of liability in this situation was not, however, a matter of Community but national law to be determined by the national court.

Directive 86/378/EEC

Following on from this discussion of the case law, it is clear that certain aspects of occupational social security schemes fall under Article 119 and the question must be raised as to the relationship of Directive 86/378 with that Article. Article 119 includes in its ambit the benefits derived from the existence of an occupational scheme and the right to join a pension scheme. Many of these issues are included in Directive 86/378 and so this section outlines the provisions of the Directive and shows how certain aspects of it can quite clearly be seen to be *ultra vires*. The proposed amendments to the Directive will, therefore, be discussed.

Directive 86/378 was intended as a parallel instrument to Directive 79/7 and, whereas the latter instrument was to introduce the principle of equal pay into statutory schemes, the former was to introduce it into occupational social security schemes. Occupational social security schemes are defined in Article 2 of the Directive as being schemes not governed by Directive 79/7 whose purpose is to provide workers, whether employed or self employed, in an undertaking or group of undertakings, area of economic activity or occupational sector or group of such sectors, with benefits intended to supplement or replace statutory schemes, whether membership of such schemes is compulsory or optional. Excluded from the scope of the Directive, however, are individual contracts, schemes having only one member, insurance contracts to which the employer is not a party in the case of salaried workers and optional elements of occupational schemes which guarantee additional benefits or a choice of dates on which normal benefits start, or a choice between benefits.

The key element of this definition is that such schemes are for the benefit of workers, whether employed or self employed. The Court of Justice, however, has held that all forms of occupational pensions and the benefits deriving from such schemes are, in the case of employees, elements of pay within the meaning of Article 119. A distinction is to be drawn, therefore, between occupational social security schemes for employees which can be defined as schemes "which originate in a contract of employment between a worker and a given employer, except statutory schemes proper and insurance and pension contracts concluded privately without the employer being involved"[43] and schemes for self employed workers.

In so far as the Directive purports to regulate occupational schemes for employees it is, therefore, potentially at odds with Article 119, especially in those provisions which seek to exclude aspects of occupational schemes and their benefits from the principle of equal treatment. Any such provisions are, therefore, invalid since a Directive cannot amend an Article of the Treaty. The Treaty is a primary source of law and the Directive a secondary source and, as such, must be consistent with the provisions of the Treaty. The Court stated this explicitly in *Moroni*[44] where it said that Directive 86/378 "cannot preclude an employee discriminated against because of the determination of different pensionable ages from relying on Article 119 . . . the provisions of Directive 86/378 could not limit the scope of Article 119".

The Commission proposes to amend Article 2 by limiting the exceptions to the principle of equal treatment in that Article to schemes which are for the benefit of self-employed workers i.e. individual contracts for self-employed workers, schemes for self-employed workers having only one member and optional provisions allowing a choice of date for the commencement of benefits for self-employed workers. The other exceptions in the Article will be allowed to stand since the definition by the Court of pay excludes contracts which do not arise out of the contract of employment and additional voluntary contributions to schemes.

Article 3 defines the personal scope of the Directive. The wording is slightly different to Directive 79/7 in that the working population includes self-employed persons, persons whose activity is interrupted by illness, maternity (not covered by 79/7) accident or involuntary unemployment and persons seeking employment, and to retired and disabled workers. The Court has not had occasion to interpret this Article as yet but it has held that survivors' benefits are pay within the meaning of Article 119. For this reason, the Commission is proposing to add the words "and to those claiming under them" to Article 3.

The material scope of the Directive is set out in Article 4. It applies to occupational schemes which provide against the risks of sickness, invalidity, old age including early retirement, industrial accidents and occupational diseases and unemployment. With the exception for early retirement this is the same scope as Directive 79/7. In addition the Directive includes the principle of equal treatment in occupational schemes which provide for other social benefits, in particular survivors' benefits and family allowances accorded to employed persons. The Commission does not intend to amend this Article

[43] See COM(95) 186 final cited in note 3 *supra*.
[44] Case C-110/91 Moroni cited in note 15 *supra*.

although it is redundant, in the case of individuals governed by a contract of employment, since the Court has ruled on the issue of survivors' benefits.

Neither does the Commission intend to amend Article 5 of the Directive which states that the principle of equal treatment must be applied in the scope of occupational schemes and conditions of access to them; the obligation to contribute and the calculation of contributions; the calculation of benefits, including supplementary benefits in respect of a spouse or dependants and the conditions governing the duration and retention of entitlement to benefits. Again this provision is redundant in respect of employees since these matters are covered by the principle of equal treatment in matters relating to pay. Article 5 excludes provisions relating to protection of women by reason of maternity from the scope of the principle of equal treatment.

Article 6 prohibits discrimination in relation to: determining the persons who may participate in a scheme, fixing the compulsory or optional nature of a scheme, having different entry rules or minimum periods of employment to obtain benefits, laying down different rules for the reimbursement of contributions on leaving a scheme early (except in relation to setting benefit levels on the basis of actuarial calculations which differ according to sex (para. h) or setting different levels of workers contributions in order to equalise leaving benefits (para. i)), setting different conditions for granting or restricting benefits to one sex only, fixing different retirement ages, suspending the retention or acquisition of rights during agreed periods of maternity leave, and laying down different standards except as provided in (h) or (i) above. Again many of these provisions are redundant in the sense that, for employees and/or paid workers, they merely spell out the decisions of the Court in respect of Article 119.

Article 7 remains unchanged. This Article requires Member States to ensure that provisions contrary to the principle of equal treatment in legally compulsory collective agreements, staff rules of undertakings or any other arrangements relating to occupational schemes are null and void, or may be declared null and void or amended and that schemes containing such provisions may not be approved or extended. Given that this Directive is for implementation by the Member States then this wording is unsurprising. However, given that Article 119 creates direct effect, then the obligation to eliminate discrimination in schemes governed under that Article is much wider in that it applies to employers and trustees as well as other administrators of occupational pension schemes.

The Directive provides for an implementation date of 1 January 1993. The proposed amendment to the Directive would provide that this is the date of implementation in schemes for self employed workers. Article 8(2) does not preclude rights and obligations relating to a period of membership of an occupational scheme from remaining in force subject to the provisions of the scheme in force during that period. This paragraph is also to be amended to cover only schemes for self-employed workers.

Article 9 provided for deferral of the compulsory application of the principle of equal treatment with regard to the determination of pensionable age for the purposes of granting old-age or retirement pensions and the possible implications for other benefits either until equality is achieved in statutory schemes or, at the latest, until equality is required by another Directive.[45] Deferral was also possible in matters relating to survivors' pensions until a Directive in matters relating to statutory social security in that regard is adopted. Deferral for a period of 13 years from the date of notification of the Directive was also possible for outlawing the use of actuarial factors in setting levels of worker contribution. These derogations are clearly contrary to the case law of the Court. The proposed amendment of the Directive will, therefore, limit such derogations to schemes for self-employed workers.

Article 10 will remain unchanged as this requires Member States to introduce measures which enable individuals to pursue their claim of discrimination in the national courts, possibly after recourse to other competent authorities.

Article 11 too will remain unchanged as this protects workers against dismissal if they seek to complain at the level of the undertaking or if they open legal proceedings in a claim of discrimination.

Article 12 allows an implementation period of three years and this period remains unchanged (i.e. until July 1989). Member States must also report to the Commission on the measures which they have taken to implement the Directive within five years (i.e. by July 1991). It is clear from the limitations imposed in *Barber* that amendment must be made to the Directive to take these factors into consideration. The Commission proposes to add an additional Article which would provide that any measure implementing the Directive as regards paid workers must cover all benefits derived from periods of employment subsequent to 17 May 1990 and shall apply retro-actively to that date without prejudice to those who had already instituted proceedings before that date. In that event, the implementation measures must apply retro-actively to 8 April 1976 (the date of *Defrenne II*) or, for Member States who acceded to the Community after that date, the date on which Article 119 became applicable in their territory. For states acceding after May 1990, the latter date is replaced by 1 January 1994.

---

[45] Equality would be required by the 1987 proposal for a Directive COM(87) 494 final of 23 October 1987. This Directive is still pending as part of the Commission's Social Action Programme see *257 European Industrial Relations Review* (1995) 12.

This Article does not affect national rules relating to time limits for bringing actions provided that such requirements are not less favourable than those which apply to actions of a domestic nature and that they do not render the exercise of Community law impossible in practice. These proposals merely write into the Directive the case law of the Court.

Member States are given until 1 July 1996 to introduce such measures and, when they adopt them, they must inform the Commission. Furthermore, they must make reference to the Directive in the implementing measures.

Implementation in the UK

Given that in the matter of occupational social security schemes European law has been in a state of some confusion, it is not surprising that there has also been confusion in the UK.[46] It is estimated that there are currently tens of thousands of cases pending before the industrial tribunals on the matter of access to pension schemes and on the question of benefits payable. UK legislation has been amended at least six times to cope with the changes in European law to bring the legislation into line with Community obligations.

Transposition in UK legislation

The Equal Pay Act 1970 section 6(1A)(b) exempted from its scope "Terms and conditions related to retirement, marriage or death or to any provision made in connection with retirement, marriage or death".[47] At this time, there were discrepancies in a number of provisions relating to occupational social security, the most obvious being that many schemes were geared to the state pensionable age. Several schemes distinguished between survivors' benefits on the assumption that a widow would be left unprovided for as the dependent of a deceased husband whereas a widower would have been the breadwinner.

Following the decision of the Court in *Defrenne I* (1971), no moves were made to amend this legislation despite the Court's view that some aspects of occupational pay did fall within the definition of pensions for the purposes of Article 119. This failure to amend the legislation is not surprising. At this time it was not clear what aspects of occupational social security were to be classified as pay and also the UK Government was as unaware as any other in

---

[46] For a discussion of the implementation of the principle of equal treatment in occupational pensions schemes see Davidson "Occupational Pensions and Equal Treatment" 5 *Journal of Social Welfare Law*" (1990) 310; "Pensions and Equal Treatment" (Labour Research Department, 1991); Richard Townshend-Smith *Sex Discrimination in Employment* (Sweet and Maxwell, 1989) chapter 10.

[47] Equal Pay Act 1970, chapter 41, section 6(1)(b).

Europe that the Court would later declare the direct effect of Article 119 (1976) thereby setting up a potential clash between the Equal Pay Act and Article 119.

The Social Security Pensions Act 1975 and the Regulations adopted under this Act created equal access requirements for men and women.[48] Section 53 of the Act provided that "equal access requirements in relation to a scheme are that membership of the scheme is open to both men and women on terms which are the same as to the age and length of service needed for becoming a member and whether membership is voluntary or obligatory". There is no mention in this Act as to whether a requirement of full-time work would be contrary to the equal access requirements but it seems that equal access was not meant to be guaranteed to part-time workers by this Act.[49] As far as European Law is concerned we know that Article 119 required equal access for part-time workers unless there was an objective justification for such refusal on the part of the employer. However, this was only known to be European Law in 1986 (*Bilka*), although the right existed (but had not been enunciated) as from 1976.

The Sex Discrimination Act[50] amended the Equal Pay Act by providing that an equality clause shall operate "in relation to terms relating to member-ship of an occupational pension scheme (within the meaning of the Social Security Pensions Act 1975) so far as those terms relate to any matter in respect of which the scheme has to conform with the equal access require-ments of Part IV." However, subject to this the Act was not to operate in relation to terms related to death or retirement.

The Social Security Pensions Act 1975 did not address the issue of equal treatment in respect of contributions or of the range of benefits available. Again this is not surprising. At the time of the adoption of the Act, the UK government was involved in negotiating Directive 76/207 which, when it was adopted in 1976, excluded from the scope of the principle of equal treatment "matters of social security". The adoption of the Act also came before the European Court's decisions in *Worringham, Liefting* and *Newstead* which, if only by implication, brought occupational social security into the scheme of Article 119.

In terms of European Law the key date for an understanding of Article 119 and its relationship to the principle of equal treatment in occupational

[48] Social Security Pensions Act 1975, chapter 60, section 53 and S.I. 1976 No. 142 Occupational Pensions Schemes (Equal Access to Membership Regulations).
[49] The debates in Parliament clearly show that 1975 Act was designed, amongst other things, to assist women. However, in introducing the Bill to Parliament, Mrs Castle made no mention of the right of access of part-time workers. At the time this did not appear to be considered as an equal treatment issue. See H.C.Deb.,18 March 1975 Cols 1485–1498.
[50] Sex Discrimination Act 1975, chapter 65 Schedule 1.

schemes must be the *Bilka* decision in 1986. However 1986 was also the year in which the Occupational Social Security Directive was adopted. It is worth recalling here that the determination of the state pensionable age had been excluded from the ambit of Directive 79/7. In the 1980s, therefore, the UK legislature was faced with two irreconcilable tasks. It was required to ensure that the principle of equal treatment was enforceable in the UK in matters relating to access to and benefits payable from occupational pensions, an obligation arising from Article 119, and it was required to introduce legislation transposing Directive 86/378 into UK law. In 1986 it should have been clear that aspects of Directive 86/378 were contrary to Article 119 and therefore illegal and, it could be argued, the Council of Ministers chose deliberately to ignore the judgment of the European Court. Whatever the reason for the confusion, the UK chose to follow the path of transposing the Directive into UK law, ignoring *Bilka*. The Directive gave the UK until January 1993 to ensure that the principle of equal treatment would be applied in matters of occupational social security and it allowed derogations in certain areas.

The method chosen to implement Directive 86/378 was the adoption of the Social Security Act 1989.[51] Section 23 of the Act states that its Schedule 5 will have effect for the purposes of implementing Directive 86/378. The 1989 Act outlaws both direct and indirect discrimination in relation to employment related benefits schemes including benefits in relation to termination of service, retirement, old age or death, interruptions of service by reasons of sickness or invalidity, accidents, injuries or diseases connected with employment, unemployment or expenses incurred in connection with children or other dependants. This list mirrors Article 4 of the Directive. The Schedule provides for the compulsory levelling up of benefits to the extent that any provision of an employment-related benefit does not comply with the principle of equal treatment. The more favourable treatment shall be accorded to persons of either sex.

As Davidson points out,[52] the UK made the most of the derogations permissible under the Directive. The most glaring example is the continuation of different pensionable ages for men and women. However the Act also allowed for the continued use of actuarial factors in determining some levels of benefit and discrimination in survivors' benefits was sanctioned. These derogations were all permissible under the terms of the Directive. However, the first and the third were contrary to Article 119.

Schedule 5 also amended the Equal Pay Act by substituting the words following 1975 (quoted above) with the following "which is also an employment related benefit scheme, within the meaning of Schedule 5 to the Social

---

[51] Social Security Act 1989, chapter 24.
[52] Davidson, cited in note 46 *supra*.

Security Act 1989, so far as those terms relate to any matter in respect of which the scheme has to comply with the principle of equal treatment in accordance with that Schedule".

Thus far, therefore, the UK legislation complied with some aspects of Community law. Occupational pension schemes were recognised as constituting pay but derogations which apparently were permissible under the Directive were introduced into UK law. These derogations themselves were, however, not permissible. This was the classic "Catch 22" situation faced by the pensions industry and by employers when the Court gave its decision in *Barber* (1990). It is hardly surprising that the reaction of the industry was to sue for damages.[53]

The extent of UK confusion is shown in the Pension Schemes Act 1993 which attempted to provide a solution.[54] Section 118 relates to equal access requirements and repeats the requirements in relation to age and length of service contained within the 1975 Social Security Pensions Act. The same section provides that regulations may make provision for the Equal Pay Act to have effect in relation to terms of employment relating to membership of an occupational pension scheme, or to impose requirements on employers as to payment of contributions in the case of their failing to comply with such amendments and for the amendment of any schemes which do not comply with the amendments to the Equal Pay Act whenever these are made. Section 153 of this Act gives power to the Secretary of State to make regulations to provide for the equal access requirements to apply, whether to an occupational pension scheme or to terms of employment relating to membership of it, or to both, with such modifications and exceptions as the Secretary of State considers necessary for particular cases or classes of case. Finally, in relation to equal access, Schedule 7(3) to this same Act repeals Section 118. Schedule 7 amends the Equal Pay Act to add a reference in section 6(1)(a) to employment-related benefits schemes within the meaning of Schedule 5 to the Social Security Act, so far as those terms relate to any matter in respect of which the scheme has to comply with the principle of equal treatment in accordance with that Schedule.

The confusion within the Act itself is attributable to the fact that it was adopted following the decision of the European Court in *Barber* but prior to the same Court's decision in *Coloroll*. The UK legislator just did not know how the Court would decide the issue of temporal limitations and just exactly when and to what extent the principle of equal treatment for men and women was to apply to occupational pensions.

---

[53] See notes 10 and 11 *supra*.
[54] Pension Schemes Act 1993, chapter 48.

In May 1995, Section 118 was amended to impose a requirement on schemes not to discriminate, either directly or indirectly, with regard to schemes' terms of admission to membership.[55] At the same time the gearing of upper age limits on membership of occupational schemes to the normal pension age of men and women was prohibited.

It is clear that European Law and UK law on occupational pensions were never synchronised from the 1970s onwards. This is partly attributable to the hapahazard way in which Community law has developed in this area, making the task of the UK legislator difficult. However, it must also be attributable to the failure of the UK legislator to grasp the implications of Community law for the UK. It is not clear whether this was deliberate tactics on the part of the UK which, throughout the 1980s, was opposed to any extension of the right to equal treatment of men and women. It was the UK delegation, in negotiating the two social security Directives, which insisted on the inclusion of deroga-tions, some of which were clearly opposed to Treaty principles. Certainly there was a failure to comprehend that when the European Court stated that the principle of equal treatment of men and women was a fundamental principle of Community law that this principle would constrain the UK legislator from introducing legislation contrary to that essential "constitu-tional" principle. The resulting confusion has introduced complete uncer-tainty into an area of law which, more than most, requires certainty since the well-being of large numbers of individuals depend on their pension rights.[56]

In contrast to earlier UK legislation in this area, the 1995 Pensions Act is a model of clarity.[57] The UK had to implement Community law arising from the decisions of the European Court. It had also recognised that the time had come to equalise the state pension age since otherwise the pensions industry and employers would be required to adhere to the principle of equal treatment whilst the State would not. Many commentators had pointed to the iniquity in this anomaly.

Section 62 of the Act provides that any pension scheme which does not contain an equal treatment rule shall be treated as including one. The equal treatment rule applies to the terms on which persons become members of the scheme or are treated by the scheme. This means that where a woman is employed on like work with a man in the same employment, or she is

---

[55] S.I. 1995 No. 1215 The Occupational Pension Schemes (Equal Access to Membership) Amendment Regulations 1995 came into force 31 May 1995. These Regulations impose the full cost of providing back dated pensions benefits on the employer (including both the employer's and the employee's contribution) for service after 31 May 1995.

[56] In 1977 the government stated that it did not accept the view that equal treatment for men and women in respect of occupational pensions was required by Article 119. This view is discussed in McCallum and Snaith "EEC Law and UK Occupational Pension Schemes" 2 *European Law Review* (1977) 266.

[57] Pensions Act 1995, chapter 26.

employed on work rated as equivalent with that of a man in the same employment or on work rated as of equal value, any less favourable term of a pension scheme must be treated as modified by the equal treatment rule.

The equal treatment rule does not operate where the difference in treatment is genuinely due to a material factor which is not due to sex and this is proved by the trustees or managers of the scheme (*Bilka*). Where managers or trustees are allowed to exercise their discretion in matters related to membership or the way in which members of the scheme are treated, then they must do so in the light of the equal treatment principle. The effect of their failure to do so is that the term granting them the discretion shall be treated as modified as not to permit the discretion to be exercised in a way less favourable to the woman than the man. Trustees and managers are empowered by Section 65 to make alterations to schemes in order to secure conformity with the principle of equal treatment by way of resolution if they do not already have sufficient powers or if the procedure for making such alterations is protracted and difficult. Trustees and managers are empowered to make such changes retrospective (*Coloroll*).

Section 63 of the Act extends the equal treatment rule to benefits paid under a scheme to dependants (*Ten Oever*). It also states that Article 62 is to be construed as one with Section 1 of the Equal Pay Act 1970 and with the disputes and enforcement sections of that Act. Article 63 also makes Article 62 retrospective, so far as it relates to terms on which members of a scheme are treated, as from 17 May 1990 (*Barber*).

Section 64 exempts from the equal treatment rule bridging pensions (*Birds Eye Walls Ltd*) and payments made on the basis of actuarial figures relating to the life expectancy of men and women (*Neath*).

The 1995 Act clearly brings UK legislation into line with European law for the first time in matters of occupational pensions. However, given the retrospective nature of some of the amendments and the reluctance of the European Court to impose a temporal limitation on the right to equal treatment in matters of access to occupational schemes, problems now abound in the UK in deciding on how to alter schemes to accord with the principle of equal treatment and how UK tribunals should deal with retrospective claims.

A number of the claims brought are in respect of the exclusion of part-time workers from occupational pension schemes. In any given enterprise, such exclusion is effectively deemed to be indirect discrimination against women if the exclusion operates to disadvantage more women than men and if there is no objective justification for the exclusion. Claimants can be divided into two groups. The first group of claimants are women currently employed and the second are those who have left their employment. There are no statutory limitations on the first group of claimants which would prevent their claim to equal access from being heard by an indistrial tribunal. For the second group, however, their claims can only be heard within six months of leaving their employment (1995 Pensions Act in Section 63 (4)(c)). This limitation is the same for other equal pay claims and therefore satisfies one of the criteria laid down by the European Court on the effect of national time limits. Whether it satisfies the criterion of allowing such women to claim their enforceable Community rights is a matter for the tribunal to determine, if necessary with the the help of a preliminary ruling from the European Court itself. If the time limit is allowed to stand then such women may very well have an action in damages, not against their employer, but against the UK government for failing to comply with a Community obligation and thereby causing them loss. Such an action would have to be based on *Francovich* principles.[58]

For claimants who can argue their case before the tribunal, the main issue is whether the limitation of two years in the Equal Pay Act on backdated claims is tenable. A part-time employee who has been excluded from a scheme, for example, for the last 15 years will wish to argue that, provided of course she is willing to pay her contributions (*Fisscher*), her employer must also pay his or her contributions. This may be the case even if she has been excluded since 1976 (*Defrenne*). Her argument will be that the two year restriction should not apply to the question of access.[59] Again, the issue of whether such time-limits are permissible under Community law is a matter for the tribunal, possibly with the assistance of the European Court.[60]

Employers or trustees of pension schemes who find that they suffer following any such decision may wish to consider attempting a *Francovich* action against the UK since they have relied on derogations and exceptions in UK legislation which we now know to be wrongful.

---

[58] Cases 6 and 9/90 *Francovich* v *Italian Republic* [1991] ECR I-5357.

[59] It has been argued that the two year limit may not be appropriate "since UK law implements the equal pay principle by a contractual route, it would be inappropriate for the courts to apply a two year limitation period to equal pay claims when the ordinary limitation period for breach of contract claims is six years". European Developments 24 *Industrial Law Journal* (1995) 194.

[60] A test-case on this issue is to be heard before the Industrial Tribunal in Birmingham in November 1995.

Questions

1. Can you reconcile the decision of the ECJ in *Newstead* with the subsequent case law on occupational pensions and Article 119?

2. To what extent has the ECJ recognised the concerns of the Member States and the pensions industry in their decisions?

3. Is there now a clear view of the scope of Article 119 in relation to occupational pensions?

Contents of Chapter 6

ATYPICAL AND PART-TIME WORKERS

Chapter 6

ATYPICAL AND PART-TIME WORKERS

Introduction

There is currently little[1] specific European legislation relating to the rights of workers who are employed either on short term or temporary contracts and none on part-time workers although proposals have been made for legislation in this area and these proposals are discussed below. It was noted in Chapter 3 that the EC, when introducing its legislation on sex-based discrimination, maintained the ideal type of worker as being full-time and in secure and regular employment. This was the solution to the recession of the 1970s. The aim of EC law in this area was to afford to women the same rights as those offered to what was then perceived to be the typical worker (male, full-time), in possession of a wide range of employment and statutorily defined rights.

Two developments occurred to change this view. One was in relation to our understanding of the very concept of discrimination. Discrimination was not merely treating a female less favourably than a male on the assumption that the two individuals were in the same situation or that the law could create the same situation for them. It came to be recognised that the male norm could not be fitted to the employment patterns of female workers, many of whom were part-time for at least part of their employment and many of whom had career breaks to care for dependants. The concept of indirect discrimination was developed in response to this realisation. Indirect discrimination did not rely on the direct comparison of a man and woman in the same situation, but on a more sophisticated analysis of situations which were in some respects

---

[1] A Directive relating to health and safety of fixed-term and agency workers was adopted in 1991. Directive 91/383, OJ 1979 L206/19.

similar but in others dissimilar. In the employment field, the most obvious such situation was in the position of part-time workers, many of whom suffered disadvantages in comparison to full-time workers and the bulk of whom were women.

Along with this understanding of the concept of indirect discrimination came significant changes in work patterns in Europe. In many countries, employers were seeking greater flexibility of the workforce. As the service sector developed and manufacturing industry declined, there was a growth in the number of part-time and temporary jobs, some seasonal. In many instances, the part-time workers lacked the ability, because of the hours worked, to acquire statutory rights and protections. Their contractual position was also weak because in many industries they were under-represented in pay or other aspects of bargaining.[2] The response of the EC was to attempt to develop specific legislation to cover these workers but this legislation has been consistently blocked in the Council of Ministers.

At the European level, therefore, the development of the concept of indirect discrimination has led to the development of rights for part-time workers where there is an element of sex discrimination. In turn this has led to the necessity on the part of the UK to introduce new legislation to enhance the status of such workers. The irony is that if the UK had not blocked the EC legislation on atypical workers (which would have created a parity of rights only for those working an average of eight hours per week) the amendments to UK legislation may not have required to be quite so dramatic. This is a classic case of a government shooting itself in the foot to maintain its ideological purity.

Indirect discrimination in European law

Indirect discrimination on the grounds of sex is explicitly prohibited by Directive 76/207 on equal treatment in working conditions and by Directive 79/7 on equal treatment in matters of social security. However, there is no definition in the legislation of the concept of indirect discrimination. As late as 1987, a group of experts established by the Commission to examine the implementation of the equality Directives indicated that there was a problem of definition in Community law and in the legal orders of the Member States

[2] See the TUC Report *The new divide – part-time workers pay in the 90s* discussed in *61 Equal Opportunities Review* (1995) 6.

of the concept of indirect discrimination.[3] The experts pointed out that there was little by way of legislation or case law in the Member States which would help in finding a Community definition. Their suggestion was to develop a European level definition based on three factors: a requirement or condition of employment, which is not essential or objectively justified, and which has a disproportionate adverse impact on members of one sex.

These factors are similar to those outlined by the European Court when it was asked to decide whether Article 119 could apply to indirect discrimination. In *Jenkins*, a case which involved differential pay rates for part-time and full-time workers, the Court held that Article 119 did outlaw indirect discrimination and that such discrimination might arise where an employer is unable to show that the difference in pay is not attributable to factors other than sex related discrimination.[4] The employer must show an objective justification for treating full-time and part-time employees differently where it is established that a considerably smaller percentage of women than men can perform the minimum number of working hours to justify the higher rates of pay, regard being had to the difficulties facing women in arranging to work that minimum number of hours. The Court stated, however, that it was for the national court to evaluate the facts to determine whether indirect discrimination arose in any particular case.

The European Court clarified its position in the case of *Bilka* which has become the leading case in European law on the question of indirect discrimination.[5] Here the Court was asked to determine whether the exclusion of part-time employees from an occupational pension scheme was indirectly discriminatory and, therefore, contrary to Article 119.[6] The Court reiterated its position in *Jenkins*, that to accord to part-time workers less favourable treatment than that accorded to full-time workers where a considerably smaller percentage of women work full-time as compared to men is indirect discrimination unless the difference in treatment can be objectively justified on grounds other than sex discrimination. The test to be applied by the national court in assessing that objective justification is that there must be a genuine need on the part of the enterprise that the means chosen are suitable for attaining the objective and are necessary for that purpose. In other words, the Court applied a proportionality test.

---

[3] Commission of the European Communities *Implementation of the Equality Directives* (1987).
[4] Case 96/80 *Jenkins* v *Kingsgate (Clothing Productions) Ltd* [1981] ECR 911.
[5] Case 70/84 *Bilka Kaufhaus GmbH* v *Karin Weber Von Hartz* [1986] ECR 1607. This case is discussed in chapter 5 *supra* in relation to access to occupational pension schemes.
[6] The question of the access of part-time employees to occupational pension schemes was also discussed by the European Court in case C-57/93 *Anna Adriaantje Vroege* v *NCIV Instituut voor Volkshuisvesting BV and Stichting Pensioenfonds NCIV* [1994] ECR I-4583. This case is discussed in Chapter 5 *supra*.

The same test was applied to the situation of part-time employees covered by a German collective agreement for the public service which provided for severance pay for full-time workers but not part-timers.[7] Salary increments paid to full-time workers but not part-timers are also in principle contrary to Article 119 unless they can be objectively justified.[8] Paying full-time employees for attendance at training courses where the same payments were not paid to part-time employees has similarly been attacked under Article 119[9] although payment of differential overtime rates for full-time and part-time workers has been held not to constitute discrimination.[10]

Two years after the Court's decision in *Bilka* it laid down a modified proportionality test where the national court was faced with legislation rather than with an employer's pay policy. In *Rinner-Kuhn* the European Court was asked whether German legislation which permitted restrictions on the right of part-time workers to sick pay was contrary to article 119.[11] The Court held that such a distinction could only be justified by objective factors unrelated to sex. Generalisations about the likelihood of the better integration of full-time over part-time employees into the workforce were insufficient justification. In order to justify such legislation, the state would have to show that the means chosen by the legislation meets a genuine social need and that the means chosen to achieve that need are suitable and requisite to achieve it. Again it was the function of the national court to make this assessment.

These cases all arose in the context of equal pay claims but it is clear from the wording of Directives 76/207, 79/7 and 86/378 that it is contrary to European law to accord to employees different and less favourable working conditions in terms of access to employment, training and vocational training, working conditions or other occupational social security benefits to part-time workers unless the employer can provide an objective justification which meets the test laid down in *Bilka*. For national legislation, the test is that of *Rinner-Kuhn*, i.e. the legislation must meet a genuine social need and be requisite and suitable to achieve the objectives set in the national legislation.[12] In both cases the European Court has said that it is the function of the national court to make the appropriate assessment.

[7] Case C-33/89 *Kowalska* v *Freie und Hansestadt Hamburg* [1990] ECR I-2591.
[8] Case C-184/89 *Nimz* v *Freie und Hansestadt Hamburg* [1991] ECR I-297.
[9] Case C-360/90 *Arbeiterwohlfahrt der Stadt Berlin* v *Botel* [1992] ECR I-3589.
[10] Joined cases C-399/92, C-409/92, C-425/92, C-34/93, C-50/93 and C-78/93 *Stadt Lengerich and others* v *Angelika Helmig and others* [1994] ECR I-5727.
[11] Case C-171/88 *Rinner-Kuhn* v *FWW Spezial-Gebaudereinigung GmbH & Co KG* [1989] ECR 2743.
[12] The indirect discrimination inherent in the Dutch system of incapacity benefits was held by the European Court to be contrary to Directive 79/7 since it excluded part-time workers. See case C-102/88 *Ruzius-Wilbrink* v *Bestuur Van de Bedrijfsvereniging Voor Overheidsdiensten* [1989] ECR 4311. This case is discussed in Chapter 4 *supra*.

Part-time workers in UK law

Statutory rights

The most dramatic change in UK legislation in relation to the rights of part-time workers did not come about as a result of an action being brought by the EC Commission under Article 169 of the Treaty alleging an infringement of EC law, or even by way of reference to the European Court of Justice under Article 177 as a question of interpretation of Community law. It was the House of Lords which held that certain provisions of the Employment Protection (Consolidation) Act 1978 were indirectly discriminatory against women and, therefore, contrary to Article 119 of the Treaty and the equality Directives.[13] It was in the light of this decision that new regulations were adopted affording equal statutory rights for part-time workers.[14]

The Equal Opportunities Commission (EOC) sought a judicial review of the Employment Protection (Consolidation) Act 1978, arguing that the provisions in that Act which imposed a requirement that part-time employees (defined as being employees working between 8 and 16 hours per week) must have five years' continuous employment before being able to bring a claim for compensation for unfair dismissal and for statutory redundancy payments, whereas full time employees (defined as being employees working not less than 16 hours per week) were subject to a requirement of two years' continuous employment, was contrary to Article 119 and the European equality Directives. Under the terms of this legislation, employees working less than eight hours per week could never qualify. The EOC argued that these requirements constituted indirect discrimination.

Two major issues fell to be decided by the House of Lords. The first was in relation to the standing of the EOC to bring such an action and the EOC was held to have sufficient interest to seek a judicial review (Lord Jauncey dissenting on this point).[15] On the substantive issue the House of Lords was

---

[13] *Equal Opportunities Commission and another* v *Secretary of State for Employment* [1994] 1 All ER 910. This case has been extensively reviewed see Morris "Rights and Remedies : part-time workers and the Equal Opportunities Commission" 17 *Journal of Social Welfare and Family Law* (1995) 1: Napier "Victory for part-time workers" *New Law Journal* (1994) 396; Harlow and Szyszczak (case report) 32 *Common Market Law Review* (1995) 641; Villiers and White "Agitating for Part-Time Workers' Rights" 58 *Modern Law Review* (1995) 560.

[14] Employment Protection (Part-time Employees) Regulations 1995 S.I. 1995 No.31. The Regulations are discussed in 60 *Equal Opportunities Review* (1995) 2 and in 524 Industrial Relations Law Bulletin (1995) 2.

[15] The question of standing is discussed extensively in the Villiers and White article cited in note 13 *supra*.

asked to determine whether the provisions of the 1978 Act could be objectively justified. Lord Keith accepted that the provisions were indirectly
discriminatory. He outlined the tests which must be applied in these cases and
quoted both the *Bilka* and *Rinner-Kuhn* tests which are outlined above. The
argument forwarded by the Secretary of State for the differential thresholds
was that government policy was aimed at increasing the amount of part-time
work available and that employers would find it less desirable to employ an
individual if faced with the possibility of having to pay compensation for
redundancy and unfair dismissal. Lord Keith accepted that the goal of
creating additional part-time jobs was a legitimate goal of government policy.
He rejected the argument that maintaining in force different thresholds was
either requisite or suitable to achieve these aims. Lord Keith pointed out that
the aim of reducing the indirect labour costs to employers by relieving them of
the burden of payment of compensation or redundancy payments was unsuit-
able as a method of achieving the stated aims of government policy. Legislation which would permit employers to save on direct costs by maintaining
wage differentials would clearly be contrary to the principle of equal pay. So
too, argued Lord Keith, is legislation aimed at lowering indirect costs of the
kind in issue. This was also contrary to the principle of equality. Neither were
the means chosen requisite. Lord Keith could find no evidence to support the
view of the Secretary of State that there had been an increase in part-time
employment as a result of the different thresholds. The evidence from other
European countries where such differences did not exist did not indicate that
part-time employment decreased, it was rather the reverse. He quoted
statistics from France to show that after legislation had been introduced
providing for equal treatment for full and part-time workers the level of part-
time work increased. On all of these points of substance the other judges
agreed with Lord Keith, and the House of Lords therefore held that the
Secretary of State had failed to provide an objective justification for the
legislation which was, therefore, contrary to European law.

In one intriguing passage in this case Lord Keith perhaps hints that there
may in fact be an objective justification for setting some qualifying thresholds.
As part of the evidence before the House of Lords, the Secretary of State had
produced the draft Commission proposal on atypical work.[16] This proposal
sets a qualifying threshold of eight hours per week so as to reduce the
disproportionate administrative burden on employers which the legislation
would otherwise impose. Lord Keith plays with this idea but rejects it as an
objective justification, not because it lacks any merit, as he does not deal with
that issue, but because the argument had not been led by the Secretary of
State. His argument had rested on the justification that the legislation would

---

[16] The Commission proposal is discussed below.

increase the volume of part-time work and this was not proved to be the case.

A further issue had arisen in respect of whether compensation for unfair dismissal constituted pay within the meaning of Article 119. The House of Lords did not decide this issue since it held that the right to claim compensation was the issue before it. The right to claim compensation fell within the Equal Treatment Directive 76/20. Subsequently, however, the EAT both in England and Scotland have held that compensation for unfair dismissal is pay within the meaning of Article 119.[17]

Following this decision, the Secretary of State issued regulations regarding the rights of part-time workers. The Regulations, which came into force on 6 February 1995, abolish the requirement to work a minimum number of hours (whether 8 or 16) in a working week to allow the week to count as a period of continuous service for qualification for statutory rights in respect of claims for unfair dismissal and redundancy payments.[18] Any employee with two years service can now qualify for redundancy pay and unfair dismissal pay[19]. The 1995 Regulations abolish all statutory provisions which exclude part-time employees such as the hours per week qualification for extended maternity absence.[20]

The decision of the House of Lords and the consequential changes brought about in legislation led to a number of cases being brought to tribunals for backdated claims or for reopening claims which had been dismissed in the past since the applicants did not meet the qualifying hours.

Ms Biggs was a part-time teacher who was dismissed in 1976. Within three months of the House of Lords decision in the EOC case, she brought a complaint to the industrial tribunal. The tribunal held that it did not have jurisdiction to entertain the complaint. The chairman held that the time limits for bringing a complaint began to run within three months of the dismissal although he readily accepted that UK law at that time prevented her from bringing such a claim. Ms Biggs appealed to the Employment Appeal Tribunal (EAT).[21] The EAT recognised that the question raised in this case

[17] *Mediguard Services Ltd* v *Thame* [1994] IRLR 504; *Methilhill Bowling Club* v *Hunter* [1995] IRLR 232.

[18] The Industrial Tribunal had already interpreted the decision of the House of Lords as meaning that both the 8 and 16 hour thresholds were contrary to European law in *Warren* v *Wylie and Wylie* [1994] IRLR 316. The EAT applied the same reasoning in respect of the dismissal of employees in the public sector in *Clifford* v *Devon County Council* [1994] IRLR 625.

[19] But see *R* v *Secretary of State for Employment ex parte Seymour Smith and Perez* [1995] IRLR 449. discussed *infra*.

[20] These provisions were contained in the Trade Union and Labour Relations (Consolidation) Act 1992 c.52.

[21] *Biggs* v *Somerset County Council* [1995] IRLR 452.

affected "thousands of other part-time workers" and the importance of its reasoning which depends in large part on the nature and effect of directly enforceable community rights and the remedies and procedures available to enforce such rights. The EAT quite rightly stated that the starting point for any analysis was the decision of the House of Lords in the EOC case, and the House of Lords had not imposed a temporal limitation on the decision. Since that decision there had been many developments in the law relating to part-time workers. The 1995 Regulations had been adopted under the European Communities Act 1972. The EAT had declared that compensation for unfair dismissal was pay within the meaning of Article 119 and that the industrial tribunal could entertain a claim for unfair dismissal relying on the direct effect of Article 119.[22] It was also the case that the tribunals had been inundated with claims from part-timers. Claims like that of Mrs Biggs had been brought claiming unfair dismissal many years ago. The question in these cases was whether the three months limit laid down in the 1978 Act should apply or whether the tribunal should exercise its discretion and apply a different time limit. If so, what was that limit? Also, certain cases had been dismissed in the past because the applicants failed to meet the qualifying requirements of weekly hours of work. The possibility now arises as to whether the tribunal should exercise its discretion to extend the time limit for appeal and to hear these cases. A related question is whether complainants whose claims had been rejected could still raise another claim on the basis of a new cause of action, namely the infringement of free standing enforceable Community rights. The last issue relates to claims before tribunals in relation to pensions. Here the EAT stated that some 50,000 applications have been presented to tribunals by part-time workers making claims of unlawful exclusion from pension schemes. Time limits in these cases had still to be decided.[23] Finally claims had been raised in industrial tribunals against the Secretary of State for damages for failure to implement the EC equality Directives fully into UK law. In all these circumstances it was imperative for the EAT to apply a proper analysis of the relevant EC law to the case in question.

The EAT examined the rationale for the imposition of national time limits: the promotion of social, economic and political stability; legal certainty and finality in disputes; and recognition of evidential, procedural and other practical difficulties in achieving a fair and just solution of a dispute long after the event. Applying a form of legitimate expectations, the EAT stated that "a claim well-founded, in fact and law, may this perish with the passing of time". It then argued that Mrs Biggs' claim is one in private law against her

---

[22] This was in *Methilhill* cited in footnote 17 *supra*.
[23] There is to be a test case in the Birmingham EAT in November 1995 on these time-limits.

employer. Her right to bring a claim for compensation for unfair dismissal is a right based in UK law and UK legislation lays down the conditions for the exercise of this right. UK law also lays down the courts in which the right can be claimed and the limits of that court's jurisdiction. A tribunal has no inherent right to hear a public law claim, for example, for a claim for compensation against the state for "wrongful" legislation. Neither does it have jurisdiction to entertain claims outside the statutory time limits unless that period is extended to a period which the tribunal considers is reasonable. Tribunals are bound to apply UK domestic law and EC law and disapply offending UK law where this is incompatible with Community law in order to safeguard enforceable Community rights. In 1976, therefore, the industrial tribunal had jurisdiction to disapply offending national legislation. The EAT examined the nature of the rights in question and concluded that the approach taken in *Rankin*[24], which had been to view the right to equal pay under Article 119 as a "free-standing" right, was a misunderstanding of the relationship between Community and national law. In *Rankin*, the EAT had held that statutory time limits on bringing cases could not apply to directly enforceable Community rights. The time limits applied in that case had been based on a balance between the principles of legal certainty and the require-ment of national courts to protect Community rights, "a reasonable period of time after the coming into force of amending legislation".

The EAT declined to adopt the *Rankin* test. It stated that Mrs Biggs' right to bring a claim was based in UK law which should only be set aside if that law was incompatible with Community law. In this case the time limits were not established to be incompatible with Community law.[25] The EAT adopted this approach since it took a different view of the relationship between the two legal orders of national and European law. The EAT argued that equal pay claims deriving from Article 119 are only free standing in the sense that they derive ultimately from "a legal order recognised as superior in force to UK domestic law". The two legal orders, however, are not independent of each other but complementary. In this case national time limits must apply to the bringing of an action which may indeed *ultimately* (the emphasis is that of Mr Justice Mummery) be based on Article 119 unless the two legal orders are incompatible on the point of time limits.

The EAT was aware of the importance of this decision and stated that it was imperative that a higher court should have the opportunity to consider the

---

[24] *Rankin* v *British Coal Corporation* [1993] IRLR 69.
[25] The EAT considered the decision of the European Court in case C-208/90 *Emmott* v *Minister for Social Welfare and another* [1991] ECR 4269 (discussed in chapter 4) but distinguished that case on the basis that it dealt with the failure to implement a Directive and was brought against the Secretary of State.

question of time limits.[26] This is clearly a matter of national law to be determined by the national courts in the light of the case law of the European Court in *Emmott, Johnson and Steenhort-Neerings*.[27] In these cases the European Court held that national time limits for claims arising under European law must be comparable to those for similar claims under national law and that national limits must not effectively deter an individual from enforcing a right arising from European law. The merit of the *Biggs* approach is that it meets the rationale outlined by the EAT for having time limits in the first place, these are the principles of certainty and stability, and the criteria of the European Court in *Steenhort-Neerings*, but it may appear unduly harsh on the claimant. If the case had been decided the other way, it would have been equally hard on employers who might have endless backdated claims to deal with. In reality the problem lies with the failure of the part of the state to reconcile domestic law with Community obligations. The solution is to attempt a public law claim against the state. If *Biggs* is followed, claimants may have a Frankovich claim against the UK Government for failure to implement Community law in the UK. If it is not, then employers may have similar claims.[28]

A question in relation to qualifying periods has still to be finally settled and this is whether the two year requirement for unfair dismissal which now applies to both full-time and part-time workers is indirectly discriminatory. The English Court of Appeal has recently held that the qualifying periods are not objectively justifiable in the case of *Seymour-Smith and Perez*.[29] This case

---

[26] The lack of certainty on this issue is illustrated by the approach taken by the EAT sitting in Scotland in *Methilhill* (cited in note 17) in which it was held that the applicant's claim for unfair dismissal had been originally denied in February 1994 on the ground that she normally worked less than 16 hours per week and did not have five years service. The following month the House of Lords declared this legislation incompatible with Community law. The applicant attempted to re-open her case and it was regarded as timeous, being brought within one month of the House of Lords decision. The EAT agreed and also argued that the case could be re-opened since the original matter application had not raised the Article 119 issue. Compare this to *Setiya* v *East Yorkshire Health Authority* (discussed in Incomes Data Service Brief 547 (1995) 14). Dr Setiya, who had originally brought an action for unfair dismissal before the Industrial Tribunal, sought to bring an appeal to the EAT some two years after the decision of the Industrial Tribunal but shortly after the decision of the House of Lords in the EAT case. The EAT declined to extend the time limit for bringing an appeal.

[27] Case C-208/90 *Emmott* v *Minister for Social Welfare and another* [1991] ECR 4269; Case C-410/92 *Elsie Rita Johnson* v *Chief Adjudication Officer* [1994] ECR I-5483; Case C-338/91 *Steenhorst-Neerings* v *Bestuur Van de Bedrijfsvereniging voor Detail handel, Ambachtenen Huisvrouwen* [1994] IRLR 244. These cases are discussed in Chapter 4 above.

[28] It was noted in the *Guardian* of 19 September 1995 that the government has paid some £34,000 plus legal costs to a woman forced to retire at the age of 60 by a private sector employer. This is an out of court settlement based on the woman's claim that the government had failed to implement the Equal Treatment Directive. This is a case from Northern Ireland where the provisions relating to retirement age were not brought into force until 1989, after the woman was sacked.

[29] Cited in note 19 *supra*.

resulted from the introduction of the Unfair Dismissal (Variation of Qualifying Period) Order 1985 which extended the qualifying period for the right to bring an unfair dismissal claim from one year to two years. The applicants had attempted to make a claim for unfair dismissal in the industrial tribunal but had been unable to since they lacked the qualifying period. They then sought a judicial review of the 1985 Order on the grounds that the percentage of women who could comply with the two year rule was considerably smaller than that of men. The Divisional Court did not accept that the proportion of qualifying women was "considerably smaller" than the proportion of men but if that adverse impact had been shown then the Secretary of State had not shown an objective justification for the change.

The Court of Appeal believed that exaggerated weight should not be given to the word considerable. It held that there had been shown to be a considerable and persistent difference in the numbers of qualifying men and women on the figures which had been presented to it.[30] Turning then to the issue of justification, the Court examined the arguments of the Secretary of State that this case could be distinguished from the EOC case. He had argued that the two year rule applies uniformly to those working more than 16 hours per week, that Lord Keith's judgment was limited to the specific facts of the case where the great majority of part-time workers were women and that, in assessing the suitability of a measure, regard should be had to the degree of discrimination; and only if the degree of discrimination was disproportionate to the good sought would the court interfere in the measure. The Court of Appeal decided to consider what good could be achieved by the discrim-inatory measure in question. It found nothing to enable it to draw the inference that the increase in the employment threshold had led to an increase in employment opportunities. Therefore, it held that the Secretary of State had not established an objective justification and that the applicants were entitled to some form of declaratory relief. It is likely that this case will now go to the House of Lords.

Contractual rights

Indirect discrimination, which is defined by the UK Sex Discrimination Act as the imposition of a requirement or condition which creates a disadvantage for

---

[30] This is a remarkable case in the approach taken by the Court of Appeal in interpreting UK legislation. The Court of Appeal not only relied on EC legal sources but on a statistical analysis of the workforce in the UK in reaching its decision. It is a judgment well worth reading in the context of analysing how judges decide on legal issues.

a considerably greater proportion of women than men and which is not reasonable, is outlawed. Part-time workers are, therefore, free to enjoy the same contractual benefits as full-time employees. On questions of pay, the Equal Pay Act has, since *Jenkins*, been interpreted in such a way as to accord part-time workers the same right as full time workers unless the pay differential has been justified. However, there has been one major problem in the UK in respect of equal pay and indirect discrimination and that has been in relation to the question of access to and benefits derived from occupational pension schemes.

The cases of *Bilka, Barber, Fisscher* and *Vroege*[31] in the European Court have made it abundantly clear that UK legislation fell far short of the Community standard on equal treatment. Recent amendments to legislation have now brought UK law into line on this issue but the question remains open on backdated claims. The 1995 Pensions Act[32] brings the substantive aspects of pensions into line with the decisions of the European Court. On questions of backdated access to membership the situation is not quite so clear cut. The Occupational Pension Schemes (Equal Access to Membership) Regulations 1995 which came into force on 31 May 1995 provide that claims for equal access to membership of schemes after that date apply the national time limits for claims under the Equal Pay Act. Claims must be brought within two years of leaving employment and can be backdated only two years. These time limits must clearly be in conformity with Community law since they apply to all questions of equal pay and they provide an opportunity for individuals to assert their Community law rights.

For claims prior to that date, it is not clear what national time limits apply.[33] The best approach is to take that of the EAT in *Biggs* and to view the question from the relationship between the national and Community legal orders. It has been clear since *Bilka* that part-time staff had the right to apply to join a pension scheme and that this right derived from Article 119, that is, it is an equal pay claim. That right could have been exercised by part-time employees and a claim could have been raised in an industrial tribunal. To do so, national time limits would have applied to the right to raise the claim. Such a claim would have had to have been raised within six months of leaving employment. A successful claim could lead to retrospective admission to a scheme but, on a parity with other equal pay claims, could only be backdated to two years prior to the claim.

---

[31] These cases are extensively discussed in Chapter 5 *supra*.

[32] The Pensions Act 1995 c.26.

[33] The degree of confusion is apparent from the suggested figure that some 75,000 cases have been raised on access to occupational schemes, see 525 *Industrial Relations Law Bulletin* (1995) 7.

Draft Directive on atypical workers

In 1990, the Commission published its latest proposal for legislation in the area of atypical workers.[34] This was one of three proposals which were to be adopted, the others being in the area of health and safety for part-time workers (discussed in Chapter 12) and the other regarding part-time and temporary employment in relation to distortions of competition.[35]

The Commission's proposal applies to part-time employment relationships (but not less than eight hours per week) which involve shorter working hours than statutory, collectively agreed or usual working hours. It also applies to temporary employment in the form of fixed term contracts (including seasonal work) and temporary employment by an agency where the employee has no contract with the undertaking where he or she performs the activities concerned. It is to apply to employed persons in the public and private sector.

Article 2 of the proposed Directive provides for access for atypical workers to vocational training initiated by the undertaking on the same terms as for other employees. Atypical workers are to be included in the computation of the number of employees for the purposes of the organisation of a works council. The workforce is to be consulted when the employer intends to introduce part-time working and an employer of more than 1000 employees must draw up an annual report on the development of the workforce as a whole. An employer must also state the grounds for recourse to part-time work. Atypical workers should enjoy the same access to benefits in cash or in kind granted under social assistance schemes or non-contributory social security schemes (Art. 3). They should have access to social services normally made available to other employees (Art. 4). Part-timers should be given information in good time about full-time posts so that consideration can be given to their applications (Art. 5). Member States must ensure that clauses prohibiting the employment of an agency worker by a user employer can be declared null and void (Art. 6). They must also ensure that the contractual obligations of an employer to a part-time worker are fulfilled, notably in respect of remuneration and social security benefits where the business cannot do so (Art. 7). The Directive applies to seasonal workers in so far as the special features of this form of work allow (Art. 8). Finally Article 9 provides that the Directive does not prevent Member States from introducing more favourable legislation.

---

[34] Proposal for a Council Directive on certain employment relationships with regard to working conditions OJ 1990 C 224/4.
[35] See COM(90) 228 final 13 August 1990 *Explanatory memorandum on the proposals for directives concerning certain employment relationships.*

It is clear from the terms of the draft Directive that the EC still sees part-time work as an exception to the rule of full-time, open ended employment. The Directive is designed to bring the status of atypical workers up to that of full-time workers. It is not surprising then that the UK government blocked this legislation in the Council of Ministers. The UK position is that part-time employment, far from being an undesirable alternative to full-time work, is desirable from the point of those individuals who prefer such a working pattern and from the point of view of employers who can benefit from the increased flexibility which part-time working can bring. The UK government argue that the introduction of equal rights for part time workers will destroy jobs and inhibit the competitiveness of British industry.[36]

The Commission has now withdrawn the proposal which had been based on Article 100/EC.[37] That Article requires unanimity in the Council but the UK effectively vetoed the proposal. The Commission is, however, considering the reintroduction of the proposal under the Social Chapter provisions which exclude the UK.[38] At the time of writing the intention of the Commission appears to be that consultation with the social partners will take place in the second half of 1995 with a view to introducing legislation in the future.[39]

---

[36] These were the arguments put forward in the EOC case cited in note 13 *supra*.

[37] The intention to withdraw the Directive is published in the Commission's Social Action Programme 1995-97. See *Social Europe 1/95*.

[38] These provisions are discussed in Chapter 14 on works councils *infra*.

[39] See the discussion in 257 *European Industrial Relations Review* (1995) 12 and Jeffery "The Commission Proposals on "Atypical Work: Back to the Drawing Board...Again" 24 *Industrial Law Journal* (1995) 296.

Questions

1. How would you define indirect discrimination in European law?

2. Why should an employer be entitled to justify indirectly discriminatory practices on the basis of an objective justification when he/she cannot do so in cases of direct discrimination?

3. Did the House of Lords in the EOC case go beyond the requirements of European law in holding that provisions of the Employment Protection (Consolidation) Act 1978 in relation to requirements on length of service were indirectly discriminatory?

4. What do you understand by the term 'free-standing Community law rights'?

Contents of Chapter 7

PREGNANT WORKERS: EQUAL TREATMENT AND EMPLOYMENT RIGHTS

Chapter 7

PREGNANT WORKERS: EQUAL TREATMENT AND EMPLOYMENT RIGHTS

Background

In the Social Action Programme of 1989 the Commission indicated an intention to take specific action in relation to pregnant workers[1] and, in October 1992, the Council of Ministers adopted a Directive on the introduction of measures to encourage improvements in the health and safety at work of pregnant workers and workers who have recently given birth or who are breastfeeding ("the Pregnancy Directive").[2] This measure sets out minimum standards of treatment to be applied to all pregnant workers. Prior to the adoption of the Pregnancy Directive, pregnancy has been considered by the European Court and the national courts in terms of the Equal Treatment Directive.[2a] In order to attempt to understand the effects of European social law on pregnant workers within the Member States it is necessary to consider both of these Directives, their implementation and interpretation.

Different philosophies and practical approaches towards tackling gender discrimination have been put forward. The traditional Aristotelian argument that "things that are alike should be treated alike, while things that are unalike should be treated unalike in proportion to their unalikeness"[3] may be seen as

---

[1] In addition to the proposed directive on the protection of pregnant women at work, the Action Programme also proposed a Recommendation concerning child care and a Recommendation concerning a code of good conduct on the protection of pregnancy and maternity. For full text see Appendix.
[2] Directive 92/85/EEC.
[2a] Directive 76/207/EEC OJ 1976 L 39/40. For text see Appendix.
[3] Aristotle, *Ethica Nicomachea* V.3. 1131a – 1131b (W.Ross trans.1925).

underlying the Equal Treatment Directive. Article 2(1) of the Equal Treatment Directive sets out the principle that men and women should be treated
equally but then goes on to permit exceptions to this principle in situations
where there are perceived to be differences based on gender. This approach
has been criticised as being based on a male norm; women should be treated
equally with men to the extent that they conform to the standard of men.[4] Its
inadequacy becomes particularly evident when it is applied to the situation of
the pregnant woman. The other side of the principle that like should be
treated alike is that those who are different should be treated differently. The
Pregnancy Directive may be seen as recognition of one particular difference
between men and women.[5] While this approach may be welcomed as tackling
an area of practical difficulty for female workers, it can be argued that it
continues to uphold the male worker as the norm. Pregnant women are given
specific employment rights because they are different from men. If different
treatment for women is seen as an exception to the equality principle, it may
be seen as providing women with a special advantage. These tensions are
evident in the legislative measures themselves, in the decisions of the European Court and the national courts and in the implementation in domestic
law of the European provisions.

Equal Treatment Directive

Article 2(1) of the Equal Treatment Directive provides that "there shall be no
discrimination whatsoever on grounds of sex either directly or indirectly by
reference in particular to marital or family status". The principle of equal
treatment applies, *inter alia*, to access to employment[6] and to working conditions, including the conditions governing dismissal.[7] An exception to the
principle of equal treatment is provided for in Article 2(3) which states that the
Directive is without prejudice to provisions concerning the protection of
women, particularly as regards pregnancy and maternity.[8]

---

[4] For a critique of EC discrimination law see Gillian C. More,"Equal Treatment of the Sexes in
European Community Law: What Does 'Equal' Mean?" (1993) Feminist Legal Studies 45;
Sandra Fredman,"European Community Discrimination Law: A Critique" (1992) Industrial Law
Journal 119.

[5] For further discussion of the inadequacy of the non-discrimination principle in relation to
pregnancy, see N.Burrows,"International Law and Human Rights: The Case of Women's Rights
in Human Rights" in Campbell, *From Rhetoric to Reality* (Blackwell, 1986).

[6] Article 3.

[7] Article 5.

[8] For further discussion of the Equal Treatment Directive, see chapter 3.

Interpretation of the Directive by the European Court – the issues

Paternity leave

Article 2(3) allows for a derogation from the principle of equal treatment by permitting measures which protect women in relation to pregnancy and maternity. The scope of this derogation has been considered by the European Court in relation to the question of paternity leave. An infringement action was brought against Italy[9] in respect of legislation which granted a period of leave to adoptive mothers. The Commission argued that this legislation was in breach of Article 5 of the Equal Treatment Directive which applied the principle of equality of treatment to working conditions. The Court accepted the argument of the Italian Government that this legislation fell within the scope of Article 2(3) in that it aimed "to assimilate as far as possible the conditions of entry of the child into the adoptive family to those of the arrival of a new born baby in the family during the very delicate initial period."

The issue of paternity leave was again considered by the Court in *Hofmann*[10] when a father challenged a legislative provision in Germany which provided for an optional period of maternity leave of six months to follow the compulsory "protective period" of eight weeks which was granted to all mothers following the birth of a child. Ulrich Hofmann, the father of a child, arranged for a period of six months unpaid leave from his employment during which he cared for the child while its mother returned to work. He sought payment of the statutory allowance which was provided to mothers during this period of maternity leave. The Court was asked to consider whether the refusal to pay such an allowance to the father of a child was in breach of Articles 1, 2 and 5(1) of the Equal Treatment Directive. Hofmann argued that the legislation was concerned, not with the health of the mother, but with the care of the child. The Court rejected this argument and held that the scheme fell within the derogation in Article 2(3). Considering the scope of the protection which may be permitted under Article 2(3), it held that it is legitimate first to protect a woman's biological condition during pregnancy and thereafter until her physiological and mental functions have returned to normal and, secondly, that it is legitimate to protect the special relationship between a woman and her child during the period which follows pregnancy and childbirth. In their interpretation of the Directive the Court made it clear that it could not be extended to cover the provision of paternity leave where

[9] Case 163/82 *Commission* v *Italian Republic* [1983] ECR 3273.
[10] Case 184/83 *Hofmann* v *Barmer Esatzkasse* [1984] ECR 3047.

no such provision was made in the Member States and it stated that "the Directive is not designed to settle questions concerned with the organisation of the family, or to alter the division of responsibility between parents".

Direct discrimination – the male comparator

The European Court has also considered, in a number of cases, the application of Articles 2, 3 and 5 to pregnant workers. *Dekker*,[11] the first of the Court's decisions in this area, came to the Court by way of an Article 177 reference from the Dutch Supreme Court. Mrs Elizabeth Dekker applied for a post of training instructor in a youth centre operated by VJV. At the time of her application she was three months pregnant and she informed the selection committee accordingly. The selection committee nevertheless recommended her to the board of management on the basis that she was the best candidate. The management did not however appoint her, giving as their reason the fact that their insurer would not reimburse the maternity allowance which VJV as the employer would be obliged to pay to Mrs Dekker during her maternity leave. Dutch law provided that the insurer could refuse to reimburse payments where "sickness was foreseeable" with no exceptions for pregnant employees.

In considering whether these facts disclosed direct discrimination in terms of Articles 2(1) and 3(1) of the Directive, the Court stated that the answer depended on the fundamental reason for the refusal of employment. If the refusal was based on a reason which applied exclusively to one sex, the refusal to employ would constitute direct discrimination. As pregnancy is unique to women, refusal to employ on the grounds of pregnancy must be direct discrimination. Where the employer gave as the reason for refusal financial disadvantage flowing from the candidate's pregnancy, that amounted to refusal to employ because of pregnancy.

The second question which the Court was asked to consider was whether or not VJV's refusal to employ constituted discrimination where there were in fact no male candidates for the post. The Court stressed that the important issue was the reason for the refusal and where that reason was pregnancy it was directly related to the sex of the candidate and in those circumstances the absence of male candidates was irrelevant. A third question related to the need to prove fault before holding an employer liable; an argument which the court firmly rejected.

In *Dekker*, the European Court held that refusal to employ on the basis of pregnancy is direct discrimination and in a second decision of the same day, in

[11] Case C-177/88 *Dekker* v *Stichting Vormingscentrum voor Jonge Volswassenen Plus* [1990] ECR I-3941.

the case commonly referred to as *Hertz* (the name of the woman involved),[12] it applied the same reasoning to the situation of dismissal because of pregnancy. Mrs Hertz resumed employment after statutory maternity leave in late 1983. In the following June, she developed health problems and during the next 12 months she was on sick leave for more than 100 days. It was accepted by both sides that her ill health resulted from pregnancy and childbirth. She was informed by her employers that they were terminating her contract on the grounds of ill health. The European Court was asked to consider whether the principle of equal treatment in respect of access to employment and working conditions applied to dismissal as a result of pregnancy-related illness and, if so, whether the protection against dismissal was unlimited in time.

The Court re-affirmed the principle of its decision in the earlier case of *Dekker* to the effect that dismissal on account of pregnancy constitutes direct discrimination. It went on to say, however, that the Directive is not intended to encompass illness resulting from pregnancy which should instead be dealt with by provision by the Member States for a period of maternity leave. During this period of leave, a woman must be protected against dismissal due to absence. Men and women are, however, equally susceptible to illness and where illness develops after the period of maternity leave there is no reason to distinguish between pregnancy and non pregnancy-related illness. It is difficult to reconcile the reasoning of the court in *Dekker* with that in *Hertz* to the extent that the fundamental reason for dismissal due to a pregnancy-related illness would seem to be pregnancy and therefore that the dismissal would constitute direct discrimination. While dismissal on the grounds of pregnancy is clearly unlawful, the scope for dismissal due to pregnancy-related illness is less clear. It is prohibited during the period of maternity leave provided for by national law. Following the period of maternity leave, no distinction need be drawn between a pregnancy-related illness and any other illness. Therefore in order to determine whether or not there has been discrimination, the woman's treatment should be compared with that which would have been given to a man in a comparable situation. What then is the position of a woman who is dismissed due to a pregnancy-related illness during pregnancy but prior to the date when her maternity leave period commences?

It is difficult to avoid the conclusion that in *Hertz* the Court was concerned with the practical inconvenience for employers of an unlimited period of protection against dismissal for pregnancy-related illness. It is in most cases the inconvenience to the employer of a woman's absence because of pregnancy rather than the fact of her pregnancy itself which prompts employers to seek

[12] Case C-179/88 *Handels-og Kontorfunktionaerernes Forbund i Danmark* v *Dansk Arbejdsgiverforening* [1990] ECR I-3980.

to dismiss pregnant employees. The line of reasoning in *Hertz* does not seem to have been followed by the Court in more recent decisions where the employer has again put forward the argument of inconvenience.

In *Habermann-Beltermann*,[13] Gabriele Habermann-Beltermann obtained employment as a night attendant in a home for the elderly and it was specified in her contract that she would work only at night. A medical certificate produced shortly after she commenced work disclosed that she was pregnant and that she had been pregnant at the date when the contract was concluded. A provision of the German law on protection of mothers prohibited night work for pregnant women and provided that any contract which infringed this provision would be treated as null. It was further provided in the German Civil Code that an employer could avoid a contract where he or she had at the time been mistaken as to the personal characteristics of the candidate. The European Court was asked to consider whether these provisions were incompatible with the principle of equal treatment in relation to access to employment and working conditions, as interpreted by the Court in *Dekker*. The employer argued that the prohibition against night work fell within the scope of Article 2(3) which allowed for protection of women in relation to pregnancy and childbirth. The Court held that a prohibition in national law against night work during pregnancy which results in the avoidance of a contract of employment, which is not for a fixed term, is in breach of the Equal Treatment Directive. The Court reiterated that the test to be applied was whether the reason for the dismissal was one which related only to one sex and it rejected the argument that in this case the reason for dismissal was not pregnancy itself but was a prohibition on night work during pregnancy which fell within the scope of Article 2(3). The Court considered the intention of Article 2(3) and found that to allow the termination of an open ended contract of employment on the basis of the prohibition against night work would in practice undermine the protective aim of Article 2(3). The operation of the prohibition should be considered in the context of the ongoing contract and it should be recognised that the woman's inability to perform night work was temporary.

Temporary inability to fulfill a fundamental requirement of the employment contract was considered again by the European Court in *Webb* v *EMO Air Cargo (UK) Ltd*.[14] Ms Webb was dismissed from employment as a replacement for another employee on maternity leave when she informed the employer that she herself was also pregnant. Although she had been appointed

---

[13] Case C-421/92 *Habermann-Beltermann* v *Arbeiterwohlfart Bezirksverband Ndb/ Opf eV* [1994] IRLR 364.
[14] Case C-32/93 *Webb* v *EMO Air Cargo (UK) Ltd* [1994] IRLR 482.

initially as a temporary replacement it was intended that her post would continue following the pregnant employee's return to work. Ms Webb complained that her dismissal constituted unlawful direct discrimination in terms of section 1(1)(a) of the Sex Discrimination Act 1975. On appeal to the House of Lords, following the decision of the European Court in *Dekker* and *Hertz*, reference was made to the European Court. The House of Lords took the view that, in terms of UK law, dismissal because of pregnancy is unlawful direct discrimination. The facts of this particular case, however, did not disclose dismissal on the grounds of pregnancy but rather as a result of the employee's unavailability for work at "the critical period". In this situation, the House of Lords considered that, in terms of the Sex Discrimination Act, the appropriate test for discrimination was one of comparison with a man who would have been similarly unavailable for work. Accepting their obligation to interpret UK law in compliance, so far as possible, with European law, the House of Lords asked the European Court whether or not dismissal in this particular situation would constitute unlawful direct discrimination contrary to Directive 76/207.

In clear terms, the European Court stated that dismissal of a woman, employed for an unlimited term as a replacement during another employee's maternity leave, who shortly after recruitment found that she was also pregnant, is contrary to the Equal Treatment Directive, regardless of the fact that a male employee engaged for the same purpose who required leave of absence during the relevant period would also have been dismissed. Several aspects of the Court's judgment are noteworthy. First, the comparison of a pregnant woman with a sick man is rejected. The Court states that:

"since pregnancy is not in any way comparable with a pathological condition, and even less so with unavailability for work on non-medical grounds, there can be no question of comparing the situation of a woman who finds herself incapable by reason of pregnancy of performing the task for which she was recruited with that of a man similarly incapable for medical or other reasons."

Secondly, following on from the decision in *Habermann-Beltermann*, the Court rejects, as a possible justification for dismissal, the woman's inability to fulfill a fundamental condition of her contract. The temporary nature of the woman's inability and thus the temporary nature of the inconvenience to the employer was emphasised. This must, however, be read in the context of a contract of employment for an unlimited term.

Although this case arose in relation to the Equal Treatment Directive, the European Court made reference to the recently adopted Pregnancy Directive and indicated that these two measures should be looked at in conjunction. The

Pregnancy Directive aims to provide protection for the health and safety of women during pregnancy and prohibits dismissal, by reason of pregnancy, during the period commencing with pregnancy until the end of statutory maternity leave. The Court stated that such protection cannot depend on whether the woman's "presence at work during maternity is essential to the proper functioning of the undertaking in which she is employed".

Despite these clear and encouraging statements from the Court, one doubt remains. The decision was given in the context of employment "for an unlimited term". The decision in *Habermann* similarly emphasised the unlimited nature of the woman's employment. Scope for use of the male comparator may exist in relation to women engaged on short or fixed term contracts. Once again it is difficult to avoid the conclusion that the Court was exercising caution based on concern for the practical inconvenience to employers. The stress placed by it upon the permanent and open ended nature of the woman's contract gives rise to the inference that the Court's decision might have been different had the contract been short term or temporary. The choice of language appears to leave open the potential for justification of direct discrimination. Having established that there is direct discrimination where the reason for the woman's treatment is pregnancy, if the Court was to reach a different decision in the context of a temporary contract, it would appear to be allowing justification of direct discrimination. This possibility throws into question the previously well established principle that there can be no objective justification of direct discrimination.

The Advocate General has recently issued his Opinion in *Gillespie* v *Northern Health and Social Services Board*.[15] In this case, referred from Northern Ireland, a group of women employed by various public health boards are disputing the level of pay which they received while on maternity leave. At the heart of this case is the question of whether or not the sick man comparator has been fully excised from the pregnancy debate. The European Court has been asked to consider whether Article 119, the Equal Pay Directive or the Equal Treatment Directive require that a woman on maternity pay should receive the full pay which she would have received had she been working. Is it unlawful discrimination to take into account a woman's absence on maternity leave when calculating her entitlement to remuneration? The Advocate General's Opinion suggests that, on the authority of *Webb*, there is no scope for comparison of a pregnant woman with a man who is incapable of working due to ill health or for some other reason. He confirms however that it would be unlawful to take account of a woman's pregnancy in relation to pay while she is working. The indications seem to be that the sick man comparison will not be revived.

---

[15] Case C-342/93 *Gillespie* v *Northern Ireland Health and Social Services Board*.

Pregnancy Directive

The Equal Treatment Directive permits Member States to introduce protective measures in relation to pregnancy and maternity and, in the Action Programme of 1989, the Commission indicated the intention to introduce a Directive setting out minimum standards of protection. Two aims can be seen as underlying the proposal; the protection of the health and safety of a particular section of the workforce[16] and the introduction of measures designed to enable women "to reconcile their occupational and family obligations".[17] The legal base for the Directive was Article 118A which allows for qualified majority voting in respect of the adoption of Directives aimed at encouraging improvements and harmonising conditions "especially in the working environment, as regards the health and safety of workers". It was issued as an individual Directive within the framework of the Health and Safety Directive 89/391/EEC.[18] The difficulty of obtaining unanimity in social measures was undoubtedly influential in the choice of Article 118A but this in turn restricted the extent to which the Directive could introduce social measures and it has been criticised as subordinating "the principle of equal opportunities between women and men . . . to the protection of their health and safety".[19] The UK Government, amongst others, has argued nonetheless that the Directive represents a misuse of Article 118A in that the provisions of the Directive extend beyond the boundaries of health and safety.[20]

Despite the use of Article 118A, and the process of qualified majority voting, the original proposals had to be substantially weakened before the Directive was finally adopted on 19 October 1992. The preamble sets out a number of concerns to be addressed by the measure; the continued improvement of the health and safety of workers and, in particular, those who are at special risk; the identification of pregnant women and women who have recently given birth as being such a special risk group; the health and safety implications not only of traditional workplace risks but also of the risk of dismissal; and the need to reconcile the protection of the health and safety of pregnant workers with their equal treatment in the labour market.

Article 1 sets out the purpose of the Directive which is the encouragement of improvements in the health and safety at work of pregnant workers and workers who have recently given birth or are breastfeeding. The Directive is

[16] Community Charter, para 19.
[17] Community Charter, para.16.
[18] OJ 1989 L 183/1. For the text see Appendix.
[19] D.Muffat-Jeandet, "Protection of Pregnancy and Maternity" (1991) 20 Industrial Law Journal 76, at 77.
[20] See chapter on Health and Safety.

intended to set minimum standards and it cannot be used to reduce existing higher levels of protection within Member States.

Article 2 provides definitions of "pregnant worker", "worker who has recently given birth" and "worker who is breastfeeding". In each case, the definition of these terms is made in accordance with national legislation and/or national practice. It is an essential element of satisfying the definition that the woman has informed her employer of her condition.

The focus of the health and safety provisions of the Directive is on the use of risk assessments and in Article 3 it is provided that the Commission, in conjunction with the Advisory Committee on Safety, Hygiene and Health Protection at Work, will draw up guidelines on assessment of hazardous materials and processes. The guidelines will take account not only of dangerous substances and processes but will also deal with "movements, postures, mental and physical fatigue and other types of physical and mental stress connected with the work."

Employers are obliged to carry out health and safety assessments based on these guidelines under Article 4. Where an assessment discloses a risk to the health and safety of a worker covered by the Directive, Article 5 sets out three stages of action which the employer should take. First, the employer shall temporarily adjust the woman's working conditions and/or working hours in order to avoid the risk. Secondly, if this is not practicable, the employer shall move the worker concerned to another job and finally, if this is not possible, the worker shall be given a period of leave. Under Article 6, the same steps shall be taken where the worker will be exposed to certain specified hazardous substances listed in Appendices to the Directive.

Night work during pregnancy and for a period after childbirth is prohibited by Article 7. Where this provision applies, the woman shall be transferred to daytime work or, where this is not practicable, she shall be given leave.

According to Article 8, Member States are required to ensure that workers covered by the Directive are given a period of maternity leave. The leave must be for a continuous period of 14 weeks and must include a period of compulsory leave of two weeks before and/or after confinement.

Article 9 requires that workers covered by the Directive must be allowed time off work, without loss of pay, for ante-natal care.

Workers covered by the Directive are protected by Article 10 from dismissal from the commencement of pregnancy to the end of the period of maternity leave provided for in Article 8. Dismissal is prohibited "save in exceptional cases not connected with their condition and which are permitted under national legislation and/or practice." Where a woman is dismissed during the protected period, she must be provided with written reasons for dismissal.

Article 11 is concerned with the maintenance of employment rights. In the situations covered by Articles 5, 6 and 7, contractual rights, including payment of an adequate allowance, must be maintained. During the period of maternity leave provided for in Article 8, contractual rights must be ensured with the exception of pay. During this period there must be an adequate allowance which must be "at least equivalent to that which the worker would receive in the event of a break in her activities on grounds connected with her state of health". Entitlement to such an allowance can be made dependent on certain conditions of eligibility provided that these do not require more than 12 months' employment prior to the expected week of confinement.

Article 12 requires that Member States shall ensure that adequate means exist whereby individuals can enforce their rights arising from this Directive.

The Directive should have been implemented within two years of its adoption, i.e. by October 1994 and Member States are required to report to the Commission every five years on its implementation. No cases have as yet been heard by the European Court arising from the Directive.

In the decision of the Court in *Webb*, reference was made to the recently adopted Pregnancy Directive and the court discussed the necessity of interpreting the principle of equal treatment in the context of the Directive. In earlier decisions,[21] the Court has referred to the relationship between Article 2(1) which requires equal treatment and Article 2(3) which allows for exceptions to the principle of equal treatment in respect of protective measures relating to pregnancy and maternity. Is the Pregnancy Directive intended to set down minimum standards of protection which must be provided as exceptions to the principle of equal treatment? Or is it intended to be a move away from the male oriented model of equal treatment to a recognition of the unique needs of the pregnant woman in the workplace?

The relationship between the two Directives may give rise to some jurisprudential and practical difficulties. Article 10 of the Pregnancy Directive prohibits dismissal of workers covered by the Directive from the beginning of their pregnancy to the end of the period of maternity leave provided for by the Directive. This is subject to an exception in respect of "exceptional cases not connected with their condition which are permitted under national legislation and/or practice". This provision must be read together with the principle of equal treatment as developed by the European Court. The interpretation of the exception will be of particular significance to the effectiveness of Article 10 and, while decisions such as *Habermann* and *Webb* indicate that the Court will construe strictly the phrase "not connected with their condition", doubts must remain in relation to, for example, women on temporary contracts. In that situation it may remain possible for an employer to argue successfully that the

---

[21] See e.g. Case 184/83 *Hofmann* cited in note 10 *supra* and Case C-421/92 *Habermann* cited in note 13 *supra*.

reason for the woman's dismissal was not her pregnancy but the fact, for example, that she was unavailable for work.

Although the Pregnancy Directive sets out a minimum standard of protection for women who are already employed, it makes no provision in relation to job applicants who are pregnant. *Dekker* has established that it is unlawful discrimination to refuse to employ a candidate on the basis that she is pregnant but this particular situation is not dealt with in the Pregnancy Directive. Practical difficulties may arise for employers in the situation where a pregnant woman applies for a post which would entail risks to her health and safety during pregnancy. According to the principle of equal treatment, the employer cannot refuse to employ her on the basis of her pregnancy but, having engaged the woman, may then be required under the Pregnancy Directive to change her working conditions or ultimately to suspend her. This may be seen as placing an undue, although only temporary, burden on the employer.[22]

Implementation in the UK – problems

Equal treatment and the pregnant worker

The Equal Treatment Directive is given effect in the UK by the Sex Discrimination Act 1975. The issue of the application of the Act to pregnant workers has given rise to difficulty in the interpretation of the Act and to doubts as to its compliance with the Directive. Section 1(1)(a) defines the concept of direct discrimination as being where an employer treats a woman less favourably, on the grounds of her sex, than he treats or would treat a man. Early attempts to apply this provision to pregnant women were rejected on the basis that the legislation requires a male comparator and there is no male comparator for a pregnant woman.[23] The argument was then developed of comparing the treatment of a pregnant woman with that of a man who was absent from work due to ill health.[24] This was the approach adopted by the UK courts in *Webb* although the House of Lords accepted that in a clear case of dismissal because of pregnancy there was no need for comparison. Following the decision of the European Court, *Webb* was referred back to the House of Lords which issued its decision in October 1995. It was hoped that the

---

[22] For a further discussion of some of these issues, see J.Jacqmain, "Pregnancy as Grounds for Dismissal" (1994) 23 Industrial Law Journal 355.

[23] *Turley* v *Allders Department Stores Ltd* [1980] IRLR 4.

[24] See, e.g. *Hayes* v *Malleable Working Men's Club* [1985] IRLR 367.

House of Lords would finally lay to rest the pregnancy/illness debate and address the issue of whether or not the Sex Discrimination Act is capable of construction in compliance with the Equal Treatment Directive. In a confusing judgment, it appears to have done neither. Lord Keith, in delivering his judgment, focussed on section 5(3) of the Act which requires that a comparison under section 1(1) "must be such that the relevant circumstances in the one case are the same, or not materially different, in the other". In the present case, the fact that Ms Webb was unavailable for work due to pregnancy was a circumstance relevant to her case which "could not be present in the case of a hypothetical man". On that basis, the appeal was allowed.

While women employed in the private sector continue to face uncertainty over interpretation of the domestic legislation, those in the public sector have been able to benefit from the direct enforceability of the Equal Treatment Directive. This in particular has benefited women who were dismissed from the armed services on becoming pregnant; a practice which was permitted by section 85(4) of the Sex Discrimination Act 1975 which excluded from the scope of the Act "service in . . . the naval, military or air forces of the Crown".[25] Women in the armed services, who were excluded from the Sex Discrimination Act and who were forced to resign on becoming pregnant, have successfully challenged their treatment and following on from the decision of the European Court in *Marshall*[26] and the removal on limits of compensation under the Sex Discrimination Act[27] a number of women have been able to obtain significant levels of compensation.[28]

Implementation of the Pregnancy Directive

Despite its opposition to the 1992 Directive, the UK Government had taken steps to implement the measures prior to the deadline of October 1994. These new provisions represent a very significant improvement in legal protection for female employees within the UK. The legal provisions are however complicated and their compliance with the Directive has not yet been tested. They have been implemented in the UK principally by means of the Trade Union Reform and Employment Rights Act 1993 (TURERA) which has amended

---

[25] This exclusion no longer operates as a result of the amendment of section 85(4) by the Sex Discrimination Act 1975 (Application to Armed Forces etc) Regulations 1994 [SI 1994 No 3276] which came into force on 1 February 1995.
[26] Case C-271/91 *Marshall* v *Southampton and South West Hampshire Area Health Authority (Teaching)* [1993] IRLR 445.
[27] Sex Discrimination and Equal Pay (Remedies) Regulations 1993.
[28] For further discussion of the claims by dismissed servicewomen against the MOD see, "Taking the Cap Off Discrimination Awards" Equal Opportunites Review No 57, September/October 1994, 11, 23; Arnull, "EC Law and the Dismissal of Pregnant Servicewomen" (1995) Industrial Law Journal 215.

the existing provisions in the Employment Protection (Consolidation) Act 1978 (EPCA). Changes to the system of maternity pay and benefits have been made by the Maternity Allowance and Statutory Maternity Pay Regulations 1994[29] and the Social Security Maternity Benefits and Statutory Sick Pay (Amendments) Regulations 1994.[30]

With the exception of the provisions relating to maternity pay, the Directive has been implemented in the UK as applying only to employees. The definitions in Article 2 of the Directive refer to a worker who is pregnant, has recently given birth or is breastfeeding and "who informs her employer of her condition, in accordance with national legislation and/or national practice". A "worker" in UK law is a broader category than an "employee" and would include an individual who works under a contract for services. Statutory definitions in the UK describe an employee as an individual who works under a contract of service, with the definition of a contract of service being left to the courts. While most employment legislation applies only to employees, the Sex Discrimination Act 1975 and the Equal Pay Act 1970 apply to the wider category of workers and it may be argued that implementation of the Pregnancy Directive should have had a similar scope. Uncertainty surrounds the status of atypical work relationships with, for example, casual workers and agency workers not always being classified as employees.[31] In view of the growth in flexible working patterns and the concentration of women in many of these atypical working relationships, the implementation of the Directive as applying only to employees may exclude from its scope a significant number of female workers.

In reviewing implementation of the Directive, provisions can be divided into four areas – maternity leave, maternity pay, protection against dismissal, and health and safety. Time off for ante-natal care was already provided for by UK law without reference to continuity of employment and this has continued unchanged.[32]

Maternity leave

Prior to the implementation of the Directive, UK law provided for women who satisfied certain conditions the right to return to work not later than the twenty-ninth week after confinement. To be entitled to the right to return to work, the woman required to have been continuously employed for at least two years and still be employed at the eleventh week prior to the expected

[29] SI 1994 No 1230.
[30] SI 1994 No 1367.
[31] See, e.g. *O'Kelly* v *Trust House Forte* [1984] QB 90.
[32] EPCA, S.31A.

week of confinement. This in effect provided for a potential period of maternity leave of 40 weeks. Article 1 of the Directive provides that it must not "have the effect of reducing the level of protection" currently existing in Member States and therefore this provision has been maintained.[33] This right is referred to as the right to return to work.

In order to comply with Article 8 of the Directive which requires a "continuous period of maternity leave of at least 14 weeks" a new general right to maternity leave has been introduced for all female employees regardless of hours of work or continuity of employment. Sections 33 to 38A EPCA provide for a period of leave of 14 weeks or until the birth of the child if that is later.[34] The period of maternity leave must include the two weeks after confinement. Section 34 EPCA sets out detailed rules as to the commencement of the period of leave and the requirement for notification to the employer. Although it is expected that maternity leave will normally commence on the date specified by the woman, there is also provision for automatic commencment where, prior to the specified date, the woman is "absent from work wholly or partly because of pregnancy or childbirth after the beginning of the sixth week before the expected week of childbirth". In its original form in the Bill, this automatic commencement was to come into effect after the eleventh week before the expected week of confinement. In the face of considerable opposition to this provision, which could have resulted in a woman's entitlement to maternity leave being almost exhausted by the date of birth, automatic commencement was delayed. If there is automatic commencement the woman must give notice to the employer that she is now on maternity leave as soon as reasonably practicable.[35] Section 33 EPCA requires the maintenance of contractual terms throughout leave although this provision applies only to the period of 14 weeks' maternity leave and not to the extended period of leave enjoyed by women who have the right to return to work.[36]

Maternity pay

Article 11 of the Directive requires that workers on maternity leave must be provided with an "adequate allowance" and further states that an allowance will be considered as adequate "if it is at least equivalent to that which the worker concerned would receive" as sick pay. Article 11(4) allows Member States to make entitlement to allowance dependent on certain conditions of

---

[33] EPCA, SS.39–44.
[34] EPCA S.35.
[35] EPCA S.36(1)(b).
[36] Contractual entitlements during the remainder of the 40 week period continue to be governed by Section 45, EPCA.

eligibility provided that there is no requirement of "periods of previous employment in excess of 12 months immediately prior to the presumed date of confinement." These provisions are given effect in two sets of Regulations, the Maternity Allowance and Statutory Maternity Pay Benefits Regulations 1994[37] and the Social Security Maternity Benefits and Statutory Sick Pay (Amendment) Regulations 1994[38] which amend the existing provisions in the Social Security Contributions and Benefits Act 1992 and the relevant Regulations.[39] The two principal sources of payment for women who are on maternity leave are Statutory Maternity Pay (SMP) and Maternity Allowance (MA).[40]

In order to be entitled to receive SMP, a woman must have been continuously employed for at least 26 weeks by the qualifying week[41] and during the previous eight weeks her average earnings must have been above the threshold for National Insurance contributions. In order to receive SMP the woman must still be pregnant at the eleventh week before the expected week of confinement, or alternatively have already given birth, and have given 21 days' notice to her employer of the date when she intends to stop work, or whatever notice is reasonably practicable. Medical evidence is required of the expected date of confinement. SMP is only payable while a woman is absent from work due to pregnancy or childbirth and therefore the final requirement for entitlement is that the woman must actually have stopped work because of pregnancy or childbirth. SMP will be payable where the woman has given birth to a stillborn child or has suffered a miscarriage after 24 weeks of pregnancy.[42] Where a woman satisfies these conditions she is entitled to SMP for a possible total of 18 weeks. During the first six weeks she is entitled to 90%t of her average weekly pay and for the remaining 13 weeks she is entitled to a weekly fixed sum of £52.50.[43]

SMP is not available earlier than 11 weeks before the expected week of childbirth and at the latest it must begin in the week following the week of birth. Payment will commence in the week following the week in which the woman stopped work. This represents a welcome change from the previous rules concerning the maternity pay period in terms of which the woman was effectively obliged to stop working by the sixth week prior to the expected

---

[37] SI 1994 No 1230.

[38] SI 1994 No 1367.

[39] Statutory Maternity Pay (General) Regulations 1986 [SI 1986 No 1960]; Statutory Maternity Allowance Regulations 1987 [SI 1987 No 416].

[40] SMP is payable by the employer whereas MA is payable by the Benefits Agency. The amount of SMP reimbursed to employers has been reduced from 100% to 92% with an exception for small businesses which continue to receive full reimbursement.

[41] i.e. the 15th week before the expected week of confinement.

[42] Stillbirth (Definition) Act 1992.

[43] This figure is linked to the upper rate of Statutory Sick Pay (SSP).

week of childbirth if she wished to receive her full 18 week entitlement. The Directive does not allow for reduction in existing provision and for that reason SMP continues to be available for 18 weeks although those women who are only entitled to the general period of maternity leave will be absent for 14 weeks and will only receive SMP during that period.

Women who do not qualify for SMP may be entitled to receive Maternity Allowance which may be claimed by those who have paid national insurance contributions in respect of at least 26 weeks out of the 66 weeks preceding the expected week of childbirth.[44] Matenity Allowance is now available at two weekly rates: £52.50 for women who are employed at the qualifying week and £44.50 for women who are self-employed or unemployed at the qualifying week.

It was recommended by the Commission that sick pay should be available to women during maternity leave where they were ill as a result of a non-pregnancy related complaint. This proposal was not adopted in the final Directive although there has been some change in the UK system with regard to the relationship between SMP and Statutory Sick Pay (SSP). Previously SMP was payable during the period of 11 weeks before and 11 weeks after the expected week of childbirth. Thus, in order to benefit from the full 18 weeks of pay, the woman required to stop work by the sixth week before the expected week of childbirth. This provision was aimed at preventing women from using sick pay provisions until the date of childbirth, thus extending their maternity pay entitlement after birth. This restriction no longer applies, although a similar result will now be achieved by the provisions relating to automatic commencement of matenity leave where a woman is absent from work for a reason related wholly or partly to pregnancy at any time after the sixth week before the expected week of childbirth. The important distinction which must now be made is between pregnancy-related and non pregnancy-related illness. Where the illness is pregnancy related, maternity leave will commence automatically and SMP will become payable whereas if the illness is not pregnancy-related the woman will be entitled to statutory (or contractual) sick pay.

Although the new provisions represent an improvement in that all women who qualify for SMP will now receive it at the higher rate for six weeks,[45] a significant number of women will fail to qualify for either SMP or Maternity Allowance. While the requirement in the Directive is considerably weaker than the requirement of maternity leave on full pay which was earlier proposed, the UK implementation may be open to criticism for further

---

[44] SSCB 1992, Section 35, as amended by Maternity Allowance and Statutory Maternity Pay Regulations 1994, reg 2(1)(b).
[45] Previously only those women with at least two years' continuous employment were entitled to six weeks at the higher rate of 90% of their average weekly earnings.

reducing the benefit. Concern has been expressed that "some of the poorest women with children, who most need to be included in the system of maternity pay, are currently excluded."[46] Eligibility for SMP depends on "employee" status, continuous employment of at least 26 weeks at the qualifying week, and earnings within the relevant period of at least the minimum threshold for National Insurance contributions.

It may be questioned whether or not the use of a minimum threshold complies with the principle of equal treatment in the situation where a significantly larger proportion of women than men receive wages below the threshold. The European Court, in a case concerning an earnings-related social security benefit, held that basing entitlement on an earnings threshold constituted indirect discrimination where a higher proportion of those below the threshold were women. In this case, a justification which was purely budgetary was rejected.[47]

SMP is only available to women who are classified as employees.[48] As discussed above, the effect of this definition as intepreted by the UK courts is to exclude not only the clearly self-employed but also possibly many workers in atypical situations including agency workers and casual workers. While Maternity Allowance is available to a wider category of workers, it provides a lower rate of pay. It may therefore be questioned whether the personal scope of the UK system of SMP is too narrow to implement the Directive properly.

Entitlement to SMP is also dependent on the woman having 26 weeks of continuous employment at the qualifying week. This appears to conform with Article 11(4) of the Directive which permits Member States to make entitlement "conditional upon the worker concerned fulfilling the conditions of eligibility for such benefits laid down under national legislation. These conditions may under no circumstances provide for previous employment in excess of 12 months immediately prior to the presumed date of confinement". The UK Government has argued that "it is wrong for a person to draw on such benefits when they have paid insufficient tax and national insurance contributions"[49] and on this basis would justify the requirement for a period of employment. The concept of continuous employment, however, requires employment with the same employer and thus the current scheme will exclude

---

[468] House of Commons Employment Select Committee, "Mothers in Employment", Volume 1: Report and Proceedings of the Committee, HMSO, 1995.

[47] See *MA Roks and others* v *Bestuur van de Bedrijfsvereniging voor de Gezondheid, Geestelijke en Maatschappelijke Belangen* Decision of the Court of 24 February 1994 n.y.r. This decision is discussed further in chapter 4.

[48] "Employee" is defined for this purpose in Section 171(1) of SSCB 1992 as being a woman over 16 who is employed under a contract of service and who is treated as an "employed earner" for the purposes of national insurance contributions.

[49] "Mothers in Employment" see note 28, *supra*.

those who have recently changed jobs. Thus, although a woman may have worked and paid national insurance contributions for many years, if she begins work with a new employer less than 26 weeks before confinement, she will not be entitled to receive SMP. The Directive does not specifically deal with this issue but in the background report for *Webb*, the Commission, in discussing the provisions of the Directive, makes it clear that the allowance should be provided to a woman provided that she has been in employment during the 12 months prior to confinement and that it is not essential that the period of employment should have been with the same employer.[50]

The rules relating to continuity for the purposes of SMP do not require a minimum number of hours per week and thus do not exclude part-time workers but in practice the requirement for both SMP and the Maternity Allowance that the woman has earned at least above the threshold for national insurance contributions will exclude the lowest paid. If a significantly larger proprtion of women could be shown to be among those who earn less than the national insurance minimum, the scheme may be open to challenge on the grounds that it is indirectly discriminatory.

Dismissal

The Directive stressed the importance of providing employment rights to back up the health and safety rights of pregnant employees and the argument that there are such employment rights has been used to calm fears as to the impact which these new provisions may have on the willingness of employers to engage women of childbearing age. While it is too early to assess whether these new maternity rights will have a deleterious effect on women's employment in general, it is clear that there has been a significant improvement in the legal protection afforded to women against unfair dismissal. Prior to October 1994, a female employee dismissed because of pregnancy could claim that such dismissal was unfair[51] but only where she satisfied the conditions as to continuity of employment.[52] This protection was further subject to exceptions where the woman, because of her pregnancy, was no longer capable of doing the work for which she was employed or it was unlawful for the employer to continue to employ her. In these situations, the woman was entitled to be offered suitable alternative employment if such work was available but otherwise could be dismissed.

---

[50] [1994] IRLR 482 at 487.
[51] EPCA, Section 60.
[52] EPCA S64: two years' continuity where she worked over 16 hours a week and five years' where she worked between 8 and 16 hours per week.

In order to comply with Article 10 of the Directive, section 60 EPCA has been amended, thus changing considerably the previous position. Article 10 requires that "Member States shall take the necessary measures to prohibit the dismissal of workers ... during the period from the beginning of their pregnancy to the end of their maternity leave ... save in exceptional cases not connected with their condition which are permitted under national legislation and/or practice". Section 60, EPCA[53] sets out a list of inadmissible reasons; reasons which will cause any dismissal to be automatically unfair. Notably, section 60 requires no period of continuity and therefore all female employees will qualify for protection against dismissal regardless of their hours of work or period of service.

An employee will be treated as unfairly dismissed if "the reason or principal reason for her dismissal is that she is pregnant or any other reason connected with her pregnancy". This provision sets out the general rule which is required by the Directive that it is unlawful to dismiss a woman because of her pregnancy. The second inadmissible reason provides that a woman will be unfairly dismissed if "her maternity leave is ended by the dismissal and the reason or principal reason for the dismissal is that she has given birth to a child or any other reason connected with her having given birth to a child". A woman will therefore be entitled to compensation for unfair dismissal where she is dismissed during her period of maternity leave because of childbirth. The implication of this "reason", when read together with the previous "reason", would seem to be that protection against unfair dismissal on grounds of pregnancy is not intended to extend beyond the end of the statutory maternity leave period. It is arguable, nonetheless, that reasons connected with pregnancy can continue after the maternity leave period but if that is the intention of the first reason then the second seems unnecessary.[54]

The effects of pregnancy and childbirth need not automatically cease to exist at the end of the 14 week period of leave. This was an issue considered by the European Court in *Hertz* where a woman was dismissed as result of pregnancy-related illness which did not affect her until after she had returned to work following childbirth. In this decision, the Court held that there was no automatic direct discrimination but rather that the woman's treatment should once again be compared with that given to a man who was absent from work due to illness. It seemed to be arguing that there was a cut off point after which pregnancy was irrelevant. This approach has been reflected in the provisions of the Pregnancy Directive and in its implementation in the UK. The decision in *Hertz* is, however, open to criticism and remains an area of uncertainty to the extent that it appears to recognise justification of direct discrimination.

---

[53] Inserted by TURERA 1993, Section 24.
[54] See discussion of Dekker, Hertz *supra*.

In addition to the possibility that pregnancy-related illness may continue beyond the 14 week period, the issue of breastfeeding, which is referred to in the title of the Directive but features little in the substantive provisions, highlights the impracticality of a cut off point for the effects of pregnancy. What if a woman returns to work after her period of maternity leave but continues to breastfeed her child? Her timekeeping deteriorates because of the demands of breastfeeding and as a result her employer dismisses her. Article 10 limits the prohibition of dismissal to the period from the commencement of pregnancy to the end of maternity leave. Could she argue that her dismissal is unfair under section 60, EPCA on the basis that she has been dismissed for a pregnancy-related reason?

Health and safety

The legal base of the Directive was Article 118A of the Treaty which deals with health and safety and consequently there is a strong emphasis in the Directive on health and safety issues and protection of the pregnant employee or employee who has recently given birth against risks in the working environment. While there was considerable disquiet, particularly within the UK Government, as to the appropriateness of Article 118A as a base for the Directive, it does have a core of traditional health and safety provisions.

There are two elements of the health and safety provisions; first, an obligation on the employer to carry out risk assessments in relation to pregnant employees and employees who have recently given birth and, secondly, a requirement that steps be taken to protect employees in situations of risk. These provisions have been implemented in the UK by TURERA, Section 25 and Schedule 3 and by the Management of Health and Safety at Work (Amendment) Regulations 1994.

The 1995 Regulations set out the obligations on the employer in respect of carrying out risk assessments. Where a risk is identified, the employer should first take any protective or preventive measures as are required by any specific legislation. If such action does not remove the risk, the employer must alter the woman's working conditions or hours if it is reasonable to do so and would avoid the risk.[55] If such alterations are not possible, the employer should consider whether the woman could be offered suitable alternative work[56] failing which she must be suspended from work for so long as is necessary in

---

[55] reg. 13.
[56] EPCA, Section 46(1).

order to avoid the risk.[57] During this period of suspension, the woman is entitled to receive her "weekly pay".[58]

As with the other areas of protection, there is an important obligation of notification placed on the woman. An employer is only obliged to take these avoidance measures where he or she has been informed in writing that the employee is a "new or expectant mother".[59]

Conclusions

While the European Court's interpretation of the Equal Treatment Directive as applied to pregnant workers and the implementation of the Pregnancy Directive represent significant improvements in the employment rights of pregnant workers in the UK, a number of issues remain unclear, and considerable change in employment philosophy and working patterns are still required. The question of who bears the cost of pregnancy is of great concern to both Government and employers and may influence the attitudes of employers towards female employees and applicants. While the Pregnancy Directive represents recognition of the unique needs of the pregnant employee, further practical measures including adequate provision for breastfeeding and childcare facilities are required. In order to avoid the perpetuation of the stereotype of mother as primary carer and to allow parents greater choice in the allocation of domestic responsibility, progress is also required in relation to the adoption of further measures on family leave.[60]

---

[57] EPCA, Section 45.

[58] This is calculated in accordance with EPCA, Schedule 14, although unlike calculations in respect of unfair dismissal and redundancy compensation there is no maximum limit.

[59] For further discussion of health and safety, see chapter 12.

[60] Note on current status of proposals.

Questions

1. What rights are provided for those women who are breastfeeding under Directive 92/85?

2. Do the provisions of Article 10 of Directive 92/85 in respect of pregnancy related dismissals square with the decisions of the ECJ in *Dekker, Hertz* and *Webb*?

3. Does the decision of the ECJ in *Habermann-Beltermann* open the possibility of the use of a justification for direct discrimination in pregnancy discrimination cases?

4. Is Article 118a the correct legal base for the introduction of measures such as Directive 92/85?

5. Compare the decision of the ECJ in *Roks* discussed in Chapter 4 above with the provisions for eligibility for SMP. Are these compatible?

Contents of Chapter 8

ACQUIRED RIGHTS

Chapter 8

ACQUIRED RIGHTS

Background

Of the three Directives which emerged from the Social Action Programme 1974 to 1976,[1] the most successful and the one which has attracted greatest interest and judicial consideration is Directive 77/187/EEC on the approximation of the laws of the Member States relating to the safeguarding of employees' rights in the event of transfers of undertakings, businesses or parts of businesses.[2] The underlying purpose of this measure, which is commonly referred to as the "Acquired Rights Directive", was to provide some security and stability to employees in the event of the business in which they worked being transferred. The concerns which resulted in the introduction of this Directive were similar to those behind the Directives on Collective Redundancies and Employer's Insolvency:[3] i.e. the potentially harmful and disruptive effect on employees and employment rights of major restructuring of business as a result of the changing European market.

The Acquired Rights Directive has had a significant and widespread effect within the UK on business negotiations, insolvency practice, commercial conveyancing and government policy, not to mention the improved protection which it offers to employees. It introduced provisions which were contrary to well established principles of the law of contract and thus disrupted normal legal practice. Unlike the Collective Redundancies Directive, which provides only for information and consultation with employees' representatives, the

---

[1] OJ 1974 C 13/1.
[2] OJ 1977 L 61/26. For text see Appendix.
[3] For a discussion of these Directives, see chapters 9 and 10.

Acquired Rights Directive also sets out clear and specific individual rights and obligations which have been the subject of much litigation before both European and national courts. Although the European Court has not been asked to rule on the direct effect of this Directive, detailed decisions on its scope and the recognition by the UK courts of their obligation to interpret domestic law in accordance with European law have resulted in the widespread application of the Directive and of the resulting UK legislation.

Directive 77/187/EEC

The Acquired Rights Directive has two aspects: it regulates the individual relationship of employer and employee in the event of a business transfer, and it provides for the involvement of employees' representatives in the process of the transfer by means of information and consultation.

Section I – scope and definitions

Article 1(1) defines the situation in which the Directive will apply as being where there is a "transfer of an undertaking, business or part of a business to another employer as a result of a legal transfer or merger". This definition has given rise to uncertainty and debate and has been interpreted on numerous occasions by the European Court of Justice. The business or the relevant part of it must be situated within the scope of the Treaty and sea-going vessels are expressly excluded.

Article 2 provides further definitions of key terms within the Directive. A "transferor" is any natural or legal person who, by reason of a transfer within the terms of Article 1(1), ceases to be the employer. A "transferee" is the person who becomes the employer following a transfer. The Directive provides for consultation with representatives and Article 2 defines "representatives of employees" as being those representatives provided for by national law or practice.[4]

Section II – safeguarding of employees' rights

The purpose of the Directive is to protect the rights of employees in the event of a transfer and Article 3 forms a substantial part of this protection. Article 3(1) provides that in the event of a transfer, the transferor's rights and obligations arising from a contract of employment or employment relationship

---

[4] The definition excludes employee representatives on administrative, governing or supervisory bodies of companies.

will be transferred to the transferee. This provision takes effect only in relation to contracts of employment or employment relationships which exist on the date of the transfer. It is open to Member States to provide for joint liability in respect of existing obligations.

Article 3(2) provides for the maintenance of terms and conditions of employment arising from a collective agreement following a transfer. Such terms and conditions are to be maintained until the expiry of the collective agreement or until another agreement comes into operation.

Article 3(3) makes an important exception to the previous protections in that it excludes the rights of employees to old age, invalidity or survivors' benefits under supplementary company pension schemes. This applies to pension schemes which are outside the statutory social security scheme. Member States are, however, required to provide for the protection of the interests of employees and former employees who have immediate or pro-spective entitlement to old age and survivors' benefits.

A relevant transfer under the Directive does not in itself provide grounds for dismissal by the transferor or transferee, according to Article 4(1). Where specific categories of employees are not protected against dismissal by national laws or practice, the Member State may also exclude them from the ambit of Article 4. An exception is permitted to the general protection against dismissal where the dismissal is for "economic, technical or organisational reasons entailing changes in the work force". There has been little judicial consider-ation of this exception by either the European or the domestic courts and in its broadest sense it has the potential to undermine the protection against dismissal.

Article 4(2) provides for the situation of constructive dismissal, where the contract or employment relationship is terminated as a result of a substantial change in working conditions to the detriment of the employee. In that situation, the employer will be treated as having terminated the employment contract or relationship.

According to Article 5, the status and function is preserved of the repre-sentatives of the employees who are affected by the transfer. This provision will apply "if the business preserves its autonomy" after the transfer. Article 5 relies to a very great extent on the existing rules in any Member State.

Section III – information and consultation

The third section of the Directive provides, in similar terms to those employed in the Collective Redundancies Directive,[5] for information to be given to employees' representatives and for consultation to take place with them about

---

[5] See chapter 9.

the transfer. Article 6(1) provides that both the transferor and the transferee must provide information to the representatives of those employees affected by a relevant transfer on the reasons for the transfer, the legal, social and economic implications of the transfer for the employees and of any measures which are proposed in respect of the employees. The transferor must provide this information "in good time" prior to the transfer and the transferee must similarly provide the information in good time and certainly before the terms and conditions of the employees are directly affected by the transfer.

Article 6(2) requires consultation with employee representatives where any measures are envisaged in relation to the employees. Consultation must take place in good time and it must be with " a view to seeking agreement". It is therefore envisaged that such consultation should be meaningful and not simply a formality.

Article 6(3) states that, where Member States provide employee representatives with access to an arbitration board in respect of measures to be taken in relation to employees, they may limit the consultation requirements in paragraphs 1 and 2 to situations where the transfer results in changes in the business which are likely to bring about serious disadvantages for a considerable number of the employees.

In recognition of the burden which these provisions may represent for small businesses, Article 6(4) allows Member States to limit further the requirements to provide information and to consult where the business or undertaking being transferred is small. Paragraph 4 appears to assume a particular system for the identification of employee representatives and it provides that the obligations to inform and consult may be limited to businesses which, in terms of employee numbers, "fulfill the conditions for the election or designation of a collegiate body representing the employees". The effect of this provision is difficult to understand in the context of national systems which have different arrangements for representation.

If there are no employee representatives in an undertaking or business, Article 6(5) enables Member States to provide that the employees concerned must be informed in advance of the transfer.

Section IV – final provisions

As with all European social measures, this Directive is intended to establish a minimum level of protection for workers and Article 7 confirms the freedom of Member States to introduce more favourable provisions.

Article 8 required implementation of the Directive within two years[6] and Article 9 required that by February 1981 all Member States should provide

---

[6] i.e. by February 1979.

relevant information about adoption of the Directive in order to enable the Commission to prepare a report on implementation.

In summary, the Directive provides for the safeguarding of employment rights and for information and consultation about the transfer. The application of the Directive is dependent upon the transfer of an undertaking, business or part of a business.

Interpretation of the Directive by the European Court – the issues

Directive 77/187, or the Acquired Rights Directive, has given rise to uncertainty and has been considered by the European Court on numerous occasions. The issues which have arisen most frequently before the Court have related to the definition of a transfer in Article 1(1) and the effect of Articles 3 and 4 on employment contracts. Although there is no specific reference in the Directive, the Court has also considered the relationship between the transfer of a business and insolvency.

Transfer of an undertaking – Article 1(1)

Article 1(1) states that the Directive will apply in relation to the "transfer of an undertaking, business or part of a business to another employer as a result of a legal transfer or merger" while giving no further guidance as to the scope of this concept. An important part of the case law of the European Court arising from the Directive has been concerned with the interpretation of this definition. The Court has tended to give a very wide construction to these words. Interpretation of Article 1(1) has focused on two elements:

– has there been a legal transfer?
– has there been a transfer of an undertaking?

Legal transfer

The definition of a legal transfer in Article 1(1) was considered by the Court in *Ny Molle Kro*.[7] A dispute relating to wage arrears arose in the context of a restaurant business – the Ny Molle Kro – which was leased by the owner to Mrs Larsen in 1980. In January 1981, the owner rescinded the lease and took over the running of the business herself, with effect from March 1981. The first question referred to the European Court related to the scope of Article

---

[7] Case 287/86 *Landsorganisationen i Danmark for Tjenerforbundet i Danmark v Ny Molle Kro* [1987] ECR 5465.

1(1) and, in particular, whether it included the situation where the owner of a property rescinded a lease agreement and then took over the operation of the business. In submissions to the Court, a distinction emerged between the owner of the business and the employer. As the Court pointed out, the preamble to the Directive refers to the safeguarding of the rights of employees "in the event of a change of employer",[8] and therefore the Directive would apply where, after the transfer, "there is a change in the legal or natural person who is responsible for carrying on the business and who by virtue of that fact incurs the obligations of an employer *vis-a-vis* the employees of the undertaking, regardless of whether or not ownership of the undertaking is transferred."[9] Article 1(1) is therefore applicable in the situation outlined provided that the lessee becomes the employer and, following the transfer, he or she is replaced by another employer. Where a lease is rescinded and the business is taken over by the owner, that constitutes a legal transfer within Article 1(1).

In *Daddy's Dance Hall*,[10] the Court held that, where a non-transferable lease is terminated and a new lease is then granted to a lessee who carries on the business with the same staff and without interruption, the Directive will apply. The test developed by the Court in relation to the definition of a transfer is not affected simply by the fact that the transfer takes place in two stages.

The transfer of a business by a lease-purchase agreement[11] was considered by the European Court, on reference from the Supreme Court of the Netherlands in *Berg*.[12] Mr Berg continued to work in a bar-discothèque which was taken over by a partnership by means of a lease-purchase agreement. Six months later the agreement was terminated by judicial decision on the grounds of non-performance and the business was restored to the owner. Mr Berg and another sought payment of wage arrears from the owner in respect of the period during which the lease-purchase agreement was in existence. The European Court confirmed the approach set out in *Ny Molle Kro*[13] which focused on a change of employer, regardless of ownership. This would apply in relation to both the transfer resulting from the coming into force of the lease-purchase agreement and the subsequent re-transfer on termination of the agreement.

---

[8] *Ibid*, p 5482.
[9] *Ibid*, p 5483.
[10] Case 324/86 *Foreningen af Arbejdsledere i Danmark* v *Daddy's Dance Hall A/S* [1988] ECR 739.
[11] A lease-purchase agreement was defined as sale on deferred payments, by which the parties agree that the object sold shall not become the property of the purchaser by mere transfer.
[12] Joined cases 144 and 145/87 *Harry Berg and Johannes Theodorus Maria Busschers* v *Ivo Marten Besselsen* [1988] ECR 2559.
[13] Case 287/86 *Ny Molle Kro* cited in note 7 *supra*.

In *Bork*,[14] the Court gave a clear statement as to the concept of a legal transfer. The Directive applies "wherever, in the context of contractual relations, there is a change in the legal or natural person who is responsible for carrying on the business and who incurs the obligations of an employer towards employees of the undertaking".[15] This test has subsequently been satisfied, in *Dr Sophie Redmond Stichting*,[16] where a local authority unilaterally withdrew funding from the Redmond Foundation, which provided assistance to drug addicts, and gave the funding instead to the Sigma Foundation which performed a similar service. In *Rask*,[17] where a company contracted out repsonsibility for operating its staff canteen to ISS Kantineservice, who took over the previous staff, the Court confirmed that there was a legal transfer.

The Court has clearly and consistently adopted a wide and purposive construction of "legal transfer". It is evident that it comprises not simply the sale and purchase of assets but any situation arising from contractual relations where there is a change in the identity of the employer. This definition, while surprising commercial practitioners who may traditionally conceive of business transfers in terms of exchange of ownership or legal title, has benefited employees. The concept of a legal transfer has been seen, by the European Court, from the viewpoint of employment.

Transfer of an undertaking

The second aspect of Article 1(1) "Has there been the transfer of an undertaking?" is concerned with the identification of an "undertaking". The European Court has developed an equally wide approach to interpretation of the concept of an "undertaking".

One of the earliest and most useful decisions of the Court on this issue was in the case of *Spijkers*.[18] Mr Spijkers was employed as an assistant manager by a company which operated an abattoir. The business of the company, and goodwill in it, ceased and the premises and machinery were subsequently purchased by Benedik Abattoir which recommenced the business of an abattoir. None of the customers of the previous company were acquired. Benedik Abattoir took over all of the former employees with the exception of Mr Spijkers and one other. In the course of proceedings by Mr Spijkers to establish that his contract, and the rights and obligations relating to it, had been transferred under the Acquired Rights Directive, the European Court

[14] Case 101/87 *P.Bork International A/S in liquidation* v *Foreningen af Arbejdsledere i Danmark, acting on behalf of Birger E Petersen and Junckers Industrier A/S* [1988] ECR 3057.
[15] *Ibid*, p 3076.
[16] Case C-29/91 *Dr Sophie Redmond Stichting* v *Hendrikus Bartol* [1992] ECR 3189.
[17] Case C-209/81 *Rask and Christensen* v *ISS Kantineservice A/S* [1993] IRLR 133.
[18] Case 24/85 *Jozef Maria Antonius Spijkers* v *Gebroeders Benedik Abattoir CV and Alfred Benedik en Zonen BV* [1986] ECR 1119.

was asked for direction in the interpretation of Article 1(1). The Court, establishing what has become an influential test, held that "the decisive criterion . . . is whether the business in question retains its identity".[19] A transfer will not occur simply because there has been a disposal of assets; instead it should be considered whether there has been the transfer of a going concern. In deciding whether these conditions have been satisfied, the Court suggested a number of factors to be considered:

- the nature of the undertaking or business

- the transfer of the tangible assets of the business, such as buildings and moveable property

- the value of its intangible assets at the time of the transfer

- whether or not the majority of employees were taken over by the new employer

- the transfer of customers

- the degree of similarity between the activities carried on before and after the transfer

- the period, if any, for which these activities were suspended.

The Court stressed, however, that these were simply factors to be considered in the overall circumstances of the case and that no one factor was determinative. The Court also confirmed that the existence of a transfer in any situation was a factual question for the national court which should make its decision with the aid of the criteria listed.

The Danish court in *Ny Molle Kro*[20] specifically asked whether there could be a transfer where the business was closed at the time of the transfer and had no employees. The European Court confirmed the test set out in *Spijkers*[21] to the effect that the business should retain its identity. This in turn may be shown where the business is "continued or resumed by the new employer, with the same or similar activities".[22] While the temporary closure of a business and the absence of employees is a factor to be taken into account in deciding whether or not there is a transfer of a going concern, in itself it will not prevent the transfer from falling within the scope of Article 1(1), particularly, as in this case, where the business is seasonal in nature. In *Bork*[23] the Court confirmed that the mere fact of a temporary closure and the absence of employees at the date of the transfer would not preclude the application of the Directive,

[19] *Ibid*, p 1228.
[20] Case 287/86 *Ny Molle Kro* cited in note 7 *supra*.
[21] Case 24/85 *Spijkers* cited in note 18 *supra*.
[22] Case 287/86 *Ny Molle Kro* cited in note 7 *supra* at 5484.
[23] Case 101/87 *Bork* cited in note 14 *supra*.

particularly where, as in this case, the closure coincided with Christmas and New Year holidays.

When public funding was withdrawn from the Redmond Foundation which provided assistance to drug addicts, and given instead to the Sigma Foundation to carry out similar work, a question arose as to whether or not this constituted the transfer of an undertaking.[24] A lease of premises from the funding body was also transferred. The decision to transfer was taken unilaterally by the public authority and was not the result of an agreement between the parties. Referring once again to *Spijkers*,[25] the European Court held that there was a legal transfer in this situation and summarised the two questions which the national court should ask in order to establish whether the transfer had taken place of an undertaking or part of an undertaking: first, following the transfer, has the entity retained its identity and, secondly, are the same or similar activities resumed or carried out by the transferee? The Court made it clear that the fact that Sigma did not carry on social and recreational activities which had been performed by Redmond was not fatal where it could be shown that these formed an independent function and that the core function continued. Although the Directive includes no reference to commercial activities, this decision made it clear that the Directive does apply to non-commercial undertakings and sent a clear signal to the UK Government that its exclusion of such bodies from the scope of the UK legislation was unlawful.

In *Redmond Stichting*,[26] only public subsidies and the lease of premises had been transferred and in *Rask*[27] the Court went further in that the transfer concerned the provision of a service. A company, Phillips, entered into an agreement with ISS Kantineservice whereby ISS would take over the operation of Philips' staff canteen in return for a fee. ISS agreed to take over the staff currently employed in the canteen and they were also given the use of Philips' premises and equipment for the purposes of running the canteen. In a dispute concerning employment conditions following this agreeement, the European Court was asked for a ruling as to whether or not these circumstances disclosed a transfer to which the Directive would apply. The Court confirmed that the national court should consider whether or not the business had retained its identity in the context of all of the relevant circumstances.[28] Individual factors, however, should not be looked at in isolation. It held that the situation where the provision of a service to an undertaking was contracted out to another undertaking was capable of being included in the scope of

[24] Case C-29/91 *Dr Sophie Redmond Stichting* cited in note 16 *supra*.
[25] Case 24/85 *Spijkers* cited in note 18 *supra*.
[26] Case C-29/91 *Dr Sophie Redmond Stichting* cited in note 16 *supra*.
[27] Case C-209/81 *Rask* cited in note 17 *supra*.
[28] Such as those discussed in *Spijkers* cited in note 18 *supra*.

Article 1(1) and the fact that "the activity transferred is only an ancillary activity of the transferor undertaking not necessarily related to its objects cannot have the effect of excluding that transaction from the scope of the Directive."[29]

Developing this approach still further, the European Court held in *Schmidt*[30] that the Directive could apply where the part of a business transferred involved only one employee. Mrs Schmidt was employed as a cleaner in a bank. When the bank decided to contract out its cleaning to another company, which offered to employ Mrs Schmidt but on different terms, the national court sought guidance from the European Court as to whether or not this constituted the transfer of part of a business. Focusing on the change of employer, the Court held that the Directive would apply where an undertaking engages another undertaking to perform one of its services, even where this service is ancillary to its main activity. The decisive criterion is whether the entity retains its identity, and this can be indicated where the new employer carries on or resumes the same or similar activities. This would clearly include the present example of cleaning a bank. Referring to the purpose of the Directive as being to protect employees, the Court held that this protection could not be dependent on the number of employees concerned. The mere fact that the service which was transferred was performed by only one employee would not exclude application of the Directive.

Throughout these decisions the Court adopted a consistently wide interpetation of an undertaking, concentrating on the need for preservation of identity. The factors highlighted in *Spijkers* have been referred to frequently but the Court has also made it clear that these should not be considered in isolation and no one factor is determinative of a transfer within the meaning of the Directive. The recent decisions in *Redmond, Rask* and *Schmidt* have particularly made it clear that the Directive applies even where all that is transferred is the provision of a service. Despite the absence of guidance in the Directive itself, the Court has created a relatively simple and practical test.

A new element of doubt has very recently been introduced by the surprising decision of the Court in *Rygaard*.[31] The specific question posed by the Danish court in this case was: is the Directive applicable when, following an agreement with Contractor A, Contractor B continues part of building works commenced by Contractor A, and it is agreed between them that some of Contractor A's workers will continue to work for Contractor B who will also take over materials already on the building site in order to complete the work,

---

[29] Case C-209/81 *Rask* cited in note 17 *supra*, at 136.

[30] Case C-392/92 *Schmidt* v *Spar-und Leihkasse der fruheren Amter Bordesholm, Kiel und Cronshagen* [1994] IRLR 302.

[31] Case C-48/94 *Ledernes Hovedorganisation, acting on behalf of Ole Rygaard* v *Dansk Arbejdsgiverforening, acting on behalf of Stro Molle Akustik A/S*, decision of 19 September 1995, n.y.r.

and there will be a period after the transfer during which both contractors will be working on the site at the same time? In this particular case, the work concerned was the completion of the building of a canteen and the work was not expected to last for more than a few months. The Advocate General reviewed the previous decisions of the European Court and, in view of the broad interpretation developed by the Court, concluded that such a situation would constitute a transfer within Article 1(1). It was clear that there was no need for the transfer of ownership of physical assets, the Directive could apply in respect of the transfer of an ancillary activity and the mere fact that only one employee was concerned was not fatal. In his view, the transfer, even of a single activity which is of a fixed term nature, could fall within the scope of the Directive. The European Court, surprisingly, disagreed with the Advocate General and in so doing introduced what appears to be a new requirement into the test for a transfer within Article 1(1). Before the Directive will apply, the subject of the transfer must be "a stable economic unit". The Court seemed to suggest that this had always been an implied requirement of the test, although previous decisions make no express reference to this factor. This decision has raised doubt as to the scope of the Directive and it seems certain that the Court will be called upon to provide further clarification in the future.

Protection of employment rights

Article 3 of the Directive provides for the transfer of rights and obligations arising from contracts or relationships of employment to the transferee. This includes rights and obligations arising from collective agreements and it applies to those who were employed on the date of the transfer. The meaning of this provision has been considered by the Court on several occasions along with the protection offered by Article 4 in respect of dismissal.

Employment on the date of the transfer

Article 3(1) provides that the transferee will take over all rights or obligations arising from contracts or relationships of employment existing on the date of the transfer. In *Wendelboe*,[32] The Danish High Court sought clarification of the application of Article 3. Employees of LJ Music had been dismissed because of the company's impending insolvency on 28 February. On 4 March, in the course of insolvency proceedings, the premises and equipment of the insolvent company were taken over by another company and the dismissed employees were re-engaged on a higher salary but with a loss of seniority. They raised an

---

[32] Case 19/83 *Knud Wendelboe v LJ Music ApS, in liquidation* [1985] ECR 457.

action against LJ Music for compensation for unfair dismissal and holiday pay. The Bankruptcy Court awarded holiday pay but rejected the claim for unfair dismissal and LJ Music appealed to the High Court which made a reference to the European Court. The Danish Court asked whether the transferee, under Directive 77/187, becomes liable in respect of holiday pay and unfair dismissal in respect of employees who were not employed on the date of the transfer? The European Court confirmed that the transferee only becomes liable in respect of contracts of employment existing on the date of the transfer. Textual analysis of the provision concentrated on the question of whether the phrase "existing at the date of transfer" qualified the words "rights and obligations" or " contract of employment or . . . employment relationship".[33] Either construction was possible in the English and Danish versions of the Directive whereas it was clear in the French, Dutch, German and Italian versions that it was the contract or relationship which must be in existence on the relevant date. The Court confirmed that this was the correct interpretation. In addition to being the literal interpretation of the provision, this also reflected the purpose of the Directive which was to ensure where possible that the employment relationship continued unchanged as a result of the transfer.

It was for the national court to decide whether or not a contract or relationship of employment was in existence on the date of the transfer. The Court did, however, indicate an important link between Articles 3 and 4. When deciding on the existence of a contract or relationship of employment, the national court must bear in mind the protection afforded to employees by Article 4 against dismissal by reason of the transfer. In *Bork* it expressly stated the link between Article 3 and the protection against dismissal in Article 4(1). The result of reading these two provisions together is that where an employee is dismissed, contrary to Article 4(1) and prior to the transfer, his or her contract or relationship of employment will be treated as still in existence at the date of the transfer.

Employment in the part of a business transferred

The Directive will only apply to employees engaged in the part of the business or undertaking which is transferred. Where, as happened in *Botzen*,[34] an insolvent company formed a new company and transferred parts of its business to the new company, only employees assigned to the parts of the business which were transferred would be covered by the Directive. Employees in the remaining departments would not be protected even where their work involved using assets of the parts of the business transferred and

[33] See Opinion of Advocate General Slynn at p 459.
[34] Case 186/83 *Arie Botzen* v *Rotterdamsche Droogdok Maatschappij BV* [1985] ECR 519.

providing services for the part transferred. The Advocate General suggested that the test should be whether the employee was "wholly engaged" in the part of the undertaking transferred[35] whereas the test adopted by the Court depended on the department to which the employee was assigned.[36]

Article 3 – its automatic effect

The scope of the protection of the rights of employees was considered by the Court in *Danmols*,[37] a reference from the Danish High Court. Danmols Inventar A/S, having suspended payment of debts, was transferred to a newly formed company of which Mr Mikkelsen, the works foreman with Danmols Inventar A/S, was a co-owner and shareholder. The Danish court sought guidance as to whether the Directive applied to an employee of the transferor who, of his own volition, did not continue to work as an employee of the transferee. Must an employee of the transferor continue to be an employee of the transferee in order to benefit from the protection of the Directive? Considering the purpose of the Directive as being to ensure the continuation of the employment relationship unchanged as a result of the transfer, the European Court held that the rights are safeguarded only of employees who continue to be employed by the transferee. Where an employee terminates the employment contract of his or her own free will, Article 3(1) of the Directive does not apply.

It is for the national court to interpret "employee" and the Directive neither expressly prescribes nor requires a Community-wide definition of the term. The Court in *Danmols* held that the intention of the Directive is to achieve only partial harmonisation by safeguarding, in the event of a transfer, whatever rights arise from an employment contract or relationship in the Member States.

In *Ny Molle Kro*,[38] a dispute arose concerning the obligation of a transferee to observe the terms of a collective agreement accepted by the transferor, in respect of an employee who commenced employment in the undertaking some time after the transfer took place. Reiterating what had been said in *Wendelboe* and *Danmols*, the Court rejected the application of the Directive in such a case since the purpose of Article 3(2), concerning the observance of collective agreements, was merely to ensure that the conditions of employees engaged in the business remained the same after a transfer.

---

[35] *Ibid*, p 521.
[36] *Ibid*, p 528.
[37] Case 105/84 *Foreningen af Arbejdsledere i Danmark* v *A/S Danmols Inventar, in liquidation* [1985] ECR 2639.
[38] Case 287/86 *Ny Molle Kro* cited in note 7.

In many legal systems, one party cannot take over another's debt without the consent of the creditor. Mr Berg argued, on this basis, that the transferor could not be discharged from his obligations under a contract of employment following a transfer without the consent of the employees. He also sought to argue that the consent of employees was required in order to achieve the aim of Directive 77/187 "to ensure that the transfer of undertakings is not effected at the expense of their employees".[39] As the Court held, however, Article 3(1) clearly provides for automatic transfer of the employer's obligation except in the event that the Member State has specifically provided for joint liability. The transferor is thus discharged from his or her obligations as a result of the transfer and without the need for the consent of all of the employees. The option of joint liability allows Member States to reconcile the requirements of the Directive with their domestic law of obligations.

Derogations

The automatic transfer of the employer's rights and obligations under the contract of employment has been confirmed by the European Court on numerous occasions. In *Daddy's Dance Hall*[40] the Court held that an employee is not permitted to waive the rights provided by the Directive even where other benefits are provided by the transferee. The Court qualified this decision by reiterating that the Directive is only intended to achieve partial harmonisation and to maintain the employment contract or relationship with the transferee as it was with the transferor. If, therefore, the contract could have been varied with the transferor it can equally be varied with the transferee, subject to the qualification that the transfer itself may not constitute the reason for the variation. This decision has been followed in *Rask*.[41]

While this decision appears correct within the terms of the Directive, it highlights a weakness in the protection afforded to employees and, in the absence of further guidance from the Court, it may be difficult to establish whether or not an amendment is made as a result of the transfer. Could the transferee change terms of the contract close to the date of the transfer or would there have to be a significant gap in time?

Employees' objections

In order to safeguard the rights of employees in the event of a transfer, the Directive provides for the automatic transfer of all rights and obligations arising from contracts or relationships of employment in existence at the date

[39] Joined cases 144 and 145/87 *Harry Berg and Johannes Theodorus Maria Busschers* cited in note 12 *supra*, at 2580.
[40] Case 324/86 *Daddy's Dance Hall* cited in note 10 *supra*.
[41] Case C-209/81 *Rask* cited in note 17 *supra*.

of the transfer. What is the position of the employee who does not wish to be transferred? The European Court has consistently confirmed the operation of Article 3(1) to transfer the employer's obligations to the transferee and discharge the transferor.

This issue was the subject of a reference to the Court from the *Arbeitsgericht* of Hamburg in *Katsikas*.[42] The principal question raised was whether an employee could object to the transfer of the rights and obligations of the transferor to the transferee. The Court confirmed that, as held in *Daddy's Dance Hall*, the protection afforded by the Directive was "independent of the will of the parties to the contract".[43] Similarly in *Berg*, it had been held that the obligations of the transferor were acquired by the transferee without the need for the consent of the employees. In *Danmols*,[44] however, it had been made clear that an employee could voluntarily decide not to continue in employment with the transferee. It was clear that the Directive could not be interpreted as forcing an employee to continue in employment with the transferee: an interpretation which would question the basic freedom of an employee. In the situation where an employee voluntarily decides not to continue the employment relationship with the transferee, it is for the Member States to provide what is to happen to the contract. Either it can be treated as having been terminated by the transferor or the employee or it may be provided that it continues with the transferor.[45]

Dismissal

The Court has had few opportunities to consider the protection against dismissal in Article 4. In *Bork*[46] it recognised the importance of the link between Article 4(1) and the automatic transfer of the employer's obligations in Article 3(1). In order to decide whether an employee has been dismissed solely as a result of the transfer, the Court indicated that account must be taken of the circumstances of the dismissal. The fact that a dismissal was effected shortly before the transfer, and the dismissed employees were subsequently re-engaged by the transferee, was a significant factor. In relation to the "economic, technical or organisational" defence, it is a general rule that it

[42] Joined Cases C-132/91 and 138-139/91 *Katsikas* v *Konstantinidis* [1993] 1 CMLR 845.
[43] Case 324/86 *Daddy's Dance Hall* cited in note 10 *supra*, at 754.
[44] Case 105/84 *Danmols* cited in note 37 *supra*.
[45] In response to this decision, the UK has provided that a contract of employment will not be transferred where the employee has objected to either the transferor or the transferee. In that event, the contract will be terminated by the transfer but the employee will not be treated as having been dismissed by the transferor: TUPE, reg 5(4A) and (4B), inserted by Trade Union Reform & Employment Rights Act 1993, Section 33(4).
[46] Case 101/87 *Bork* cited in note 14 *supra*.

cannot be accepted where the employees were in fact rehired by the transferee.

Transfers and insolvency

No specific mention was made in the Directive of transfers in the context of insolvency and they were not expressly excluded from the scope of protection. The application of the Directive in relation to insolvent undertakings has, however, been restricted by the European Court. In *Abels*[47] the Court held that Article 1(1) of the Directive does not apply to the transfer of an undertaking, business or part of a business where the transferor has been adjudged insolvent and where the undertaking or business forms part of the assets of the transferor. Article 1(1) provides that the Directive is to apply where there is a transfer of an undertaking or business "as a result of a legal transfer". Whereas the protection of workers in the case of a transfer was the purpose of the Acquired Rights Directive, insolvency law was intended to take account of and weigh up the interests of different classes of creditors. It concluded that, in view of the diversity of national rules applying to insolvency, and in view of the existence of specific rules, both national and European,[48] an express provision would have been included in the Directive if it had been intended that it should apply to transfers which arose in the context of insolvency.

The Court went on to justify this interpretation in light of the purpose of the Directive and considered the view that its application in the context of insolvency might in fact undermine the protection of employees which the Directive was designed to achieve. It concluded that the impact on employees of the application of the Directive in insolvency situations was uncertain and that therefore it should not be held to apply. It was open to Member States, however, to choose to include transfers resulting from insolvency within the scope of all or part of the provisions.

The Dutch court also asked whether the Directive applied to a transfer in the course of a procedure such as *"surseance van betaling"* (judicial leave to suspend payment of debts) which was available under Dutch law. The European Court distinguished this type of procedure from liquidation proceedings on the basis that the object of such a procedure was to protect the property of the insolvent undertaking and, where possible, to enable the business to continue. In that situation the reasons outlined above for excluding application of the Directive should not apply. In reaching this conclusion, it

---

[47] Case 135/83 *HBM Abels* v *The Administrative Board of the Bedrijfsvereniging voor de Metaalindustrie en de Electrotechnische Industrie* [1985] ECR 469.

[48] e.g. Directive 80/987/EEC on the approximation of the laws of the Member States relating to the protection of the rights of employees in the event of the insolvency of their employer.

may be argued that the Court overlooked the fact that one of the reasons for seeking judicial protection against creditors by "*surseance van betaling*" (or Administration in the UK) is the hope of finding a buyer for the business. The application of the Acquired Rights Directive to such sales might act as a disincentive to prospective purchasers. In reaching this conclusion, the Court also highlighted as important the greater role and supervision of the court in relation to the commencement of liquidation.

Although insolvency was not expressly excluded from the scope of the Directive, the Court in *Abels* held that it was. At the same time the Court drew a distinction between insolvency or liquidation proceedings and other types of judicial process, such as suspension of the payment of debts, which might take place at an earlier stage. In view of the diversity of procedures and terminology in the Member States this decision could be foreseen as causing some difficulties to the national courts. The Court confirmed its decision in *Abels* in three other judgments issued on the same day.[49]

In *Abels*, the Court attempted to distinguish between different types of legal proceedings for dealing with insolvency, classifying some as being concerned with the liquidation of the business and the disposal of assets and others with continued trading. This approach has a number of difficulties within the context of the diverse national systems. As the use of different terms by the Court, such as insolvency, liquidation, bankruptcy and administration, demonstrates, there is a wide variety of legal processes in operation and national courts may have difficulty in deciding where the Directive should or not be applied in the context of a range of domestic insolvency procedures. The distinction in *Abels* also assumes that each legal procedure has a single purpose.

In *d'Urso*,[50] the Court reviewed the considerations set out in *Abels* and concluded that the decisive test for the application of the Directive in the context of insolvency and other similar proceedings was "the purpose of the procedure in question". The procedure under review in this case was the Italian law on administration which could have a variety of effects. It could provide for compulsory administration which would have effects very similar to those of liquidation or, alternatively, it might provide for special administration whereby the undertaking would continue trading under supervision.

In summary, the application of the Directive depends on the purpose of the insolvency process. It will not apply where the purpose is the liquidation and disposal of assets but it will apply where the purpose is the continuation of the

---

[49] Case 19/83 *Knud Wendelboe, supra* note 32; Case 179/83 *Industriebond FNV and Federatie Nederlandse Vakbeweging (FNV)* v *The Netherlands State* [1985] ECR 511; Case 186/83 *Botzen, supra* note 34. See also Case 105/84 *Danmols* cited in note 37 *supra*.

[50] Case C-362/89 *Giuseppe d'Urso, Adriana Ventadori* v *Ercole Marelli Elettromeccanica Generale SpA* [1991] ECR I-4105.

business. While this interpretation provides more scope for the accommodation of diverse national systems and it reflects the intention of the Directive to protect the interests of the employees, it might still be argued that it can in fact produce harmful results for employees. The aim of proceedings, such as the UK system of Administration (which suspends debts and assists companies in their bid to continue trading) is very often to find a buyer for the business. It may be argued that it will be more difficult to sell the business if it is burdened with employment obligations, and that ultimately the application of the Directive will result in the loss of employment.[51]

Implementation in the UK – TUPE Regulations

At common law, the contract of employment is a personal contract which cannot be transferred from one employer to another without the consent of the employee.[52] While theoretically this confirms the freedom of the employee and protects against enforced labour, in practice it fails to address the vulnerability of an employee in the situation of a business transfer. Some limited provision was made in the UK for the preservation of an employee's continuity of employment in the situation where he or she was re-engaged by a transferee.[53] The transferee was, however, under no obligation to hire the employees of the business and nor was there any requirement to maintain working terms and conditions.

The provisions of the Acquired Rights Directive represented a radical change for UK law and as such they were accepted reluctantly. They were finally implemented by the Transfer of Undertakings (Protection of Employment) Regulations 1981[54] (TUPE Regs) "with a remarkable lack of enthusiasm".[55] The UK failed to give effect to the Directive within the time limit of

---

[51] These concerns have persuaded the Commission to suggest amendments to the Directive in relation to transfers in the context of insolvency: Proposal for a Council Directive on the approximation of the laws of the Member States relating to the safeguarding of employees' rights in the event of transfers of undertakings, businesses or parts of businesses, OJ 1994 C 274/10.
[52] *Nokes* v *Doncaster Amalgamated Collieries* [1940] AC 1014.
[53] Employment Protection (Consolidation) Act 1978, Schedule 13, para 17(2). When the Acquired Rights Directive was implemented in the UK, no attempt was made to integrate the existing provisions on continuity in the 1978 Act and the relationship between continuity and acquired rights has proved another source of uncertainty. For a full discussion of both Schedule 13 and the TUPE Regs, see McMullen, *Business Transfers and Employee Rights* (2nd ed), Butterworths, 1992.
[54] SI 1981 No 1794.
[55] Mr David Waddington (Under Secretary of State for Employment) 991 Hansard HC Deb col 680.

two years and, when the Regulations finally appeared, there were a number of differences between their terms and those of the Directive which, together with subsequent inconsistencies in interpretation of the measures by the European Court and the UK courts, have made this a very controversial and uncertain area of law.

In 1992, the Commission presented an Implementation Report[56] on Directive 77/187 to the Council in which it highlighted a number of problems in implementation, particularly in the UK. The UK Government accepted a number of criticisms and introduced appropriate amendments in the Trade Union Reform and Employment Rights Act 1993. Proceedings were nonetheless initiated by the Commission and on 8 June 1994 the European Court gave its decision in *European Commission* v *United Kingdom*[57] on the basis of five complaints. TUPE has now been amended to take account of this decision.

Transfer of an undertaking

Regulation 3 of TUPE defines a "relevant transfer" in words similar to those employed in the Directive. It specifically includes a transfer which is brought about by a series of two or more linked transactions. A significant restriction was placed on the definition of an undertaking[58] which excluded "any undertaking or part of an undertaking which is not in the nature of a commercial venture". This restriction is not applied in the Directive and its inclusion in the Regulations was challenged by the Commission.[59] This point was conceded by the UK and the exclusion of non-commercial ventures has been deleted.

The second complaint raised by the Commission was that the UK definition of a transfer, as interpreted by the domestic courts and tribunals, did not apply to transfers where there was no transfer of property. This complaint was rejected by the Court on the basis that the TUPE Regulations must be interpreted in accordance with the Directive and with the decisions of the European Court and that, certainly since the decision of the House of Lords in *Litster*,[60] the UK decisions appeared to be consistent. For the avoidance of doubt, Regulation 3(4) has now been amended to state that a relevant transfer may occur whether or not any property is transferred.[61]

---

[56] SEC (92) 857.
[57] Case C-382/92 *European Commission* v *United Kingdom* [1994] IRLR 392.
[58] Reg 2(1).
[59] *European Commission* v *United Kingdom*, note 57, *supra*.
[60] *Litster* v *Forth Dry Dock & Engineering Co Ltd* [1989] IRLR 161.
[61] TURERA 1993, section 33(3)(b).

Transfer of rights

Regulation 5 of TUPE gives effect to Article 3 of the Directive and deals with the consequences of a relevant transfer for contracts of employment. The contracts of employees engaged by the transferor will not be terminated by the transfer, but they will be treated as if they had been concluded between the employee and the transferee. All of the rights, powers, duties and obligations of the transferor in relation to these contracts will be transferred to the transferee.[62] This provision does not affect the right of an employee to terminate his or her contract if there is a significant and detrimental change in working conditions.[63] The application of Regulation 5 is restricted to any person who is employed in the undertaking "immediately before the transfer"[64] or immediately before any of the transactions where the transfer results from a series of transactions. Interpretation of this phrase has given rise to a number of important UK decisions and, for a time, significantly reduced the impact of the Regulations.[65]

Dismissal

Regulation 8 provides that the dismissal of an employee either before or after the transfer will be regarded as an unfair dismissal in terms of the Employment Protection (Consolidation) Act 1978 where the reason or principal reason for the dismissal is the transfer or a reason connected with it. Dismissal resulting from a transfer will therefore be treated as automatically unfair. Section 57 of the 1978 Act sets out the potentially fair reasons for dismissal, the final category being a "substantial reason". Regulation 8(2) provides that where there is an "economic, technical or organisational" reason for the dismissal before or after the transfer, that will be treated as a substantial reason for the dismissal. In such a situation the court or tribunal would still require to be satisfied that the employer acted reasonably in making the dismissal.

Information and consultation

Regulation 10 provides for the duty to inform and consult trade union representatives. Information must be provided to the representatives "long

---

[62] Personal liability for any offence is not affected: Reg 5(4).

[63] The mere fact of a change of employer will not justify the employee in terminating the contract unless it can in itself be shown to represent a substantial change to the detriment of the employee: Reg 5(5).

[64] Reg 5(3).

[65] See discussion below.

enough before a relevant transfer to enable consultations to take place".[66] This form of words seems to be a rather grudging implementation of "in good time".[67] While Regulation 10(5) provides for the obligation of an employer to consult with representatives in relation to any measures proposed in respect of employees, unlike the Directive it did not expressly require these consultations to take place with "a view to seeking agreement".[68] Regulation 10(6) does, however, require that the employer shall consider representations made by the representatives and reply to them, stating reasons for rejecting any of the representations. This provision was the cause of another of the Commission's complaints.The UK conceded that the Regulations did not require consultation to take place with a view to seeking agreement, as stipulated in the Directive, and Regulation 10(5) of TUPE has now been amended to include these words.[69]

The most important restriction on the requirements in Regulations 10 and 11 is that they only apply to representatives of an independent trade union recognised by the employer in respect of the affected employees. A recognised trade union is one recognised by the employer for the purposes of collective bargaining.[70] There is no legal procedure for recognising trade unions and no obligation on an employer to do so. The requirements of information and consultation are, therefore, set on very insecure foundations. This provision formed the basis for the Commission's principal complaint against the UK and it was the only point which was not conceded prior to the Court's decision. TUPE required such information and consultation only in respect of representatives of a recognised trade union which in effect provided employers with a very simple way of avoiding the application of this requirement – by refusing to recognise any trade union. The UK Government argued that the Directive was intended to achieve partial harmonisation and that it was for the Member State to define the term "employee representative". The European Court firmly rejected this argument and held that, although the aim of the Directive was only partial harmonisation, this must not be allowed to destroy the effectiveness of the provisions. It was therefore incumbent on the UK to take all necessary steps to ensure the existence of representatives within the context of the obligations to inform and consult. This complaint was also raised against the UK Government in relation to Collective Redundancies and amendments have now been introduced.[71]

---

[66] Reg 10(2).
[67] See e.g. *Melon* v *Hector Powe Ltd* [1980] IRLR 477.
[68] Art 6(2).
[69] TURERA 1993, section 33(6).
[70] Reg 2(1).
[71] Case C-383/942. *European Commission* v *UK* [1994] IRLR 412. The response of the government to this decision is discussed in chapter 9 *infra*.

Sanctions

Where an employer has failed to inform or consult, as required by Regulation 10 of TUPE, the union concerned may complain to an industrial tribunal.[72] If the tribunal finds the complaint well founded, the employer may be ordered to pay compensation to the employees concerned. In response to such a complaint, the employer may show that there were special circumstances which prevented compliance[73] with Regulation 10 and that all reasonable steps in the circumstances were taken to comply. It seems that there is nothing expressly stated in the Directive which allows the employer to put forward special circumstances for failure to inform or consult, although this provision has not been challenged.

The Commission's final complaint related to the sanctions for failure to inform and consult. Compensation was payable under Regulation 11 subject to a maximum amount and it could also be set off against any compensation payable under the Employment Protection Act 1975 for failure to inform and consult in respect of collective redundancies.[74] The Court held that where no specific sanction was specified in the Directive, Article 5 of the Treaty required Member States to take all necessary measures to ensure the application and effectiveness of Community law. Thus, while the choice of sanction was left to the Member State, it must at least be "effective, proportionate and dissuasive". The UK sanctions did not meet these criteria and Regulation 11 has now been amended by removing the possibility of set-off against compensation for failure to consult in respect of redundancy and by raising the limit on the amount of compensation. The maximum limit of compensation is now four weeks' pay for each employee and it may be argued that this still does not represent a sufficient deterrent to employers.

Interpretation of the Directive and the Regulations in the UK – issues arising

"Relevant transfer"

Prior to the introduction of the Transfer Regulations, the only protection for employees in the event of a transfer of business was in respect of their

---

[72] Reg 11.
[73] Reg 11(2). These provisions in relation to information and consultation are very similar to those provided in relation to collective redundancies: see chapter 9 *infra*.
[74] See chapter 9 *infra*.

continuity of employment under the Employment Protection (Consolidation) Act 1978, Schedule 13. In defining the concept of a business transfer under this Act, the classic approach adopted by the courts was to distinguish between the transfer of a going concern, which was covered by the Act, and an assets sale, which was not.[75] In early decisions under the TUPE Regulations,[76] it became clear that the definition of a transfer of an undertaking would be interpreted in accordance with the meaning of a transfer of a business under the 1978 Act. The transfer of goodwill was often seen as being of particular importance in indicating the existence of a going concern.[77] While decisions of the European Court have also confirmed the requirement of more than a simple transfer of assets, a difference could be detected in the UK courts' tendency to adopt the viewpoint of the conveyancer rather than the employee.[78] Gradually, however, the UK courts have accepted the necessity of interpreting the UK Regulations in accordance with the Directive and with the case law of the European Court and this is reflected in the recent decision of the EAT in *Brintel Helicopters*.[79] The EAT attempted to set out guidance to practitioners, and to industrial tribunals, as to the meaning of a transfer of an undertaking or business within Regulation 3(1) and Article 1(1) of the Directive. A reminder was given about the requirements of interpreting UK legislation in accordance with the interpretation of the Directive by the European Court and of adopting a purposive approach. Summarising the decisions of the European Court, the EAT concluded that the decisive criterion in identifying a transfer was whether the business retained its identity. An economic entity may be made up only of activities and employees. There may be no transfer of assets. Tribunals were advised that there may be no single factor which will be present in all relevant transfers and the absence of one factor, such as goodwill, should not in itself prevent the application of the Regulations. While the transfer of employees and the number of employees concerned may be important, the absence of employees will not prevent the transaction from being a transfer within Regulation 3 and the Directive.

This decision indicates a clear recognition by the EAT of the relationship between the Regulations and the Directive and of the obligations of the UK courts and tribunals in respect of interpretation and application of the Regulations. In light of the Court's recent decision in *Rygaard*[80] it may even be

---

[75] See, e.g, *Kenmir Ltd* v *Frizzell* [1968] 1 All ER 414.

[76] See, e.g, *Premier Motors (Medway) Ltd* v *Total Oil Great Britain Ltd* [1983] IRLR 471.

[77] See, e.g, *Melon* cited in note 67 *supra*.

[78] For detailed discussion of the distinction between business and asset transfers see McMullen, *Business Transfers and Employee Rights* (2nd ed), Butterworths, 1992, 48–54.

[79] *Council of the Isles of Scilly* v *Brintel Helicopters and Ellis* [1995] IRLR 6.

[80] Case C-48/94 *Rygaard* cited in note 31 *supra*.

suggested that the current UK definition of a relevant transfer is slightly wider than that of the European Court.

"Immediately before the transfer"

Regulation 5 provides that contracts of employment shall not be terminated in the event of a transfer and that all rights and obligations relating to such contracts shall be transferred to the transferee. Paragraph 3 states that this applies to any person employed "immediately before the transfer". For a while, the effectiveness of the Regulations was severely limited in the UK due to the literal interpretation by the courts of this requirement. In *Apex Leisure Hire*[81] the EAT held that it was a question of fact in each case whether a dismissal prior to a transfer was sufficiently close to the time of the transfer for the employee to be treated as employed immediately before the transfer. They upheld the decision of the industrial tribunal that a gap of two days between the dismissal and the transfer could be disregarded.

The Court of Appeal in *Spence*,[82] stating that *Apex Leisure Hire* had been wrongly decided, held that the Regulations applied only to those employed at the moment of the transfer. In delivering the Opinion of the Court, Balcombe LJ quoted extensively from the Advocate General's Opinion in *Wendelboe*.[83] Although in that Opinion, the Advocate General referred to the need to read Article 3 of the Directive (safeguarding of employee's rights) subject to Article 4 (protection against dismissal), the Court of Appeal devoted little attention to this link except to comment that those dismissed prior to the transfer could rely on the protection against dismissal in the Regulations.

The decision in *Spence* looked set to undermine the intended impact of the Regulations and left the way open to those involved in business transfers to agree that the workforce should be dismissed shortly before any transfer, thus allowing the transferee the choice as to whether or not to re-engage any of the workers, and at what rates. This was a flaw in the Regulations, from the employee's perspective, which was widely and openly exploited.

The gap was firmly closed by the House of Lords in *Litster*,[84] one of the most important UK decisions on transfers and a significant decision in the general development of the relationship between domestic legislation and courts and European law. Oliver LJ began by restating the important rule that, where UK legislation can be reasonably construed in a way which conforms with European law, a purposive interpretation should be applied even where "it

---

[81] *Apex Leisure Hire* v *Barratt* [1985] IRLR 224.
[82] *Secretary of State for Employment* v *Spence* [1986] IRLR 248.
[83] Case 19/83 *Wendelboe* cited in note 32 *supra*.
[84] *Litster* cited in note 60 *supra*.

may involve some departure from the strict and literal application of the words which the legislature has elected to use".[85] He then went on to trace the development of the link between Articles 3 and 4 of the Directive in the case law of the European Court, concluding with the decision in *Bork*. While recognising that Regulation 8 provides only for the treatment of a dismissal linked to a transfer as an unfair dismissal and does not have "the same prohibitory effect as that attributed by the European Court to Article 4",[86] he proceeded nonetheless to follow the decision of *Bork* and to apply Regulation 5 in the light of Regulation 8. In view of the purpose of the Directive, the court had greater flexibility in interpretation than it would have under the normal domestic rules of construction. The phrase "immediately before the transfer" in Regulation 5 should therefore be read as if it was followed by the words "or would have been so employed if he had not been unfairly dismissed" by reason of the transfer.

This decision firmly established the close relationship between the Regulations and the Directive and it gave renewed life to the Regulations, the effect of which had been seriously weakened by the decision of the Court of Appeal in *Spence*. Following *Litster* it was clear that agreements concerning the dismissal of staff could no longer lawfully be incorporated into sale and purchase or other transfer transactions.

Safeguarding of rights or enhanced rights?

The European Court has consistently stated that one of the purposes of the Directive is to maintain the employment rights of the employee after the transfer although it is not designed to provide better rights in the event of a transfer than would otherwise be available in national law. This issue has recently been considered by the EAT in relation to Regulation 8 of TUPE which provides that "an employee shall be treated for the purposes of Part V of the Employment Protection (Consolidation) Act 1978 . . . as unfairly dismissed". The right not to be unfairly dismissed conferred by section 54 of that Act is dependent on the employee having a period of two years' continuous employment, and the accepted view has been that an employee dismissed by reason of a transfer will have no greater right than one dismissed in other circumstances. This provision has, however, been challenged in *Milligan*[87] and the traditional view has been rejected by the EAT. In a decision based on close statutory interpretation of Article 4 of the Directive and Regulation 8 of TUPE, the EAT held that while the Directive permits the

---

[85] *Ibid*, 165.
[86] *Ibid*, 172.
[87] *Milligan* v *Securicor Cleaning Ltd* [1995] IRLR 288.

exclusion by the Member States of certain categories of workers from protection against dismissal, Regulation 8 does not make any specific exemptions. The reference to the provisions of the 1978 Act is intended simply as a short hand way of referring to the remedies available for unfair dismissal and cannot be read as incorporating the continuity requirements in relation to Regulation 8. Although this may be a correct literal interpretation of Article 4 and Regulation 8, it is surprising in that it suggests a construction more favourable to the employee than that adopted by the European Court.

The Government has now taken steps to reverse the effect of this decision by means of a provision in the Collective Redundancies and Transfer of Undertakings (Protection of Employment) Regulations 1995[88] which expressly states that the two year qualifying period will apply to dismissals which are connected with a transfer of an undertaking. A question remains as to how this is to be reconciled with the decision of the English Court of Appeal in *R* v *Secretary of State for Employment, ex parte Seymour Smith and Perez*.[89]

TUPE and CCT

In recent years, the area of greatest controversy in the UK in relation to the application of the Directive and Regulations has been that of contracting out of public services and the programme of compulsory competitive tendering (CCT).[90] Through the process of CCT it was intended that private organisations should bid to provide public services more cheaply than could be done by the local authority. One of the principal ways in which the private firm could provide cheaper services was by reducing wage costs. It was not originally foreseen that the Acquired Rights Directive and TUPE would apply to contracting out but the decisions of the European Court in *Redmond, Rask* and *Schmidt*[91] have made it clear that their application extends to this process. This has caused consternation to the Government and has been highlighted as one of the reasons for a disappointingly low number of bids from the private sector. Decisions such as that of the Court of Appeal in *Dines*[92] indicate that the UK courts and tribunals have now accepted the application of the acquired rights provisions to contracting out. It seems inevitable that the

---

[88] SI 1995 No 2587.

[89] [1995] IRLR 449. This case is discussed in chapter 6 in the context of indirect discrimination and part time workers.

[90] CCT was introduced in relation to local authorities by the Local Government Planning and Land Act 1980 and extended by the Local Government Acts 1988 and 1992.

[91] Case C-29/91 *Redmond Stichting* cited in note 16 *supra*, case C-209/81 *Rask* cited in note 17 *supra* and case C-392/92 *Schmidt* cited in note 30 *supra*.

[92] *Dines* v *Initial Health Care Services Ltd* [1994] IRLR 336. See also *Kenny* v *South Manchester College* [1993] ICR 934, *Brintel Helicopters, supra* at note 79 , *Kelman* v *Care Contract Services Ltd* [1995] ICR 260.

growing certainty which is evident in legal decisions in this area will be disturbed by the decision of the European Court in *Rygaard*.[93] Although it may be argued that the peculiar facts of that case, and in particular the very short term nature of the contract, were highly influential in the decision, services which are contracted out may also be of a specific and fixed term nature and there is once again a doubt as to whether all instances of contracting out will be covered by the Directive and the UK Regulations.

Proposed amendments to the Directive

In September 1994, the Commission submitted a proposal for amendment of the Acquired Rights Directive.[94] Among the reasons put forward for the proposed revisions were the adoption of a revised Directive on Collective Redundancies, the case law of the European Court and the legislation of Member States in relation to corporate rescue. The future of the proposal is uncertain but, nonetheless, it provides an interesting indication of areas of potential development.

Although the Court has done much to clarify the scope of Article 1(1) and the definition of a relevant transfer, the Commission has suggested that the definition in the Directive should be revised and further clarified. A number of changes are proposed, the most controversial of which is a new distinction between the transfer of an economic entity and the transfer of a mere activity. The latter would not constitute a relevant transfer for the purposes of the legislation. This new distinction may be seen as an attempt to restrain the increasingly wide definition adopted by the Court and, if adopted, it is certain to give rise to renewed uncertainty and increased litigation as to its meaning. The European Court in *Rygaard*[95] may have had such a development in mind.

The decisions of the Court have made it clear that the Directive applies to both profit and non profit-making organisations, public and private, and it is proposed that this be expressly stated in the revised definition of a "transfer".

The existing Directive makes no specific provision as to its application in the context of insolvency proceedings although it has been clearly stated by the Court that it does not apply in that situation unless the Member State provides for it. This approach, it is proposed, should be expressly set out in the

[93] Case C-48/94 *Rygaard* cited in note 31 *supra*.
[94] OJ 1994 C 274/10.
[95] Case C-48/94 *Rygaard* cited in note 31 *supra*.

Directive. Member States would have the option of choosing whether or not to apply the Directive to transfers arising in the context of liquidation. This was considered necessary by the Commission to provide flexibility in situations of economic difficulty. While this provision may provide flexibility and assist in the transfer of the assets of insolvent businesses, it may be argued that it is in such situations that the employees are particularly vulnerable and that there is a danger of false or unnecessary insolvency proceedings as a means of avoiding the application of the transfer rules.

The Acquired Rights Directive is intended to provide only partial harmonisation in that the substantial "rights and obligations" to be transferred are dependent on the employment rules and practices of each Member State. Similarly, while the Directive provides for protection against dismissal in the event of a transfer it does not prescribe what that protection should be, leaving these matters to the domestic law of the Member States. While the Commission has rejected the need to introduce uniform rights, it has been proposed that workers should not be excluded from the personal scope of the Directive simply on the basis of hours of work, fixed term or temporary contracts.

Conclusions

Following the amendments to TUPE Regulations in 1993, the written word of the UK provisions now appears to be in closer harmony with the European Directive. Recent decisions of domestic courts and tribunals also suggest acceptance of the need to interpret the Regulations in accordance with the Directive.[96] After a period of considerable uncertainty as to the scope of the Directive and the Regulations, to some extent there is greater clarity and understanding of their application. Uncertainties, however, still exist. Even if the proposed amendments are not introduced, a renewed question mark hangs over the scope of the Directive and there may be a suggestion that its ever widening application has reached the limit.

---

[96] See, e.g, *Council of the Isles of Scilly* v *Brintel Helicopters* cited in note 79 *supra.*

Questions

1. Directives 77/187, 75/129, 533/91 specifically exclude crews of sea-going vessels. Why should this be the case? What purpose does such exclusion serve?

2 Examine the case law of the ECJ in relation to the definition of a "legal transfer". Summarise the definition of the ECJ and explain.

3 Should the Acquired Rights Directive apply in the context of the transferor's insolvency? To what extent has the court resolved this issue?

Contents of Chapter 9

COLLECTIVE REDUNDANCIES

Chapter 9

COLLECTIVE REDUNDANCIES

Background

The first of the three Directives to emerge from the 1974 to 1976 Social Action Programme[1] was Directive 75/129/EEC on the approximation of the laws of the Member States relating to Collective Redundancies.[2] This Directive has recently been amended by Council Directive 92/56/EEC.[3] There was diversity among the Member States in relation to the labour costs of restructuring and this was seen as a threat to continued economic integration. The Collective Redundancies Directive, and the others which emerged from the Social Action Programme,[4] were examples of the Community's desire to avoid inequality of competition and these measures can be "traced to the economic liberalism of the Treaty directed against disparities in the conditions of competition, the dangers to balanced regional development, and restrictions on the free movement of workers."[5] This objective is set out in the preamble to the Directive where it is stated that "it is important that greater protection should be afforded to workers in the event of collective redundancies while taking into account the need for balanced economic and social development within the Community." The aim of the original Directive was to harmonise, to some extent, the procedures to be followed in relation to large scale dismissals. It is a Directive which may be seen to have had

[1] OJ 1974 C 13/1.
[2] OJ 1975 L 48/29. See Appendix for full text of the Directive.
[3] OJ 1992 L 245/3. For full text see Appendix.
[4] See chapters 8 and 10.
[5] Hepple, "Community Measures for the Protection of Workers against Dismissal" (1977) 14 *Common Market Law Review* 489.

relatively limited impact, its principal weakness perhaps being the absence of substantive individual rights. For the UK, the Directive was much less controversial than the Acquired Rights Directive which emerged from the same Action Programme. To a large extent, the provisions of the Directive were already catered for in UK employment law although recent developments have once again shown the inadequacy of the UK provision.

The aim of this chapter is to consider the provisions of the original Directive, the amendments introduced in 1992, and some of the issues which have arisen in respect of their implementation in the UK.

Directive 75/129/EEC and its interpretation by the European Court

The Directive has three main sections: the first is concerned with the scope of the Directive and defines "collective redundancies"; the second sets out the obligation on an employer to consult prior to making redundancies, and the third relates to notification of redundancies.

Definitions

Article 1 provides Member States with a choice of definition for the concept of "collective redundancies". There are two elements to the definition: first, the reason behind the dismissal and secondly, the number of such dismissals. A "redundancy" is defined as a dismissal "effected by an employer for one or more reasons not related to the individual workers concerned".[6] The aim of the Directive is to regulate the treatment of workers who are dismissed for business reasons and not for any personal reason. In order for such dismissals to qualify as "collective" there must be:

"– either, over a period of 30 days:
(1) at least 10 in establishments normally employing more than 20 and less than 100 workers;
(2) at least 10% of the number of workers in establishments normally employing at least 100 but less than 300 workers;
(3) at least 30 in establishments normally employing 300 workers or more;

---

[6] Article 1(1)(a).

– or, over a period of 90 days, at least 20, whatever the number of workers normally employed in the establishments in question".

Paragraph 2 provides a number of exceptions, the most significant being an exception in relation to workers who are "affected by the termination of an establishment's activities where that is the result of a judicial decision". The inclusion of this exception reflected concern about the relationship between the protection of employment rights and insolvency proceedings. The Directive expressly excludes the need for consultation and notification in the event of the business being terminated and the employees dismissed as a consequence of a court decree. The Acquired Rights Directive made no such express provision although the Directive has been interpreted by the European Court to the effect that it was not intended to apply in the context of liquidation.[7]

Consultation procedure

The Directive aimed to harmonise the procedures adopted in Member States in relation to carrying out collective dismissals rather than to harmonise the remedies available to those who had been dismissed. The intention was not to interfere with the discretion accorded to employers under national law to make redundancies. Its somewhat limited aim was merely to make provision for uniform requirements of consultation prior to the dismissals and notification of the proposed dismissals to the relevant public authority. Article 2 sets out the requirements for consultation.

An employer is obliged to consult with workers' representatives "with a view to reaching an agreement" and such consultation should begin when "an employer is contemplating collective redundancies". The consultations must include ways of avoiding or reducing the redundancies and of "mitigating the consequences". It is clearly intended that these should be meaningful consultations and not simply a formality; Article 2(1) expressly states that consultation should be undertaken "with a view to reaching an agreement". In order to enable the workers' representatives to play a constructive part it is provided that they must be given relevant information which must include, at least, the reasons for the redundancies, the number of workers to be made redundant, the number of workers normally employed and the period of time during which the redundancies are to be made.

[7] See discussion of Transfer of Undertakings and Insolvency in chapter 8. See further on the difficult relationship between employment rights and insolvency, Davies "Acquired Rights, Creditors' Rights, Freedom of Contract and Industrial Democracy" (1989) 9 *Yearbook of European Law* 21.

Notification of a public authority

The third element of the Directive has the title "Procedure for Collective Redundancies" although its substance is limited in that it provides only for notification to a competent public authority that such collective redundancies are proposed. An employer must notify the authority of proposed collective redundancies within the definition of the Directive and the redundancies must not take effect earlier than 30 days after the notification. The intention is that this period of 30 days should be used by the authority to consider ways of solving the problems or mitigating the consequences which will result from the redundancies. The public authority may also be given the power to postpone the dismissals for a period of up to 60 days after the notification, where the initial period is thought to be inadequate, to allow for solution of the problems.

The final provisions of the Directive state that it is intended to set a minimum standard[8] and that implementation should be completed within two years.[9] No mention is made of measures for enforcement of rights under the Directive and there is no express provision for sanctions against employers who fail to comply with their obligations. This omission may be explained by the lack of individual rights under the Directive but it casts doubt on the strength of the provisions. Article 4(1), for example, provides that "projected collective redundancies notified to the competent public authority shall take effect not earlier than 30 days after notification" but it is silent on the question of enforcement of this rule. If an employer purports to carry out the dismissals at an earlier date, are the dismissals ineffective? Is the employer obliged to continue paying wages? Can the public authority countermand the employer's action?

The scope of the Directive and its objectives were considered by the European Court in *Dansk* .[10] This case arose from an action by two trade unions against a company in liquidation (Nielsen). In February 1980 the company informed the workers' representatives that it was in financial difficulty. On 14 March, the company informed the Bankruptcy Court that it was suspending payment of its debts. At this time the trade unions sought a bank guarantee from the company to cover future wages. When the company refused, the unions advised their members to stop working which they duly did on 19 March. The company informed the relevant public authority on 21 March that it was contemplating dismissing all of its workers. On 25 March the company was declared insolvent and on the following day the workers

---

[8] Article 5.
[9] Article 6.
[10] Case 284/83 *Dansk Metarbejderforbund* v *Specialarbejderforbundet i Danmark* [1985] ECR 553.

were given notice of dismissal. The trade unions sought allowances which were available under Danish law where an employer failed to give the requisite period of 30 days' notice to the authority. These Danish provisions were intended to implement the requirements of Directive 75/129. The Danish Supreme Court referred two questions to the European Court.

The first question related to the fact that the workers in this case had stopped working prior to their being given notice of dismissal. "May a termination of employment which is effected by the employees . . . be treated as dismissal by the employer"? In other words, did the Directive encompass the concept of constructive dismissal? The second question dealt with the issue of when an employer should begin consultation. Article 2 requires an employer to begin consultation when he or she "is contemplating collective redundancies". The second question asked by the Danish Court was whether or not an employer is also obliged to embark on consultation when he or she *ought* to have contemplated collective redundancies. Does the Directive encompass the standard of a "reasonably prudent employer"? In answering no to both questions, the European Court confirmed the relatively limited ambitions of this Directive.

The trade unions argued that in the situation where workers were no longer guaranteed payment they were entitled to regard themselves as having been constructively dismissed. They were therefore "dismissed" on the date when they gave notice to the employer that they were terminating their contracts and as such fell within the scope of the Directive. Their argument was rejected, with the Court refusing to accept the notion of constructive dismissal as falling within the term "dismissal". The Court stated that the Directive was not intended to interfere in any way with an employer's freedom to dismiss and that, further, to allow workers themselves to decide when they had been "dismissed" would have the effect of preventing the employer from complying with his or her obligations under the Directive.

The only way in which the obligations of the Directive could therefore be brought into force was by the employer "contemplating" redundancies. It seems that the Directive places no obligation on an employer to contemplate redundancies and nor does it provide any test as to when the reasonable employer would contemplate redundancies. It is an entirely subjective test. In its answer to this question the Court considered the exception in the Directive which excluded "the termination of an establishment's activities where that is the result of a judicial decision".[11] An employer whose enterprise was subsequently declared insolvent and who failed to contemplate redundancies might be found to be in breach of the Directive, on the ground that he or she ought to have contemplated redundancies. If, however, the business had been

---

[11] Article 1(2)(d).

terminated by judicial decision, then the consequent dismissals would not fall within the scope of the Directive.

This decision of the Court highlights the difficulty of reconciling the interests of employees with the discretion of employers, in particular in relation to the financial management of the business. It may be argued that requiring employers to consult in the face of impending financial collapse will hasten the failure of the business. At a sensitive time, employers may be understandably reluctant to publicise the economic instability of the business. This direct clash between workers' rights and business needs does, nonetheless, highlight the very shaky foundations of the provisions of this Directive. Although written in the language of legal obligations, in effect it seems closer to a code of good practice.

Directive 92/56/EEC[12]

The proposal

A proposal for a revised Directive[13] emerged from the Commission's Action Programme of 1989, the principal purpose of which was to take account of the transnational nature of many enterprises and the effect of this type of business structure on decision-making. The proposal did not extend the scope of the Directive by way of introducing individual rights but simply amended it to take account of the transnational context of many business enterprises. The proposed revisions were designed to deal with the situation where the decision to make redundancies was taken by the head office or controlling undertaking which was located in another Member State. The proposal included a number of other amendments to the original Directive, one of them being that dismissals should be treated as null if they were effected in breach of the procedures. The amending Directive was adopted on 24 June 1992, its provisions having been restricted in a number of ways from those originally proposed. It made some amendments to the requirement of consultation, introduced a transnational element to the provisions, and inserted a requirement as to enforcement.

The Directive

The basic requirements of the Directive remain consultation and notification with some minor modifications. The phrase "in good time" has been added to

[12] OJ 1992 L 245/3.
[13] OJ 1991 C 31/5.

the requirement to consult and the information to be made available to workers' representatives has been expanded to include categories of workers to be made redundant, the method of selection for redundancy, and the method for calculating redundancy payments.

It is now provided that the obligation to consult applies regardless of whether or not the decision to make the dismissals has been taken by the immediate employer or by a controlling undertaking. The immediate employer cannot plead in defence a lack of information from the controlling body.

The substance of the Directive has not been significantly broadened, although the scope of those affected by it has been changed. The definition of redundancies in Article 1(1) of the original Directive has been amended to include "terminations of an employment contract which occur to the individual workers concerned" provided that there are at least five redundancies. This change should now encompass, for example, negotiated terminations as opposed to dismissals. In the original Directive, collective redundancies which resulted from the closure of a business "as a result of a judicial decision" were excluded. Such redundancies are now included for the purposes of consultation, although Member States may choose to continue to exclude them from the requirement of notification. It is suggested that this change may cast doubt on the decision of the European Court in *Dansk*[14] where one of the reasons given for rejection of the argument that an employer ought reasonably to have foreseen collective redundancies was that it would run counter to the wording of the Directive which excluded workers affected by the closure of a business as the result of a judicial decision. The proposed inclusion of crews of seagoing vessels within the scope of the Directive was rejected.

The original Directive was criticised for its lack of substantive rights and its failure to provide for any remedies. This has been addressed to a very limited extent in that the amending Directive requires that: "Member States shall ensure that judicial and/or administrative procedures for the enforcement of obligations under this Directive are available to the workers' representatives and/or workers." The proposal that dismissals made contrary to the procedural requirements should be declared null did not make it into the final provisions of the Directive.

Implementation in the UK

The provisions of Directive 75/129 were given effect in Part IV of the Employment Protection Act 1975 and are now contained in sections 188 to 198 of the Trade Union and Labour Relations (Consolidation) Act 1992.

---

[14] Case 284/83 *Dansk* cited in note 10 *supra*.

These provisions have been further amended to comply with the 1992 Directive[15] and as a result of proceedings against the UK by the Commission. A significant development for implementation of the Collective Redundancies Directive in the UK employment context has been the decision of the European Court in *European Commission* v *UK*.[16] The Commission commenced proceedings against the UK on the basis that it had failed to fulfil its obligations under Article 5 of the Treaty and under both Directives. Four complaints were made about the UK implementation concerning:

(1) the definition of redundancy;
(2) absence of a requirement that consultations by an employer who is contemplating collective redundancies should be "with a view to reaching an agreement" and should cover all matters specified in the Directive;
(3) lack of effective sanctions in case of failure to consult workers' representatives; and
(4) failure to provide for the designation of workers' representatives where this does not occur voluntarily in practice.

The UK government conceded the first three complaints prior to the decision of the Court and amended the legislation accordingly.[17]

Recently, therefore, a number of amendments have, been introduced to the UK provisions on consultation and notification prior to redundancies. These have been in response both to the 1992 Directive and the decision of the European Court. Some of these areas have also been subject to interpretation by the domestic courts. While the wording of the UK legislation is now closer to that of the Directives, some areas of uncertainty continue and the underlying weakness of these provisions remains.

Definition of redundancy

An employer is required to consult with a recognised trade union where he or she intends to make redundancies.[18] As originally implemented, the definition of redundancy for the purposes of consultation was the standard definition used for the purposes of unfair dismissal and entitlement to redundancy payment. The definition as set out in Section 195 was that redundancy will occur where the employer ceases to carry on the business for the purposes of which the employee was employed or at the place where the employee was

---

[15] Council Directive 92/56/EEC.
[16] Case C-383/92 [1994] IRLR 412. The Court's decision in this case was given on the same day as that in Case C-382/92 [1994] IRLR 392 which is discussed in chapter 9.
[17] Trade Union Relations (Consolidation) Act 1992, Part IV, Chapter II, as amended by Trade Union Reform and Employment Rights Act 1993, Section 34.
[18] 1992 Act, Section 188.

employed, or where the needs of the business for employees to carry out the relevant work have diminished or ceased. It has been argued for some time that this definition is narrower than that used in the Directive and it was amended following the Commission's indication that it intended to commence proceedings against the UK for failure to implement the Directive properly. The definition of redundancy as being dismissals "not related to the individual workers concerned" has now been incorporated into the UK legislation for the purposes of redundancy consultation.[19]

The 1992 amendments to the Directive included a provision to the effect that "terminations of an employment contract . . . shall be assimilated to redundancies provided that there are at least five redundancies". This would allow for the inclusion of negotiated terminations of employment, perhaps by means of voluntary early retirement, which would not fall within the concept of "dismissal". This provision does not appear to have been implemented in the UK legislation although there is a provision to the effect that dismissals will be presumed to be dismissals for redundancy.

When to consult?

Section 188 places an obligation on an employer to consult with a recognised trade union where he or she intends to make redundancies. Such consultation should begin "at the earliest opportunity", with minimum periods in respect of the number of proposed redundancies and the duration of time over which they will be effected. The inclusion of the phrase "at the earliest opportunity" in the UK legislation is as vague as the formula of "in good time" which was added to the Directive by the 1992 amendment.

The question of when an employer is obliged to consult was discussed by the High Court in *R v British Coal Corporation, ex parte Vardy,*[20] the facts of which demonstrate the ineffectiveness of the consultation requirements. The lack of attention paid by employers to the obligations to consult and notify was particularly evident in 1992 when British Coal announced the immediate closure of 31 collieries with the loss of approximately 30,000 jobs. Following the announcement, the President of the Board of Trade declared that the closure of ten would proceed, after the elapse of the statutory consultation period, with the viability of the others being reviewed. The National Union of Miners (NUM) sought judicial review of the closure decisions of British Coal

---

[19] Trade Union and Labour Relations (Consolidation) Act 1992, Section 196, as amended by Trade Union Reform and Employment Rights Act 1993, Section 34.
[20] *R v British Coal Corporation and the Secretary of State for Trade and Industry ex parte Vardy* [1993] 1 CMLR 721.

and the President of the Board of Trade without having conducted proper consultation.

It was argued that there had been a breach of Section 188 of the Trade Union Relations (Consolidation) Act 1992, the Directive and of the Modified Colliery Review Procedure which had been agreed in 1985. The alleged breach of Section 188 and of the Directive was not pursued as British Coal undertook to carry out consultation in accordance with these provisions but Glidewell LJ discussed *obiter* the interpretation of Section 188 and its compatibility with the Directive. He stated that the "difference between the wording of the Directive and the wording of Section 188 of the Act of 1992 is such that the Section cannot be interpreted as having the same meaning as the Directive."[21] Whereas the Directive requires consultation when the employer is "contemplating" redundancies, Section 188 requires it only where redundancies are "proposed": " a state of mind which is much more certain and further along the decision making process".[22]

The question of when an employer is required to commence consultation was also considered by Blackburne J in *Griffen v South West Water Services Ltd*[23] and, in this case, a later date was considered appropriate. Consultation was not required until an employer had identified which workers were likely to be affected and thus was in a position to provide the information which was required in relation to the number and categories of workers likely to be affected. While this interpretation fits well with the information to be given to the workers' representatives, it seems unlikely that consultation at this stage could lead to the avoidance of redundancies or a significant reduction in the number of workers likely to be affected.

Nature of the consultation

In its original form, the only requirements imposed by the UK legislation as to the nature of the consultation were that the employer should consider and respond to any representations made by the trade union representatives and state reasons for rejecting them. The Commission indicated in its action against the UK that this very limited provision did not adequately implement the obligation set out in the Directive. Section 188 has now been amended to include the general exhortation that the consultation must "be undertaken by the employer with a view to reaching agreement with the trade union representatives." In the context of these more positive talks, there must be consultation as to ways of avoiding the dismissals, reducing the number of

---

[21] *Ibid,* p 751.
[22] *Ibid.*
[23] [1995] IRLR 15.

employees to be dismissed and mitigating the consequences of the dismissals.[24]

Certain written information was required to be disclosed by the employer to the union.[25] This provision has been amended to include a requirement that the employer provide details of the proposed method of calculating redundancy payments if it differs from the statutory method. This brought the UK provision into line with changes made by the 1992 Directive.

Special circumstances

The obligations in the Directive, as they have been implemented in the UK, have on a number of occasions been quite evidently ignored. Their strength is further weakened by the UK provision which excuses an employer from full compliance with either consultation or notification where there are "special circumstances". The requirement of consultation is limited by Section 188(7) which provides that in "special circumstances", the employer is required only to take reasonably practicable steps towards compliance. There is no further guidance as to what might constitute "special circumstances" and this is a provision which has no express basis in either of the Directives. Attempts have been made to argue that there are special circumstances in the situation where the employer is in receivership or administration, although this argument has been rejected by the courts.[26]

Notification

The duty to notify a public authority of proposed redundancies is set out in Section 193. Similar time periods to those in Section 188 apply to the duty of notification and, within these time limits, an employer must give written notification to the Secretary of State of proposed redundancies. Where there is a recognised trade union in respect of the employees affected, a copy of the notice should be given to it. There is once again a provision to the effect that full compliance is not necessary in special circumstances where it is not reasonably practicable.

Sanctions

One of the weaknesses of Directive 75/129 is its lack of substantive rights and its failure to provide for enforcement of the provisions. This was addressed to

[24] Trade Union and Labour Relations (Consolidation) Act 1992, Section 188(6).
[25] *Ibid*, Section 188.
[26] See, for example, *Hartlebury Printers* [1992] IRLR 516.

some extent by the 1992 Directive which provided that "Member States shall ensure that judicial and/or administrative procedures for the enforcement of obligations under this Directive are available to the workers' representatives and/or workers". The UK legislation already made some provision for an enforcement mechanism which was reliant for implementation on the trade union. Where the employer fails to consult in accordance with Section 188, the relevant trade union may complain to an industrial tribunal.[27] Where the complaint is well founded, the tribunal may make a "protective award" which is a requirement that the employer continue to pay remuneration to the employees concerned throughout a "protected period".[28] A protective award cannot be sought by individual employees but only by the trade union which represents them and which is recognised by the employer. Once such an award has been made, however, an individual employee can complain to the tribunal where the employer has failed to make the proper payment in terms of the award.[29] The Commission indicated in its action against the UK[30] that this provision was an inadequate sanction on the basis that an employer could set off the protective award against other payments due under the contract of employment or in respect of damages payable for breach of the contract. By virtue of allowing this set-off, the sanction was largely deprived "of its practical effect and its deterrent value".[31] Section 190 has now been amended to remove the rule against double payment.[32]

The original Directive made no mention of sanctions for non-compliance with the obligations placed on an employer but in its judgment in *Commission v UK*,[33] the European Court made it clear that:

"where a Community Directive does not specifically provide any penalty for an infringement ... Article 5 of the Treaty requires Member States to take all measures necessary to guarantee the application and effectiveness of Community Law".[34]

---

[27] Trade Union and Labour Relations (Consolidation) Act 1992, Section 189.

[28] For calculation of the employee's entitlement to remuneration under a protective award, see 1992 Act, Section 190.

[29] Trade Union and Labour Relations (Consolidation) Act 1992 Section 192. No remedy is provided for either the individual or the trade union where the employer has failed to give written notification to the Secretary of State: the only sanction against the employer is a fine: 1992 Act, Section 194.

[30] Case C-383/92 *European Commission v UK* cited in note 16 *supra*.

[31] *Ibid*, p 422.

[32] This provision was considered by the Employment Appeal Tribunal in *Secretary of State for Employment v Mann*, [1996] IRLR 4, in relation to Section 122 of the Employment Protection (Consolidation) Act 1978: see chapter 10.

[33] Case C-383/92 *European Commission v UK* cited in note 16 *supra*.

[34] *Ibid*, p 421.

The UK conceded that its provisions on sanctions were inadequate and they have been amended. The position remains however that the only remedy for workers is a limited amount of financial compensation. The proposal for the 1992 Directive put forward the suggestion that Member States should be required to provide for dismissals to be null and void if they were made in breach of the procedures set out in the Directive. This proposal was rejected and all that was included in the 1992 Directive was a requirement that enforcement procedures be made available. While such a provision might have been seen as exceeding the limited scope of the Directives which were concerned only with consultation and notification, the absence of a real sanction has resulted in some employers taking little notice of the requirements.

Workers' representatives

By the time the European Court considered the complaints made by the Commission against the UK, the only outstanding complaint related to the problem of lack of workers' representation. The nature of this complaint was very similar to that made against the UK in respect of implementation of the consultation provisions of the Acquired Rights Directive.[35] The Directive requires consultation with workers' representatives and this was translated into UK law as representatives of recognised trade unions. The limited scope of this method of implementation is clear in the definition of "trade union representative" which is given in Section 196 of the Trade Union and Labour Relations (Consolidation) Act 1992. A trade union representative is an official or other person authorised by a union which is recognised by the employer for the purposes of collective bargaining. In the absence of any obligation on employers to recognise any trade union the weakness of the protection for workers in this situation is obvious.

The UK government argued that the domestic legislation provided for consultation with a recognised trade union and that the process of recognition was a voluntary matter for individual employers. Where no such recognition existed, the employer was not obliged to follow the requirements set down by the Directive. The Court decisively rejected this argument while at the same time making it clear that it did not require compulsory recognition of trade unions. What was required was the provision of workers' representatives in situations covered by the Directive and the UK legislation. The Court reiterated that the Directive only provided for partial harmonisation but it "is not simply a *renvoi* to the rules in force in the Member States on the

---

[35] Case C-382/92 *European Commission* v *UK* in note 16 *supra*. This is considered further in chapter 9.

designation of workers representatives".[36] The matter was referred back to the UK government to produce proposals for compliance with the Directive.

Following the decision of the European Court, but prior to the introduction of new rules governing representation, this issue was considered by the High Court in *Griffen*.[37] An action was raised by the trade union, UNISON, arising out of redundancies made by South West Water (SWW). Following privatisation, SWW refused to recognise UNISON, instead setting up staff consultative committees and a staff council. When it subsequently proposed to make redundancies, it consulted with these bodies. UNISON raised the question of whether or not the Directive was directly enforceable against SWW as an emanation of the state and if so whether SWW were obliged to consult with them.

The European Court in *European Commission* v *UK* had decided that provision must be made for workers' representatives in terms of the Directive and, in the absence of Government steps to give effect to this decision, UNISON sought to rely directly on the Directive. The Court held that this aspect of the Directive was not sufficiently unconditional and precise to give rise to direct effect and that the State required to take action to provide for workers' representatives in the situation where there was no voluntary agreement between employer and employees. Had the Directive been directly enforceable, however, who would have been the "workers' representatives"? Despite the creation of special staff committees, it was concluded, on the basis of expert evidence as to industrial relations practices in the UK, that officials of the union and not the staff committees would have been the "workers' representatives".[38]

More than a year after the finding of the European Court that the UK did not adequately provide for consultation, Section 188 of the 1992 Act has been amended to provide for representation where there is no recognised trade union.[39] The Collective Redundancies and Transfer of Undertakings (Protection of Employment) (Amendment) Regulations 1995[40] came into force on 26 October 1995 although they will not be fully effective until March 1996. The requirement on an employer to provide information and to consult will now apply to "appropriate representatives". Appropriate representatives are representatives of a trade union which is recognised by the employer in respect of

[36] Case C-383/92 *European Commission* v *UK* cited in note 16 *supra* at 420.
[37] *Griffen* v *South West Water Services Ltd* [1995] IRLR 15.
[38] The inherent contradiction in the court's finding that the provisions of the Directive were not clear, precise and unambiguous and its subsequent ability to decide who were the workers' representatives is discussed in Skidmore "Enforcement of Rights to Worker Representation in Community Law" (1995) 58 *Modern Law Review* 744.
[39] Similar amendments have been made to the Transfer of Undertakings (Protection of Employment) Regulations 1981.
[40] SI 1995 No 2587.

the employees concerned or employees elected by the employees. If there are both trade union representatives and elected representatives, the employer may choose to consult with either. Elected representatives must be employed in the undertaking concerned at the time of their election. While the Regulations now allow for elected representatives, they set down no procedure for their election. The Regulations further provide that, where the employer has allowed sufficient time for election of representatives, he or she will not be in breach of the periods for consultation if the reason is a delay in the election.

The Regulations make a number of other amendments, including the exclusion of the need for consultation where only a limited number of redundancies are to be made. In respect of dismissals taking place after 1 March 1996, an employer will not be required to consult where he or she proposes to make less than 20 dismissals over a period of 90 days. The existing legislation required consultation regardless of the number of dismissals, although defined periods for consultation were dependent on the scale of the redundancies.[41]

Although steps have finally been taken to satisfy the requirement of consultation with workers' representatives, they may still be open to challenge. There is a lack of guidance as to how representatives should be elected and it is unlikely that elections will be a priority for either employer or employees when faced with news of impending dismissals. While employers are now obliged to consult with elected representatives, they are under no obligation to organise the elections and it is unclear what will happen if no representatives are elected. The burden appears firmly placed upon the workers to ensure that the new requirement to consult is not as easily avoided as it was prior to the amendments.

[41] Trade Union and Labour Relations (Consolidation) Act 1992, Section 188.

Questions

1. Why do you think that Directive 75/129 requires notification to a public authority of proposed collective redundancies? What function could such notification fulfil?

2   Examine the view by Glidewell LJ in *Vardy* that the 1992 Act cannot be interpreted consistently with Directive 75/129. What legal effect can this inconsistency, if there is one, produce?

3   In the context of section 188(7) TURERA, what do you understand by the phrase "special circumstances"? and in section 188, "reasonably practicable"? Do these provisions undermine the aim of Directive 75/129?

Contents of Chapter 10

INSOLVENCY

Chapter 10

INSOLVENCY

Background

The third Directive which emerged from the Social Action Programme of 1974 to 1976 was the Directive protecting the rights of workers on the insolvency of their employer: Council Directive 80/987/EEC.[1] It was foreseen that the Common Market would result in restructuring of businesses and companies and that restructuring in turn could result in economic disadvantages, at least in the short term. The need for social provision within the Community became evident within the context of the developing economic market. One particular area of concern, which was closely allied to the issues of collective redundancies and acquired rights, was that of the effect of insolvency of an employer on the workers in the enterprise. It was therefore proposed that workers should have some guarantee of money owing to them by the insolvent employer. As with the Directives on collective redundancies and acquired rights, the intention was to introduce a minimum floor of rights. Based on Article 100, the Directive aims to promote the approximation of laws and to improve living and working conditions by protecting employees in the event of the insolvency of their employer.

A variety of methods might be adopted in order to provide some financial protection for employees in the event of their employer's insolvency. In the UK, as part of the law of insolvency, employees are given preferential status and rank as preferential creditors in the employer's insolvency. In this way,

---

[1] OJ 1980 L 283/23. For full text see Appendix.

their claims are placed above those of ordinary and secured creditors.[2] An employee is treated as a preferential creditor in respect of the following debts: remuneration payable in respect of the period of four months prior to the commencement of sequestration or winding up; guarantee payment; medical suspension pay; pay during suspension on maternity grounds; pay during time off; statutory sick pay; and pay due under a protective award.[3] While these debts are classed as preferred debts, the employee may still fail to recover what he or she is due as a result of the employer's financial situation. In that event, an alternative scheme of protection is required and it is that which the Directive aims to provide. The effect of the Directive is to shift some of the responsibility for the employer's insolvency to an independent authority which acts as guarantor.

Directive 80/987/EEC

The aim of the Directive is to provide for a scheme which ensures that the payment of employees' outstanding contractual claims is guaranteed by guarantee institutions independent from the employer. The provisions of the Directive can be divided into four sections:

- definitions
- guaranteed pay
- guarantee institutions
- relationship between insolvency protection and statutory social security schemes.

Definitions

Article 1 defines the scope of the application of the Directive. It applies to employees' claims arising from contracts of employment or employment relationships and existing against employers who are in a state of insolvency.[4] The definitions of "employer", "employee", "contract of employment" and "employment relationship" are left to Member States.[5] An employer is to be treated as being in a state of insolvency in two situations. The first is where a

---

[2] Employees have preferential creditor status under the Companies Act 1985 and the Insolvency Act 1986, Section 175 and Sched 6.
[3] Insolvency Act 1986, Schedule 6, as amended by Trade Union Reform and Employment Rights Act 1993, Schedule 8, para 34 to take account of introduction of suspension on maternity grounds.
[4] Article 1(1).
[5] Article 2(2).

request has been made for the opening of proceedings involving the employer's assets in order to satisfy collectively the claims of creditors and which make it possible to take into account the claims of employees. Alternatively, there will be a state of insolvency where a competent authority in the Member State has decided to open proceedings or has established that the employer's business has been definitively closed down and that there are insufficient assets to warrant the opening of proceedings.[6]

The scope of the Directive is limited in a number of situations set out in Article 1. Article 1(2) allows Member States to exclude certain categories of employees from the scope of the Directive. Exclusions may be based on the "special nature" of the contract or employment relationship or on the fact that other equivalent forms of protection apply to these employees. Details of these excluded categories are provided in the Annex to the Directive and the exclusions are clearly divided into two separate categories. Those in the first category are excluded on the basis of the nature of their contract or employment relationship and there is no requirement that they be provided with alternative forms of protection. Those in the second category, however, are excluded from the application of the Directive precisely because they are covered by an alternative guarantee scheme.[7] Those excluded in the UK include the spouse of the employer and crews of sea-going vessels.

Guaranteed pay

The second aspect of the Directive deals with those claims of an employee which are to be protected by guarantee. Outstanding claims by employees for payments resulting from contracts of employment or employment relationships and relating to pay must be guaranteed in respect of a certain period of time "prior to a given date".[8] Member States can choose to define this date as that of:

- the onset of the employer's insolvency.
- the notice of dismissal issued to the employee concerned on account of the employer's insolvency.
- the onset of the employer's insolvency or the date on which the contract or relationship of employment was discontinued on account of the employer's insolvency.[9]

Guaranteed claims are to be calculated in terms of this date.

---

[6] Article 2(1).
[7] This distinction between the two categories of excluded workers was confirmed by the European Court in Case C-53/88 *Commission* v *Hellenic Republic* [1990] ECR I-3917.
[8] Article 3(1).
[9] Article 3(2).

The aim of the Directive is to guarantee payment of outstanding claims to employees and in its widest sense the protection offered is generous. Article 4 provides, however, that Member States may limit the scope of the claims. Definition of the minimum guaranteed claim will depend on the definition of the "given date" which has been adopted. Article 4(2) provides that Member States may limit liability as follows:

- if the given date is the onset of the employer's insolvency, they must ensure the payment of outstanding claims relating to pay for the last three months of the contract of employment or employment relationship occurring within a period of six months preceding the date of the onset of the employer's insolvency.
- if the given date is that of notice of dismissal to the employee, they must ensure the payment of outstanding claims relating to pay for the last three months of the contract of employment or employment relationship preceding the date of the notice of dismissal issued to the employee on account of the employer's insolvency.
- if the given date is that of the onset of the employer's insolvency or that on which the contract of employment was discontinued on account of the employer's insolvency, they must ensure payment of claims relating to pay for the last 18 months of the contract or employment relationship preceding the date of the onset of the employer's insolvency or the date on which the contract of employment or employment relationship was discontinued on account of the employer's insolvency. In this case, Member States may limit the liability to make payment to pay corresponding to a period of eight weeks or to several shorter periods totalling eight weeks.[10]

In addition to limiting the temporal scope of the Directive, Member States may place an upper limit on claims guaranteed by setting a financial ceiling to the liability.[11]

Guarantee institutions

The third element of the Directive provides for the establishment of guarantee institutions which will have liability for payment of the employees' claims. Article 5 provides that it is for the Member States to establish the detailed

---

[10] Article 4(2).
[11] Article 4(3). The Commission must be informed of the method used to set such a limit on liability.

rules relating to these institutions but sets out three guiding principles which must be observed. The first principle is that the assets of the guarantee institution must be independent from those of the employer and must not be accessible to the insolvency proceedings. The second principle is that, while the guarantee institution should be separate, employers should contribute to its financing. The Member State may decide, however, that it will be entirely state funded. The third principle is that, where employers are required to contribute to the financing of the institution, the institution's liability should not be affected by the failure of an employer to meet his or her obligation to contribute.

Overlap with social security

The Directive aims to provide social protection for employees and to some extent there could be overlap with social security schemes. There may also be overlap in that employers may be obliged to make payments to social security schemes in respect of the relevant employees. Article 6 allows Member States to provide that guarantee institutions will not be liable in respect of contributions which have not been paid under statutory social security schemes or company pension schemes. Article 7, however, protects the employee in the situation where the employer has failed to make compulsory contributions to a national social security scheme despite the fact that the employee's contributions have been deducted at source from his or her remuneration. Article 8 offers protection to employees who have already left the employer's service prior to insolvency and who are entitled to "immediate or prospective entitlement to old-age benefits" from a supplementary company pension scheme. [12]

Final provisions

In keeping with the aim of social law measures as being to establish a minimum floor of rights, it is stated that Member States may provide more favourable provisions and they may also introduce measures designed to avoid abuse. Member States were given three years within which to implement the

---

[12] Italy was found not to have implemented these Articles by failing to provide for the payment of benefits to employees where contributions had been deducted at source and by failing to protect pension rights under supplementary pension schemes: Case 22/87 *Commission* v *Italian Republic* [1989] ECR 143.

Directive and actions were raised against both Italy and Greece for failure to carry out proper implementation.[13]

Interpretation of the Directive by the European Court

The question of whether or not Directive 80/987/EEC was capable of direct effect was considered by the European Court in *Francovich and Bonifaci* v *Italy,*[14] in which a number of questions were referred by two magistrates' courts in Italy to the Court. The applicants were owed substantial arrears of salary when their employers became insolvent and sought payment under the Directive or, alternatively, damages from the State for failure to implement the relevant provisions of the Directive. The first issue to be considered by the Court was whether the Directive could be directly enforced by the individual employees. In other words, did the Directive give rise to unconditional and sufficiently precise rights. The Court's conclusion was that, while the personal scope of the Directive and the extent of the guaranteed payments were precise and unconditional, the identity of the guarantee institution was not. They further held that, in the absence of a guarantee institution, the State itself would not be treated as having to adopt the role of the guarantee institution.

Having concluded that the provisions of the Directive did not give rise to direct effect, the Court went on to consider the potentially far reaching issue of State compensation. Italy had already been held to be in breach of its obligation to implement the Directive within the set time limit of three years.[15] The Court stated that as a matter of principle Member States were obliged to make good damage suffered by individuals as a result of breaches of Community law for which the State was responsible. The Court went on to set down conditions of liability to apply in situations, as in this case, where a Member State had failed to fulfil its obligation under Article 169 of the Treaty to implement fully a Community measure. In such a situation the Member State should be liable provided that the Directive was intended to confer individual rights, the content of those rights could be identified on the basis of the Directive and there was a causal link between the failure of the Member State

---

[13] Case 22/87 *Commission* v *Italy* [1989] ECR 143; Case C-53/88 *European Commission* v *Greece* [1990] ECR I-3917.

[14] Joined cases C-6/90 and C-9/90 *Francovich & Bonifaci* v *Italy.*

[15] Case 22/87 *Commission* v *Italy* cited at note 13 *supra.*

and the damage suffered by the individual. All three conditions were satisfied.[16]

Implementation in the UK

The Insolvency Directive is implemented in UK law by Sections 122 to 127 of the Employment Protection (Consolidation) Act 1978. Provision is made for employees to apply directly to the Secretary of State for payment of certain debts which are owed by the employer at the time of insolvency. These debts can be paid by the Secretary of State out of the National Insurance Fund.

Section 122 sets out the rights of the employee in the case of the employer's insolvency. Application must be made to the Secretary of State who should be satisfied that the employer is insolvent, the employment has terminated and that the employee is entitled to payment of a debt which is covered by Section 122. The debts which are covered are arrears of pay, payment in respect of notice periods, holiday pay, the basic award of compensation for unfair dismissal and reimbursement of a reasonable sum in respect of training fees.[17] Arrears of pay are defined as including guarantee payments, remuneration during suspension on maternity or medical grounds, payment for time off work and remuneration under a protective award.[18] These payments are subject to temporal limitation[19] and are calculated in terms of a maximum weekly pay.[20]

The EAT in *Secretary of State for Employment* v *Mann*[21] has recently considered the compatibility of these limits and has concluded that they are permitted by the Directive. The social objective of the Directive is to provide protection for employees but this does not require an absolute guarantee of payments. This decision also challenged the right of the Secretary of State to make deductions from one element of the guaranteed payment to take account of another. A number of employees, dismissed by administrative receivers, sought payment from the Secretary of State under Section 122 of various sums including

---

[16] The UK Employment Appeal Tribunal has declined jurisdiction in a *Francovich* type claim for damages in respect of failure to implement properly the Insolvency Directive. Such actions should instead be raised before the English High Court: *Secretary of State for Employment* v *Mann* [1996] IRLR 4.
[17] Employment Protection (Consolidation) Act 1978, Section 122(3).
[18] *Ibid*, Section 122(4), as amended by Trade Union Reform and Employment Rights Act 1993, Schedule 8, para 18 to take account of introduction of suspension on maternity grounds.
[19] *Ibid*, Section 122(3).
[20] *Ibid*, Section 122(5).
[21] [1996] IRLR 4.

protective awards[22] and wage arrears. At the time when these claims were considered, an employer would have been entitled to set these payments off against each other[23] although this right has subsequently been repealed[24] as a result of the decision of the European Court in *European Commission* v *United Kingdom*.[25] Following the decision of the Court, the EAT concluded that they were obliged to interpret Section 122 in accordance with European law and therefore held that the Secretary of State was not entitled to make deductions from one element of pay in respect of another.

Section 123 provides for the Secretary of State to make payments into an occupational pension scheme of unpaid contributions due by the employer. This section applies to contributions due on behalf of the employer or the employee although in respect of employee contributions payment will not be made in excess of the contributions deducted from the employee's pay during the last 12 months. Application to the Secretary of State in respect of unpaid contributions should be made on behalf of the fund.

Provision is made under Section 124 for complaint to the industrial tribunal in respect of the Secretary of State's decision. The employee or a representative of the pension fund who is aggrieved at the Secretary of State's decision not to pay or at the level of payment to be made may, within three months of receiving the Secretary of State's decision, complain to an industrial tribunal which can issue a declaration as to the amount which should have been paid.[26] Where payment has been made by the Secretary of State to an employee or to an individual on behalf of the pension fund, the Secretary of State will then acquire any rights or remedies which that person had against the insolvent employer and any money recovered under these rights or remedies should be paid into the National Insurance Fund.[27]

Conclusions

In general, the Insolvency Directive seems to have given rise to few problems and it has aroused little interest in the UK. This may reflect the fact that, unlike other social law Directives, the provisions of the Insolvency Directive fit well with existing UK law and were generally welcomed. A recent Report

---

[22] An employer may be ordered by an industrial tribunal to pay protective awards in the event of failure to consult prior to redundancy dismissals: Trade Union and Labour Relations (Consolidation) Act 1992, Section 189.

[23] *Ibid*, Section 190.

[24] Trade Union Reform and Employment Rights Act 1993, Section 34(3).

[25] Case C-383/92 *European Commission* v *UK* [1994] IRLR 412. For further discussion of this decision see chapter 9, *supra*.

[26] Employment Protection (Consolidation) Act 1978, Section 124.

[27] *Ibid*, Section 125.

from the Commission on Transposition of the Directive[28] shows that there have been few problems in any of the Member States, with the most common criticism being a difference between the concept of insolvency in the national law and that used in the Directive. The only criticism of the UK legislation relates to the exclusion of merchant seamen from the scope of the guarantee. The Commission has indicated that it will decide in the first half of 1996 whether and to what extent the Directive should be revised.[29]

[28] Report from the Commission : Transposition of Council Directive 80/987/EEC of 20 October 1980 on the Approximation of the Laws of the Member States Relating to the Protection of Employees in the Event of the Insolvency of their Employer: COM (95) 164 final.
[29] Commission Medium Term Social Action Programme 1995 – 1997: COM (95) 134 final.

Questions

1. What is the rationale, in UK law, for excluding the spouse of an employer and the crew of a sea-going vessel from the application of Directive 80/987?

2. Why should European law permit the imposition of a statutory upper limit to liability in the case of insolvency of the employer when it does not do so in the case of sex discrimination?

3. Does the decision of the ECJ in *Francovich and Bonifaci* have implications for other areas of social law?

Contents of Chapter 11

CONTRACT OF EMPLOYMENT

Chapter 11

CONTRACT OF EMPLOYMENT

Background

Throughout the European Union in recent years, there have been changes in the pattern of working relationships, with interest focused on the growing use of "atypical workers" and flexible working.[1] These developments may lead to uncertainty among workers as to their legal status and their employment rights. In the UK there has also been a recent trend towards encouraging the use of personal contracts or individually bargained contracts. This has increased the already considerable importance of the contract of employment as a source of employment rights and obligations. The concentration on individual bargaining, while in theory placing the employee at the centre of the process, may in practice exacerbate his or her vulnerability. One area, albeit limited, in which new measures have been adopted which are aimed at strengthening the position of the employee in relation to working terms is that of provision of information about the contract of employment to the employee.

On 14 October 1991, Council Directive 533/91/EEC on an employer's obligation to inform employees of the conditions applicable to the contract or employment relationship was adopted.[2] This Directive, based on Article 100, has attracted relatively little attention in the UK with this lack of interest being attributable to the fact that the Directive, to a large extent, reflects provisions

---

[1] For discussion of the growth of new forms of work and some of the related legal issues see Kravaritou-Manitakis, *New Forms of Work: labour law and social security aspects in the European Community* (European Foundation for the Improvement of Living and Working Conditions, 1988).
[2] OJ 1991 L 288/32. For full text see Appendix.

which already existed in domestic legislation. The Directive nonetheless has required some changes to be made to the UK provisions and discussion of it provides an opportunity to consider its limited scope and the potential in this area for further development. Although, unlike many social law measures, this Directive presented little threat to existing UK labour law, the UK abstained from the final vote on the ground that it objected to the choice of legal base.

The Directive

Directive 533/91 is clearly concerned with form as opposed to substance and it sets out no requirements as to the level of employment rights to be enjoyed by workers in the Member States. It does however prescribe a number of issues in relation to which the employee should be informed of his or her legal rights and obligations. One of its aims, as set out in the preamble, is to "create greater transparency on the labour market" and its effect is intended to be the provision of certain information by the employer to the employee.

Personal scope

The Directive applies to every paid employee who has a contract or relationship of employment defined or governed by the law in force in a Member State.[3] Member States are permitted to limit the application of the obligations in the Directive by excluding employees who have a contract or employment relationship not exceeding one month in total and those who are required to work less than eight hours a week.[4] Employees engaged on work of a casual or specific nature may also be excluded provided that their exclusion can be objectively justified.

Obligation to provide information

Article 2(1) requires the employer to provide the employee with notification of "the essential aspects of the contract or employment relationship". The information must include at least the following:

- identities of the parties
- place of work – where there is no fixed place of work it must be stated that the employee is required to work at various places
- job title or brief job description

[3] Article 1(1).
[4] Article 1(2).

- date of commencement of the contract or employment relationship
- where the employment is temporary, its expected duration
- amount of paid leave or method for calculating entitlement
- notice periods
- amount and frequency of payment of remuneration
- length of normal working day or week
- details of collective agreements governing the employee's conditions of work.

Although the aim of the Directive is to ensure that each employee is provided with notification of the terms of his or her employment, Article 2(3) provides that all of this information need not be given to the employee in a single, personal document. In respect of information concerning paid leave, notice, remuneration and working hours, the employee may be referred to "laws, regulations and administrative or statutory provisions or collective agreements governing these particular points". While it is argued that this provision lessens the administrative burden on employers, to some extent it also undermines the effectiveness of the Directive as the employee will not necessarily have a single, complete and easily understood statement containing all of the relevant information.

Means of information

Subject to the provision in Article 2(3) for reference to legislation or collective agreements, the basic principle set out in Article 3 is that each employee should receive a written copy of the essential information. The information may be given to the employee in a variety of forms; a written contract of employment, a letter of engagement or one or more written documents provided that one of the documents contains at least information relating to the identity of the parties, the place of work, the job description, remuneration and working hours.[5] If the employer has failed to provide information in any of these forms then he or she must provide the employee with a signed written declaration containing all of the information required by Article 2 by the end of two months of employment.[6] This information must be provided within two months even where the employment has already terminated.

While this provision offers flexibility to Member States and to individual employers in terms of the way in which they choose to provide the required information to each employee, the diversity of documents may in effect create confusion.

[5] Article 3(1).
[6] Article 3(2).

Expatriate employees

Additional information must be given to employees who are required to work in a country other than the Member State whose law governs the contract. This information, required by Article 3, must include the duration of the employment abroad, the currency in which he or she is to be paid, any benefits in cash or in kind in relation to the period of employment abroad and any conditions governing the employee's repatriation. This information is only required in respect of periods of work abroad of more than one month and it must be given to the employee before his or her departure. Reference may be made to relevant legislation and collective agreements in respect of information concerning the currency of remuneration and the provision of any benefits.

Modification of terms

In order to protect the employee's rights and to encourage transparency, an employee is entitled not only to initial notification of the terms of employment but also to notification of any subsequent changes in these terms. Once again the Directive is not concerned with the process of modification of contractual terms or the freedom of an employer to institute such changes, but simply with the flow of information about such changes to the employee. An employer must give written notification to the employee of any changes to aspects of employment referred to in Articles 2(2) and 4(1). Notification should be provided as soon as possible but not later than one month after the change has taken effect. No written notification is required where change has been made in the statutory provision or collective agreements to which an employee has been referred. Where, for example, the rate of remuneration is set out in a collective agreement to which an employee has been referred in terms of Article 2, and that collective agreement is amended, the employer is not required to provide the employee with written notification.

Form and proof of the contract or employment relationship

The Directive is concerned solely with the provision of information to the employee and does not affect the legal status of the individual. The form of a contract of employment, the proof of its existence and the proof of its terms remain matters for the law of the Member State.[7] The provision by an

---

[7] Article 6.

employer of a written declaration of terms in accordance with Article 3 does not establish the legal status of the recipient as an employee and nor does it provide conclusive evidence of the terms of the contract. This provision, which reflects the statutory measures already in existence in the UK, highlights the very limited nature of the Directive and also creates the potential for further confusion.

Enforcement

Some limited provision is made in the Directive for enforcement of the obligations imposed on the employer in that Member States are required to provide means by which employees may pursue claims arising from the Directive by judicial process.

Final provisions

The Directive is intended to establish a minimum standard and Member States are therefore entitled to provide higher levels of protection. Implementation of the Directive was required by 30 June 1993 and it is expressly provided by Article 9(1) that such implementation may be by means of collective agreement between employers and workers' representatives. Where implementation is by means of collective agreement, reference to the Directive must be made in the agreement. It is further provided that employees who are already engaged at the time of coming into force of these provisions may request that the employer provides them with the information required by the Directive and that on receipt of such a request the employer must provide the relevant documents within two months.[8]

Implementation – issues arising

This Directive reflects to a large extent the provisions which already existed in UK law. Sections 1 to 11 of the Employment Protection (Consolidation) Act 1978 provided for the issue to an employee of a written statement of terms within 13 weeks of the commencement of employment. A number of relatively minor amendments have now been made to these provisions by the Trade Union Reform and Employment Rights Act 1993 in order to bring them into compliance with the Directive.

The legislative history of this Directive demonstrates the difficulty in achieving consensus in areas of social law and the lack of interest in its

[8] Article 9(2).

adoption might prompt the question – "was it worth the effort?". In many ways the final product appears a faint shadow of the original idea. The value, and indeed the appropriateness, of such social measures may be questioned. Experience in the UK has highlighted a number of difficulties and defects with the system of a written statement of terms, and it is disappointing that few of these issues have been addressed.

Proof of contract or statement of terms?

The original proposal introduced by the Commission[9] envisaged that each employee would be given a written declaration of the main terms of his or her employment. The title of the proposed Directive referred to a "form of proof of an employment relationship" and it was stated in the preamble that each employee was to be entitled to a form of proof of the main terms of his or her employment relationship. In their Opinion on the Directive[10] the Economic and Social Committee raised concern about the effect of this requirement in view of the flexibility which currently existed in many national systems and which allowed the existence of an employment contract to be proved by any means. By introducing a requirement of writing to prove the terms of the contract, the effect might be to exclude individuals who had not received such a document from being able to establish that they were in fact employed. In the Directive which was finally adopted by the Council, the title referred simply to the provision of information concerning the conditions applicable to the contract or employment relationship. The obligation placed on the employer is to notify the employee of "the essential aspects of the contract or employment relationship".[11] The obligation arises only in respect of paid employees who have a contract or relationship of employment as defined by national law[12] and it is clearly stated that the Directive is without prejudice to national law and practice regarding proof of the existence and content of a contract.[13]

The original proposal presented certain dangers for individual workers. The lack of a written declaration might prevent proof of employment status by other means. A written document issued by the employer may not accurately reflect the bargain made between the parties. The absence of reference to "proof" in the final document would seem sufficient to allay these fears. It might be suggested, however, that the final Directive makes so much provision

[9] Proposal for a Council Directive on a form of proof of an employment relationship, OJ 1991 C 24/3.
[10] OJ 1991 C 159/32.
[11] Article 2(1).
[12] Article 1(1).
[13] Article 6.

for flexibility that it becomes almost meaningless. Article 3 provides that the required information may be given to the employee by means of:

- a written contract
- a letter of engagement
- one or more other written documents
- a written declaration signed by the employer.

There is clearly scope for confusion. While lawyers may understand the difference between a contract, the terms of which can be enforced, and a written document providing information as to the terms of the contract, which in the UK has been held to constitute strong evidence of the contract, it is unlikely to be a distinction which is clear to all employees.[14] It is questionable whether the Directive achieves the objective of greater transparency set out in the preamble.

Entitlement to information about the contract is dependent on the worker having "employment" status, according to national law. In the UK, this has traditionally been left to the courts to decide on the basis of the distinction between a contract of service and a contract for services.[15] The application of this distinction has in several cases resulted in atypical workers such as casual workers[16] and temporary or agency workers[17] being denied employment status. These workers would not qualify within the Directive. European social law lacks a uniform definition of an employee and even within social legislation itself there is inconsistent use of terms. The Equal Pay Directive, for example, refers to employees whereas the Pregnancy Directive refers to workers.[18] With the growth of atypical work relationships, it may be argued that the scope of the Directive is too limited and in many cases it will be those workers engaged on a casual basis who would benefit most from clear information as to their terms and conditions.

Discrimination?

Article 1(2) permits Member States to exclude from the scope of the Directive employees who do not work more than eight hours a week and those who have a contract of a casual or specific nature. The hours threshold has not

[14] *System Floors (UK) Ltd* v *Daniel* [1981] IRLR 475.
[15] For an indication of the judicial test see *Ready Mixed Concrete* v *Minister of Pensions and National Insurance* [1968] 1 All ER 433.
[16] *O'Kelly* v *Trusthouse Forte* [1984] QB 90.
[17] *Wickens* v *Champion Employment* [1984] ICR 365; *Ironmonger* v *Movefield Ltd* [1988] IRLR 461; but *cf McMeechan* v *Secretary of State for Employment* [1995] IRLR 461.
[18] Interestingly the opposite approach has been used in their implementation in the UK with equal pay applying to the wider category of "workers" whereas maternity rights are available only to employees.

been implemented into UK legislation and nor has the restriction concerning the nature of the contract although, as discussed above, workers engaged on a casual or fixed term basis may fail to establish employment status. The restrictions in the Directive may be open to challenge on the basis that they constitute indirect discrimination.[19] The Directive requires objective justification for the exclusion of casual or specific contracts but it is not clear from textual analysis of the provision whether this justification is also required in relation to the eight hours limit. The case law of the European Court in relation to indirect discrimination and part time workers seems to suggest that such justification would be required.

Essential aspects of the contract

This Directive demonstrates many of the difficulties inherent in the attempt to introduce partial harmonisation of employment law. In addition to differing concepts of employment, there is also a lack of uniformity in respect of the essential aspects of the contract. The Social Committee in its Opinion on the proposed Directive recommended that the requirement to provide information should be defined in general terms. The identification of what was essential to the contract should be left to the laws and practices of each Member State. This view was rejected and instead the Directive represents a compromise list of what is essential.[20] While those elements specified in the Directive are likely to be important no matter what the legal system, there may be other terms which are essential in particular States but which are not included in the list.

Effective remedies

Article 8 requires Member States to introduce measures to enable employees to enforce their rights under the Directive by means of judicial process. Section 11 of the Employment Protection Consolidation Act 1978 already provides for limited enforcement of the right to a written statement of terms within the UK and this provision has not been amended as a result of the Directive. In practice the weakness of the enforcement provisions has made the right to a written statement illusory in situations where the employer does not voluntarily comply. A complaint to an industrial tribunal can currently produce merely a declaration as to what should have been included in the written statement. Not surprisingly, few employees make use of this provision.

---

[19] For full discussion of the development of the concept of indirect discrimination in relation to part time workers, see chapter 6.
[20] Article 2(2).

In the absence of effective sanctions against employers who fail to provide the required information, these provisions are destined to remain weak.

For those employers who already consider it good practice to provide full information to employees, this Directive will require little change while, for those who fail to provide information, the Directive poses no threat. This Directive has attracted scant attention in the UK[21] and experience of similar provisions in national law suggest that it will be of limited effect. The issues which it raises are, nonetheless, of fundamental importance to social law and employment rights.

---

[21] This lack of interest has resulted in it being dubbed "The Cinderella Directive": see Clark and Hall, "The Cinderella Directive? Employee Rights to Information about Conditions Applicable to their Contract or Employment Relationship" (1992) 21 *Industrial Law Journal* 106.

Questions

1. What do you understand by the term "employee" in the context of Directive 533/91? Does this term have an equivalent in UK labour law?

2. What do you understand by the concept of trancparency as a stated aim of Directive 533/91? Does this concept have other meanings in other areas of European law?

3. Examine the case law of the ECJ in relation to hours of work thresholds discussed in Chapters 6 and 13. In the light of this case law would you agree that Directive 533/91 may itself be inherently discriminatory?

4. What other elements, essential to the contract of employment, do you believe should be provided by employers to their employees?

Contents of Chapter 12

HEALTH AND SAFETY

Chapter 12

HEALTH AND SAFETY

This chapter explores the development of European health and safety legislation and its impact on the UK structure of health and safety law. The volume of legislation at the European level and its technical detail make a study of each Directive impossible within a book of this size. The chapter will, therefore, provide a description of the framework of the legislation, concentrating on its underlying principles, before showing the impact that such principles have in the UK.

The place of health and safety in European Community law

The relationship with other Community policies

The health and safety provisions of the Treaty are to be found in the Title of the Treaty of Rome dealing with social policy. However, there are certain other policy areas which overlap with health and safety issues. The most important of these areas are the harmonisation of technical standards and environmental law and policy. Technical standards legislation affects the design and manufacture of equipment and imposes standardisation. The Directives are based on Article 100 (or 100a) of the Treaty and are intended to assist in the free movement of goods whilst providing protection for the user of the equipment. Such legislation has obvious implications for health and safety but, because it is not primarily designed to promote a safe working environment, it is not dealt with in this chapter.[1] The environmental policy also imposes standards of care in environmentally sensitive areas. Again, since this legislation is not designed as health and safety legislation it is not dealt with in this chapter.

Treaty Articles on health and safety

Article 118 of the Treaty of Rome originally provided that the Commission had the task of promoting close co-operation between Member States in matters relating to the prevention of occupational accidents and diseases and occupational hygiene. Article 118, however, is an insufficient legal base for legislation in the field of health and safety. In order to move forward on these matters the Commission had to show that legislation at the European level was necessary in order to attain one of the objectives of the Community so that it could use as a legal base the power to adopt Directives to harmonise national law in Article 100 or the power to adopt any measures necessary to attain the objectives of the Community contained in Article 235. A Directive was adopted on the packaging of dangerous materials[2] in 1967 but there was little activity in this field until 1974 when the Community's first social action programme envisaged activity which aimed to improve safety and health conditions at work.[3] In the same year, the Council set up an Advisory Committee on Safety, Hygiene and Health Protection at work.[4] The task of the Committee was to conduct studies and assist the Commission to develop policy. Two programmes on health and safety were adopted leading to the adoption of seven Directives relating to specific risks at work such as exposure to chemicals or working with lead.[5] These seven Directives were adopted on the basis of Article 100 as measures necessary to ensure the proper functioning of the common market.

In these Directives the approach of the Commission was to provide detailed guidelines as to the content of national provisions. They were examples of the

---

[1] Burrows, "Harmonisation of technical standards: *reculer pour mieux sauter?*" 53 *Modern Law Review* (1990) 597.

[2] Directive 67/548 on the classification, labelling and packaging of certain dangerous substances OJ (1967) L 196/1.

[3] The Social Action Programme is to be found in OJ (1974) C13/1.

[4] Council Decision on the setting up of an Advisory Committee on Safety, Hygiene and Health Protection at Work OJ (1974) L 185/15.

[5] Directive 77/576 on the provision of safety signs at places of work OJ (1977) L 229/12; Directive 78/610 on the protection from risks related to exposure to vinyl chloride monomer OJ (1978) L 197/12; Directive 82/501 on major hazards connected with industrial activity OJ (1982) L 230/1; Directive 82/605 on the protection from the risks of exposure at work to metallic lead and its ionic compounds OJ (1982) L 247/12; Directive 83/477 on the protection from the risks related to exposure to asbestos at work OJ (1983) L 263/25; Directive 86/188 on the protection from risks related to exposure to noise at work OJ (1986) L 137/28; Directive 88/379 on the classification, packaging and labelling of dangerous preparations OJ (1988) L 187/14.

so-called vertical harmonising Directives which were to go out of fashion with the plan to complete the single market.[6] These Directives laid down specific rules relating to specific risks at work. The negotiation process for such Directives was long and complex so that harmonisation proved to be slow and cumbersome. One exception to the principle was Directive 80/107 on the protection from risks related to exposure to chemical, physical and biological agents at work.[7] This Directive was more general in approach and provided guidelines for whole sections of industry.

The project for the completion of the Single European Market provided the impetus for a new approach to harmonisation of health and safety legislation on the basis of an amended Article 118. Article 118a required Member States to pay particular attention to encouraging improvements in the working environment as regards health and safety, and to set as an objective the harmonisation of conditions. Directives were to be adopted setting minimum requirements to be gradually implemented by the Member States. These new requirements were to take into consideration the particular needs of small and medium sized undertakings and were without prejudice to the right of any Member State to adopt more stringent standards. Crucially, they were to be adopted on the basis of the co-operation procedure laid down in the new Article 189c. This procedure involved a greater input from the European Parliament and required only a qualified majority vote on the part of the Council. The way was therefore laid for the development of a new approach to health and safety.

The new approach

In its Communication on health and safety the Commission indicated that it would move forward in this area on the basis of Article 118a taking into account the need to promote dialogue between the two sides of industry.[8] The Council accepted the Commission's proposals but added that in adopting Community measures the Commission should adopt the substitutability principle whereby dangerous substances (or procedures) should be replaced by non or less dangerous.[9] The Council also stressed the need for legislation outlining the main provisions for the elimination of risks at work.

---

[6] Vertical harmonising directives create specific and detailed rules to be implemented by national legislation. They proved difficult to negotiate and the approach of the Community to the process of harmonisation after the Single European Act was to adopt horizontal directives setting out guidelines and frameworks for action at the national level. See Daintith, *Implementing EC Law in the UK; Structures for Indirect Rule*, (Wiley, 1995) for case studies of this kind of legislation and a discussion of horizontal and vertical harmonising directives.

[7] OJ (1980) L 327/8.

[8] *Commission communication on its programme concerning safety, hygiene and health at work* 88/C 28/02 OJ (1988) C 28/3.

[9] *Council Resolution on safety, hygiene and health at work* 88/C 28/01 OJ (1988) C 28/1.

Directive 89/391/EC – the Framework Directive

Following discussion within the Parliament and the Council, Directive 89/391 on the introduction of measures to encourage improvements in the safety and health of workers at work was adopted.[10] The Directive contains general principles concerning risk and its elimination, protection of workers, information and consultation of workers' representatives and guidelines on implementation. It imposes obligations on and divides responsibility for the health and safety of workers between Member States, employers and employees.

Obligations of the Member States

Member States are obliged to ensure that there is a legal framework for health and safety applicable to all sectors of industry, both public and private. There are certain exceptions to this rule where there is an inevitable conflict between the Directive and the activities concerned, such as work within the police service or the armed forces. This does not mean to say that health and safety is not a factor in these cases. Here the principles of health and safety are to be implemented so far as possible in the light of the Directive. National provisions which limit or exclude the liability of employers under unusual or unforeseeable circumstances are permitted. Member States must set standards of expertise and training required of safety representatives. They should also ensure that health surveillance is provided, possibly as part of the national health service. Particular risk-sensitive groups (as defined by national law) must be protected against specific risks. Member States were given until 31 December 1992 to transpose the provisions of the Directive into national law and to inform the Commission of the measures taken. The Directive does not impose any further obligations on the Member States such as the establishment of research, advice or information centres which might assist employers or employees to determine risk in the workplace.

Employers' obligations

A general obligation to ensure the safety and health of workers is imposed on employers. This general obligation extends to prevention of risks, provision of

[10] OJ (1989) L 183/1. For text see Appendix. The Commission's initial proposal is at OJ (1988) C 141/1. ECOSOC suggested certain improvements, see OJ (1988) C 175/22. The European Parliament made extensive amendments at its first reading, see OJ (1988) C 326/102 and a common position was achieved fairly quickly, see OJ (1988) C 158/131.

training of employees and reorganisation of the undertaking where required. The Directive provides for nine principles of prevention;

- avoiding risks
- evaluating risks which cannot be avoided
- combatting risks at source
- adapting the work to the individual
- adapting to technical progress
- replacing the dangerous by the less on non dangerous (substitutability)
- adoption of a coherent safety policy
- giving collective measures priority over individual measures
- giving appropriate instructions to employees.

With these principles in mind the employer must evaluate risks to employees and, where necessary, introduce preventative measures. The employer must take into consideration the workers' capabilities in respect of health and safety, ensure that consultation takes place before the introduction of new technologies, and limit access to dangerous areas to those workers who have undergone training.

Safety representatives should be chosen to assist the employer in introducing safe working conditions. Such workers must not be placed at risk and they should have adequate time to allow them to fulfill their safety duties. If internal staff lack the relevant competence, employers must buy in appropriate experts who must be given the information required to carry out the tasks entrusted to them. In all cases, safety representatives must meet the standards prescribed by national law in terms of training and expertise.

Employers must advise employees of the necessary precautions to be taken in the event of accidents (in respect of first aid), fire and of serious and imminent danger. All necessary training must be provided.

Employers must be in possession of a risk assessment. They must decide on protective measures. They must keep a record of accidents which result in a worker being unfit for more than three days and report such accidents in accordance with national law.

Employees have the right to be informed by employers of any risks involved in the workplace and the measures taken by the employer to minimise the risks. This obligation to inform extends to any worker on the premises of an employer including those from other undertakings. Full information on safety must be provided to safety representatives.

Employers are obliged to consult workers or their representatives on all matters relating to health and safety. Workers must have the right to make proposals. The Directive speaks of consultation taking part in a balanced way which seems to imply that workers or their representatives have an equal part to play in the development of safety policy or at least that their view is taken seriously by the employer. Workers must have a right of appeal to national safety organisations if they feel that safety is jeopardised in their organisation and they have the right to speak with national safety inspectors when such inspectors visit sites.

Employers are obliged to provide adequate training on safety matters to employees on recruitment, on transfer or change of job, or on the introduction of new technology, and training must be repeated periodically if necessary. Safety representatives are to be provided with adequate training. All such training must be at the employer's expense and during working hours.

Workers' obligations

Each worker is obliged as far as possible to take care of his or her own health and safety and that of other workers affected by his or her acts in accordance with training given by the employer. Workers must use equipment correctly, refrain from interfering with safety devices, and inform their employer or safety representative of situations of danger. They have a duty to co-operate with employers and safety representatives on health and safety matters.

Future legislation

Article 16 of Directive 89/391 provides for the adoption of further legislation on work places, work equipment, personal protective equipment, visual display units, handling of heavy loads, temporary or mobile work sites and fisheries or agriculture. These daughter Directives are subject to the overall principles of protection provided in the mother Directive and can only be adopted with a view to enforcing more stringent provisions.

Adjustments to European legislation can only be made after consultation of a committee of representatives of the Member States chaired by the Commission, whose establishment is foreseen by the Directive itself.

Daughter directives

The six-pack

The Framework Directive was adopted in June 1989. Between November of that year and May 1990 five other daughter Directives were adopted based on the Framework Directive. These Directives together have come to be known, in the UK, as the "six-pack". Directive 89/654 on Work Places[11] introduces

[11] OJ (1989) L 393/1.

rules governing the design of work places with provisions covering such matters as design of windows, ventilation, or provision of toilet facilities. Directive 89/655 on the Use of Work Equipment[12] imposes obligations on employers to provide safe equipment and to train workers in its use, and provides fairly detailed guidelines on controls, guards, and so on. Directive 89/656 on the use of personal protective equipment imposes duties on employers to assess, provide and ensure the use of personal protective equipment and to provide training to employees on its use.[13] Directive 90/269 imposes an obligation on the employer to avoid manual handling of loads, but where this is impossible employers must attempt to reduce risks associated with the handling of such loads.[14] Finally, Directive 90/270 requires employers to assess the risks associated with display screens and to ensure that work stations comply with any risk assessment, including the rights of workers to eye tests and the provision of glasses where necessary.[15]

Further directives

Following the adoption of the six-pack, nine additional Directives were adopted and four more are still pending.[16] All these Directives are individual Directives within the meaning of Article 16 of the Framework Directive and their passage has been relatively trouble free. Only one of the Directives has been controversial, that relating to the rights of breast feeding and pregnant workers which is discussed in Chapter 7. Controversy arose in this case due to

[12] OJ (1989) L 393/13.
[13] OJ (1989) L 393/18.
[14] OJ (1989) L 156/9.
[15] OJ (1990) L 156/14.
[16] Directive 90/394 on the protection of workers from the risks related to exposure to carcinogens at work OJ (1990) L 196/1; Directive 90/679 on the protection of workers from risks related to exposure to biological agents OJ (1990) 374/1; Directive 93/88 amending Directive 90/679 on the protection of workers from the risks related to exposure to biological agents at work OJ (1993) L 268/71; Directive 92/57 on the implementation of minimum safety and health requirements at temporary mobile construction sites OJ (1992) L 245/6; Directive 92/58 on the minimum requirements for the provision of safety and/or health signs at work OJ (1992) L 245/23; Directive 92/85 on the introduction of measures to encourage improvements in the safety and health at work of pregnant workers and workers who have recently given birth OJ (1992) L 348/1; Directive 92/91 concerning the minimum requirements for improving the safety and health protection of workers in the miner-extracting industries through drilling OJ (1992) L 348/9; Directive 92/104 on the minimum requirements for improving the safety and health protection of workers in surface and underground mineral-extracting industries OJ (1992) L 404/10; Directive 93/103 concerning the minimum health and safety requirements of work on board fishing vessels OJ (1993) L 307/1. The current proposals are for a Directive concerning the minimum health and safety requirements for transport activities and work places on the means of transport OJ (1993) C 25/17; proposal for a Directive exposure of workers arising from the risks of physical against OJ (1993) C 77/12; proposal for a Directive regarding the exposure of workers to chemical agents OJ C (1993) 191/94 and a proposed Directive on the use of work equipment OJ C 104/94.

the incorporation within the Directive of provisions relating to the employment rights of pregnant workers within a text on health and safety.

European Agency for Safety and Health at Work

The European Agency for Health and Safety at Work, which is now situated in Bilbao, was established in 1994 to co-ordinate a network of national monitoring agencies to collect information on health and safety matters.[17] The Agency will provide the Community institutions, the Member States and those involved in the field with the technical, scientific and economic information of use to them. The Agency is intended to collect and disseminate information, create a European network of agencies, organise seminars and conferences, liaise with other international organisations active in the field and contribute to the future development of Community policy without prejudice to the Commission's sphere of competence.

The protection of young people at work

Baldwin notes that, in the UK, the earliest concerns were not with safety as such but with child labour and working hours.[18] In the light of this it is perhaps ironic that the UK was opposed to the adoption of a Directive on protecting young people at work.[19] Directive 94/33 on the Protection of Young People at Work was adopted on the basis of Article 118a and it cites the Framework Directive as authority for the need to protect "particularly sensitive risk groups". It is not, however, a daughter Directive within the meaning of Article 16 of the Framework Directive.

Children and young people are ripe for exploitation by unscrupulous employers. Their lack of experience, the limited understanding of the adult workplace, and the need to ensure that their education and training is not disrupted, provide the "moral" reasoning for the adoption of the Directive and these reasons are recited in the preamble. So too is the Community Charter of the Fundamental Rights of Workers which had set as a minimum

[17] Council Regulation 2062/94 establishing a European Agency for Safety and Health at Work OJ (1994) L 216/1.
[18] Baldwin, in *Harmonization and Hazard* Baldwin and Daintith (eds)(London, 1992), chapter 7.
[19] Council Directive 94/33/EEC on the protection of young people at work OJ (1994) L216/12.

school leaving age of 15 and had foreseen a limitation on working hours and the prohibition of night work for young people.[20]

The Directive makes provision for three groups; children (defined as being under 15 years of age), adolescents (defined as being over 15 years and no longer subject to compulsory schooling) and young persons (defined as being under 18 and having an employment contract or employment relationship defined by national law). Member States are free to exclude from the ambit of the Directive occasional or short-term work involving domestic service in a private household or work which is not harmful, damaging or dangerous within a family undertaking.

Children

Member States must prohibit work by children. Such a prohibition can exclude certain categories of work. Cultural activities may be excluded subject to authorization being given by the relevant national authority in each case. Cultural activities are defined as being the employment of children for the purposes of cultural, artistic, sports or advertising activities. Member States must ensure that authorization will not be given for harmful activities or activities which would disrupt educational opportunities. Member States which operate a system of licensing for modelling agencies for children are allowed to keep these arrangements. Work/training or work experience schemes for children of 14 and over may also be excluded as can certain "light work" as defined by national legislation. In the latter case, children as young as 13 may be allowed to work for a limited number of hours per week in categories of work defined by national law.

Obligations on employers

Employers must assess the workplace in order to provide a safe working environment for young people. Such an assessment must be made before a young person begins work and must include such things as exposure to physical, biological or chemical agents. Young people are entitled to free health assessments if there is any risk in the workplace. Young people and their representatives must be informed of possible risks and the measures taken to avoid them.

---

[20] The Charter was adopted by 11 of the then 12 members of the European Council in Strasbourg on 9 December 1989. The UK abstained. The Charter has no legal force itself but it declares the intentions of the Member States to incorporate social policy as an integral element of the Community. For text see Appendix.

Young people

The Directive provides that there are certain forms of work prohibited for young people, such as work involving the risk of accidents which would be difficult to avoid owing to the lack of training or experience. Again derogations are possible from this prohibition in the case of vocational training schemes. However, young people on these schemes must be under the supervision of a competent person. Member States must always ensure that young people are protected from danger which arises due to their inexperience.

Working time

Whenever a Member State permits children to undertake work by making use of the derogations outlined above they must limit working hours. These hours are laid down in detail within the Directive.

Night work

Night work is prohibited for children and adolescents although Member States may provide for certain exceptions for specific activities undertaken by adolescents. These, however, must be supervised by an adult. Certain sectors are exempted from this provision in the case of adolescents such as police work or work within the shipping or fishing industries.

Rest periods

Detailed rules are provided within the Directive on the need to ensure adequate rest periods, breaks and holidays.

Implementation

Member States must adopt effective and proportionate measures to ensure that the Directive is complied with. They may adopt more stringent standards but the Directive insists that its implementation must not provide an excuse to Member States to lower their existing standards. The Directive is to be implemented by 22 June 1996. The UK was given a four year extension to the implementation period in the case of the requirements relating to hours of work and night work. The Council may decide to extend this opt-out.

UK opposition to this Directive can only be more symbolic than real. The Directive itself adds very little to the protection of young people at work because it is so full of exceptions, derogations and loopholes. As it stands, the

Directive is an extremely weak and disappointing device for the protection of a group which the Community recognises as being sensitive and in need of protection. Such protection is recognised in the UK although there is no systematic legislation on the employment of children and young persons. The Children and Young Persons Act 1933 and the Children and Young Persons (Scotland) Act 1937 provide that children between 13 and 16 may engage in part-time work provided that this amounts to no more than 2 hours per school day or on Sundays. They cannot engage in work during school hours or before 7 a.m. or after 7 p.m.. Under the Employment of Children Act 1973, local authorities (education authorities in Scotland) have certain supervisory powers over the employment of children. They may make bye-laws restricting the employment of children. They are prohibited entirely, under the Factories Acts and the Employment of Women, Young Persons and Childrens Act, from engaging in employment in certain sectors such as mines and quarries or sea-going vessels. Children in entertainment are protected under the 1938 Young Persons (Employment) Act and those attempting to gain work experience may only do so in the school term preceding the start of the school year in which they become entitled to leave school under the terms of the Education (Work Experience) Act 1973.

It is not clear how the UK intends to implement the Community Directive. However, this could provide the opportunity to rationalise UK law on the employment of children to make it more comprehensible to them, to employers and to parents. Such a move would be a welcome step.

The current approach to health and safety

In September 1994, the Commission set up a group of independent experts to assess the impact of Community and national legislation on employment and competitiveness with a view to finding ways of reducing and simplifying legislation. Part of the remit of the group was to examine the health and safety provisions. The group reported back to the Commission in June 1995.[21] Several problems with the Community approach were identified by the group. In particular the risk management strategies dictated by European Directives were not thought to be suited to the needs and resources of small and medium sized undertakings. It also questioned whether there was a need to reiterate specific obligations in the daughter Directives when the Framework Directive already imposed stringent obligations on employers. However, the group

---

[21] *Report of the group of independent experts on legislative and administrative simplification*, COM (95) 288 final/2.

recognised the need for Community legislation on the basis that those States which did not have effective laws in this area would benefit from a comparative advantage over those States which did have such systems.

Several key recommendations were made in the report, notably that the Commission should review its existing legislation and future proposals and, until the review is completed, the presumption should be against any new regulatory initiatives. Implementation and enforcement of existing legislation should be strengthened and clarification should be given where there is overlap between provisions. As part of the review, the group recommended that, where obligations are imposed, they should be written in general terms supplemented by guidelines or recommendations.

Shortly after this review was completed, the Commission adopted its Fourth Action Programme concerning safety, hygiene and health at work.[22] The Fourth Programme does not envisage the adoption of a significant number of new Directives although it does state that the three outstanding Directives on transport and on physical and chemical agents should be completed and adopted. The emphasis in the programme is on education and training and envisages the adoption of a number of non-legislative measures to assist firms under the SAFE Programme (Safety Actions for Europe). Implementation and enforcement of existing law is also a priority.

On the same day the Fourth Action Programme was announced, the Commission adopted a Decision setting up a Committee of Senior Labour Inspectors.[23] The adoption of this Decision is a formalisation of an existing arrangement whereby members of national labour inspectorates meet together to discuss common problems of implementation and enforcement. The Committee is intended to assist administrative co-operation based on obligations of mutual assistance and transparency. The Commission hopes that the Committee will be of assistance in ensuring uniform application of Community standards within the Member States.

In October 1995, the Commission put forward its proposals for non-legislative measures in the area of health and safety.[24] This programme of non-legislative measurers is to consist of two aspects. The first is the provision of guidance and information to help in the correct application of Community law. The second is the SAFE programme which is particularly aimed at small businesses to assist them in complying with health and safety requirements.

---

[22] *Communication from the Commission on a Community programme concerning safety, hygiene and health at work* (1996-2000) COM (95) 282 final.
[23] Commission Decision of 12 July 1955 setting up a Committee of Senior Labour Inspectors OJ (1995) L 188/11.
[24] Proposal for a Council Decision adopting a programme of non-legislative measures to improve health and safety at work OJ (1995) C 262/18.

The division of competence in international health and safety standards

The European Community is not the sole standard bearer of internationally defined health and safety norms. The ILO is responsible for the elaboration of international conventions on health and safety matters. The question has now arisen, therefore, as to whether the Community or the Member States have responsibility for concluding ILO conventions and assuming obligations under them. The European Court has been asked to give an Opinion on these questions.[25]

The European Community is not a member of the ILO, although all of the Member States are. However, it has observer status. In 1990, the ILO adopted a Convention on the use of chemicals at work and the Commission sought the views of the European Court as to whether the Community has exclusive competence to conclude the Convention or whether this competence lay within the jurisdiction of the Member States. The Court held that the field covered by the ILO Convention falls within the social provisions of the EEC Treaty. The Community enjoys an internal legislative competence which, however, is shared with the Member States in this particular matter since the ILO Convention does not affect the rule in Article 118a that the Community may lay down minimum standards for health and safety without prejudice of the right of the Member States to adopt more stringent protection. The ILO Convention would not require a Member State to lower its standards below those set out in the relevant EEC Directives and, indeed, Contracting Parties to the ILO are always free to adopt standards more stringent than those contained in ILO Conventions. The Community does not, therefore, have exclusive competence.

However, the Court then argued that certain specific Directives adopted by the Community provided more extensive protection for workers than the ILO Convention, particularly in the case of labelling requirements. In the circumstances where extensive Community legislation has been adopted with a view to achieving harmonisation then the Community had exclusive competence to conclude any international agreement and consequently the Member States could not undertake commitments outside the Community framework. Under all these circumstances, therefore, the Court held that the conclusion of the Convention is a matter falling under the joint competence of the Community and the Member States and that there is a duty of mutual co-operation in the

---

[25] Opinion 2/91 *Re ILO Convention No.170* [1994] IRLR 135.

process of negotiation, conclusions and implementation of the ILO Convention. The Court stressed that this duty of co-operation was all the more relevant since, under the current state of international law, the Community is unable to conclude an ILO Convention other than through the medium of the Member States.

From the point of view of the UK this ruling means that involvement in negotiating health and safety conventions and the decision as to whether to accede to such conventions is a matter governed by Community principles, if not law. The UK could not unilaterally decide to ratify an ILO Convention on health and safety and could not, without consulting the Commission and the other Member States, participate in the negotiations leading to the development of new conventions. Similarly, if the Community, through the medium of the Member States, decides to ratify any such Convention then one Member State would not be free thereafter to deratify as this would affect Community participation as a whole. The importance of this latter point will become obvious in the discussion of deregulation of health and safety discussed below as it will tie the hands of any minister wishing to deregulate health and safety in areas covered by any such ILO conventions.

Health and safety in the UK

The basic framework for health and safety law in the UK was established following the Robens Committee Report published in 1972.[26] Robens had recommended a simplification of the existing rather fragmented law on health and safety and sought to provide a modern framework for action. The Health and Safety at Work Act (1974) introduced a form of self-regulation by imposing general duties on employers, employees and the self-employed, enforced by a Health and Safety Executive which was given powers of inspection of premises and powers to issue notices.[27] The Health and Safety Commission, responsible to the Secretary of State, was given investigative powers. The 1974 Act repealed some existing statutory provisions as set down in Schedules to the Act. Section 15 enabled the Secretary of State to make regulations, including amendment and repeal of existing legislation, for matters governed by the Act (excluding agriculture which was covered separately). Schedule 3 of the Act, however, laid down the areas in which such regulations might be adopted. The purpose behind such regulations was to be the maintenance of improvements of standards of health, safety and welfare. It

---

[26] *Report of the Robens Committee on Safety and Health at Work*, Cmnd.5034. See Craig and Miller, *Law of Health and Safety at Work in Scotland*, (W. Green, 1995) for the most recent outline.
[27] Health and Safety at Work Act 1974. Chapter 37. See Baldwin cited in note 18 supra.

was anticipated that the Secretary of State would issue such regulations after consultation with the Health and Safety Commission.

No specific power was given in this Act to allow the Secretary of State to introduce regulations to transpose Community Directives into UK law. Such a power is provided in Section 2(2) of the European Communities Act 1972 which provides that any designated minister may, by regulations, make provision for the purpose of implementing any Community obligation.[28]

One important feature of the 1974 Act was the stress placed on the concept of reasonable practicability as far as the general duties of employers were concerned. This concept acted as a way of avoiding the imposition of an absolute duty on the employer to provide a safe healthy workplace. He or she was only required to do so in so far as it was reasonably practicable. This framework allowed a margin of discretion both for employers and, perhaps more importantly, law enforcers.

Implementation of Community health and safety law

When it came to implementation of Community Directives, the UK had little difficulty in incorporating them into the structure outlined above until the Framework Directive was adopted. Then, the change in direction of Community law towards the adoption of horizontal Directives covering a wider scope than our own legislation meant that the UK was faced with difficult problems of implementation.[29] In particular, the UK found difficulty with the absolute nature of the duties to be imposed on employers in terms of risk assessment and the avoidance of risk. For these reasons the UK had attempted to include a clause equivalent to the reasonable practicability test in the Framework Directive but had been unsuccessful in these attempts.

The Framework Directive

The choice was open to the UK to implement the Framework Directive either by amending the Health and Safety at Work Act to change the nature of the obligations imposed on employers according to the terms of Articles 5 to 12 of the Directive or by introducing new domestic regulations. In the latter case, the choice was to copy out the terms of the Directive, that is, to repeat the

---

[28] The European Communities Act 1972 Chapter 68.
[29] *Review of the implementation and enforcement of EC law in the UK* (DTI, 1993). This report contains a remarkably frank account of the difficulties faced by the UK in negotiating and implementing the health and safety provisions, particularly the six-pack.

language of the Directive in the domestic regulations or to rewrite the directive for the purposes of national law. It was this third option which was chosen by the UK.[30]

The implementation technique chosen has now been adjudged to be misplaced but, at the time, "the threat to the UK health and safety system was perceived...to be so fundamental" that other options were discarded.[31] This means that the basic framework of the Health and Safety at Work Act still governs the obligations imposed on employers but they are also subject to the regulations which impose a slightly different regime. Implementation meant the repeal of certain existing provisions and the amendment of others. This means that the Framework Directive is now implemented in the UK by a combination of Acts of Parliament, including the Health and Safety at Work Act 1974, the Employment Protection (Consolidation) Act 1978 (as amended by the Trade Union Reform and Employment Rights Act 1993) and a number of Statutory Instruments making a total of nine different pieces of legislation. This means that the "overall effect was to make the implementation package more voluminous than the Directives.[32]

The six-pack

The other five Directives which make up the six-pack were also implemented by the adoption of regulations.[33] Their implementation did provide the opportunity for the Government to repeal certain outdated existing legislation and to bring other aspects up to date. The Workplace Regulations, for example, repeal aspects of the Factories Act 1961 and, overall, 42 sections of Acts, 25 sets of regulations and 28 parts of regulations were repealed.[34]

Deregulation and health and safety

October 1992 saw the launch of a major deregulation initiative by the Conservative Government. Eight task forces were established to question the value of existing regulations across the spectrum of business activity. The think tanks reported to the Government that a number of regulations should be abolished, including some recommendations in relation to the work of the

[30] Management of Health and Safety at Work Regulations SI 1992/2051.
[31] The quotation is taken from the DTI report cited in note 29 *supra.*
[32] *Ibid* 106-110 for a complete list of domestic provisions which now apply.
[33] Workplace (Health, Safety and Welfare) Regulations SI 1992/3004 ; Provision and Use of Work Equipment Regulations SI 1992/2932; Manual Handling Operations Regulations SI 1992/2793; Health and Safety (Display Screen Equipment) Regulations SI 1992/2792.
[34] These figures are quoted in the DTI report cited in note 29 supra at 96.

Health and Safety Executive (HSC).[35] At the same time, the Employment Minister asked the HSC to assess existing law to see whether it was still relevant or whether simplification was possible. In view of the belief propounded by the Government that much of the necessary burdens on business arising from over regulation were the result of over implementing EC Directives, a review was also established to consider the assertion that the UK over-implements Community law and, in doing so, is stricter in enforcement than other Member States of the Community.[36] This latter review was commissioned by the Board of Trade and is addressed to all government departments.

The result of the deregulation initiative as far as health and safety is concerned was the adoption in 1994 of Section 37 of the Deregulation and Contracting Out Act.[37] That section gives power to the Secretary of State to repeal legislation or regulations adopted prior to 1974 by the adoption of a Statutory Instrument subject to an affirmative resolution procedure in Parliament. Before issuing any order, the Secretary of State must consult with the Health and Safety Commission.[38] Before the enactment of this Act, the Secretary of State only had power to repeal existing provisions if they were to be replaced by provisions designed to maintain or improve standards. It has been said that "nowhere in the Act has the deregulatory net been cast with so few safeguards as in Section 37".[39] It seems entirely possible for the Secretary of State to repeal legislation under the terms of Section 37 merely if he deems it desirable. There is no requirement on his part to take the advice given to him on consultation with the HSC.

The Secretary of State has begun to make use of these powers to remove "obsolete and out of date legislation".[40] The HSC had reported to the Government in 1994 that the broad framework of legislation and practice was well understood by business and that it commanded widespread support.[41] However, the HSC did identify certain areas which it considered ought to be

---

[35] Woolfson, *Deregulation: The Politics of Health and Safety* (University of Glasgow, 1995). Holgate, "Workplace Health and Safety: The Deregulatory Riddle, Parts I and II" *Business Law Review* (1995) 57 and 81.

[36] *Review of the implementation and enforcement of EC law in the UK* (DTI, 1993).

[37] Deregulation and Contracting Out Act 1994 Chapter 40.

[38] The Act is discussed in Williams, "Deregulating Occupational Health and Safety" 24 *Industrial Law Journal* (1995) 133. In the annotation to the Act in Current Law Statutes, Page suggests that repeal or revocation of pre-1974 legislation should be on the ground that "it no longer serves a useful purpose". In fact the Act does not specify the grounds for repeal, leaving the Secretary of State free to determine which legislation should be repealed.

[39] *Ibid.*

[40] Letter from Michael Portillo to the Chairman of the Health and Safety Commission, reproduced in Health and Safety Commission consultative document, *The proposed removal of outdated health and safety legislation*, (HSC, 1995).

[41] Woolfson cited in note 35 *supra.*

revoked without replacement; homework legislation, slaughterhouse legislation, railway running sheds legislation, the Hours of Employment (Conventions) Act 1936 and the regulations concerning Horizontal Milling Machines. The HSC has gone to consultation on these issues and, unless there is opposition to their revocation, will advise the Secretary of State to proceed with repeal. In the future the HSC intends to examine regulations relating to textile factories and ceratin agricultural provisions.

It is clear that Section 37 of the 1994 Act can be a useful device to "clean up" the statute book in an area where it is over complex and cluttered with outdated provisions. However, the Secretary of State cannot use Section 37 to repeal regulations or legislation which incorporates Community law without putting the UK into the position of breaching its Community obligations. Legislation which is adopted to satisfy ILO standards may also be beyond the grasp of the Secretary of State. However other aspects of health and safety law may be more vulnerable.[42]

The Governments's deregulation initiative comes at a time when many experts are pointing to the increasing incidence of very serious accidents at work in this country[43] and in Europe.[44] The deregulation initiative may bring some improvements in terms of cleaning up but what is really required is a review of the Health and Safety at Work Act together with a serious commitment to implementation and enforcement of EC Directives.

---

[42] Whether the Secretary of State needed such swingeing powers is open to debate. In *R* v *Secretary of State ex parte NACODS* the Divisional Court held that a court could not make the decision whether new regulations were better than old. It held that the requirement in the Health and Safety Act 1974 that new measures must "maintain or improve the standards of health, safety and welfare" was a matter for the legislature and the Secretary of State, not for the courts. Discussed in Holgate, "Workplace Health and Safety: Challenging Regulatory Standards" 23 *Industrial Law Journal* (1994) 246. Significant changes have been made in matters of health and safety where privatisation has occurred. For example, in relation to railway privatisation, new regulations have been adopted, apparently without reference to the high level of safety demanded by the 1974 Act. See the discussion of the rail regulations by Holgate, "Health and Safety Review", *Business Law Review* (1994) 150. No full study has been done on the effects of privatisation on health and safety standards.
[43] James, "Reforming British Health and Safety Law: a framework for discussion" 21 *Industrial Law Journal* (1992) 83.
[44] The Commission's fourth action programme notes that in 1992 some 8,000 people died in work-related accidents. 10 million cases of occupational diseases were recorded and 27 billion ECU was lost to the economy of the EC.

Questions

1. What do you understand by the term "the substitutability principle" in health and safety law? Is this an adequate standard in protecting the safety and health of workers?

2. If you were asked to codify a law on the employment of children and young persons to comply with Directive 94/33, which provisions of existing UK law would you repeal and which provisions would you concolidate? Would new legislative provisions be required?

3. Examine section 37 of the Deregulation and Contracting Out Act 1994. Define the precise scope available to the Secretary of State to repeal existing legislative provisions in relation to health and safety.

4. Can an employer still rely on the "so far as is reasonably practicable" test in the 1974 Health and Safety at Work Act?

Contents of Chapter 13

WORKING TIME

Chapter 13

WORKING TIME

If ever a Community provision was destined to irritate the current UK administration it is Directive 93/104 concerning certain aspects of the organisation of working time.[1] Within the entire framework of legislation designed to harmonise labour law and standards, the Directive on Working Time is the one which is least suited to contemporary UK practice and which runs counter to UK policy of introducing flexibility into the workplace by relaxing regulatory controls. It is not surprising, therefore, that the UK Government has instituted proceedings before the European Court of Justice challenging the validity of the Directive on the grounds that it has been adopted on the wrong legal base. Until such time as the Court gives its decision in this case, the UK has determined not to transpose the Directive into UK law.

UK opposition

The legal basis

Directive 93/104 is a Directive which is based on Article 118a of the Treaty. This Article allows the Community to adopt Directives, on the basis of qualified majority voting, which set minimum requirements, especially in the working environment, to ensure a better level of protection of the safety and health of workers. The UK has argued, with respect to this Directive and the Directive on Pregnant Workers, that Article 118a is an inappropriate legal base for Directives which, in the view of the UK, go beyond the concept of the

[1] OJ 1994 L 307/18. For text see Appendix.

working environment as foreseen in Article 118a. The UK is ready to accept that Directives relating purely and simply to health and safety matters, in a fairly strictly defined ambit, can be adopted on the basis of Article 118a. Other Directives, particularly those which concern workers' rights, should be adopted, according to the UK, on the basis of Article 100a which would require unanimity in the Council. This latter Article specifically refers to the rights and interests of employed persons.

The UK commenced legal proceedings against the Council in March 1994.[2] The UK Government has requested the European Court to annul certain provisions of Directive 93/104. These are the provisions which relate to breaks, weekly rest periods, the principle of Sunday as a rest day, the fixing of a maximum working week of 48 hours and the requirement to provide four weeks holiday. The UK rests its case on the basis of four arguments.

Lack of competence/ defective legal base

The UK has challenged the view that the Working Time Directive is properly a measure regulating health and safety. This argument is based on the scope of Article 118a read in conjunction with Article 3b (the principle of subsidiarity). According to the UK the enactment of the Directive on that base is incompetent and unlawful. The matter of the legal base was discussed by the House of Lords Select Committee on the European Communities when the Commission's first proposal was published.[3] Several witnesses had raised the appropriateness of Article 118a particularly in view of the fact that "the proposals had not been discussed with the Commission's own Health and Safety Advisory Committee" and that they had been rushed through without appropriate consultation.[4]

Breach of the principle of proportionality

Here the UK argues that Article 118a only permits the adoption of minimum requirements and that the Community legislature must have regard to the principle of proportionality so that measures adopted must not go beyond that aim. In the view of the UK, the framework Directive applies to all the areas

---

[2] Case C-84/94 *UK v Council of the European Union* OJ C (1994) 120/13.
[3] HL Paper 12, Select Committee on the European Communities on Working Time, Session 1990-91 fourth report.
[4] This latter point is part of a wider concern for absence of democracy in the legislative processes in Europe. It is a matter which will be discussed at the forthcoming 1996 Inter-Governmental Conference see "The 1996 Intergovernmental Conference: The Agenda; Democracy and Efficiency; The Role of National Parliaments". Twenty fourth report, Volume I; Select Committee on European Legislation: Session 1994-95 (HMSO, 1995).

covered by the Working Time Directive and there was, therefore, no impera-tive need for legislation.[5] In view of this, the UK argues, "the Council manifestly acted unlawfully in enacting the Working Time Directive".

Misuse of power

The UK argues here that the Directive covers areas which are unconnected with its aims. The Directive as a whole should be seen, therefore, as an abuse of the Council's powers.

Infringement of an essential procedural requirement

This argument is based on the lack of reasoning or, alternatively, the defective reasoning given in the Directive.

This action by the UK demonstrates that it holds a different view as to the concept of the working environment than that which is held by the Commis-sion and some of the Member States. Szyszczak has argued that the term "working environment" in Article 118a can be seen in some of the Member States as a "broad and wide ranging idea governing such matters as, *inter alia*, the arrangement of the workplace, and the physical and the socio-psychological conditions under which work is carried out, such as monotony, rapid work pace, lack of social contact, the use of equipment and machinery and the exposure of workers to toxic and other dangerous substances at work".[6]

The European Court has not yet come to any conclusion on the meaning to be accorded to the term "working environment" as it appears in Article 118a and the case brought before it by the UK will give it an opportunity to show how far the Community can extend the concept.

The practical basis

It may be that other Member States share with the UK the reservations as to the extent of Article 118a and the Commission's approach in using Article 118a as the legal base for action simply because of qualified majority voting. They will be able to intervene in the case to present their views to the Court. It is unlikely, however, that any Member State will share the practical and ideological problems which are faced by the UK when it comes to the transposition of the Directive into national law.

[5] The framework Directive is discussed in chapter 12 *supra*.
[6] Szyszczak, "1992 and the Working Environment", *Journal of Social Welfare and Family Law* (1992) 13.

The terms of the Directive are outlined below but in essence it seeks to regulate the hours worked per day, week or year. The UK is one of the very few European countries which does not have legislation in this area and which has taken steps recently to introduce even greater flexibility in the working environment in relation to working time with the abolition of prohibition of night work for women and young people, the lifting of restrictions on Sunday working and the attempt to deregulate as many aspects of the working environment as possible. Without a fundamental shift in policy, it would be ideologically impossible for the UK to introduce the kind of legislation which would be required to transpose the Directive into UK law.

It would be equally difficult on a more practical level. UK patterns of work are very different from our European neighbours. Bercusson[7] has summarised research in this area and concludes that full-time workers in the UK work the highest number of hours in the Community; for instance, they work 5.1 hours more than Italians and 3.8 hours more than Germans. Part-time workers, by contrast, work the lowest number of hours, for instance they work 7.4 hours less than Italians and 1.9 hours less than Germans. For employees working more than 48 hours per week, the UK has the highest percentage (16%) as compared with Italy at 3.5% and Germany 4.8%. The UK has the highest percentage of workers employed on shift work and night work. In the UK, according to Bercusson, 43.8% of the workforce usually work overtime every week, 23.4% paid and 17% unpaid. The proportion of unpaid overtime is highest amongst women, 58% as compared to 40% of men. Again according to Bercusson, when working hours are banded together to assess the proportion of employees working 38-40 hours per week, the UK and Portugal have less than 50% of the workforce within these hours.

Taking these statistics together, it is possible to conclude that the UK workforce is out of step with the rest of the Community in terms of their working hours. This is true for full-time employees and part-time, for men and for women. Any Community harmonisation programme will therefore have a greater disruptive effect on employment practices in the UK than in any other Community country. It must be concluded that this is the real reason behind UK opposition to the Directive and that the argument over the legal base is the only means possible open to the UK to attempt to block this particular Community provision. After all, the UK did intend to block the Pregnancy Directive on the same ground but did not proceed.

The UK position on the legal base is rendered more difficult as a number of studies produced in the UK have demonstrated the link between stress, lack of productivity, and the disintegration of family life and the long hours worked in

---

[7] Bercusson, *Working Time in Britain: Towards a European Model, Part II Collective Bargaining in Europe and the UK* (Institute of Employment Rights, 1994).

the UK.[8] It has also been suggested that the UK Government is seeking to suppress evidence which might contradict its standpoint on the link between hours and ill health.[9]

The Directive

The Directive is based on Article 118a of the Treaty which means that it could be adopted on the basis of a qualified majority.[10] It also makes reference to the Charter of Fundamental Social Rights, points 7, 8 and 19 which specifically refer to the duration and organisation of working time and recognise the right to weekly rest and annual leave and the right to a safe and healthy working environment.[11] The Directive applies to both public and private sector workers except transport workers, fishing and other work at sea and doctors in training. It applies to minimum periods of daily and weekly rest, annual leave, to breaks, maximum weekly working time and aspects of night work and shift work. It is without prejudice to other Community legislation which imposes more specific requirements concerning certain occupational activities and it does not affect the right of Member States to introduce legislation providing more favourable protection of the health and safety of workers.

Daily rest

Every worker is entitled to a rest period of 11 hours per 24 hour period of work. In a working day which is longer than six hours, a worker is entitled to a break , the details of which may be provided in collective agreements or national legislation.

Weekly rest

For every seven day period, a worker is entitled to a minimum uninterrupted rest period of 24 hours to be added to the 11 hours daily rest period. The reference period may be extended to 14 days by Member States. The 24 hour

---

[8] See *The Independent* 26 October 1995 for a discussion of the study *The Family Friendly Workplace*. The same article discusses figures from the Confederation of British Industry and states "almost eight working days per worker were lost due to sick leave in 1994".

[9] See *Financial Times* 6 October 1995 for an article in which it is suggested that a study demonstrating the link between long hours at work and coronary heart disease has been suppressed by the health secretary.

[10] Proposal for a Council Directive concerning certain aspects of the organisation of working time OJ 1990 C 254/4. The European Parliament's first reading is at OJ 1991 C72/95. ECOSOC's opinion is at OJ 1991 C 60/26. The Council's common position is at OJ 1993 C 315/125.

[11] For full text of the Charter see Appendix.

period is said to include, in principle, Sunday although the preamble states that account should be taken in deciding whether Sunday should be the rest period of cultural, ethnic, religious or other factors. Where technical or organisational factors require, the overall weekly rest period may be limited to 24 hours in total.

Maximum weekly working time

Member States must ensure that a limit is placed on the maximum weekly working time either through collective agreements or by laws or other provisions. In each seven day period, the maximum weekly working time is 48 hours. In order to calculate the average working week, a Member State may provide for the application of a reference period not exceeding 4 months. Periods of paid leave or sick leave may not be included in the calculation.

Annual leave

Each worker is entitled to four weeks' annual paid leave in accordance with national law and/or practice. This period may not be taken in lieu except where the employment relationship is terminated.

Night shift

Normal hours of work for night shift workers must not exceed eight hours in any 24 hour period. Where national law or practice determines that work involves special hazards, physical or mental strain then the eight hour limit must be observed. An appropriate reference period for the calculation of these hours may be laid down in collective agreements or after consultation with both sides of industry. The minimum weekly rest period of 24 hours may not, however, be included in the calculation. Night workers are entitled to a free health assessment both before going on to night working and at regular intervals. This assessment is to be confidential and may be part of national health service provision. Where health problems arise connected to night shift working, workers must be transferred to day shifts wherever possible. National law may provide certain guarantees to categories of night workers (for example young people or pregnant women) if such workers incur risks to their health and safety.[12] The competent national authority may request any

---

[12] In the UK, the Institute of Personnel Management suggested that workers under 18 should be excluded from night work altogether and that employers should be required to provide safe transport facilities . The proposals would be permitted under the terms of the Directive. See Institute of Personnel Management, press release September 1990.

employer who regularly uses night workers to report this. Appropriate health and safety protection measures must be available for night workers and must be equivalent to those available for day shift workers.

Patterns of work

In deciding on patterns of work, employers must take account of the principle of adapting work to the worker. This is particularly aimed at alleviating monotony at work and laying down strict health and safety standards. Bercusson has called this principle the "humanization of work" and it imposes a duty on the employer to create a working environment to suit the workforce rather than *vice versa*.[13]

Derogations

There is a general power of derogation for managing executives or others with autonomous decision-taking powers, family workers or workers officiating in religious ceremonies. Member States are also free to introduce derogations for particular categories of workers in respect of daily rest periods, breaks, weekly rest periods and length of night shifts provided that equivalent periods of compensatory rest are provided and that workers are afforded appropriate protection. The Directive lists these categories of workers in Article 17. They include: workers whose work is far from their home such as workers on oil-rigs, security personnel, workers in hospitals, residential institutions and prisons, or providing particular services where continuity of service is re-quired. Derogations are also permitted where there is a foreseeable surge in activity such as in agriculture or tourism. A derogation is also possible in regard to the rules on shift work for the changeover to day and night shift and where the day might be divided into shorter periods of work such as cleaners who may work early in the morning and later at night.

Derogations may also be negotiated by means of collective agreements, concluded by both sides of industry on condition that equivalent compensat-ing rest periods are granted or, where this is not possible, that the workers concerned are afforded adequate protection. Member States must ensure that the framework for the negotiation of such collective agreements is in place. This derogation may also be applied to the reference periods for the calcula-tion of the rest and break periods provided for in the Directive on condition that this is on the basis of a collective agreement and it is adopted for objective

---

[13] Bercusson, *Working Time in Britain: Towards a European Model, Part I The European Union Directive* (Institute of Employment Rights, 1994).

or technical reasons. Under no circumstances, however, can the reference period be extended beyond 12 months.

Implementation

The Directive is to be implemented by November 1996. Member States can opt out of the requirement to limit the average working week to 48 hours provided that national legislation or practice:

- requires the consent of the worker to a longer working week than 48 hours
- no worker is subject to a detriment for refusing to work longer hours
- records are kept so as to allow the competent authorities to restrict the working week on grounds of health and safety
- the employer provides the competent authorities with information on cases of employees working more than 48 hours.

The Commission will re-examine these restrictions within seven years of the implementation date of the Directive.

An opt-out is also provided for the provisions of the Directive which guarantee a period of annual paid leave of four weeks. Member States here are given a transitional period of up to three years during which every worker is entitled to three weeks annual paid leave which cannot be replaced by an allowance in lieu, except where the employment relationship is terminated.

National implementation measures must refer to the Directive as being their source and the process of implementation cannot be used to excuse the reduction in the general level of protection afforded to workers.

The approach of Directive 93/104

It is clear from the description of the terms of the Directive that its approach is flexible. Effectively, it lays down two options for successful implementation by the Member States. They may introduce legislation or they may provide the necessary framework for the conclusion of collective agreements. This latter approach is in conformity with the Agreement on Social Policy which lays stress on the importance of social dialogue and the involvement of the two sides of industry, management and labour. The Directive itself is neutral as to how best to achieve the goals set down, leaving implementation entirely in the hands of the Member States.

It is also clear from the terms of the Directive that there are a number of permissible derogations as to the scope of the Directive and its application to specific categories of workers. However, even where such derogations are provided for, the Directive still demands protection for the health and safety of workers.

Implementation problems for the UK

The UK Government has indicated that it will take no steps to implement the Working Time Directive until after the case which it has brought in the European Court has been heard. However implementation will cause major policy and legal changes if the Court decides that the Directive has been adopted in accordance with Community law. These problems have been summarised by Hepple who says that "it is a distinctive feature of British labour law that there is no general legislation regulating working time".[14] Furthermore, he argues, "there is a multiplicity of levels of bargaining about working time. There are no national, multi-industry agreements on the subject".[15] The British position is completely out of step with our European partners, most of which either have legislation or collective agreements covering sectors of industry and limiting the working week, providing for annual holidays and generally regulating those areas covered by the Directive.

In the total absence of regulation, the UK will be faced with the choice of either legislating or persuading the two sides of industry to achieve agreement on the matters covered by the Directive. Both of these approaches would signify a turnaround from the deregulatory policies pursued in the 1980s and 1990s and would require the Government to interfere in the relationship between employers and employees. Such an interventionist stand is likely to prove difficult. Of course, it would also be possible for the UK Government to refuse to implement the Directive, thereby putting itself in breach of Community obligations and Community law. This latter scenario is possible given the increasing tendency to Euro-phobia within the UK establishment.

Assuming however that the UK is required to implement the Directive and is willing to do so, the most desirable approach is the introduction of legislation laying down minimum requirements, a so-called "floor of rights."[16] This approach is favoured by Hepple who calls for a new Working Time Act to reconcile three objectives; flexibility for employers, reduction in working time to increase employment, and the demands by individuals for autonomy

---

[14] Hepple, *Working Time: A New Legal Framework?*, (Institute for Public Policy Research, 1990).
[15] *Ibid* p 11.
[16] Muckenberger and Deakin, "From deregulation to a European floor of rights: Labour law, flexibilisation and the single market," 3 *Zeitschrift für auslandisches und internationales Arbeits und Sozialrecht* (1989) 153.

in their own working environment. Hepple's proposals would also incorporate the rights of part-time workers and, to some extent, have been incorporated into recent changes adopted in response to developments in sex equality law.[17] Any such legislation would, as does the Directive, lay down minimum standards leaving collective bargaining to adapt the general principles to specific circumstances.

Hepple's work, however, must be seen in the context in which it is written: it is a proposal for a future Labour Government. In the absence of a Labour Government, any legislation is likely to be hedged with enormous difficulties and exceptions.

Bercusson advocates a different approach with greater reliance on the traditional British approach to collective bargaining.[18] He argues that "collective bargaining has received a major stimulus in the Working Time Directive" and "this is an important opportunity for trade unions to re-think traditional bargaining packages".[19] The UK cannot rely on such bargaining as being correct implementation of the Directive as it is not a systematic transposition of the Directive's principles into national law.

The future of the Directive?

True to its word, the UK Government shows no signs of implementing the Working Time Directive in the UK. There are only plans for deregulation and none for reregulation. The cut off date for implementation is November 1996. It is likely that the Court of Justice will have given its decision on the legality of the Directive by then. Difficult choices will have to be made on how to implement the Directive in the UK if the case goes against the UK stand.[20] Full implementation may have to await a change of government or, at least, a change of government policy.

---

[17] See chapter 6 on atypical workers.

[18] Bercusson cited in notes 7 and 13 *supra*.

[19] At the time of completing this manuscript, October 1995, Ford workers were in the process of negotiating for a two hour reduction in the working week.

[20] There may be a kind of personal bar argument against the UK in this case. The UK had initially threatened to challenge the legality of the pregnancy Directive on the grounds that Article 118a was insufficient legal base. In the event this threat was not carried through. It could be argued, therefore, that the UK has accepted that certain workers' rights, provided that they have some relationship with health and safety matters, can be legislated for under the terms of Article 118a.

Questions

1. Compare the wording of Articles 118a and 100a of the Treaty of Rome. In the light of the wording of these Articles how would you assess the arguments of the UK?

2. What do you understand by the term "the humanisation of work"? Do you think that any of the other directives discussed in this book advance that concept or is Directive 93/104 the only one to whichit might apply?

3. Examine the derogations provided for in the Directive. Taking these derogations into consideration, how far can it be said that Directive 93/104 provides European regulation of hours of work?

Contents of Chapter 14

WORKS COUNCIL

Chapter 14

WORKS COUNCILS

Introduction

Directive 94/45 on the Establishment of Works Councils is the first Community Directive in the area of social law which does not apply to the UK. This chapter therefore adopts a different approach from others in this book. It outlines the procedures adopted as part of the Treaty on European Union for legislation which is to be followed according to the terms laid down in the Protocol and Agreement on Social Policy adopted at Maastricht. This forms the background to the legislative history of Directive 94/45. The chapter then outlines the main provisions of the Directive. This Directive will not be implemented in UK law but its provisions have guided several UK companies which have decided, for whatever purpose, to implement its provisions in the internal management structure of their companies. Implementation in the UK, therefore, is at the level of organisations rather than at the level of the State.

The Maastricht Treaty

Directive 94/45 on the Establishment of Works Councils was the first Directive to be adopted on the basis of the procedures set down in the opt-out provisions provided in the Maastricht Treaty.[1] This means that it is a

---

[1] Council Directive 94/45/EEC of 22 September 1994 on the establishment of a European Works Council or a procedure in Community -scale undertakings and Community-scale groups of undertakings for the purposes of informing and consulting employees OJ (1994) L 254/64. For text see Appendix.

Directive which is addressed to all the Member States of the Community with the exception of the UK.

The Maastricht opt-out

The rather tortuous negotiations which preceded the adoption of the Treaty on European Union in 1992 led to the inclusion in that Treaty of an opt-out for the UK from additional provisions relating to social policy. Whilst existing Treaty provisions remained largely unchanged, a Protocol and Agreement were added giving the then 11 Member States the right to use the institutional framework of the Community to move forward on social policy.

The Protocol on Social Policy

In the Protocol, all 12 Member States agreed that 11 of them would "continue along the path" of the Social Charter which had been adopted as a solemn declaration in 1989.[2] Action by the 11 was not to affect the existing Treaty regime nor would it affect legislation adopted up to that date by the Community. The Protocol authorised the 11 to utilise the institutional structure provided for in the Treaty in order to give effect to the Agreement itself. In other words the 11 Member States agreed to use the Charter as a guide to the legislation which they would adopt in the future. The UK was not to take part in the deliberations and the adoption of Council proposals and an adjustment was inserted into the Protocol to the rules on qualified majority voting for decisions to be taken by the 11. Acts adopted by the Council following these procedures were not to be applicable to the UK. This Protocol was accepted by the three new Member States so that now 14 of the 15 Member States will take part in the deliberations and adoption of law on social policy.[3]

The Agreement on Social Policy

The Agreement on Social Policy asserts the desire of the 11 (now 14) to implement the Social Charter. The Agreement relates the objectives of social policy and balances the need to promote employment and secure enhanced conditions, promote social dialogue and work towards the combating of social exclusion with the need to ensure competitiveness of European industry and the recognition of national diversity in labour law.

[2] For text of the Protocol see Appendix. For a discussion of the Social Charter see Hepple, "The Implementation of the Community Charter of Fundamental Social Rights", 53 *Modern Law Review* (1990) 643; Bercusson, "The European Community's Charter of Fundamental Social Rights for Workers" 53 *Modern Law Review* (1990) 624.
[3] Council Decision 95/1 adjusting the Treaty of Accession OJ (1995) L 1/1.

The fields covered by the Agreement are health and safety, working conditions, equality of men and women and the integration of individuals into the workforce. Directives which avoid the imposition of undue costs may be adopted setting minimum requirements for the Member States. Directives in these areas can be adopted on the basis of qualified majority voting. However, on matters of social security, protection of workers on the termination of employment, representation and collective bargaining, conditions of employment for third country nationals and financial contribution to job creation the Council must act on the basis of unanimity. The Agreement cannot be used to introduce measures in relation to pay, the right of association, the right to strike or the right to impose lock-outs.

Directives adopted on the basis of the Agreement may be implemented in the Member States by a common agreement of management and labour without necessarily involving the State in taking any legislative measures. However, after the date of transposition of the Directive has passed, each State must be in a position to ensure effective implementation of its provisions. Member States remain free to adopt measures going beyond the minimum standards laid down in Directives.

The Commission remains responsible for proposing measures to be adopted under the terms of the Agreement but it is also made responsible for promoting dialogue between both sides of industry and, to assist in this, the Commission must consult management and labour before proposing any new Directives. Management and labour must also be consulted on the content of proposals. After such consultation, one of two procedures may be followed.

The first procedure results in the agreement between management and labour to conclude contractual relations at Community level to be implemented at the national level in accordance with national procedures. Alternatively such contractual relations might be implemented through the adoption of a Council decision where there is a joint request by both parties. The process of achieving agreement can last for up to nine months, to be extended if management, labour and the Commission so agree.

Where no agreement can be reached in this way, the Commission may proceed to propose a Directive according to the procedures outlined above.

The Commission is also given a proactive role in the encouragement of dialogue between the Member States in order to co-ordinate social policy in all the fields covered by the Agreement.

Finally, the Member States agree to modify the definition of equal pay by adding an additional paragraph which would allow them to make provision for positive discrimination which would make it easier for women to pursue a vocational activity or to compensate for disadvantages to women's professional careers. This is a difficult provision in legal terms since it appears to be an attempt to modify Article 119 of the Treaty. However the Protocol to the

Treaty specifically states that it is without prejudice to the existing *acquis communautaire* of which Article 119 is a part. It is probably true to say that this specific aspect of the Agreement therefore carries no legal force.[4]

Legislative implications

The legislative implications of the adoption of the Protocol and Agreement for social law matters are wide ranging. It is apparent that the Agreement covers areas which are already provided for in the Treaty such as health and safety, equality of men and women, and working conditions. In these areas the Commission would wish to legislate for the entire Community otherwise the whole purpose of the introduction of social legislation, the avoidance of social dumping, would be thwarted. The Commission will, therefore, introduce a proposal following the procedures provided for in the Treaty and only if the proposal is blocked or rejected will it open the opt-out procedures. At this stage, the Commission proposal will have been subject to the amendment of Parliament and ECOSOC as well as amendments suggested by Member States and may well be a watered down version of the original proposal. Nonetheless, it is this proposal which then goes to the two sides of industry for consultation. At this stage the proposal may not gain approval and the Commission must then go for legislation in the form of a Directive to be adopted by the Council. This is obviously an unsatisfactory and cumbersome legislative process which can only lead to the adoption of unsatisfactory legislation. It was the procedure which was followed in the case of the Works Council Directive.

Directive 94/45

Background

Students of Community law in the 1980s would have been familiar with some of the ideas which are incorporated in the 1994 Directive since it was as early as 1980 that the then Commissioner for Social Affairs, a Mr Vredeling, proposed what came to be known as the Vredeling Directive on Worker Participation and Consultation.[5] Cressey has said that "there is a long, overlapping and confusing history regarding the proposals on worker participation".[6] He identifies the Vredeling Directive as part of a number of Directives which would create a German type model of worker consultation

---

[4] See also chapter 2 *supra*.
[5] OJ (1980) C 297/3.
[6] Cressey "Employee participation" in Gold (ed), *The Social Dimension*, (MacMillan, 1993).

and participation. Others were the early drafts of a European Company Statute, and the fifth draft Directive on Company Law (amended twice) on public limited liability companies. Cressey also demonstrates that the level of opposition to these proposals from business was the reason why they were stalled.[7]

The Community returned to the idea of consultation and participation of workers in the late 1980s and early 1990s with proposals for a new Directive on the establishment of a European Works Council.[8] These proposals were blocked by the UK.

Following the adoption of the Treaty on European Union, the Commission came forward with a revised version of the 1990 Directive in May 1994.[9] The legislative history of this proposal is outlined in the preamble to the Directive and can be summarised as follows. In 1991 there was a broad consensus within the Council for the need for a Directive on works councils. However, no agreement was reached on its content. The Commission's proposal was based on Article 100 of the Treaty which requires unanimity in the Council and the UK opposed the adoption of legislation. Therefore, following the Maastricht Agreement, the Commission consulted management and labour both on the advisability of action and on the content of its proposals. Management and labour did not wish to proceed by way of a Europe wide agreement, therefore the Commission resorted to the introduction of a Directive.

Ideas underlying the Directive

The Directive is aimed only at Community-scale undertakings on the basis that the creation of a single European market has entailed increasing trans-nationalization of activities of undertakings and groups of undertakings. National provisions very often fail to address the problem of transnationalization and Community-wide legislation is appropriate. The right of workers to adequate consultation and participation on these matters is therefore not guaranteed. The Directive recognises the twin principles of autonomy of the parties to determine how works councils should operate and of subsidiarity

[7] The Vredeling Directive, its substance and the implications of it for the UK are discussed in Docksey, "Information and Consultation of Employees: The United Kingdom and the Vredeling Directive", 49 *Modern Law Review* (1986) 281.
[8] The Commission proposal for a Council Directive on the establishment of a European Works Council in Community-scale undertakings for the purposes of informing and consulting employees is contained in COM (90) 581 final and OJ (1991) C 39/10. The amended proposal is in COM (91) 345 and OJ (1991) C 336/11.
[9] OJ (1994) C 135/8 and OJ (1994) C 199/10. ECOSOC delivered its opinion in June 1994 see OJ (1994) C 295/64 and Parliament at the same time see OJ C 205/00. The Council's common position is found at OJ C 244/37.

which leaves it to the Member States to decide who are the workers' representatives for the purposes of the Directive.

Provisions of the Directive

The Directive recognises the right of information and consultation of employees in Community-scale undertakings and, to that end, provides that either a works council or other procedure for consultation should be established in such undertakings or groups of undertakings.

The undertakings covered by the Directive are those with at least 1000 employees in the Member States and at least 150 in each of two Member States. A group of undertakings is the controlling undertaking and its controlled undertakings. In the latter case there must be at least 1000 employees in the Member States with at least two undertakings having at least 150 employees in different Member States. Article 3 of the Directive defines the controlling undertaking for the purposes of this Directive alone as being one which can exercise a dominant influence over the others within a group.

One group of researchers has attempted to estimate the number of companies which will be required to establish a European Works Council or alternative consultation structure.[10] In the European Economic Area (EEA) as a whole to which the Directive applies, it is estimated that 458 corporate groups meet the threshold defined in the Directive. In the UK, it is estimated that 326 companies would have been directly required by the Directive, if it had been applicable to the UK, to establish a European Works Council (these figures are additional to the 458). Some of these companies will, nonetheless, be required to comply with the Directive since their European operations would require this. The same research estimates that possibly two in five of the UK companies are covered. Seventy six companies with headquarters outside the EEA will also be required to establish a European Works Council.

Responsibilities of central management

Central management is responsible for facilitating the creation of either a works council or some form of consultation mechanism. To do so it must initiate negotiations either on is own initiative or at the written request of 100 employees in at least two undertakings in different Member States. A special negotiating body must be established along the lines provided in the Directive,

---

[10] Hall, Carley, Gold, Marginson and Sisson, *European Works Councils Planning for the Directive* (Eclipse, 1995) Chapter 3. The Works Council Directive is one which has European Economic Area relevance i.e. it applies not just to the EC members but also to the two EEA members. This research is therefore based on a "Community" of 16.

e.g. there must be not less than three and not more than 17 members. National law is to determine who may participate in this body. The task of the negotiating body is to reach written agreement determining the scope, composition and functions of the works council or system of consultation. Experts may be drafted in to assist at the expense of management.

The agreement

Certain matters must be covered in the written agreement:

- which undertakings are covered
- the composition of the works council
- its functions and procedures
- the venue and frequency of meetings
- the resources to be allocated to the works council
- the duration of the agreement.

Where a works council as such is not established then the agreement must lay down the details of the appropriate consultation procedures.

Employee representatives

Nothing in the Directive specifies that employees are to be represented by trade unions. The Directive leaves it to national law and/or practice to define the appropriate representatives.[11] The use of the word "representative" does, however, imply that the employees have participated in some way in the election or selection of their representatives and that the latter carry some authority to speak on behalf of fellow workers.

Failure to achieve an agreement

Where an agreement is not adopted because the central management and special negotiating groups so decide, or where central management refuses to open negotiations after being requested to do so or where they are unable to conclude an agreement, the subsidiary requirements laid down in the Directive come into play. These requirements are to be laid down by national law which must comply with the detailed rules contained in the Annex of the Directive as to the competence, composition, election or appointment of members, timing of meetings and matters to be discussed by the works

[11] See chapters 8, 9 and 10 *supra* for a discussion of representation and consultation of workers in respect of specific policies.

council. In effect, the subsidiary requirements provide a model framework for a European Works Council law.[12]

Confidentiality

Member States must ensure the confidentiality of information provided to members of special negotiating groups, works councils members or experts brought in to assist in achieving an agreement on the creation of a works council where relevant. National legislation may also provide for the protection of information, disclosure of which might prove to be harmful to undertakings. In these cases, Member States must arrange for administrative or judicial procedures to determine what level of information may be withheld. Member States may retain in force any existing arrangements for enterprises which "pursue directly and essentially the aim of ideological guidance with respect to information and the expression of opinions". In its context this appears to mean that specific national legislation might apply to the kind of enterprise covered by the above definition. Such enterprises may be the press or political or religious organisations such as the Catholic Church. It is not clear what specific national provisions are to be protected by this provision but it may be that such organisations are exempted from the obligation to establish a European Works Council.

Co-operation

Central management and works councils (or alternative consultation structures) must work in a spirit of co-operation. Employees' representatives must not be victimised by their participation in the creation or operation of works councils.

Obligations on the Member States

Member States (excluding the UK) must ensure that all relevant parties abide by the provisions of the Directive, and where they do not so comply Member States must ensure that adequate administrative or judicial procedures are available to ensure effective compliance. Where national legislation provides that management may withhold certain information on the grounds of confidentiality then employees' representatives must have recourse to appropriate procedures for appeal.

---

[12] The subsidiary requirements are set out in full in the Appendix as part of the Directive.

Pre-existing arrangements

The date of implementation of the Directive is 22 September 1996. If, before that date, a Community scale undertaking has a pre-existing agreement covering the entire workforce and which provides for the transnational information and consultation of employees, it is exempted from the provisions of the Directive. Going for a "pre-emptive agreement" on the basis of this provision has several attractions and it appears that a number of enterprises have availed themselves of this option.[13] The attraction of the option is that it allows complete freedom to operate an agreement without needing to fulfill the requirements of the Directive. Nonetheless, some companies, whilst claiming the exemption under Article 13, appear to be following the requirements of the Directive to the letter.[14] Other agreements, which appear to have been established as pre-emptive agreements, do not seem to meet all the requirements of the Directive and, it has been claimed, have been imposed by management without the appropriate level of consultation taking place.[15] Certain of these agreements have been boycotted by trade union organisations, either nationally or at the European level. The "virtual European Works Council" established by Digital may be a pre-emptive procedure rather than a structure, since it provides for "an electronic dialogue and exchange of views". Workers' representatives appear to be opposed to this procedure.[16]

Agreements which conform to the spirit of the Directive clearly fall within the Article 13 exemption. Others which do not conform, perhaps because they are management-imposed and do not represent a genuine agreement between management and worker representatives, are likely to be insufficient to exempt a Community-scale enterprise from the requirements of the Directive.

Links with other provisions

This Directive is not intended to disturb the procedures for consultation and participation of workers laid down in other Directives.[17] Nor is it intended to prejudice existing rights to consultation and participation under national

---

[13] The phrase "going for a pre-emptive agreement" is taken from Hall and others, cited in note 10 *supra*.

[14] See the ISS agreement discussed in 259 *European Industrial Relations Review* 4. The agreement has been described as "exemplary".

[15] See the discussion of the Marks and Spencer and Honda agreements discussed in 256 *European Industrial Relations Review* (1995) 16.

[16] *Ibid* p 18.

[17] Such as Directive 75/129 on collective redundancies discussed in Chapter 9 *supra* or Directive 77/187 on transfer of undertakings discussed in Chapter 8 *supra*.

law.[18] Neither does it apply to Community-scale undertakings which already have in place an agreement on consultation and participation covering the entire workforce.

Implementation of the Directive

The European Works Council Directive requires no legislative action on behalf of the UK since it is based on the opt-out provisions of the Maastricht Treaty. Any discussion of implementation in the UK must, therefore, centre on the activities of enterprises.

The most recent available statistics suggest that some 54 agreements on the establishment of European Works Councils have been reached.[19] Some of these have been initiated by companies based in the UK but which have trading operations in several European states, such as Marks and Spencer. Other agreements bring in representatives from the UK since UK operations are part of the group as a whole, such as the Eridania Beghin-Say agreement. Another category of agreements which involve UK representation is that of non European corporations. Honda, for example, is a Japanese company with widespread European operations. Its main European workforce is based in Britain but it has operations in other European countries.

Alternatives to participation

Directive 94/45 prescribes some form of representative participation within Community-scale undertakings. It has been suggested that other forms of participation might be equally effective in terms of improving motivation and commitment of workers and of improving the decision-making process. Alternative methods of participation other than European Works Councils have been the subject of recent investigation but the conclusion has been that alternatives to organised and representative participation are limited "in particular that the legitimate expression of the collective views of employees can be carried out only through representational forms of participation".[20]

---

[18] Legislation exists on works councils at the national level in France, Germany, the Netherlands, and Portugal. In Denmark works councils are voluntary. See D'Sa and Woolridge, "Directive on the Establishment of European Works Councils: Effect on UK and Non-EU Companies" *Business Law Review* (1994) 295.

[19] 256 *European Industrial Relations Review* (1995) 14.

[20] See the discussion of the report by Gold, *Direct Communications in European multinationals: A case study approach*, in *253 European Industrial Relations Review* (1995) 25.

Conclusions

It has been said that the regime provided for under the Directive is a flexible one.[21] It is certainly the case that Community-scale undertakings are given a great deal of autonomy in devising procedures for consultation and participation of their workforce. The terms of the Directive really only come into play when an agreement proves impossible to achieve. Given that the aim of the Directive is to facilitate communication it may be that its mere existence will encourage undertakings to develop lines of communication and provide them with ideas on how they might proceed. It seems to have been the case in the UK that, despite the UK opt-out, certain companies have voluntarily complied with the Directive and those which have are reporting the success of the experiment. Compliance with a law which does not apply directly to undertakings is an interesting phenomenon and seems to suggest that the antagonism which was displayed by UK-based companies to the whole concept of works councils in the 1980s has been replaced by a cautious welcome.

---

[21] *Ibid.*

Questions

1. Which areas of social policy contained in the Agreement on Social Policy already have a legal base within the Treaty of Rome?

2. Did the Community have the competence to adopt a directive, under the terms of the Maastricht Agreement and Protocol, which would have applied to all undertakings in the Member States, as opposed to Community-scale undertakings?

3. If you were asked to draft a model works council agreement for use by companies in the UK, what areas would you include within it?

4. If, at some stage in the future, the UK were to sign up to Directive 94/45 what kind of legislation or other action would be needed to ensure that UK law complies with the Directive?

APPENDICES

EEC TREATY EXTRACTS

Article 100[1]

The Council shall, acting unanimously on a proposal from the Commission and after consulting the European Parliament and the Economic and Social Committees, issue directives for the approximation of such laws, regulations or administrative provisions of the Member States as directly affect the establishment or functioning of the common market.

Article 100a

1. By way of derogation from Article 100 and save where otherwise provided in this Treaty, the following provisions shall apply for the achievement of the objectives set out in Article 8a. The Council shall, acting by a qualified majority on a proposal from the Commission in co-operation with the European Parliament and after consulting the Economic and Social Committee, adopt the measures for the approximation of the provisions laid down by law, regulation or administrative action in Member States which have as their object the establishment and functioning of the internal market.

2. Paragraph 1 shall not apply to fiscal provisions, to those relating to the free movement of persons nor to those relating to the rights and interests of employed persons.

3. The Commission, in its proposals envisaged in paragraph 1 concerning health, safety, environmental protection and consumer protection, will take as a base a high level of protection.

[1] As amended by Article G(21) TEU.

4. If, after the adoption of a harmonization measure by the Council acting by a qualified majority, a Member State deems it necessary to apply national provisions on grounds of major needs referred to in Article 36, or relating to protection of the environment or the working environment, it shall notify the Commission of these provisions.

The Commission shall confirm the provisions involved after having verified that they are not a means of arbitrary discrimination or a disguised restriction on trade between Member States.

By way of derogation from the procedure laid down in Articles 169 and 170, the Commission or any Member State may bring the matter directly before the Court of Justice if it considers that another Member State is making improper use of the powers provided for in this Article.

5. The harmonization measures referred to above shall, in appropriate cases, include a safeguard clause authorizing the Member States to take, for one or more of the non-economic reasons referred to in Article 36, provisional measures subject to a Community control procedure.

Article 117

Member States agree upon the need to promote improved working conditions and an improved standard of living for workers, so as to make possible their harmonisation while the improvement is being maintained.

They believe that such a development will ensue not only from the functioning of the common market, which will favour the harmonisation of social systems, but also from the procedures provided for in this Treaty and from the approximation of provisions laid down by law, regulation or administrative action.

Article 118

Without prejudice to the other provisions of this Treaty and in conformity with its general objectives, the Commission shall have the task of promoting close co-operation between Member States in the social field, particularly in matters relating to:

- employment;
- labour law and working conditions;
- basic and advanced vocational training;
- social security;
- prevention of occupational accidents and diseases;
- occupational hygiene;

- the right of association, and collective bargaining between employers and workers.

To this end, the commission shall act in close contact with Member States by making studies, delivering opinions and arranging consultations both on problems arising at national level and on those of concern to international organisations.

Before delivering the opinions provided for in this Article, the Commission shall consult the Economic and Social Committee.

Article 118a EEC

1. Member States shall pay particular attention to encourage improvements, especially in the working environment, as regards the health and safety of workers, and shall set as their objective the harmonization of conditions in this area, while maintaining the improvements made.

2. In order to help achieve the objective laid down in the first paragraph, the Council, acting by a qualified majority on a proposal from the Commission, in co-operation with the European Parliament and after consulting the Economic and Social Committee, shall adopt, by means of directives, minimum requirements for gradual implementation, having regard to the conditions and technical rules obtained in each of the Member States.

Such directives shall avoid imposing administrative, financial and legal constraints in a way which would hold back the creation and development of small- and medium-sized undertakings.

3. The provisions adopted pursuant to this Article shall not prevent any Member State from maintaining or introducing more stringent measures for the protection of working conditions compatible with this Treaty.

Article 119[2]

Each Member State shall during the first stage ensure and subsequently maintain the application of the principle that men and women should receive equal pay for equal work.

For the purpose of this Article, 'pay' means the ordinary basic or minimum wage or salary and any other consideration, whether in cash or in kind, which the worker receives, directly or indirectly, in respect of his employment from his employer.

[2] See the Agreement on Social Policy. Article 6.

Equal pay without discrimination based on sex means:

(a) that pay for the same work at piece rates shall be calculated on the basis of the same unit of measurement;

(b) that pay for work at time rates shall be the same for the same job.

Article 235

If action by the Community should prove necessary to attain, in the course of the operation of the common market, one of the objectives of the Community and this Treaty has not provided the necessary powers, the Council shall, acting unanimously on a proposal from the Commission and after consulting the Assembly, take the appropriate measures.

COUNCIL DIRECTIVE
of 10 February 1975

on the approximation of the laws of the Member States relating to the application of the principle of equal pay for men and women (75/117/EEC)

THE COUNCIL OF THE EUROPEAN COMMUNITIES,
 Having regard to the Treaty establishing the European Economic Community, and in particular Article 100 thereof;
 Having regard to the proposal from the Commission;
 Having regard to the Opinion of the European Parliament;[1]
 Having regard to the Opinion of the Economic and Social Committee;[2]
 Whereas implementation of the principle that men and women should receive equal pay contained in Article 119 of the Treaty is an integral part of the establishment and functioning of the common market;
 Whereas it is primarily the responsibility of the Member States to ensure the application of this principle by means of appropriate laws, regulations and administrative provisions;
 Whereas the Council resolution of 21 January 1974[3] concerning a social action programme, aimed at making it possible to harmonize living and

---

[1] OJ No C 55, 13.5.1974, p. 43.
[2] OJ No C 88, 26.7.1974, p. 7.
[3] OJ No C 13, 12.2.1974, p. 1.

working conditions while the improvement is being maintained and at achieving a balanced social and economic development of the Community, recognized that priority should be given to action taken on behalf of women as regards access to employment and vocational training and advancement, and as regards working conditions, including pay;

Whereas it is desirable to reinforce the basic laws by standards aimed at facilitating the practical application of the principle of equality in such a way that all employees in the Community can be protected in these matters;

Whereas differences continue to exist in the various Member States despite the efforts made to apply the resolution of the conference of the Member States of 30 December 1961 on equal pay for men and women and whereas, therefore, the national provisions should be approximated as regards application of the principle of equal pay,

HAS ADOPTED THIS DIRECTIVE:

Article 1

The principle of equal pay for men and women outlined in Article 119 of the Treaty, hereinafter called 'principle of equal pay', means, for the same work or for work to which equal value is attributed, the elimination of all discrimination on grounds of sex with regard to all aspects and conditions of remuneration.

In particular, where a job classification system is used for determining pay, it must be based on the same criteria for both men and women and so drawn up as to exclude any discrimination on grounds of sex.

Article 2

Member States shall introduce into their national legal systems such measures as are necessary to enable all employees who consider themselves wronged by failure to apply the principle of equal pay to pursue their claims by judicial process after possible recourse to other competent authorities.

Article 3

Member States shall abolish all discrimination between men and women arising from laws, regulations or administrative provisions which is contrary to the principle of equal pay.

Article 4

Member States shall take the necessary measures to ensure that provisions appearing in collective agreements, wage scales, wage agreements or individual contracts of employment which are contrary to the principle of equal pay shall be, or may be declared, null and void or may be amended.

Article 5

Member States shall take the necessary measures to protect employees against dismissal by the employer as a reaction to a complaint within the undertaking or to any legal proceedings aimed at enforcing compliance with the principle of equal pay.

Article 6

Member States shall, in accordance with their national circumstances and legal systems, take the measures necessary to ensure that the principle of equal pay is applied. They shall see that effective means are available to take care that this principle is observed.

Article 7

Member States shall take care that the provisions adopted pursuant to this Directive, together with the relevant provisions already in force, are brought to the attention of employees by all appropriate means, for example at their place of employment.

Article 8

1. Member States shall put into force the laws, regulations and administrative provisions necessary in order to comply with the Directive within one year of its notification and shall immediately inform the Commission thereof.
2. Member States shall communicate to the Commission the texts of the laws, regulations and administrative provisions which they adopt in the field covered by this Directive.

Article 9

Within two years of the expiry of the one-year period referred to in Article 8, Member States shall forward all necessary information to the Commission to enable it to draw up a report on the application of this Directive for submission to the Council.

Article 10

This Directive is addressed to the Member States.
Done at Brussels, 10 February 1975.

For the Council
The President
G. FITZGERALD

COUNCIL DIRECTIVE
of 17 February 1975

on the approximation of the laws of Member States relating to collective redundancies (75/129/EEC)

THE COUNCIL OF THE EUROPEAN COMMUNITIES,

Having regard to the Treaty establishing the European Economic Community, and in particular Article 100 thereof;

Having regard to the proposal from the Commission;

Having regard to the Opinion of the European Parliament[1];

Having regard to the Opinion of the Economic and Social Committee[2];

Whereas it is important that greater protection should be afforded to workers in the event of collective redundancies while taking into account the need for balanced economic and social development within the Community;

Whereas, despite increasing convergence, differences still remain between the provisions in force in the Member States of the Community concerning the practical arrangements and procedures for such redundancies and the measures designed to alleviate the consequences of redundancy for workers;

Whereas these differences can have a direct effect on the functioning of the common market;

Whereas the Council resolution of 21 January 1974[3] concerning a social action programme makes provision for a Directive on the approximation of Member States' legislation on collective redundancies;

[1] OJ No C 19, 12.4.1973, p. 10.
[2] OJ No C 100, 22.11.1973, p. 11.
[3] OJ No C 13, 12.2.1974, p. 1.

Whereas this approximation must therefore be promoted while the improvement is being maintained within the meaning of Article 117 of the Treaty,

HAS ADOPTED THIS DIRECTIVE:

SECTION 1
Definitions and scope

Article 1

1. For the purposes of this Directive:

(a) 'collective redundancies' means dismissals effected by an employer for one or more reasons not related to the individual workers concerned where, according to the choice of the Member States, the number of redundancies is:
   - either, over a period of 30 days:
     (1) at least 10 in establishments normally employing more than 20 and less than 100 workers;
     (2) at least 10% of the number of workers in establishments normally employing at least 100 but less than 300 workers;
     (3) at least 30 in establishments normally employing 300 workers or more;
   - or, over a period of 90 days, at least 20, whatever the number of workers normally employed in the establishments in question;
(b) 'workers' representatives' means the workers' representatives provided for by the laws or practices of the Member States.

2. This Directive shall not apply to:

(a) collective redundancies affected under contracts of employment concluded for limited periods of time or for specific tasks except where such redundancies take place prior to the date of expiry or the completion of such contracts;
(b) workers employed by public administrative bodies or by establishments governed by public law (or, in Member States where this concept is unknown, by equivalent bodies);
(c) the crews of sea-going vessels;
(d) workers affected by the termination of an establishment's activities where that is the result of a judicial decision.

SECTION 2
Consultation procedure

Article 2

1. Where an employer is contemplating collective redundancies, he shall begin consultations with the workers' representatives with a view to reaching an agreement.
2. These consultations shall, at least, cover ways and means of avoiding collective redundancies or reducing the number of workers affected, and mitigating the consequences.
3. To enable the workers' representatives to make constructive proposals the employer shall supply them with all relevant information and shall in any event give in writing the reasons for the redundancies, the number of workers to be made redundant, the number of workers normally employed and the period over which the redundancies are to be effected.

The employer shall forward to the competent public authority a copy of all the written communications referred to in the preceding subparagraph.

SECTION 3
Procedure for collective redundancies

Article 3

1. Employers shall notify the competent public authority in writing of any projected collective redundancies.

This notification shall contain all relevant information concerning the projected collective redundancies and the consultations with workers' representatives provided for in Article 2, and particularly the reasons for the redundancies, the number of workers to be made redundant, the number of workers normally employed and the period over which the redundancies are to be effected.
2. Employers shall forward to the workers' representatives a copy of the notification provided for in paragraph 1.

The workers' representatives may send any comments they may have to the competent public authority.

Article 4

1. Projected collective redundancies notified to the competent public authority shall take effect not earlier than 30 days after the notification referred to in Article 3(1) without prejudice to any provisions governing individual rights with regard to notice of dismissal.

Member States may grant the competent public authority the power to reduce the period provided for in the preceding subparagraph.

2. The period provided for in paragraph 1 shall be used by the competent public authority to seek solutions in the problems raised by the projected collective redundancies.

3. Where the initial period provided for in paragraph 1 is shorter than 60 days, Member States may grant the competent public authority the power to extend the initial period to 60 days following notification where the problem raised by the projected collective redundancies are not likely to be solved within the initial period.

Member States may grant the competent public authority wider powers of extension.

The employer must be informed of the extension and the grounds for it before expiry of the initial period provided for in paragraph 1.

SECTION 4
Final provisions

Article 5

This Directive shall not affect the rights of Member States to apply or introduce laws, regulations or administrative provisions which are more favourable to workers.

Article 6

1. Member States shall bring into force the laws, regulations and administrative provisions needed in order to comply with this Directive within two years following its notification and shall forthwith inform the Commission thereof.

2. Member States shall communicate to the Commission the texts of the laws, regulations and administrative provisions which they adopt in the field covered by this Directive.

Article 7

Within two years following expiry of the two year period laid down in Article 6, Member States shall forward all relevant information to the Commission to enable it to draw up a report for submission to the Council on the application of this Directive.

Article 8

This Directive is addressed to the Member States.
Done at Brussels, 17 February 1975.

For the Council
The President
R. RYAN

COUNCIL DIRECTIVE
of 9 February 1976

on the implementation of the principle of equal treatment for men and women as regards access to employment, vocational training and promotion and working conditions (76/207/EEC)

THE COUNCIL OF THE EUROPEAN COMMUNITIES,

Having regard to the Treaty establishing the European Economic Community, and in particular Article 235 thereof,

Having regard to the proposal from the Commission,

Having regard to the Opinion of the European Parliament[1]

Having regard to the Opinion of the Economic and Social Committee,[2]

Whereas the Council, in its resolution of 21 January 1974 concerning a social action programme,[3] included among the priorities action for the purpose of achieving equality between men and women as regards access to employment and vocational training and promotion and as regards working conditions, including pay;

Whereas, with regard to pay, the Council adopted on 10 February 1975 Directive 75/117/EEC on the approximation of the laws of the Member States relating to the application of the principle of equal pay for men and women;[4]

---

[1] OJ No C 111, 20.5.1975, p. 14.
[2] OJ No C 286, 15.12.1975, p. 8.
[3] OJ No C 13, 12.2.1974, p. 1.
[4] OJ No L 45, 19.2.1975, p. 19.

Whereas Community action to achieve the principle of equal treatment for men and women in respect of access to employment and vocational training and promotion and in respect of other working conditions also appears to be necessary; whereas, equal treatment for male and female workers constitutes one of the objectives of the Community, in so far as the harmonization of living and working conditions while maintaining their improvement are *inter alia* to be furthered; whereas the Treaty does not confer the necessary specific powers for this purpose;

Whereas the definition and progressive implementation of the principle of equal treatment in matters of social security should be ensured by means of subsequent instruments,

HAS ADOPTED THIS DIRECTIVE:

Article 1

1. The purpose of this Directive is to put into effect in the Member States the principle of equal treatment for men and women as regards access to employment, including promotion, and to vocational training and as regards working conditions and, on the conditions referred to in paragraph 2, social security. This principle is hereinafter referred to as 'the principle of equal treatment'.

2. With a view to ensuring the progressive implementation of the principle of equal treatment in matters of social security, the Council, acting on a proposal from the Commission, will adopt provisions defining its substance, its scope and the arrangements for its application.

Article 2

1. For the purposes of the following provisions, the principle of equal treatment shall mean that there will be no discrimination whatsoever on grounds of sex either directly or indirectly by reference in particular to marital or family status.

2. This Directive shall be without prejudice to the right of Member States to exclude from its field of application those occupational activities and, where appropriate, the training leading thereto, for which, by reason of their nature or the context in which they are carried out, the sex of the worker constitutes a determining factor.

3. This Directive shall be without prejudice to provisions concerning the protection of women, particularly as regards pregnancy and maternity.

4. This Directive shall be without prejudice to measures to promote equal opportunity for men and women, in particular by removing existing inequalities which affect women's opportunities in the areas referred to in Article 1(1).

Article 3

1. Application of the principle of equal treatment means that there shall be no discrimination whatsoever on grounds of sex in the conditions, including selection criteria, for access to all jobs or posts, whatever the sector or branch of activity, and to all levels of the occupational hierarchy.

2. To this end, Member States shall take the measures necessary to ensure that:

(a) any laws, regulation and administrative provisions contrary to the principle of equal treatment shall be abolished;

(b) any provisions contrary to the principle of equal treatment which are included in collective agreements, individual contracts of employment, internal rules of undertakings or in rules governing the independent occupations and professions shall be, or may be declared, null and void or may be amended;

(c) those laws, regulations and administrative provisions contrary to the principle of equal treatment when the concern for protection which originally inspired them is no longer well founded shall be revised; and that where similar provisions are included in collective agreements labour and management shall be requested to undertake the desired revision.

Article 4

Application of the principle of equal treatment with regard to access to all types and to all levels, of vocational guidance, vocational training, advanced vocational training and retraining, means that Member States shall take all necessary measures to ensure that:

(a) any laws, regulations and administrative provisions contrary to the principle of equal treatment shall be abolished;

(b) any provisions contrary to the principle of equal treatment which are included in collective agreements, individual contracts of employment, internal rules of undertakings or in rules governing the independent occupations and professions shall be, or may be declared, null and void or may be amended;

(c) without prejudice to the freedom granted in certain Member States to certain private training establishments, vocational guidance, vocational training, advanced vocational training and retraining shall be accessible on the basis of the same criteria and at the same levels without any discrimination on grounds of sex.

Article 5

1. Application of the principle of equal treatment with regard to working conditions, including the conditions governing dismissal, means that men and women shall be guaranteed the same conditions without discrimination on grounds of sex.
2. To this end, Member States shall take the measures necessary to ensure that:

(a) any laws, regulations and administrative provisions contrary to the principle of equal treatment shall be abolished;
(b) any provisions contrary to the principle of equal treatment which are included in collective agreements, individual contracts of employment, internal rules of undertakings or in rules governing the independent occupations and professions shall be, or may be declared null and void or may be amended.
(c) those laws, regulations and administrative provisions contrary to the principle of equal treatment when the concern for protection which originally inspired them is no longer well founded shall be revised; and that where similar provisions are included in collective agreements labour and management shall be requested to undertake the desired revision.

Article 6

Member States shall introduce into their national legal systems such measures as are necessary to enable all persons who consider themselves wronged by failure to apply to them the principle of equal treatment within the meaning of Articles 3, 4 and 5 to pursue their claims by judicial process after possible recourse to other competent authorities.

Article 7

Member States shall take the necessary measures to protect employees against dismissal by the employer as a reaction to a complaint within the undertaking or to any legal proceedings aimed at enforcing compliance with the principle of equal treatment.

Article 8

Member States shall take care that the provisions adopted pursuant to this Directive, together with the relevant provisions already in force, are brought to the attention of employees by all appropriate means, for example at their place of employment.

Article 9

1. Member States shall put into force the laws, regulations and administrative provisions necessary in order to comply with this Directive within 30 months of its notification and shall immediately inform the Commission thereof.

However, as regards the first part of Article 3(2)(c) and the first part of Article 5(2)(c), Member States shall carry out a first examination and if necessary a first revision of the laws, regulations and administrative provisions referred to therein within four years of notification of this Directive.

2. Member States shall periodically assess the occupational activities referred to in Article 2(2) in order to decide, in the light of social developments, whether there is justification for maintaining the exclusions concerned. They shall notify the Commission of the results of this assessment.

3. Member States shall also communicate to the Commission the texts of laws, regulations and administrative provisions which they adopt in the field covered by this Directive.

Article 10

Within two years following expiry of the 30-month period laid down in the first subparagraph of Article 9(1), Member States shall forward all necessary information to the Commission to enable it to draw up a report on the application of this Directive for submission to the Council.

Article 11

This Directive is addressed to the Member States.
  Done at Brussels, 9 February 1976.

For the Council
The President
G. THORN

COUNCIL DIRECTIVE
of 19 December 1978

on the progressive implementation of the principle of equal treatment for men and women in matters of social security (79/7/EEC)

THE COUNCIL OF THE EUROPEAN COMMUNITIES,

Having regard to the Treaty establishing the European Economic Community, and in particular Article 235 thereof,

Having regard to the proposal from the Commission,[1]

Having regard to the Opinion of the European Parliament,[2]

Having regard to the Opinion of the Economic and Social Committee,[3]

Whereas Article 1(2) of Council Directive 76/207/EEC of 9 February 1976 on the implementation of the principle of equal treatment for men and women as regards access to employment, vocational training and promotion, and working conditions[4] provides that, with a view to ensuring the progressive implementation of the principle of equal treatment in matters of social security, the Council, acting on a proposal from the Commission, will adopt provisions defining its substance, its scope and the arrangement for its application; whereas the Treaty does not confer the specific powers required for this purpose;

Whereas the principle of equal treatment in matters of social security should be implemented in the first place in the statutory schemes which provide protection against the risks of sickness, invalidity, old age, accidents at work, occupational diseases and unemployment, and in social assistance in so far as it is intended to supplement or replace the above mentioned schemes;

Whereas the implementation of the principle of equal treatment in matters of social security does not prejudice the provisions relating to the protection of women on the grounds of maternity; whereas, in this respect, Member States may adopt specific provisions for women to remove existing instances of unequal treatment,

HAS ADOPTED THIS DIRECTIVE:

---

[1] OJ No C 34, 11.2.1977, p. 3.
[2] OJ No C 299, 12.12.1977, p. 13.
[3] OJ No C 180, 28.7.1977, p. 36.
[4] OJ No L 39, 14.2.1976, p. 40.

Article 1

The purpose of this Directive is the progressive implementation, in the field of social security and other elements of social protection provided for in Article 3, of the principle of equal treatment for men and women in matters of social security, hereinafter referred to as 'the principle of equal treatment'.

Article 2

This Directive shall apply to the working population – including self-employed persons, workers and self-employed persons whose activity is interrupted by illness, accident or involuntary unemployment and persons seeking employment – and to retired or invalided workers and self-employed persons.

Article 3

1. This Directive shall apply to:

(a) statutory schemes which provide protection against the following risks:
    – sickness,
    – invalidity,
    – old age,
    – accidents at work and occupational diseases,
    – unemployment;
(b) social assistance, in so far as it is intended to supplement or replace the schemes referred to in (a).

2 This Directive shall not apply to the provisions concerning survivors' benefits nor to those concerning family benefits, except in the case of family benefits granted by way of increases of benefits due in respect of the risks referred to in paragraph 1 (a).

3. With a view to ensuring implementation of the principle of equal treatment in occupational schemes, the Council, acting on a proposal from the Commission, will adopt provisions defining its substance, its scope and the arrangements for its application.

Article 4

1. The principle of equal treatment means that there shall be no discrimination whatsoever on grounds of sex either directly, or indirectly by reference in particular to marital or family status, in particular as concerns:

– the scope of the schemes and the conditions of access thereto,

- the obligation to contribute and the calculation of contributions,
- the calculation of benefits including increases due in respect of a spouse and for dependants and the conditions governing the duration and retention of entitlement to benefits.

2. The principle of equal treatment shall be without prejudice to the provisions relating to the protection of women on the grounds of maternity.

Article 5

Member States shall take the measures necessary to ensure that any laws, regulations and administrative provisions contrary to the principle of equal treatment are abolished.

Article 6

Member States shall introduce into their national legal systems such measures as are necessary to enable all persons who consider themselves wronged by failure to apply the principle of equal treatment to pursue their claims by judicial process, possibly after recourse to other competent authorities.

Article 7

1. This Directive shall be without prejudice to the right of Member States to exclude from its scope:

(a) the determination of pensionable age for the purposes of granting old-age and retirement pensions and the possible consequences thereof for other benefits;
(b) advantages in respect of old-age pension schemes granted to persons who have brought up children; the acquisition of benefit entitlements following periods of interruption of employment due to the bringing up of children;
(c) the granting of old-age or invalidity benefit entitlements by virtue of the derived entitlements of a wife;
(d) the granting of increases of long-term invalidity, old-age, accidents at work and occupational disease benefits for a dependent wife;
(e) the consequences of the exercise, before the adoption of this Directive, of a right of option not to acquire rights or incur obligations under a statutory scheme.

2. Member States shall periodically examine matters excluded under paragraph 1 in order to ascertain, in the light of social developments in the matter

concerned, whether there is justification for maintaining the exclusions concerned.

Article 8

1. Member States shall bring into force the laws, regulations and administrative provisions necessary to comply with this Directive within six years of its notification. They shall immediately inform the Commission thereof.
2. Member States shall communicate to the Commission the text of laws, regulations and administrative provisions which they adopt in the field covered by this Directive, including measures adopted pursuant to Article 7(2).

They shall inform the Commission of their reasons for maintaining any existing provisions on the matter referred to in Article 7(1) and of the possibilities for reviewing them at a later date.

Article 9

Within seven years of notification of this Directive, Member States shall forward all information necessary to the Commission to enable it to draw up a report on the application of this Directive for submission to the Council and to propose such further measures as may be required for the implementation of the principle of equal treatment.

Article 10

This Directive is addressed to the Member States.
Done at Brussels, 19 December 1978.

For the Council
The President
H.-D. GENSCHER

COUNCIL DIRECTIVE
of 14 February 1977

on the approximation of the laws of the Member States relating to the safeguarding of employees' rights in the event of transfers of undertakings, businesses or parts of businesses (77/187/EEC)

THE COUNCIL OF THE EUROPEAN COMMUNITIES,

Having regard to the Treaty establishing the European Economic Community, and in particular Article 100 thereof,

Having regard to the proposal from the Commission,

Having regard to the Opinion of the European Parliament,[1]

Having regard to the Opinion of the Economic and Social Committee:[2]

Whereas economic trends are bringing in their wake, at both national and Community level, changes in the structure of undertakings, through transfers of undertakings, businesses or parts of businesses to other employers as a result of legal transfers or mergers;

Whereas it is necessary to provide for the protection of employees in the event of a change of employer, in particular, to ensure that their rights are safeguarded;

Whereas differences still remain in the Member States as regards the extent of the protection of employees in this respect and these differences should be reduced;

Whereas these differences can have a direct effect on the functioning of the common market;

Whereas it is therefore necessary to promote the approximation of laws in this field while maintaining the improvement described in Article 117 of the Treaty,

HAS ADOPTED THIS DIRECTIVE:

SECTION 1
Scope and definitions

Article 1

1. This Directive shall apply to the transfer of an undertaking, business or part of a business to another employer as a result of a legal transfer or merger.
2. This Directive shall apply where and in so far as the undertaking, business or part of the business to be transferred is situated within the territorial scope of the Treaty.

---

[1] OJ No C 95, 28.4.1975, p. 17.
[2] OJ No C 255, 7.11.1975, p. 25.

3. This Directive shall not apply to sea-going vessels.

Article 2

For the purposes of this Directive:

(a) 'transferor' means any natural or legal person who, by reason of a transfer within the meaning of Article 1(1) ceases to be the employer in respect of the undertaking, business or part of the business;
(b) 'transferee' means any natural or legal person who, by reasons of a transfer within the meaning of Article 1(1), becomes the employer in respect of the undertaking, business or part of the business;
(c) 'representatives of the employees' means the representatives of the employees provided for by the laws or practice of the Member States, with the exception of members of administrative, governing or supervisory bodies of companies who represent employees on such bodies in certain Member States.

SECTION 2
Safeguarding of employees' rights

Article 3

1. The transferor's rights and obligations arising from a contract of employment or from an employment relationship existing on the date of a transfer within the meaning of Article 1(1) shall, by reason of such transfer, be transferred to the transferee.

Member States may provide that, after the date of transfer within the meaning of Article 1(1) and in addition to the transferee, the transferor shall continue to be liable in respect of obligations which arose from a contract of employment or an employment relationship.

2. Following the transfer within the meaning of Article 1(1), the transferee shall continue to observe the terms and conditions agreed in any collective agreement on the same terms applicable to the transferor under that agreement, until the date of termination or expiry of the collective agreement or the entry into force or application of another collective agreement.

Member States may limit the period for observing such terms and conditions, with the provision that it shall not be less than one year.

3. Paragraphs 1 and 2 shall not cover employees' rights to old-age, invalidity or survivors' benefits under supplementary company or inter-company pension schemes outside the statutory social security schemes in Member States.

Member States shall adopt the measures necessary to protect the interests of employees and persons no longer employed in the transferor's business at the time of the transfer within the meaning of Article 1(1) in respect of rights conferring on them immediate or prospective entitlement to old-age benefits, including survivors benefits, under supplementary schemes referred to in the first subparagraph.

Article 4

1. The transfer of an undertaking, business or part of a business shall not in itself constitute grounds for dismissal by the transferor or the transferee. This provision shall not stand in the way of dismissals that may take place for economic, technical or organizational reasons entailing changes in the workforce.

Member States may provide that the first subparagraph shall not apply to certain specific categories of employees who are not covered by the laws or practice of the Member States in respect of protection against dismissal.
2. If the contract of employment or the employment relationship is terminated because the transfer within the meaning of Article 1(1) involves a substantial change in working conditions to the detriment of the employee, the employer shall be regarded as having been responsible for termination of the contract of employment or of the employment relationship.

Article 5

1. If the business preserves its autonomy, the status and function, as laid down by the laws, regulations or administrative provisions of the Member States, of the representatives or of the representation of the employees affected by the transfer within the meaning of Article 1(1) shall be preserved.

The first subparagraph shall not apply if, under the laws, regulations, administrative provisions or practice of the Member States, the conditions necessary for the re-appointment of the representatives of the employees or for the reconstitution of the representation of the employees are fulfilled.
2. If the term of office of the representatives of the employees affected by a transfer within the meaning of Article 1(1) expires as a result of the transfer, the representatives shall continue to enjoy the protection provided by the laws, regulations, administrative provisions or practice of the Member States.

SECTION 3
Information and consultation

Article 6

1. The transferor and the transferee shall be required to inform the representatives of their respective employees affected by a transfer within the meaning of Article 1(1) of the following:

- the reasons for the transfer,
- the legal, economic and social implications of the transfer for the employees,
- measures envisaged in relation to the employees.

The transferor must give such information to the representatives of his employees in good time before the transfer is carried out.

The transferee must give such information to the representatives of his employees in good time, and in any event before his employees are directly affected by the transfer as regards their conditions of work and employment.

2. If the transferor or the transferee envisages measures in relation to his employees, he shall consult his representatives of the employees in good time on such measures with a view to seeking agreement.

3. Member States whose laws, regulations or administrative provisions provide that representatives of the employees may have recourse to an arbitration board to obtain a decision on the measures to be taken in relation to employees may limit the obligations laid down in paragraphs 1 and 2 to cases where the transfer carried out gives rise to a change in the business likely to entail serious disadvantages for a considerable number of the employees.

The information and consultations shall cover at least the measures envisaged in relation to the employees.

The information must be provided and consultations take place in good time before the change in the business as referred to in the first subparagraph is effected.

4. Member States may limit the obligations laid down in paragraphs 1, 2 and 3 to undertakings or businesses which, in respect of the number of employees, fulfil the conditions for the election or designation of a collegiate body representing the employees.

5. Member States may provide that where there are no representatives of the employees in an undertaking or business, the employees concerned must be informed in advance when a transfer within the meaning of Article 1(1) is about to take place.

SECTION 4
Final Provisions

Article 7

This Directive shall not affect the right of Member States to apply or introduce laws, regulations or administrative provisions which are more favourable to employees.

Article 8

1. Member States shall bring into force the laws, regulations and administrative provisions needed to comply with this Directive within two years of its notifications and shall forthwith inform the Commission thereof.
2. Member States shall communicate to the Commission the texts of the laws, regulations and administrative provisions which they adopt in the field covered by this Directive.

Article 9

Within two years following expiry of the two-year period laid down in Article 8, Member States shall forward all relevant information to the Commission in order to enable it to draw up a report on the application of this Directive for submission to the Council.

Article 10

This Directive is addressed to the Member States.
   Done at Brussels, 14 February 1977.

For the Council
The President
J. SILKIN

COUNCIL DIRECTIVE
of 20 October 1980

on the approximation of the laws of the Member States relating to the protection of employees in the event of the insolvency of their employer (80/987/EEC)

THE COUNCIL OF THE EUROPEAN COMMUNITIES,

Having regard to the Treaty establishing the European Economic Community, and in particular Article 100 thereof,

Having regard to the proposal from the Commission,[1]

Having regard to the Opinion of the European Parliament,[2]

Having regard to the Opinion of the Economic and Social Committee:[3]

Whereas it is necessary to provide for the protection of employees in the event of the insolvency of their employer, in particular in order to guarantee payment of their outstanding claims, while taking account of the need for balanced economic and social developments in the Community;

Whereas differences still remain between the Member States as regards the extent of the protection of employees in this respect; whereas efforts should be directed towards reducing these differences, which can have a direct effect on the functioning of the common market;

Whereas the approximation of laws in this field should, therefore, be promoted while the improvement within the meaning of Article 117 of the Treaty is maintained;

Whereas as a result of the geographical situation and the present job structure in that area, the labour market in Greenland is fundamentally different from the other areas of the Community;

Whereas to the extent that the Hellenic Republic is to become a member of the European Community on 1 January 1981, in accordance with the Act concerning the Conditions of Accession of the Hellenic Republic and the Adjustments to the Treaties, it is appropriate to stipulate in the Annex to the Directive under the heading 'Greece', those categories of employees whose claims may be excluded in accordance with Article 1(2) of the Directive,

HAS ADOPTED THIS DIRECTIVE:

SECTION 1
Scope and definitions

Article 1

1. This Directive shall apply to employees' claims arising from contracts of employment or employment relationships and existing against employers who are in a state of insolvency within the meaning of Article 2(1).

---

[1] OJ No C 135, 9.6.1978, p. 2.
[2] OJ No C 39, 12.2.1979, p. 26.
[3] OJ No C 105, 26.4.1979, p. 15.

2. Member States may, by way of exception, exclude claims by certain categories of employee from the scope of this Directive, by virtue of the special nature of the employee's contract of employment or employment relationship or of the existence of other forms of guarantee offering the employee protection equivalent to that resulting from this Directive.

The categories of employee referred to in the first sub-paragraph are listed in the Annex.

3. This Directive shall not apply to Greenland. This exception shall be re-examined in the event of any development in the job structures in that region.

Article 2

1. For the purposes of this Directive, an employer shall be deemed to be in a state of insolvency:

(a) Where a request has been made for the opening of proceedings involving the employer's assets, as provided for under the laws, regulations and administrative provisions of the Member State concerned, to satisfy collectively the claims of creditors and which make it possible to take into consideration the claims referred to in Article 1(1), and

(b) where the authority which is competent pursuant to the said laws, regulations and administrative provisions has:
   – either decided to open the proceedings,
   – or established that the employer's undertaking or business has been definitively closed down and that the available assets are insufficient to warrant the opening of the proceedings.

2. This Directive is without prejudice to national law as regards the definition of the terms 'employee', 'employer', 'pay', 'right conferring immediate entitlement' and 'right conferring prospective entitlement.'

SECTION 2
Provisions concerning guarantee institutions

Article 3

1. Member States shall take the measures necessary to ensure that guarantee institutions guarantee, subject to Article 4, payment of employees' outstanding

claims resulting from contracts of employment or employment relationships and relating to pay for the period prior to a given date.

2. At the choice of the Member States, the date referred to in paragraph 1 shall be:

- either that of the onset of the employer's insolvency;
- or that of the notice of dismissal issued to the employee concerned on account of the employer's insolvency;
- or that of the onset of the employer's insolvency or that on which the contract of employment or the employment relationship with the employee concerned was discontinued on account of the employer's insolvency.

Article 4

1. Member States shall have the option to limit the liability of guarantee institutions, referred to in Article 3.

2. When Member States exercise the option referred to in paragraph 1, they shall:

- in the case referred to Article 3(2), first indent, ensure the payment of outstanding claims relating to pay for the last three months of the contract of employment or employment relationship occurring within a period of six months preceding the date of the onset of the employer's insolvency;
- in the case referred to in Article 3(2), second indent, ensure the payment of the outstanding claims relating to pay for the last three months of the contract of employment or employment relationship preceding the date of the notice of dismissal issued to the employee on account of the employer's insolvency;
- in the case referred to in Article 3(2), third indent, ensure the payment of outstanding claims relating to pay for the last 18 months of the contract of employment or employment relationship preceding the date of the onset of the employer's insolvency or the date on which the contract of employment or the employment relationship with the employee was discontinued on account of the employer's insolvency. In this case, Member States may limit the liability to make payment to pay corresponding to a period of eight weeks or to several shorter periods totalling eight weeks.

3. However, in order to avoid the payment of sums going beyond the social objective of this Directive, Member States may set a ceiling to the liability for employees' outstanding claims.

When Member States exercise this option, they shall inform the Commission of the methods used to set the ceiling.

Article 5

Member States shall lay down detailed rules for the organisation, financing and operation of the guarantee institutions, complying with the following principles in particular:

(a) the assets of the institutions shall be independent of the employers' operating capital and be inaccessible to proceedings for insolvency;

(b) employers shall contribute to financing, unless it is fully covered by the public authorities;

(c) the institutions' liabilities shall not depend on whether or not obligations to contribute to financing have been fulfilled.

SECTION 3
Provisions concerning social security

Article 6

Member States may stipulate that Articles 3, 4 and 5 shall not apply to contributions due under national statutory social security schemes or under supplementary company or inter-company pension schemes outside the national statutory social security schemes.

Article 7

Member States shall take the measures necessary to ensure that nonpayment of compulsory contributions due from the employer, before the onset of his insolvency, to their insurance institutions under national statutory social security schemes, does not adversely affect employees' benefit entitlement in respect of these insurance institutions inasmuch as the employees' contributions were deducted at source from the remuneration paid.

Article 8

Member States shall ensure that the necessary measures are taken to protect the interests of employees and of persons having already left the employer's undertaking or business at the date of the onset of the employer's insolvency in respect of rights conferring on them immediate or prospective entitlement to old age benefits, including survivors' benefits, under supplementary company or inter-company pension schemes outside the national statutory social security schemes.

SECTION 4
General and final provisions

Article 9

This Directive shall not affect the option of Member States to apply or introduce laws, regulations or administrative provisions which are more favourable to employees.

Article 10

This Directive shall not affect the option of Member States:

(a) to take the measures necessary to avoid abuses;
(b) to refuse or reduce the liability referred to in Article 3 or the guarantee obligation referred to in Article 7 if it appears that fulfilment of the obligation is unjustifiable because of the existence of special links between the employee and the employer and of common interests resulting in collusion between them.

Article 11

1. Member States shall bring into force the laws, regulations and administrative provisions necessary to comply with this Directive within 36 months of its notification. They shall forthwith inform the Commission thereof.
2. Member States shall communicate to the Commission the texts of the laws, regulations and administrative provisions which they adopt in the field governed by this Directive.

Article 12

Within 18 months of the expiry of the period of 36 months laid down in Article 11(1), Member States shall forward all relevant information to the Commission in order to enable it to draw up a report on the application of this Directive for submission to the Council.

Article 13

This Directive is addressed to the Member States.
   Done at Luxembourg, October 20, 1980.

For the Council
The President
J. SANTER

ANNEX

Categories of employees whose claims may be excluded from the scope of this Directive, in accordance with Article 1(2)
I. Employees having a contract of employment, or an employment relationship, of a special nature

a. Greece

The master and the members of a crew of a fishing vessel, if and to the extent that they are remunerated by a share in the profits or gross earnings of the vessel.

b. Ireland

1. Out-workers (ie. persons doing piece-work in their own homes), unless they have a written contract of employment.
2. Close relatives of the employer, without a written contract of employment, whose work has to do with a private dwelling or farm in, or on, which the employer and the close relatives reside.
3. Persons who normally work for less than 18 hours a week for one or more employers and who do not derive their basic means of subsistence from the pay for this work.
4. Persons engaged in share fishing on a seasonal, casual or part-time basis.
5. The spouse of the employer.

c. Netherlands

Domestic servants employed by a natural person and working less than three days a week for the natural person in question.

d. United Kingdom

1. The master and the members of the crew of a fishing vessel who are remunerated by a share in the profits or gross earnings of the vessel.
2. The spouse of the employer.

II.Employees covered by other forms of guarantee

a. Greece

The crews of sea-going vessels.

b. Ireland

1. Permanent and pensionable employees of local or other public authorities or statutory transport undertakings.
2. Pensionable teachers employed in the following: national schools, secondary schools, comprehensive schools, teachers' training colleges.
3. Permanent and pensionable employees of one the voluntary hospitals funded by the Exchequer.

c. Italy

1. Employees covered by benefits laid down by law guaranteeing that their wages will continue to be paid in the event that the undertaking is hit by an economic crisis.
2. The crews of sea-going vessels.

d. United Kingdom

1. Registered dock workers other than those wholly or mainly engaged in work which is not dock work.
2. The crews of sea-going vessels.

COUNCIL DIRECTIVE
of 24 July 1986

on the implementation of the principle of equal treatment for men and women in occupational social security schemes (86/378/EEC)

THE COUNCIL OF THE EUROPEAN COMMUNITIES

Having regard to the Treaty establishing the European Economic Community, and in particular Articles 100 and 235 thereof,

Having regard to the proposal from the Commission[1],

Having regard to the opinion of the European Parliament[2],

Having regard to the opinion of the Economic and Social Committee[3],

Whereas the Treaty provides that each Member State shall ensure the application of the principle that men and women should receive equal pay for equal work; whereas 'pay' should be taken to mean the ordinary basic or minimum wage or salary and any other consideration, whether in cash or in kind, which the worker receives, directly or indirectly, from his employer in respect of his employment;

Whereas, although the principle of equal pay does indeed apply directly in cases where discrimination can be determined solely on the basis of the criteria of equal treatment and equal pay, there are also situations in which implementation of this principle implies the adoption of additional measures which more clearly define its scope;

Whereas Article 1(2) of Council Directive 76/207/EEC of 9 February 1976 on the implementation of the principle of equal treatment for men and women as regards access to employment, vocational training and promotion, and working conditions[4] provides that, with a view to ensuring the progressive implementation of the principle of equal treatment in matters of social security, the Council, acting on a proposal from the Commission, will adopt provisions defining its substance, its scope and the arrangements for its application; whereas the council adopted to this end Directive 79/7/EEC of 19 December 1978 on the progressive implementation of the principle of equal treatment for men and women in matters of social security[5];

Whereas Article 3(3) of Directive 79/7/EEC provides that, with a view to ensuring implementation of the principle of equal treatment in occupational schemes, the Council, acting on a proposal from the Commission, will adopt provisions defining its substance, its scope and the arrangements for its application;

Whereas the principle of equal treatment should be implemented in occupational social security schemes which provide protection against the risks specified in Article 3(1) of Directive 79/7/EEC as well as those which provide employees with any other consideration in cash or in kind within the meaning of the Treaty;

[1] OJ No C 134, 21.5.1983, p. 7.
[2] OJ No C 117, 30.4.1984, p. 169.
[3] OJ No C 35, 9.2.1984, p. 7.
[4] OJ No L 39, 14.2.1976, p. 40
[5] OJ No L 6, 10.1.1979, p. 24

Whereas implementation of the principle of equal treatment does not prejudice the provisions relating to the protection of women by reason of maternity,

HAS ADOPTED THIS DIRECTIVE:

Article 1

The object of this Directive is to implement, in occupational social security schemes, the principle of equal treatment for men and women, hereinafter referred to as 'the principle of equal treatment'.

Article 2

1. 'Occupational social security schemes' means schemes not governed by Directive 79/7/EEC whose purpose is to provide workers, whether employees or self-employed, in an undertaking or group of undertakings, area of economic activity or occupational sector or group of such sectors with benefits intended to supplement the benefits provided by statutory social security schemes or to replace them, whether membership of such schemes is compulsory or optional.
2. This Directive does not apply to:

(a) individual contracts,
(b) schemes having only one member,
(c) in the case of salaried workers, insurance contracts to which the employer is not a party;
(d) the optional provisions of occupational schemes offered to participants individually to guarantee them:
  – either additional benefits, or
  – a choice of date on which the normal benefits will start, or a choice between several benefits.

Article 3

This Directive shall apply to members of the working population including self-employed persons, persons whose activity is interrupted by illness, maternity, accident or involuntary unemployment and persons seeking employment, and to retired and disabled workers.

Article 4

This Directive shall apply to:

(a) occupational schemes which provide protection against the following risks:
    - sickness,
    - invalidity,
    - old age, including early retirement,
    - industrial accidents and occupational diseases,
    - unemployment;
(b) occupational schemes which provide for other social benefits, in cash or in kind, and in particular survivors' benefits and family allowances, if such benefits are accorded to employed persons and thus constitute a consideration paid by the employer to the worker by reason of the latter's employment.

Article 5

1. Under the conditions laid down in the following provisions, the principle of equal treatment implies that there shall be no discrimination on the basis of sex, either directly or indirectly, by reference in particular to marital or family status, especially as regards:
-    the scope of the schemes and the conditions of access to them;
-    the obligation to contribute and the calculation of contributions;
-    the calculation of benefits, including supplementary benefits due in respect of a spouse or dependants, and the conditions governing the duration and retention of entitlement to benefits.

2. The principle of equal treatment shall not prejudice the provisions relating to the protection of women by reason of maternity.

Article 6

1. Provisions contrary to the principle of equal treatment shall include those based on sex, either directly or indirectly, in particular by reference to marital or family for:

(a) determining the persons who may participate in an occupational scheme;

(b) fixing the compulsory or optional nature of participation in an occupational scheme;

(c) laying down different rules as regards the age of entry into the scheme or the minimum period of employment or membership of the scheme required to obtain the benefits thereof;

(d) laying down different rules, except as provided for in subparagraphs (h) and (i), for the reimbursement of contributions where a worker leaves a scheme without having fulfilled the conditions guaranteeing him a deferred right to long-term benefits;

(e) setting different conditions for the granting of benefits or restricting such benefits to workers of one or other of the sexes;

(f) fixing different retirement ages;

(g) suspending the retention or acquisition of rights during periods of maternity leave or leave for family reasons which are granted by law or agreement and are paid by the employer;

(h) setting different levels of benefit, except insofar as may be necessary to take account of actuarial calculation factors which differ according to sex in the case of benefits designated as contribution-defined;

(i) setting different levels of worker contribution;
setting different levels of employer contribution in the case of benefits designated as contribution-defined, except with a view to making the amount of those benefits more nearly equal;

(j) laying down different standards or standards applicable only to workers of a specified sex, except as provided for in subparagraphs (h) and (i), as regards the guarantee or retention of entitlement to deferred benefits when a worker leaves a scheme.

2. Where the granting of benefits within the scope of this Directive is left to the discretion of the scheme's management bodies, the latter must take account of the principle of equal treatment.

Article 7

Member States shall take all the necessary steps to ensure that:

(a) Provisions contrary to the principle of equal treatment in legally compulsory collective agreements, staff rules of undertakings or any other arrangements relating to occupational schemes are null and void, or may be declared null and void or amended;

(b) schemes containing such provisions may not be approved or extended by administrative measures.

Article 8

1. Member States shall take all necessary steps to ensure that the provisions of occupational schemes contrary to the principle of equal treatment are revised by 1 January 1993.

2. This Directive shall not preclude rights and obligations relating to a period of membership of an occupational scheme prior to revision of that scheme from remaining subject to the provisions of the scheme in force during that period.

Article 9

Member States may defer compulsory application of the principle of equal treatment with regard to:

(a) determination of pensionable age for the purposes of granting old-age or retirement pensions, and the possible implications for other benefits:
- either until the date on which such equality is achieved in statutory schemes,
- or, at the latest, until such equality is required by a directive.
(b) survivors' pensions until a directive requires the principle of equal treatment in statutory social security schemes in that regard;
(c) the application of the first subparagraph of Article 6 (1)(i) to take account of the different actuarial calculation factors, at the latest until the expiry of a thirteen-year period as from the notification of this Directive.

Article 10

Member States shall introduce into their national legal systems such measures as are necessary to enable all persons who consider themselves injured by failure to apply the principle of equal treatment to pursue their claims before the courts, possibly after bringing the matters before other competent authorities.

Article 11

Member States shall take the necessary steps to protect the worker against dismissal where this constitutes a response on the part of the employer to a complaint made at undertaking level or to the institution of legal proceedings aimed at enforcing compliance with the principle of equal treatment.

Article 12

1. Member States shall bring into force such laws, regulations and administrative provisions as are necessary in order to comply with this Directive at the latest three years after notification thereof (1). They shall immediately inform the Commission thereof.

2. Member States shall communicate to the Commission at the latest five years after notification of this Directive all information necessary to enable the Commission to draw up a report on the application of this Directive for submission to the Council.

Article 13

This Directive is addressed to the Member States.
Done at Brussels, 24 July 1986.

For the Council
The President
A. CLARK

(1) This Directive was notified to the Member States on 30 July 1986.

COUNCIL DIRECTIVE
of 11 December 1986

on the application of the principle of equal treatment between men and women engaged in an activity, including agriculture, in a self-employed capacity, and on the protection of self-employed women during pregnancy and motherhood (86/613/EEC)

THE COUNCIL OF THE EUROPEAN COMMUNITIES,

Having regard to the Treaty establishing the European Economic Community, and in particular Articles 100 and 235 thereof,

Having regard to the proposal from the Commission[1],

Having regard to the Opinion of the European Parliament[2],

Having regard to the Opinion of the Economic and Social Committee[3],

[1] OJ No C 113, 27.4.1984, p. 4.
[2] OJ No C 172, 2.7.1984, p. 90.
[3] OJ No C 343, 24.12.1984, p. 1.

Whereas, in its resolution of 12 July 1982 on the promotion of equal opportunities for women[4], the Council approved the general objectives of the Commission communication concerning a new Community action programme on the promotion of equal opportunities for women (1982 to 1985) and expressed the will to implement appropriate measures to achieve them;

Whereas action 5 of the programme referred to above concerns the application of the principle of equal treatment to self-employed women and to women in agriculture;

Whereas the implementation of the principle of equal pay for men and women workers, as laid down in Article 119 of the Treaty, forms an integral part of the establishment and functioning of the common market;

Whereas on 10 February 1975 the Council adopted Directive 75/117/EEC on the approximation of the laws of the Member States relating to the application of the principle of equal pay for men and women[5];

Whereas, as regards other aspects of equality of treatment between men and women, on 9 February 1976 the Council adopted Directive 76/207/EEC on the implementation of the principle of equal treatment for men and women as regards access to employment, vocational training and promotion, and working conditions[6] and on 19 December 1978 Directive 79/7/EEC on the progressive implementation of the principle of equal treatment for men and women in matters of social security[7];

Whereas, as regards persons engaged in a self-employed capacity, in an activity in which their spouses are also engaged, the implementation of the principle of equal treatment should be pursued through the adoption of detailed provisions designed to cover the specific situation of these persons;

Whereas differences persist between the Member States in this field, whereas, therefore it is necessary to approximate national provisions with regard to the application of the principle of equal treatment;

Whereas in certain respects the Treaty does not confer the powers necessary for the specific actions required;

Whereas the implementation of the principle of equal treatment is without prejudice to measures concerning the protection of women during pregnancy and motherhood,

HAS ADOPTED THIS DIRECTIVE:

[4] OJ No C 186, 21.7.1982, p. 3.
[5] OJ No L 45, 19.2.1975, p. 19.
[6] OJ No L 39, 14.2.1975, p. 40.
[7] OJ No L 6, 10.1.1979, p. 24.

SECTION 1
Aims and scope

Article 1

The purpose of this Directive is to ensure, in accordance with the following provisions, application in the Member States of the principle of equal treatment as between men and women engaged in an activity in a self-employed capacity, or contributing to the pursuit of such an activity as regards those aspects not covered by Directives 76/207/EEC and 79/7/EEC.

Article 2

This Directive covers:

(a) self-employed workers, ie. all persons pursuing a gainful activity for their own account, under the conditions laid down by national law, including farmers and members of the liberal professions;

(b) their spouses, not being employees or partners, where they habitually, under the conditions laid down by national law, participate in the activities of the self-employed worker and perform the same tasks or ancillary tasks.

Article 3

For the purposes of this Directive the principle of equal treatment implies the absence of all discrimination on grounds of sex, either directly of indirectly, by reference in particular to marital or family status.

SECTION 2

Equal treatment between self-employed male and female workers – position of the spouses without professional status of self-employed workers – protection of self-employed workers or wives of self-employed workers during pregnancy and motherhood

Article 4

As regards self-employed persons, Member States shall take the measures necessary to ensure the elimination of all provisions which are contrary to the principle of equal treatment as defined in Directive 76/207/EEC, especially in respect of the establishment, equipment or extension of a business or the launching or extension of any other form of self-employed activity including financial facilities.

Article 5

Without prejudice to the specific conditions for access to certain activities which apply equally to both sexes, Member States shall take the necessary measures to ensure that the conditions for the formation of a company between spouses are not more restrictive than the conditions for the formation of a company between unmarried persons.

Article 6

Where a contributory social security system for self-employed workers exists in a Member State, that Member State shall take the necessary steps to enable the spouses referred to in Article 2(b) who are not protected under the self-employed worker's social security scheme to join a contributory social security scheme voluntarily.

Article 7

Member States shall undertake to examine under what conditions recognition of the work of the spouses referred to in Article 2(b) may be encouraged and, in the light of such examination, consider any appropriate steps for encouraging such recognition.

Article 8

Member States shall undertake to examine whether, and under what conditions, female self-employed workers and the wives of self-employed workers may, during interruptions in their occupational activity owing to pregnancy or motherhood,

- have access to services supplying temporary replacements or existing national social services, or
- be entitled to cash benefits under a social security scheme or under any other public social protection system.

SECTION 3
General and final provisions

Article 9

Member States shall introduce into their national legal systems such measures as are necessary to enable all persons who consider themselves wronged by failure to apply the principle of equal treatment in self-employed activities to pursue their claims by judicial process, possibly after recourse to other competent authorities.

Article 10

Member States shall ensure that the measures adopted pursuant to this Directive, together with the relevant provisions already in force, are brought to the attention of bodies representing self-employed workers and vocational training centres.

Article 11

The Council shall review this Directive, on a proposal from the Commission, before 1 July 1993.

Article 12

1. Member States shall bring into force the laws, regulations and administrative provisions necessary to comply with this Directive not later than 30 June 1989.

However, if a Member State which, in order to comply with Article 5 of this Directive, has to amend its legislation on matrimonial rights and obligations, the date on which such Member State must comply with Article 5 shall be 30 June 1991.

2. Member States shall immediately inform the Commission of the measures taken to comply with this Directive.

Article 13

Member States shall forward to the Commission, not later than 30 June 1991, all the information necessary to enable it to draw up a report on the application of this Directive for submission to the Council.

Article 14

This Directive is addressed to the Member States.
Done at Brussels, 11 December 1986.

> *For the Council*
> *The President*
> A. CLARKE

COUNCIL DIRECTIVE
of 12 June 1989

on the introduction of measures to encourage improvements in the safety and health of workers at work (89/391/EEC)

THE COUNCIL OF THE EUROPEAN COMMUNITIES,

Having regard to the Treaty establishing the European Economic Community, and in particular Article 118a thereof,

Having regard to the proposal from the Commission,[1] drawn up after consultation with the Advisory Committee on Safety, Hygiene and Health Protection at Work,

In co-operation with the European Parliament,[2]

Having regard to the opinion of the Economic and Social Committee,[3]

Whereas Article 118a of the Treaty provides that the Council shall adopt, by means of Directives, minimum requirements for encouraging improvements, especially in the working environment, to guarantee a better level of protection of the safety and health of workers;

Whereas this Directive does not justify any reduction in levels of protection already achieved in individual Member States, the Member State being committed, under the Treaty, to encouraging improvements in conditions in this area and to harmonizing conditions while maintaining the improvements made;

Whereas it is known that workers can be exposed to the effects of dangerous environmental factors at the work place during the course of their working life;

Whereas, pursuant to Article 118a of the Treaty, such Directives must avoid imposing administrative, financial and legal constraints which would hold back the creation and development of small and medium-sized undertakings;

[1] OJ No C 141, 30.5.1988, p. 1.
[2] OJ No C 326, 19.12.1988, p. 102, and OJ No C 158, 26.6.1989.
[3] OJ No C 175, 4.7.1988, p. 22.

Whereas the communication from the Commission on its programme concerning safety, hygiene and health at work[4] provides for the adoption of Directives designed to guarantee the safety and health of workers;

Whereas the Council, in its resolution of 21 December 1987 on safety, hygiene and health at work,[5] took note of the Commission's intention to submit to the Council in the near future a Directive on the organization of the safety and health of workers at the work place;

Whereas in February 1988 the European Parliament adopted four resolutions following the debate on the internal market and worker protection; whereas these resolutions specifically invited the Commission to draw up a framework Directive to serve as a basis for more specific Directives covering all the risks connected with safety and health at the work place;

Whereas Member States have a responsibility to encourage improvements in the safety and health of workers on their territory; whereas taking measures to protect the health and safety of workers at work also helps, in certain cases, to preserve the health and possibly the safety of persons residing with them;

Whereas Member States' legislative systems covering safety and health at the work place differ widely and need to be improved; whereas national provisions on the subject, which often include technical specifications and/or self-regulatory standards, may result in different levels of safety and health protection and allow competition at the expense of safety and health;

Whereas the incidence of accidents at work and occupational diseases is still too high; whereas preventive measures must be introduced or improved without delay in order to safeguard the safety and health of workers and ensure a higher degree of protection;

Whereas, in order to ensure an improved degree of protection, workers and/or their representatives must be informed of the risks to their safety and health and of the measures required to reduce or eliminate these risks; whereas they must also be in a position to contribute, by means of balanced participation in accordance with national laws and/or practices, to seeing that the necessary protective measures are taken;

Whereas information, dialogue and balanced participation on safety and health at work must be developed between employers and workers and/or their representatives by means of appropriate procedures and instruments, in accordance with national laws and/or practices;

Whereas the improvement of workers' safety, hygiene and health at work is an objective which should not be subordinated to purely economic considerations;

[4] OJ No C 28, 3.2.1988, p. 3.
[5] OJ No C 28, 3.2.1988, p. 1.

Whereas employers shall be obliged to keep themselves informed of the latest advances in technology and scientific findings concerning work-place design, account being taken of the inherent dangers in their undertaking, and to inform accordingly the workers' representatives exercising participation rights under this Directive, so as to be able to guarantee a better level of protection of workers' health and safety;

Whereas the provisions of this Directive apply, without prejudice to more stringent present or future Community provisions, to all risks, and in particular to those arising from the use at work of chemical, physical and biological agents covered by Directive 80/1107/EEC,[6] as last amended by Directive 88/642/EEC;[7]

Whereas, pursuant to Decision 74/325/EEC,[8] the Advisory Committee on Safety, Hygiene and Health Protection at Work is consulted by the Commission on the drafting of proposals in this field;

Whereas a Committee composed of members nominated by the Member States needs to be set up to assist the Commission in making the technical adaptations to the individual Directives provided for in this Directive.

HAS ADOPTED THIS DIRECTIVE:

SECTION 1
General provisions

Article 1

Object

1. The object of this Directive is to introduce measures to encourage improvements in the safety and health of workers at work.
2. To that end it contains general principles concerning the prevention of occupational risks, the protection of safety and health, the elimination of risks and accident factors, the informing, consultation, balanced participation in accordance with national laws and/or practices and training of workers and their representatives, as well as general guidelines for the implementation of the said principles.

---

[6] OJ No L 327, 3.12.1980, p. 8.
[7] OJ No L 356, 24.12.1988, p. 74.
[8] OJ No L 185, 9.7.1974, p. 15.

3. This Directive shall be without prejudice to existing or future national and Community provisions which are more favourable to protection of the safety and health of workers at work.

Article 2

Scope

1. This Directive shall apply to all sectors of activity, both public and private (industrial, agricultural, commercial, administrative, service, educational, cultural, leisure, etc.).

2. This Directive shall not be applicable where characteristics peculiar to certain specific public service activities, such as the armed forces or the police, or to certain specific activities in the civil protection services inevitably conflict with it.

In that event, the safety and health of workers must be ensured as far as possible in the light of the objectives of this Directive.

Article 3

Definitions

For the purposes of this Directive, the following terms shall have the following meanings:

(a) worker: any person employed by an employer, including trainees and apprentices but excluding domestic servants;
(b) employer: any natural or legal person who has an employment relationship with the worker and has responsibility for the undertaking and/or establishment;
(c) workers' representative with specific responsibility for the safety and health of workers: any person elected, chosen or designated in accordance with national laws and/or practices to represent workers where problems arise relating to the safety and health protection of workers at work;
(d) prevention: all the steps or measures taken or planned at all stages of work in the undertaking to prevent or reduce occupational risks.

Article 4

1. Member States shall take the necessary steps to ensure that employers, workers and workers' representatives are subject to the legal provisions necessary for the implementation of this Directive.

2. In particular, Member States shall ensure adequate controls and supervision.

SECTION 2
Employers' obligations

Article 5

General provision

1. The employer shall have a duty to ensure the safety and health of workers in every aspect related to the work.
2. Where, pursuant to Article 7(3), an employer enlists competent external services or persons, this shall not discharge him from his responsibilities in this area.
3. The workers' obligations in the field of safety and health at work shall not affect the principle of the responsibility of the employer.
4. This Directive shall not restrict the option of Member States to provide for the exclusion or the limitation of employers' responsibility where occurrences are due to unusual and unforeseeable circumstances, beyond the employers' control, or to exceptional events, the consequences of which could not have been avoided despite the exercise of all due care.

Member States need not exercise the option referred to in the first subparagraph.

Article 6

General obligations on employers

1. Within the context of his responsibilities, the employer shall take the measures necessary for the safety and health protection of workers, including prevention of occupational risks and provision of information and training, as well as provision of the necessary organization and means.

The employer shall be alert to the need to adjust these measures to take account of changing circumstances and aim to improve existing situations.
2. The employer shall implement the measures referred to in the first subparagraph of paragraph 1 on the basis of the following general principles of prevention:

(a) avoiding risks;
(b) evaluating the risks which cannot be avoided;
(c) combating the risks at source;

(d) adapting the work to the individual, especially as regards the design of work places, the choice of work equipment and the choice of working and production methods, with a view, in particular, to alleviating monotonous work and work at a predetermined work-rate and to reducing their effect on health.

(e) adapting to technical progress;

(f) replacing the dangerous by the non-dangerous or the less dangerous;

(g) developing a coherent overall prevention policy which covers technology, organization of work, working conditions, social relationships and the influence of factors related to the working environment;

(h) giving collective protective measures priority over individual protective measures;

(i) giving appropriate instructions to the workers.

3. Without prejudice to the other provisions of this Directive, the employer shall, taking into account the nature of the activities of the enterprise and/or establishment:

(a) evaluate the risks to the safety and health of workers, *inter alia* in the choice of work equipment, the chemical substances or preparations used, and the fitting-out of work places.

Subsequent to this evaluation and as necessary, the preventive measures and the working and production methods implemented by the employer must:
- assure an improvement in the level of protection afforded to workers with regard to safety and health,
- be integrated into all the activities of the undertaking and/or establishment and at all hierarchical levels;

(b) where he entrusts tasks to a worker, take into consideration the worker's capabilities as regards health and safety;

(c) ensure that the planning and introduction of new technologies are the subject of consultation with the workers and/or their representatives, as regards the consequences of the choice of equipment, the working conditions and the working environment for the safety and health of workers;

(d) take appropriate steps to ensure that only workers who have received adequate instructions may have access to areas where there is serious and specific danger.

4. Without prejudice to the other provisions of this Directive, where several undertakings share a work place, the employers shall co-operate in implementing the safety, health and occupational hygiene provisions and, taking into account the nature of the activities, shall coordinate their actions in matters of the protection and prevention of occupational risks, and shall

inform one another and their respective workers and/or workers' representatives of these risks.

5. Measures related to safety, hygiene and health at work may in no circumstances involve the workers in financial cost.

Article 7

Protective and preventive services

1. Without prejudice to the obligations referred to in Articles 5 and 6, the employer shall designate one or more workers to carry out activities related to the protection and prevention of occupational risks for the undertaking and/ or establishment.

2. Designated workers may not be placed at any disadvantage because of their activities related to the protection and prevention of occupational risks.

Designated workers shall be allowed adequate time to enable them to fulfill their obligations arising from this Directive.

3. If such protective and preventive measures cannot be organized for lack of competent personnel in the undertaking and/or establishment, the employer shall enlist competent external services or persons.

4. Where the employer enlists such services or persons, he shall inform them of the factors known to affect, or suspected of affecting, the safety and health of the workers and they must have access to the information referred to Article 10(2).

5. In all cases:

- the workers designated must have the necessary capabilities and the necessary means,
- the external services or persons consulted must have the necessary aptitudes and the necessary personal and professional means, and
- the workers designated and the external services or persons consulted must be sufficient in number to deal with the organization of protective and preventive measures, taking into account the size of the undertaking and/or establishment and/or the hazards to which the workers are exposed and their distribution throughout the entire undertaking and/or establishment.

6. The protection from, and prevention of, the health and safety risks which form the subject of this Article shall be the responsibility of one or more workers, of one service or of separate services whether from inside or outside the undertaking and/or establishment.

The worker(s) and/or agency(ies) must work together whenever necessary.

7. Member States may define, in the light of the nature of the activities and size of the undertakings, the categories of undertakings in which the employer,

provided he is competent, may himself take responsibility for the measures referred to in paragraph 1.

8. Member States shall define the necessary capabilities and aptitudes referred to in paragraph 5.

They may determine the sufficient number referred to in paragraph 5.

Article 8

First aid, fire-fighting and evacuation of workers, serious and imminent danger

1. The employer shall:
- take the necessary measures for first aid, fire-fighting and evacuation of workers, adapted to the nature of the activities and the size of the undertaking and/or establishment and taking into account other persons present,
- arrange any necessary contacts with external services, particularly as regards first aid, emergency medical care, rescue work and fire-fighting.

2. Pursuant to paragraph 1, the employer shall, *inter alia*, for first aid, fire-fighting and the evacuation of workers, designate the workers required to implement such measures.

The number of such workers, their training and the equipment available to them shall be adequate, taking account of the size and/or specific hazards of the undertaking and/or establishment.

3. The employer shall:

(a) as soon as possible, inform all workers who are, or may be, exposed to serious and imminent danger of the risk involved and of the steps taken or to be taken as regards protection;

(b) take action and give instructions to enable workers in the event of serious, imminent and unavoidable danger to stop work and/or immediately to leave the work place and proceed to a place of safety;

(c) save in exceptional cases for reasons duly substantiated, refrain from asking workers to resume work in a working situation where there is still a serious and imminent danger.

4. Workers who, in the event of serious, imminent and unavoidable danger, leave their workstation and/or a dangerous area may not be placed at any disadvantage because of their action and must be protected against any harmful and unjustified consequences, in accordance with national laws and/or practices.

5. The employer shall ensure that all workers are able, in the event of serious and imminent danger to their own safety and/or that of other persons, and

where the immediate superior responsible cannot be contacted, to take the appropriate steps in the light of their knowledge and the technical means at their disposal, to avoid the consequences of such danger.

Their actions shall not place them at any disadvantage, unless they acted carelessly or there was negligence on their part.

Article 9

Various obligations on employers

1. The employer shall:

(a) be in possession of an assessment of the risks to safety and health at work, including those facing groups of workers exposed to particular risks;
(b) decide on the protective measures to be taken and, if necessary, the protective equipment to be used;
(c) keep a list of occupational accidents resulting in a worker being unfit for work for more than three working days;
(d) draw up, for the responsible authorities and in accordance with national laws and/or practices, reports on occupational accidents suffered by his workers.

2. Member States shall define, in the light of the nature of the activities and size of the undertakings, the obligations to be met by the different categories of undertakings in respect of the drawing-up of the documents provided for in paragraph 1(a) and (b) and when preparing the documents provided for in paragraph 1(c) and (d).

Article 10

Worker information

1. The employer shall take appropriate measures so that workers and/or their representatives in the undertaking and/or establishment receive, in accordance with national laws and/or practices which may take account, *inter alia*, of the size of the undertaking and/or establishment, all the necessary information concerning:

(a) the safety and health risks and protective and preventive measures and activities in respect of both the undertaking and/or establishment in general and each type of workstation and/or job;
(b) the measures taken pursuant to Article 8(2).

2. The employer shall take appropriate measures so that employers of workers from any outside undertakings and/or establishments engaged in work in his

undertaking and/or establishment receive, in accordance with national laws and/or practices, adequate information concerning the points referred to in paragraph 1(a) and (b) which is to be provided to the workers in question.

3. The employer shall take appropriate measures so that workers with specific functions in protecting the safety and health of workers, or workers' representatives with specific responsibility for the safety and health of workers shall have access, to carry out their functions and in accordance with national laws and/or practices, to:

(a) the risk assessment and protective measures referred to in Article 9(1)(a) and (b);
(b) the list and reports referred to in Article 9(1)(c) and (d);
(c) the information yielded by protective and preventive measures, inspection agencies and bodies responsible for safety and health.

Article 11

Consultation and participation of workers

1. Employers shall consult workers and/or their representatives and allow them to take part in discussions on all questions relating to safety and health at work.

This presupposes:

− the consultation of workers
− the right of workers and/or their representatives to make proposals,
− balanced participation in accordance with national laws and/or practices.

2. Workers or workers' representatives with specific responsibility for the safety and health of workers shall take part in a balanced way, in accordance with national laws and/or practices, or shall be consulted in advance and in good time by the employer with regard to:

(a) any measure which may substantially affect safety and health;
(b) the designation of workers referred to in Articles 7(1) and 8(2) and the activities referred to in Article 7(1);
(c) the information referred to in Articles 9(1) and 10;
(d) the enlistment, where appropriate, of the competent services or persons outside the undertaking and/or establishment, as referred to in Article 7(3);
(e) the planning and organization of the training referred to in Article 12.

3. Workers' representatives with specific responsibility for the safety and health of workers shall have the right to ask the employer to take appropriate

measures and to submit proposals to him that to that end to mitigate hazards for workers and/or to remove sources of danger.

4. The workers referred to in paragraph 2 and the workers' representatives referred to in paragraphs 2 and 3 may not be placed at a disadvantage because of their respective activities referred to in paragraphs 2 and 3.

5. Employers must allow workers' representatives with specific responsibility for the safety and health of workers adequate time off work, without loss of pay, and provide them with the necessary means to enable such representatives to exercise their rights and functions deriving from this Directive.

6. Workers and/or their representatives are entitled to appeal, in accordance with national law and/or practice, to the authority responsible for safety and health protection at work if they consider that the measures taken and the means employed by the employer are inadequate for the purposes of ensuring safety and health at work.

Workers' representatives must be given the opportunity to submit their observations during inspection visits by the competent authority.

Article 12

Training of workers

1. The employer shall ensure that each worker receives adequate safety and health training, in particular in the form of information and instructions specific to his workstation or job:

- on recruitment,
- in the event of a transfer or a change of job,
- in the event of the introduction of new work equipment or a change in equipment,
- in the event of the introduction of any new technology.

The training shall be:

- adapted to take account of new or changed risks, and
- repeated periodically if necessary.

2. The employer shall ensure that workers from outside undertakings and/or establishments engaged in work in his undertaking and/or establishment have in fact received appropriate instructions regarding health and safety risks during their activities in his undertaking and/or establishment.

3. Workers' representatives with a specific role in protecting the safety and health of workers shall be entitled to appropriate training.

4. The training referred to in paragraphs 1 and 3 may not be at the workers' expense or at that of the workers' representatives.

The training referred to in paragraph 1 must take place during working hours.

The training referred to in paragraph 3 must take place during working hours or in accordance with national practice either within or outside the undertaking and/or the establishment.

SECTION 3
Workers' obligations

Article 13

1. It shall be the responsibility of each worker to take care as far as possible of his own safety and health and that of other persons affected by his acts or omissions at work in accordance with his training and the instructions given by his employer.

2. To this end, workers must in particular, in accordance with their training and the instructions given by their employer:

(a) make correct use of machinery, apparatus, tools, dangerous substances, transport equipment and other means of production;

(b) make correct use of the personal protective equipment supplied to them and, after use, return it to its proper place;

(c) refrain from disconnecting, changing or removing arbitrarily safety devices fitted, eg. to machinery, apparatus, tools, plant and buildings, and use such safety devices correctly;

(d) immediately inform the employer and/or the workers with specific responsibility for the safety and health of workers of any work situation they have reasonable grounds for considering represents a serious and immediate danger to safety and health and of any shortcomings in the protection arrangements;

(e) co-operate, in accordance with national practice, with the employer and/or workers with specific responsibility for the safety and health of workers, for as long as may be necessary to enable any tasks or requirements imposed by the competent authority to protect the safety and health of workers at work to be carried out;

(f) co-operate, in accordance with national practice, with the employer and/or workers with specific responsibility for the safety and health of workers, for as long as may be necessary to enable the employer to ensure that the working environment and working conditions are safe and pose no risk to safety and health within their field of activity.

SECTION 4
Miscellaneous provisions

Article 14

Health surveillance

1. To ensure that workers receive health surveillance appropriate to the health and safety risks they incur at work, measures shall be introduced in accordance with national laws and/or practices.
2. The measures referred to in paragraph 1 shall be such that each worker, if he so wishes, may receive health surveillance at regular intervals.
3. Health surveillance may be provided as part of a national health system.

Article 15

Particularly sensitive risk groups must be protected against the dangers which specifically affect them.

Article 16

Individual Directives – Amendments – General scope of this Directive

1. The Council, acting on a proposal from the Commission based on Article 118a of the Treaty, shall adopt individual Directives, *inter alia*, in the areas listed in the Annex.
2. This Directive and, without prejudice to the procedure referred to in Article 17 concerning technical adjustments, the individual Directives may be amended in accordance with the procedure provided for in Article 118a of the Treaty.
3. The provisions of this Directive shall apply in full to all the areas covered by the individual Directives, without prejudice to more stringent and/or specific provisions contained in these individual Directives.

Article 17

Committee

1. For the purely technical adjustments to the individual Directives provided for in Article 16(1) to take account of:

- the adoption of Directives in the field of technical harmonization and standardization, and/or
- technical progress, changes in international regulations or specifications, and new findings,

The Commission shall be assisted by a committee composed of the representatives of the Member States and chaired by the representative of the Commission.

2. The representative of the Commission shall submit to the committee a draft of the measures to be taken.

The committee shall deliver its Opinion on the draft within a time limit which the chairman may lay down according to the urgency of the matter.

The Opinion shall be delivered by the majority laid down in Article 148(2) of the Treaty in the case of decisions which the Council is required to adopt on a proposal from the Commission.

The votes of the representatives of the Member States within the committee shall be weighted in the manner set out in that Article. The chairman shall not vote.

3. The Commission shall adopt the measures envisaged if they are in accordance with the opinion of the committee. If the measures envisaged are not in accordance with the opinion of the committee, or if no opinion is delivered, the Commission shall, without delay, submit to the Council a proposal relating to the measures to be taken. The Council shall act by a qualified majority.

If, on the expiry of three months from the date of the referral to the Council, the Council has not acted, the proposed measures shall be adopted by the Commission.

Article 18

Final provisions

1. Member States shall bring into force the laws, regulations and administrative provisions necessary to comply with this Directive by 31 December 1992.

They shall forthwith inform the Commission thereof.

2. Member States shall communicate to the Commission the texts of the provision of national law which they have already adopted or adopt in the field covered by this Directive.

3. Member States shall report to the Commission every five years on the practical implementation of the provisions of this Directive, indicating the points of view of employers and workers.

The Commission shall inform the European Parliament, the Council, the Economic and Social Committee and the Advisory Committee on Safety, Hygiene and Health Protection at Work.

4. The Commission shall submit periodically to the European Parliament, the Council and the Economic and Social Committee a report on the implementation of this Directive, taking into account paragraphs 1 to 3.

Article 19

This Directive is addressed to the Member States.

Done at Luxembourg, 12 June 1989.

For the Council
The President
M. Chaves Gonzales

ANNEX
List of areas referred to in Article 16(1)

- Work places
- Work equipment
- Personal protective equipment
- Work with visual display units
- Handling of heavy loads involving risk of back injury
- Temporary or mobile work sites
- Fisheries and agriculture

COUNCIL DIRECTIVE
of 14 October 1991

on an employer's obligation to inform employees of the conditions applicable to the contract or employment relationship (91/533/EEC)

THE COUNCIL OF THE EUROPEAN COMMUNITIES,

Having regard to the Treaty establishing the European Economic Community, and particular Article 100 thereof,

Having regard to the proposal from the Commission,[1]

---

[1] OJ No C 24, 31.1.1991, p. 3.

Having regard to the opinion of the European Parliament,[2]

Having regard to the opinion of the Economic and Social Committee,[3]

Whereas the development, in the Member States, of new forms of work has led to an increase in the number of types of employment relationship;

Whereas, faced with this development, certain Member States have considered it necessary to subject employment relationships to formal requirements; whereas these provisions are designed to provide employees with improved protection against possible infringements of their rights and to create greater transparency on the labour market;

Whereas the relevant legislation of the Member States differs considerably on such fundamental points as the requirement to inform employees in writing of the main terms of the contract or employment relationship;

Whereas differences in the legislation of Member States may have a direct effect on the operation of the Common Market;

Whereas Article 117 of the Treaty provides for the Member States to agree upon the need to promote improved working conditions and an improved standard of living for workers, so as to make possible their harmonization while the improvement is being maintained;

Whereas point 9 of the Community Charter of Fundamental Social Rights for Workers, adopted at the Strasbourg European Council on 9 December 1989 by the Heads of State and Government of 11 Member States, states:

'The conditions of employment of every worker of the European Community shall be stipulated in laws, a collective agreement or a contract of employment, according to arrangements applying in each country.';

Whereas it is necessary to establish at Community level the general requirement that every employee must be provided with a document containing information on the essential elements of his contract or employment relationship;

Whereas, in view of the need to maintain a certain degree of flexibility in employment relationships, Member States should be able to exclude certain limited cases of employment relationship from this Directive's scope of application;

Whereas the obligation to provide information may be met by means of a written contract, a letter of appointment or one or more other documents or, if they are lacking, a written statement signed by the employer;

Whereas, in the case of expatriation of the employee, the latter must, in addition to the main terms of his contract or employment relationship, be supplied with relevant information connected with his secondment;

[2] OJ No C 240, 16.9.1991, p. 21.
[3] OJ No C 159, 17.6.1991, p. 32.

Whereas, in order to protect the interests of employees with regard to obtaining a document, any change in the main terms of the contract or employment relationship must be communicated to them in writing;

Whereas it is necessary for Member States to guarantee that employees can claim the rights conferred on them by this Directive;

Whereas Member States are to adopt the laws, regulations and legislative provisions necessary to comply with this Directive or are to ensure that both sides of industry set up the necessary provisions by agreement, with Member States being obliged to take the necessary steps enabling them at all times to guarantee the results imposed by this Directive,

HAS ADOPTED THIS DIRECTIVE:

Article 1

Scope

1. This Directive shall apply to every paid employee having a contract or employment relationship defined by the law in force in a Member State and/ or governed by the law in force in a Member State.
2. Member States may provide that this Directive shall not apply to employees having a contract or employment relationship:

(a)   – with a total duration not exceeding one month, and/or
     – with a working week not exceeding eight hours; or
(b)   – of a casual and/or specific nature provided, in these cases, that its non-application is justified by objective considerations.

Article 2

Obligation to provide information

1. An employer shall be obliged to notify an employee to whom this Directive applies, hereinafter referred to as 'the employee', of the essential aspects of the contract or employment relationship.
2. The information referred to in paragraph 1 shall cover at least the following:

(a) the identities of the parties;
(b) the place of work; where there is no fixed or main place of work, the principle that the employee is employed at various places and the registered place of business or, where appropriate, the domicile of the employer;
(c) (i) the title, grade, nature or category of the work for which the employee is employed; or

(ii) a brief specification or description of the work;

(d) the date of commencement of the contract or employment relationship;

(e) in the case of a temporary contract or employment relationship, the expected duration thereof;

(f) the amount of paid leave to which the employee is entitled or, where this cannot be indicated when the information is given, the procedures for allocating and determining such leave;

(g) the length of the periods of notice to be observed by the employer and the employee should their contract or employment relationship be terminated or, where this cannot be indicated when the information is given, the method for determining such periods of notice;

(h) the initial basic amount, the other component elements and the frequency of payment of the remuneration to which the employee is entitled;

(i) the length of the employee's normal working day or week;

(j) where appropriate;

(i) the collective agreements governing the employee's conditions of work;

or

(ii) in the case of collective agreements concluded outside the business by special joint bodies or institutions, the name of the competent body or joint institution within which the agreements were concluded.

3. The information referred to in paragraph 2 (f), (g), (h), and (i) may, where appropriate, be given in the form of a reference to the laws, regulations and administrative or statutory provisions or collective agreements governing those particular points.

Article 3

Means of information

1. The information referred to in Article 2(2) may be given to the employee, not later than two months after the commencement of employment, in the form of:

(a) a written contract of employment; and/or

(b) a letter of engagement; and/or

(c) one or more other written documents, where one of these documents contains at least all the information referred to in Article 2(2)(a), (b), (c), (d), (h), and (i).

2. Where none of the documents referred to in paragraph 1 is handed over to the employee within the prescribed period, the employer shall be obliged to give the employee, not later than two months after the commencement of

employment, a written declaration signed by the employer and containing at least the information referred to in Article 2(2).

Where the document(s) referred to in paragraph 1 contain only part of the information required, the written declaration provided for in the first subparagraph of this paragraph shall cover the remaining information.

3. Where the contract or employment relationship comes to an end before expiry of a period of two months as from the date of the start of work, the information provided for in Article 2 and this Article must be made available to the employee by the end of this period at the latest.

Article 4

Expatriate employees

1. Where an employee is required to work in a country or countries other than the Member State whose law and/or practice governs the contract of employment relationship, the document(s) referred to in Article 3 must be in his/her possession before his/her departure and must include at least the following additional information:

(a)   the duration of the employment abroad;
(b)   the currency to be used for the payment of remuneration;
(c)   where appropriate, the benefits in cash or kind attendant on the employment abroad;
(d)   where appropriate, the conditions governing the employees's repatriation.

2. The information referred to in paragraph 1(b) and (c) may, where appropriate, be given in the form of a reference to the laws, regulations and administrative or statutory provisions or collective agreements governing those particular points.

3. Paragraphs 1 and 2 shall not apply if the duration of the employment outside the country whose laws and/or practice governs the contract or employment relationship is one month or less.

Article 5

Modification of aspects of the contract or employment relationship

1. Any change in the details referred to in Article 2(2) and 4(1) must be the subject of a written document to be given by the employer to the employee at the earliest opportunity and not later than one month after the date of entry into effect of the change in question.

2. The written document referred to in paragraph 1 shall not be compulsory in the event of a change in the laws, regulations and administrative or statutory provisions or collective agreements cited in the documents referred to in Article 3, supplemented, where appropriate, pursuant to Article 4(1).

Article 6

Form and proof of the existence of a contract or employment relationship and procedural rules

This Directive shall be without prejudice to national law and practice concerning:

- the form of the contract or employment relationship,
- proof as regards the existence and content of a contract or employment relationship,
- the relevant procedural rules.

Article 7

More favourable provisions

This Directive shall not affect Member States' prerogative to apply or to introduce laws, regulations or administrative provisions which are more favourable to employees or to encourage or permit the application of agreements which are more favourable to employees.

Article 8

Defence of rights

1. Member States shall introduce into their national legal systems such measures as are necessary to enable all employees who consider themselves wronged by failure to comply with the obligations arising from this Directive to pursue their claims by judicial process after possible recourse to other competent authorities.

2. Member States may provide that access to the means of redress referred to in paragraph 1 are subject to the notification of the employer by the employee and the failure by the employer to reply within 15 days of notification.

However, the formality of prior notification may in no case be required in the cases referred to in Article 4, neither for workers with a temporary contract or employment relationship, nor for employees not covered by a collective agreement or by collective agreements relating to the employment relationship.

Article 9

Final provisions

1. Member States shall adopt the laws, regulations and administrative provisions necessary to comply with this Directive no later than 30 June 1993 or shall ensure by that date that the employers' and workers' representatives introduce the required provisions by way of agreement, the Member States being obliged to take the necessary steps enabling them at all times to guarantee the results imposed by this Directive.

They shall forthwith inform the Commission thereof.

2. Member States shall take the necessary measures to ensure that, in the case of employment relationships in existence upon entry into force of the provisions that they adopt, the employer gives the employee, on request, within two months of receiving that request, any of the documents referred to in Article 3, supplemented, where appropriate, pursuant to Article 4(1).

3. When Member States adopt the measures referred to in paragraph 1, such measures shall contain a reference to this Directive or shall be accompanied by such reference on the occasion of their official publication. The methods of making such a reference shall be laid down by the Member States.

4. Member States shall forthwith inform the Commission of the measures they take to implement the Directive.

Article 10

This Directive is addressed to the Member States.

Done at Luxembourg, 14 October 1991.

For the Council
The President
B. de Vries

COUNCIL DIRECTIVE 92/56 EEC of 24 June 1992

amending Directive 75/129/EEC on the approximation of the laws of the Member States relating to collective redundancies

THE COUNCIL OF THE EUROPEAN COMMUNITIES,

Having regard to the Treaty establishing the European Economic Community, and in particular Article 100 thereof,

Having regard to the proposal from the Commission[1],

Having regard to the Opinion of the European Parliament[2],

Having regard to the Opinion of the Economic and Social Committee[3],

Whereas the Community Charter of the Fundamental Social Rights of Workers, adopted at the Regulation Council meeting held in Strasbourg on 9 December 1989 by the Heads of State or Government of eleven Member States, states *inter alia* in point 7, first paragraph, first sentence, and second paragraph; in point 17, first paragraph; and in point 18, third indent:

7. The completion of the internal market must lead to an improvement in the living and working conditions of workers in the European Community (...).

    The improvement must cover, where necessary, the development of certain aspects of employment regulations such as procedures for collective redundancies and those regarding bankruptcies.

17. Information, consultation and participation for workers must be developed along appropriate lines, taking account of the practices in force in the various Member States.

    (...)

18. Such information, consultation and participation must be implemented in due time, particularly in the following cases:

    (−...)

    (−...)

    − in cases of collective redundancy procedures;

    (−...)';

Whereas, in order to calculate the number of redundancies provided for in the definition of collective redundancies within the meaning of Council Directive 75/129/EEC of 17 February 1975 on the approximation of the laws of the Member States relating to collective redundancies[4], other forms of termination of employment contracts on the initiative of the employer should be equated to redundancies, provided that there are at least five redundancies;

Whereas it should be stipulated that Directive 75/129/EEC applies in principle also to collective redundancies resulting where the establishment's activities are terminated as a result of a judicial decision;

Whereas the Member States should be given the option of stipulating that workers' representatives may call on experts on grounds of the technical complexity of the matters which are likely to be the subject of the informing and consulting;

[1] OJ No C 310, 30.11.1991, p. 5 and OJ No C 117, 8.5.1992, p. 10.
[2] OJ No C 94, 13.4.1992, p. 157.
[3] OJ No C 79, 30.3.1992, p. 12.
[4] OJ No L 48, 22.2.1975, p. 29.

Whereas the provisions of Directive 75/129/EEC should be clarified and supplemented as regards the employers's obligations regarding the informing and consulting of workers' representatives;

Whereas it is necessary to ensure that employers' obligations as regards information, consultation and notification apply independently of the fact that the decision on collective redundancies emanates from the employer or from an undertaking which controls that employer;

Whereas Member States should ensure that workers' representatives and/ or workers have at their disposal administrative and/or judicial procedures in order to ensure that the obligations laid down in Directive 75/129/EEC are fulfilled,

HAS ADOPTED THIS DIRECTIVE:

Article 1

Directive 75/129/EEC is hereby amended as follows:

1. Article 1 shall be amended as follows:
    (a) the following subparagraph shall be added to paragraph 1:
        'For the purpose of calculating the number of redundancies provided for in the first subparagraph of point (a), terminations of an employment contract which occur to the individual workers concerned shall be assimilated to redundancies, provided that there are at least five redundancies.';
    (b) subparagraph 2 (d) shall be deleted.
2. Section II shall be replaced by the following:

    'SECTION II

Information and consultation

Article 2

1. Where an employer is contemplating collective redundancies, he shall begin consultations with the workers' representatives in good time with a view to reaching an agreement.

2. These consultations shall, at least, cover ways and means of avoiding collective redundancies or reducing the numbers of workers affected, and of mitigating the consequences by recourse to accompanying social measures aimed, *inter alia*, at aid for redeploying or retraining workers made redundant.

Member States may provide that the workers' representatives may call upon the services of experts in accordance with national legislation and/or practice.

3. To enable workers' representatives to make constructive proposals, the employers shall in good time during the course of the consultations:

(a) supply them with all relevant information and
(b) in any event notify them in writing of:
    (i)   the reasons for the projected redundancies;
    (ii) the number of categories of workers to be made redundant;
    (iii) the number and categories of workers normally employed;
    (iv) the period over which the projected redundancies are to be effected;
    (v) the criteria proposed for the selection of the workers to be made redundant in so far as national legislation and/or practice confers the power therefore upon the employer;
    (vi) the method for calculating any redundancy payments other than those arising out of national legislation and/or practice.

The employer shall forward to the competent authority a copy of, at least, the elements of the written communication which are provided for in the first subparagraph, point (b), subpoints (i) to (v).

4. The obligations laid down in paragraphs 1, 2 and 3 shall apply irrespective of whether the decision regarding collective redundancies is being taken by the employer or by an undertaking controlling the employer.

In considering alleged breaches of the information, consultation and notification requirements laid down by this Directive, account shall not be taken of any defence on the part of the employer on the ground that the necessary information has not been provided to the employer by the undertaking which took the decision leading to collective redundancies.';

3. in Article 3(1) the following subparagraph shall be added after the first subparagraph:

'However, Member States may provide that in the case of planned collective redundancies arising from termination of the establishment's activities as a result of a judicial decision, the employer shall be obliged to notify the competent public authority in writing only if the latter so requests.';

4. in Article 4, the following paragraph shall be added after paragraph 3:

'4. Member States need not apply this Directive to collective redundancies arising from termination of the establishment's activities where this is the result of a judicial decision.';

5. the following phrase shall be inserted at the end of Article 5:
    'or to promote or to allow the application of collective agreements more favourable to workers.';
6. the following text shall be inserted after Article 5:
    '*Article 5a*
    Member States shall ensure that judicial and/or administrative procedures for the enforcement of obligations under this Directive are available to the workers' representatives and/or workers.'

Article 2

1. Member States shall bring into force the laws, regulations and administrative provisions necessary to comply with this Directive at the latest two years after its adoption or shall ensure, at the latest two years after adoption, that the employers' and workers' representatives introduce the required provisions by way of agreement, the Member States being obliged to take the necessary steps enabling them at all times to guarantee the results imposed by this Directive.

They shall immediately inform the Commission thereof.

2. When Member States adopt the provisions referred to in paragraph 1, such provision shall contain a reference to this Directive or shall be accompanied by such reference at the time of their official publication. The procedure for such reference shall be adopted by Member States.

3. Member States shall forward to the Commission the text of any fundamental provisions of national law already adopted or being adopted in the area governed by this Directive.

Article 3

This Directive is addressed to the Member States.

Done at Luxembourg, 24 June 1992.

For the Council
The President
José da SILVA PENEDA

COUNCIL DIRECTIVE 92/85/EEC of 19 October 1992*

on the introduction of measures to encourage improvements in the safety and health at work of pregnant workers and workers

who have recently given birth or are breastfeeding (tenth individual Directive within the meaning of Article 16 (1) of Directive 89/391/EEC)

THE COUNCIL OF THE EUROPEAN COMMUNITIES

Having regard to the Treaty establishing the European Economic Community, and in particular Article 118a thereof,

Having regard to the proposal from the Commission, drawn up after consultation with the Advisory Committee on Safety, Hygiene and Health Protection at work[1],

In co-operation with the European Parliament[2],

Having regard to the opinion of the Economic and Social Committee[3],

Whereas Article 118a of the Treaty provides that the Council shall adopt, by means of directives, minimum requirements for encouraging improvements, especially in the working environment, to protect the safety and health of workers;

Whereas this Directive does not justify any reduction in levels of protection already achieved in individual Member States, the Member States being committed, under the Treaty, to encouraging improvements in conditions in this area and to harmonizing conditions while maintaining the improvements made;

Whereas, under the terms of Article 118a of the Treaty, the said directives are to avoid imposing administrative, financial and legal constraints in a way which would hold back the creation and development of small and medium-sized undertakings;

Whereas, pursuant to Decision 74/325/EEC[4], as last amended by the 1985 Act of Accession, the Advisory Committee on Safety, Hygiene and Health protection at Work is consulted by the Commission on the drafting of proposals in this field;

* Annex omitted

Whereas the Community Charter of the fundamental social rights of workers, adopted at the Strasbourg European Council on 9 December 1989 by the Heads of State or Government of 11 Member States, lays down, in paragraph 19 in particular, that:

[1] OJ No C 281, 9.11.1990, p. 3; and OJ No C 25, 1.2.1991, p. 9.
[2] OJ No C 19, 28.1.1991, p. 177; and OJ No C 150, 15.6.1992, p. 99
[3] OJ No C 41, 18.2.1991, p. 29.
[4] OJ No L 185, 9.7.1974, p. 15.

'Every worker must enjoy satisfactory health and safety conditions in his working environment. Appropriate measures must be taken in order to achieve further harmonization of conditions in this area while maintaining the improvements made';

Whereas the Commission, in its action programme for the implementation of the Community Charter of the fundamental social rights of workers, has included among its aims the adoption by the Council of a Directive on the protection of pregnant women at work;

Whereas Article 15 of Council Directive 89/391/EEC of 12 June 1989 on the introduction of measures to encourage improvements in the safety and health of workers at work[5] provides that particularly sensitive risk groups must be protected against the dangers which specifically affect them;

Whereas pregnant workers, workers who have recently given birth or who are breastfeeding must be considered a specific risk group in many respects, and measures must be taken with regard to their safety and health;

Whereas the protection of the safety and health of pregnant workers, workers who have recently given birth or workers who are breastfeeding should not treat women on the labour market unfavourably nor work to the detriment of directives concerning equal treatment for men and women;

Whereas some types of activities may pose a specific risk, for pregnant workers, workers who have recently given birth or workers who are breast-feeding, of exposure to dangerous agents, processes or working conditions; whereas such risks must therefore be assessed and the result of such assessment communicated to female workers and/or their representatives;

Whereas, further, should the result of this assessment reveal the existence of a risk to the safety or health of the female worker, provision must be made for such worker to be protected;

Whereas pregnant workers and workers who are breastfeeding must not engage in activities which have been assessed as revealing a risk of exposure, jeopardizing safety and health, to certain particularly dangerous agents or working conditions;

Whereas provision should be made for pregnant workers, workers who have recently given birth or workers who are breastfeeding not to be required to work at night where such provision is necessary from the point of view of their safety and health;

Whereas the vulnerability of pregnant workers, workers who have recently given birth or are breastfeeding makes it necessary for them to be granted the right to maternity leave of at least 14 continuous weeks, allocated before and/

[5] OJ No L 183, 29.6.1989, p. 1.

or after confinement, and renders necessary the compulsory nature of maternity leave of at least two weeks, allocated before and/or after confinement;

Whereas the risk of dismissal for reasons associated with their condition may have harmful effects on the physical and mental state of pregnant workers, workers who have recently given birth or who are breastfeeding; whereas provision should be made for such dismissal to be prohibited;

Whereas measures for the organization of work concerning the protection of the health of pregnant workers, workers who have recently given birth or workers who are breastfeeding would serve no purpose unless accompanied by the maintenance of rights linked to the employment contract, including maintenance of payment and/or entitlement to an adequate allowance;

Whereas, moreover, provision concerning maternity leave would also serve no purpose unless accompanied by the maintenance of rights linked to the employment contract and/or entitlement to an adequate allowance;

Whereas the concept of an adequate allowance in the case of maternity leave must be regarded as a technical point of reference with a view to fixing the minimum level of protection and should in no circumstances be interpreted as suggesting an analogy between pregnancy and illness,

HAS ADOPTED THIS DIRECTIVE

SECTION 1

PURPOSE AND DEFINITIONS

Article 1

Purpose

1. The purpose of this Directive, which is the tenth individual Directive within the meaning of Article 16(1) of Directive 89/391/EEC, is to implement measures to encourage improvements in the safety and health at work of pregnant workers and workers who have recently given birth or who are breastfeeding.

2. The provisions of Directive 89/391/EEC, except for Article 2(2) thereof, shall apply in full to the whole area covered by paragraph 1, without prejudice to any more stringent and/or specific provisions contained in this Directive.

3. This Directive may not have the effect of reducing the level of protection afforded to pregnant workers, workers who have recently given birth or who are breastfeeding as compared with the situation which exists in each Member State on the date on which this Directive is adopted.

Article 2

Definitions

For the purposes of this Directive:

(a) *pregnant worker* shall mean a pregnant worker who informs her employer of her condition, in accordance with national legislation and/or national practice;

(b) *worker who has recently given birth* shall mean a worker who has recently given birth within the meaning of national legislation and/or national practice and who informs her employer of her condition, in accordance with that legislation and/or practice;

(c) *worker who is breastfeeding* shall mean a worker who is breastfeeding within the meaning of national legislation and/or national practice and who informs her employer of her condition, in accordance with that legislation and/or practice.

SECTION 2

GENERAL PROVISIONS

Article 3

Guidelines

1. In consultation with the Member States and assisted by the Advisory Committee on Safety, Hygiene and Health Protection at Work, the Commission shall draw up guidelines on the assessment of the chemical, physical and biological agents and industrial processes considered hazardous for the safety or health of workers within the meaning of Article 2.

The guidelines referred to in the first subparagraph shall also cover movements and postures, mental and physical fatigue and other types of physical and mental stress connected with the work done by workers within the meaning of Article 2.

2. The purpose of the guidelines referred to in paragraph 1 is to serve as a basis for the assessment referred to in Article 4(1).

To this end, Member States shall bring these guidelines to the attention of all employers and all female workers and/or their representatives in the respective Member State.

Article 4

Assessment and information

1. For all activities liable to involve a specific risk of exposure to the agents, processes or working conditions of which a non-exhaustive list is given in Annex 1, the employer shall assess the nature, degree and duration of exposure, in the undertaking and/or establishment concerned, of workers within the meaning of Article 2, either directly or by way of the protective and preventive services referred to in Article 7 of Directive 89/391/EEC, in order to:

- assess any risks to the safety or health and any possible effect on the pregnancies or breastfeeding of workers within the meaning of Article 2,
- decide what measures should be taken.

2. Without prejudice to Article 10 of Directive 89/391/EEC, workers within the meaning of Article 2 and workers likely to be in one of the situations referred to in Article 2 in the undertaking and/or establishment concerned and/or their representatives shall be informed of the results of the assessment referred to in paragraph 1 and of all measures to be taken concerning health and safety at work.

Article 5

Action further to the results of the assessment

1. Without prejudice to Article 6 of Directive 89/391/EEC, if the results of the assessment referred to in Article 4(1) reveal a risk to the safety or health or an effect on the pregnancy or breastfeeding of a worker within the meaning of Article 2, the employer shall take the necessary measures to ensure that, by temporarily adjusting the working conditions and/or the working hours of the worker concerned, the exposure of that worker to such risks is avoided.
2. If the adjustment of her working conditions and/or working hours is not technically and/or objectively feasible, or cannot reasonably be required on duly substantiated grounds, the employer shall take the necessary measures to move the worker concerned to another job.
3. If moving her to another job is not technically and/or objectively feasible or cannot reasonably be required on duly substantiated grounds, the worker concerned shall be granted leave in accordance with national legislation and/or national practice for the whole of the period necessary to protect her safety or health.

4. The provisions of this Article shall apply *mutatis mutandis* to the case where a worker pursuing an activity which is forbidden pursuant to Article 6 becomes pregnant or starts breastfeeding and informs her employer thereof.

Article 6

Cases in which exposure is prohibited

In addition to the general provisions concerning the protection of workers, in particular those relating to the limit values for occupational exposure:

1. pregnant workers within the meaning of Article 2(a) may under no circumstances be obliged to perform duties for which the assessment has revealed a risk of exposure, which would jeopardize safety or health, to the agents and working conditions listed in Annex II, Section A;
2. workers who are breastfeeding, within the meaning of Article 2(c), may under no circumstances be obliged to perform duties for which the assessment has revealed a risk of exposure, which would jeopardize safety or health, to the agents and working conditions listed in Annex II, Section B.

Article 7

Night Work

1. Member States shall take the necessary measures to ensure that workers referred to in Article 2 are not obliged to perform night work during their pregnancy and for a period following childbirth which shall be determined by the national authority competent for safety and health, subject to submission, in accordance with the procedures laid down by the Member States, of a medical certificate stating that this is necessary for the safety or health of the worker concerned.
2. The measures referred to in paragraph 1 must entail the possibility, in accordance with national legislation and/or national practice, of:

(a) transfer to daytime work; or
(b) leave from work or extension of maternity leave where such a transfer is not technically and/or objectively feasible or cannot reasonably be required on duly substantiated grounds.

Article 8

Maternity leave

1. Member States shall take the necessary measures to ensure that workers within the meaning of Article 2 are entitled to a continuous period of maternity leave of at least 14 weeks allocated before and/or after confinement in accordance with national legislation and/or practice.
2. The maternity leave stipulated in paragraph 1 must include compulsory maternity leave of at least two weeks allocated before and/or after confinement in accordance with national legislation and/or practice.

Article 9

Time off for ante-natal examinations

Member States shall take the necessary measures to ensure that pregnant workers within the meaning of Article 2(a) are entitled to, in accordance with national legislation and/or practice, time off, without loss of pay, in order to attend ante-natal examinations, if such examinations have to take place during working hours.

Article 10

Prohibition of dismissal

In order to guarantee workers, within the meaning of Article 2, the exercise of their health and safety protection rights as recognized under this Article, it shall be provided that:

1. Member States shall take the necessary measures to prohibit the dismissal of workers, within the meaning of Article 2, during the period from the beginning of their pregnancy to the end of the maternity leave referred to in Article 8(1), save in exceptional cases not connected with their condition which are permitted under national legislation and/or practice and, where applicable, provided that the competent authority has given its consent;
2. if a worker, within the meaning of Article 2, is dismissed during the period referred to in point 1, the employer must cite duly substantiated grounds for her dismissal in writing;
3. Member States shall take the necessary measures to protect workers, within the meaning of Article 2, from consequences of dismissal which is unlawful by virtue of point 1.

Article 11

Employment rights

In order to guarantee workers within the meaning of Article 2 the exercise of their health and safety protection rights as recognized in this Article, it shall be provided that:

1. in the cases referred to Articles 5, 6 and 7, the employment rights relating to the employment contract, including the maintenance of a payment to, and/or entitlement to an adequate allowance for, workers within the meaning of Article 2, must be ensured in accordance with national legislation and/or national practice;
2. in the cases referred to Article 8, the following must be ensured:
    (a) the rights connected with the employment contract of workers within the meaning of Article 2, other than those referred to in point (b) below;
    (b) maintenance of a payment to, and/or entitlement to an adequate allowance for, workers within the meaning of Article 2;
3. the allowance referred to in point 2(b) shall be deemed adequate if it guarantees income at least equivalent to that which the worker concerned would receive in the event of a break in her activities on grounds connected with her state of health, subject to any ceiling laid down under national legislation;
4. Member States may make entitlement to pay or the allowance referred to in points 1 and 2(b) conditional upon the worker concerned fulfilling the conditions of eligibility for such benefits laid down under national legislation.
    These conditions may under no circumstances provide for periods of previous employment in excess of 12 months immediately prior to the presumed date of confinement.

Article 12

Defence of rights

Member States shall introduce into their national legal systems such measures as are necessary to enable all workers who should consider themselves wronged by failure to comply with the obligations arising from this Directive to pursue their claims by judicial process (and/or, in accordance with national laws and/or practices) by recourse to other competent authorities.

Article 13

Amendments to the Annexes

1. Strictly technical adjustments to Annex I as a result of technical progress, changes in international regulations or specifications and new findings in the area covered by this Directive shall be adopted in accordance with the procedure laid down in Article 17 of Directive 89/391/EEC.

2. Annex II may be amended only in accordance with the procedure laid down in Article 118a of the Treaty.

Article 14

Final provisions

1. Member States shall bring into force the laws, regulations and administrative provisions necessary to comply with this Directive not later than two years after the adoption thereof or ensure, at the latest two years after adoption of this Directive, that the two sides of industry introduce the requisite provisions by means of collective agreements, with Member States being required to make all the necessary provisions to enable them at all times to guarantee the results laid down by this Directive. They shall forthwith inform the Commission thereof.

2. When Member States adopt the measures referred to in paragraph 1, they shall contain a reference of this Directive or shall be accompanied by such reference on the occasion of their official publication. The methods of making such a reference shall be laid down by the Member States.

3. Member States shall communicate to the Commission the texts of the essential provisions of national law which they have already adopted or adopt in the field governed by this Directive.

4. Member States shall report to the Commission every five years on the practical implementation of the provisions of this Directive, indicating the points of view of the two sides of industry.

However, Member States shall report for the first time to the Commission on the practical implementation of the provisions of this Directive, indicating the points of view of the two sides of industry, four years after its adoption.

The Commission shall inform the European Parliament, the Council, the Economic and Social Committee and the Advisory Committee on Safety, Hygiene and Health Protection at Work.

5. The Commission shall periodically submit to the European Parliament, the Council and the Economic and Social Committee a report on the implementation of this Directive, taking into account paragraphs 1, 2 and 3.

6. The Council will re-examine this Directive on the basis of an assessment carried out on the basis of the reports referred to in the second subparagraph of paragraph 4 and, should the need arise, of a proposal, to be submitted by the Commission at the latest five years after adoption of the Directive.

Article 15

This Directive is addressed to the Member States.
Done at Luxembourg, 19 October 1992.

For the Council
The President
D. CURRY

COUNCIL DIRECTIVE 93/104/EEC of 23 November 1993

concerning certain aspects of the organization of working time

THE COUNCIL OF THE EUROPEAN UNION,
Having regard to the Treaty establishing the European Community, and in particular Article 118a thereof,
Having regard to the proposal from the Commission[1],
In co-operation with the European Parliament[2],
Having regard to the Opinion of the Economic and Social Committee[3],
Whereas Article 118a of the treaty provides that the Council shall adopt, by means of directives, minimum requirements for encouraging improvements, especially in the working environment, to ensure a better level of protection of the safety and health of workers;
Whereas, under the terms of that Article, those directives are to avoid imposing administrative, financial and legal constraints in a way which would hold back the creation and development of small and medium-sized undertakings;
Whereas the provisions of Council Directive 89/391/EEC of 12 June 1989 on the introduction of measures to encourage improvements in the safety and

[1] OJ No C 254, 9.10.1990, p. 4.
[2] OJ No C 72, 18.3.1991, p. 95; and OJ No C 315, 27.10.1993, p.125.
[3] OJ No C 60, 8.3.1991, p. 26.

health of workers at work[+] are fully applicable to the areas covered by this Directive without prejudice to more stringent and/or specific provisions contained therein;

Whereas the Community Charter of the Fundamental Social Rights of Workers, adopted at the meeting of the European Council held at Strasbourg on 9 December 1989 by the Heads of State or of Government of 11 member States, and in particular points 7, first subparagraph, 8 and 19, first subparagraph, thereof, declared that:

'7. The completion of the internal market must lead to an improvement in the living and working conditions of workers in the European Community. This process must result from an approximation of these conditions while the improvement is being maintained, as regards in particular the duration and organization of working time and forms of employment other than open-ended contracts, such as fixed-term contracts, part-time working, temporary work and seasonal work.

8. Every worker in the European Community shall have a right to a weekly rest period and to annual paid leave, the duration of which must be progressively harmonized in accordance with national practices.

19. Every worker must enjoy satisfactory health and safety conditions in his working environment. Appropriate measures must be taken in order to achieve further harmonization of the conditions in this area while maintaining the improvements made.';

Whereas the improvement of workers' safety, hygiene and health at work is an objective which should not be subordinated to purely economic considerations;

Whereas this Directive is a practical contribution towards creating the social dimension of the internal market;

Whereas laying down minimum requirements with regard to the organization of working time is likely to improve the working conditions of workers in the Community;

Whereas, in order to ensure the safety and health of Community workers, the latter must be granted minimum daily, weekly and annual periods of rest and adequate breaks; whereas it is also necessary in this context to place a maximum limit on weekly working hours;

Whereas account should be taken of the principles of the International Labour Organization with regard to the organization of working time, including those relating to night work;

Whereas, with respect to the weekly rest period, due account should be taken of the diversity of cultural, ethnic, religious and other factors in the Member States;

[+] OJ No L 183, 29.6.1989, p.1.

Whereas, in particular, it is ultimately for each Member State to decide whether Sunday should be included in the weekly rest period, and if so to what extent;

Whereas research has shown that the human body is more sensitive at night to environmental disturbances and also to certain burdensome forms of work organization and that long periods of night work can be detrimental to the health of workers and can endanger safety at the workplace;

Whereas there is a need to limit the duration of periods of night work, including overtime, and to provide for employers who regularly use night workers to bring this information to the attention of the competent authorities if they so request;

Whereas it is important that night workers should be entitled to a free health assessment prior to their assignment and thereafter at regular intervals and that whenever possible they should be transferred to day work for which they are suited if they suffer from health problems;

Whereas the situation of night and shift workers requires that the level of safety and health protection should be adapted to the nature of their work and that the organization and functioning of protection and prevention services and resources should be efficient;

Whereas specific working conditions may have detrimental effects on the safety and health of workers; whereas the organization of work according to a certain pattern must take account of the general principle of adapting work to the worker;

Whereas, given the specific nature of the work concerned, it may be necessary to adopt separate measures with regard to the organization of working time in certain sectors or activities which are excluded from the scope of this Directive;

Whereas, in view of the question likely to be raised by the organization of working time within an undertaking, it appears desirable to provide for flexibility in the application of certain provisions of this Directive, whilst ensuring compliance with the principles of protecting the safety and health of workers;

Whereas it is necessary to provide that certain provisions may be subject to derogations implemented, according to the case, by the Member States or the two sides of industry; whereas, as a general rule, in the event of a derogation, the workers concerned must be given equivalent compensatory rest periods,

HAS ADOPTED THIS DIRECTIVE:

SECTION 1

SCOPE AND DEFINITIONS

Article 1

Purpose and scope

1. This Directive lays down minimum safety and health requirements for the organization of working time.

   2. This Directive applies to:

(a) minimum periods of daily rest, weekly rest and annual leave, to breaks and maximum weekly working time; and

(b) certain aspects of night work, shift work and patterns of work.

3. This Directive shall apply to all sectors of activity, both public and private, within the meaning of Article 2 of Directive 89/391/EEC, without prejudice to Article 17 of this Directive, with the exception of air, rail, road, sea, inland waterway and lake transport, sea fishing, other work at sea and the activities of doctors in training;

4. The provisions of Directive 89/391/EEC are fully applicable to the matters referred to in paragraph 2, without prejudice to more stringent and/or specific provisions contained in this Directive.

Article 2

Definitions

For the purposes of this Directive, the following definitions shall apply:

1. *working time* shall mean any period during which the worker is working, at the employer's disposal and carrying out his activity or duties, in accordance with national laws and/or practice;

2. *rest period* shall mean any period which is not working time;

3. *night time* shall mean any period of not less than seven hours, as defined by national law, and which must include in any case the period between midnight and 5 a.m.;

4. *night worker* shall mean:

   (a) on the one hand, any worker, who, during night time, works at least three hours of his daily working time as a normal course; and

   (b) on the other hand, any worker who is likely during night time to work a certain proportion of his annual working time, as defined at the choice of the Member State concerned:

      (i)   by national legislation, following consultation with the two sides of industry; or

     (ii)   by collective agreements or agreements concluded between the two sides of industry at national or regional level;

5.   *shift work* shall mean any method of organizing work in shifts whereby workers succeed each other at the same work stations according to a certain pattern, including a rotating pattern, and which may be continuous or discontinuous, entailing the need for workers to work at different time over a given period of days or weeks;

6.   *shift worker* shall mean any worker whose work schedule is part of shift work.

SECTION 2

MINIMUM REST PERIODS – OTHER ASPECTS OF THE ORGANIZATION OF WORKING TIME

Article 3

Daily rest

Member States shall take the measures necessary to ensure that every worker is entitled to a minimum daily rest period of 11 consecutive hours per 24-hour period.

Article 4

Breaks

Member States shall take the measures necessary to ensure that, where the working day is longer than six hours, every worker is entitled to a rest break, the details of which, including duration and the terms on which it is granted, shall be laid down in collective agreements or agreements between the two sides of industry or, failing that, by national legislation.

Article 5

Weekly rest period

Member States shall take the measures necessary to ensure that, per each seven-day period, every worker is entitled to a minimum uninterrupted rest period of 24 hours plus the 11 hours' daily rest referred to in Article 3.

The minimum rest period referred to in the first subparagraph shall in principle include Sunday.

If objective, technical or work organization conditions so justify, a minimum rest period of 24 hours may be applied.

Article 6

Maximum weekly working time

Member States shall take the measures necessary to ensure that, in keeping with the need to protect the safety and health of workers:

1. the period of weekly working time is limited by means of laws, regulations or administrative provisions or by collective agreements or agreements between the two sides of industry;
2. the average working time for each seven-day period, including overtime, does not exceed 48 hours.

Article 7

Annual leave

1. Member States shall take the measures necessary to ensure that every worker is entitled to paid annual leave of at least four weeks in accordance with the conditions for entitlement to, and granting of, such leave laid down by national legislation and/or practice.
2. The minimum period of paid annual leave may not be replaced by an allowance in lieu, except where the employment relationship is terminated.

SECTION 3

NIGHT WORK – SHIFT WORK – PATTERNS OF WORK

Article 8

Length of night work

Member States shall take the measures necessary to ensure that:

1. normal hours of work for night workers do not exceed an average of eight hours in any 24-hour period;
2. night workers whose work involves special hazards or heavy physical or mental strain do not work more than eight hours in any period of 24 hours during which they perform night work.

   For the purpose of the aforementioned, work involving special hazards or heavy physical or mental strain shall be defined by national legislation and/or practice or by collective agreements or agreements concluded between the two sides of industry, taking account of the specific effects and hazards of night work.

Article 9

Health assessment and transfer of night workers to day work

1. Member States shall take the measures necessary to ensure that:

(a) night workers are entitled to a free health assessment before their assignment and thereafter at regular intervals;

(b) night workers suffering from health problems recognized as being connected with the fact that they perform night work are transferred whenever possible to day work to which they are suited.

2. The free health assessment referred to in paragraph 1
(a) must comply with medical confidentiality.

    3. The free health assessment referred to in paragraph 1
(a) may be conducted within the national health system.

Article 10

Guarantees for night-time working

Member States may make the work of certain categories of night workers subject to certain guarantees, under conditions laid down by national legislation and/or practice, in the case of workers who incur risks to their safety or health linked to night-time working.

Article 11

Notification of regular use of night workers

Member States shall take the measures necessary to ensure that an employer who regularly uses night workers brings this information to the attention of the competent authorities if they so request.

Article 12

Safety and health protection

Member States shall take the measures necessary to ensure that:

1.   night workers and shift workers have safety and health protection appropriate to the nature of their work;

2.   appropriate protection and prevention services or facilities with regard to the safety and health of night workers and shift workers are equivalent to those applicable to other workers and are available at all times.

Article 13

Pattern of work

Member States shall take the measures necessary to ensure that an employer who intends to organize work according to a certain pattern takes account of the general principle of adapting work to the worker, with a view, in particular, to alleviating monotonous work and work at a predetermined work-rate, depending on the type of activity, and of safety and health requirements, especially as regards breaks during working time.

SECTION 4

MISCELLANEOUS PROVISIONS

Article 14

More specific Community provisions

The provisions of this Directive shall not apply where other Community instruments contain more specific requirements concerning certain occupations or occupational activities.

Article 15

More favourable provisions

This Directive shall not affect Member State' rights to apply or introduce laws, regulations or administrative provisions more favourable to the protection of the safety and health of workers or to facilitate or permit the application of collective agreements or agreements concluded between the two sides of industry which are more favourable to the protection of the safety and health of workers.

Article 16

Reference periods

Member States may lay down:

1. for the application of Article 5 (weekly rest period), a reference period not exceeding 14 days;
2. for the application of Article 6 (maximum weekly working time), a reference period not exceeding four months.

   The periods of paid annual leave, granted in accordance with Article 7, and the periods of sick leave shall not be included or shall be neutral in the calculation of the average.
3. for the application of Article 8 (length of night work), a reference period defined after consultation of the two sides of industry or by collective agreements or agreements concluded between the two sides of industry at national or regional level.

   If the minimum weekly rest period of 24 hours required by Article 5 falls within that reference period, it shall not be included in the calculation of the average.

Article 17

Derogations

1. With due regard for the general principles of the protection of the safety and health of workers, Member States may derogate from Articles 3, 4, 5, 6, 8 or 16 when, on account of the specific characteristics of the activity concerned, the duration of the working time is not measured and/or predetermined or can be determined by the workers themselves, and particularly in the case of:

(a) managing executives or other persons with autonomous decision-making powers;
(b) family workers; or
(c) workers officiating at religious ceremonies in churches and religious communities.

2. Derogations may be adopted by means of laws, regulations or administrative provisions or by means of collective agreements or agreements between the two sides of industry provided that the workers concerned are afforded equivalent periods of compensatory rest or that, in exceptional cases in which it is not possible, for objective reasons, to grant such equivalent periods of compensatory rest, the workers concerned are afforded appropriate protection:

   2.1. from Article 3, 4, 5, 8 and 16:

(a) in the case of activities where the worker's place of work and his place of residence are distant from one another or where the worker's different places of work are distant from one another;

(b) in the case of security and surveillance activities requiring a permanent presence in order to protect property and persons, particularly security guards and caretakers or security firms;

(c) in the case of activities involving the need for continuity of service or production, particularly:

    (i) services relating to the reception, treatment and/or care provided by hospitals or similar establishments, residential institutions and prisons;

    (ii) dock or airport workers;

    (iii) press, radio, television, cinematographic production, postal and telecommunications services, ambulance, fire and civil protection services;

    (iv) gas, water and electricity production, transmission and distribution, household refuse collection and incineration plants;

    (v) industries in which work cannot be interrupted on technical grounds;

    (vi) research and development activities;

    (vii) agriculture;

(d) where there is a foreseeable surge of activity, particularly in:

    (i) agriculture;

    (ii) tourism;

    (iii) postal services;

2.2. from Articles 3, 4, 5, 8 and 16:

    (a) in the circumstances described in Article 5(4) of Directive 89/391/EEC;

    (b) in cases of accident or imminent risk of accident;

2.3. from Article 3 and 5:

    (a) in the case of shift work activities, each time the worker changes shift and cannot take daily and/or weekly rest periods between the end of one shift and the start of the next one;

    (b) in the case of activities involving periods of work split up over the day, particularly those of cleaning staff.

3. Derogations may be made from Articles 3, 4, 5, 8 and 16 by means of collective agreements or agreements concluded between the two sides of industry at national or regional level or, in conformity with the rules laid down by them, by means of collective agreements or agreements concluded between the two sides of industry at a lower level.

Member States in which there is no statutory system ensuring the conclusion of collective agreements or agreements concluded between the two sides of industry at national or regional level, on the matters covered by this Directive, or those Member States in which there is a specific legislative framework for this purpose and within the limits thereof, may, in accordance with national legislation and/or practice, allow derogations from Articles 3, 4, 5, 8 and 16 by way of collective agreements or agreements concluded between the two sides of industry at the appropriate collective level.

The derogations provided for in the first and second subparagraphs shall be allowed on condition that equivalent compensating rest periods are granted to the workers concerned, or, in exceptional cases where it is not possible for objective reasons to grant such periods, the workers concerned are afforded appropriate protection.

Member States may lay down rules:

−   for the application of this paragraph by the two sides of industry, and
−   for the extension of the provisions of collective agreements or agreements concluded in conformity with this paragraph to other workers in accordance with national legislation and/or practice.

4. The option to derogate from point 2 of Article 16, provided in paragraph 2, points 2.1. and 2.2. and in paragraph 3 of this Article, may not result in the establishment of a reference period exceeding six months.

However, Member States shall have the option, subject to compliance with the general principles relating to the protection of the safety and health of workers, of allowing, for objective or technical reasons or reasons concerning the organization of work, collective agreements or agreements concluded between the two sides of industry to set reference periods in no event exceeding 12 months.

Before the expiry of a period of seven years from the date referred to in Article 18(1)(a), the Council shall, on the basis of a Commission proposal accompanied by an appraisal report, re-examine the provisions of this paragraph and decide what action to take.

Article 18

Final provisions

1. (a) Member States shall adopt the laws, regulations and administrative provisions necessary to comply with this Directive by 23 November 1996, or shall ensure by that date that the two sides of industry establish the necessary measures by agreement, with Member States being obliged to take any necessary steps to enable them to guarantee at all times that the provisions laid down by this Directive are fulfilled.

   (b) (i)   However, a Member State shall have the option not to apply Article 6, while respecting the general principles of the protection

of the safety and health of workers, and provided it takes the
necessary measures to ensure that:

- no employer requires a worker to work more than 48 hours
  over a seven-day period, calculated as an average for the
  reference period referred to in point 2 of Article 16, unless he
  has first obtained the worker's agreement to perform such
  work.
- no worker is subjected to any detriment by his employer
  because he is not willing to give his agreement to perform such
  work,
- the employer keeps up-to-date records of all workers who carry
  out such work,
- the records are placed at the disposal of the competent authorities, which may, for reasons connected with the safety and/or
  health of workers, prohibit or restrict the possibility of exceeding the maximum weekly working hours,
- the employer provides the competent authorities at their request with information on cases in which agreement has been
  given by workers to perform work exceeding 48 hours over a
  period of seven days, calculated as an average for the reference
  period referred to in point 2 of Article 16.

Before the expiry of a period of seven years from the date referred
to in (a), the Council shall, on the basis of a Commission proposal
accompanied by an appraisal report, re-examine the provisions of
this point (i) and decide on what action to take.

(ii) Similarly, Member States shall have the option, as regards the
application of Article 7, of making use of a transitional period of
not more than three years from the date referred to in (a),
provided that during that transitional period:

- every worker receives three weeks' paid annual leave in accordance with the conditions for the entitlement to, and granting of,
  such leave laid down by national legislation and/or practice,
  and
- the three-week period of paid annual leave may not be replaced
  by an allowance in lieu, except where the employment relationship is terminated.

(c) Member States shall forthwith inform the Commission thereof.

2. When Member States adopt the measures referred to in paragraph 1, they
shall contain a reference to this Directive or shall be accompanied by such
reference on the occasion of their official publication. The methods of making
such a reference shall be laid down by the Member States.

3. Without prejudice to the right of Member States to develop, in the light of changing circumstances, different legislative, regulatory or contractual provisions in the field of working time, as long as the minimum requirements provided for in this Directive are complied with, implementation of this Directive shall not constitute valid grounds for reducing the general level of protection afforded to workers.

4. Member States shall communicate to the Commission the texts of the provisions of national law already adopted or being adopted in the field governed by this Directive.

5. Member States shall report to the Commission every five years on the practical implementation of the provisions of this Directive, indicating the viewpoints of the two sides of industry.

The Commission shall inform the European Parliament, the Council, the Economic and Social Committee and the Advisory Committee on Safety, Hygiene and Health Protection at work thereof.

6. Every five years, the Commission shall submit to the European Parliament, the Council and the Economic and Social Committee a report on the application of this Directive taking into account paragraphs 1, 2, 3, 4 and 5.

Article 19

This Directive is addressed to the Member States.
  Done at Brussels, 23 November 1993.

For the Council
The President
M. SMET

COUNCIL DIRECTIVE
of 22 September 1994

on the establishment of a European Works Council or a procedure in Community-scale undertakings and Community-scale groups of undertakings for the purposes of informing and consulting employees (94/45/EEC)

THE COUNCIL OF THE EUROPEAN UNION,

  Having regard to the Agreement on social policy annexed to Protocol 14 on social policy annexed to the Treaty establishing the European Community, and in particular Article 2(2) thereof,

Having regard to the proposal from the Commission[1],

Having regard to the Opinion of the Economic and Social Committee[2],

Acting in accordance with the procedure referred to in Article 189c of the Treaty[3],

Whereas, on the basis of the Protocol on Social Policy annexed to the Treaty establishing the European Community, the Kingdom of Belgium, the Kingdom of Denmark, the Federal Republic of Germany, the Hellenic Republic, the Kingdom of Spain, the French Republic, Ireland, the Italian Republic, the Grand Duchy of Luxembourg, the Kingdom of the Netherlands and the Portuguese Republic (hereinafter referred to as 'the Member States'), desirous of implementing the Social Charter of 1989, have adopted an Agreement on Social Policy;

Whereas Article 2(2) of the said Agreement authorizes the Council to adopt minimum requirements by means of directives;

Whereas, pursuant to Article 1 of the Agreement, one particular objective of the Community and the Member States is to promote dialogue between management and labour;

Whereas point 17 of the Community Charter of Fundamental Social Rights of Workers provides, *inter alia*, that information, consultation and participation for workers must be developed along appropriate lines, taking account of the practices in force in different Member States; whereas the Charter states that 'this shall apply especially in companies or groups of companies having establishments or companies in two or more Member States';

Whereas the Council, despite the existence of a broad consensus among the majority of Member States, was unable to act on the proposal for a Council Directive on the establishment of a European Works Council in Community-scale undertakings or groups of undertakings for the purposes of informing and consulting employees[4], as amended on 3 December 1991[5];

Whereas the Commission, pursuant to Article 3(2) of the Agreement on Social Policy, has consulted management and labour at Community level on the possible direction of Community action on the information and consultation of workers in Community-scale undertakings and Community-scale groups of undertakings;

Whereas the Commission, considering after this consultation that Community action was advisable, has again consulted management and labour on the

---

[1] OJ No C 135, 18.5.1994, p. 8 and OJ No C 199, 21.7.1994, p. 10.

[2] OJ No C 295, 22.10.1994, p. 64.

[3] Opinion of the European Parliament of 4 May 1994 (OJ No C 205, 25.7.1994) and Council common position of 18 July 1994 (OJ No C 244, 31.8.1994, p. 37).

[4] OJ No C 39, 15.2.1991, p. 10.

[5] OJ No C 336, 31.12.1991, p. 11.

content of the planned proposal, pursuant to Article 3(3) of the said Agreement, and management and labour have presented their opinions to the Commission;

Whereas, following this second phase of consultation, management and labour have not informed the Commission of their wish to initiate the process which might lead to the conclusion of an agreement, as provided for in Article 4 of the Agreement;

Whereas the functioning of the internal market involves a process of concentrations of undertakings, cross-border mergers, take-overs, joint ventures and, consequently, a transnationalization of undertakings and groups of undertakings; whereas, if economic activities are to develop in a harmonious fashion, undertakings and groups of undertakings operating in two or more Member States must inform and consult the representatives of those of their employees that are affected by their decisions;

Whereas procedures for informing and consulting employees as embodied in legislation or practice in the Member States are often not geared to the transnational structure of the entity which takes the decisions affecting those employees; whereas this may lead to the unequal treatment of employees affected by decisions within one and the same undertaking or group of undertakings;

Whereas appropriate provisions must be adopted to ensure that the employees of Community-scale undertakings are properly informed and consulted when decisions which affect them are taken in a Member State other than that in which they are employed;

Whereas, in order to guarantee that the employees of undertakings or groups of undertakings operating in two or more Member States are properly informed and consulted, it is necessary to set up European Works Councils or to create other suitable procedures for the transnational information and consultation of employees;

Whereas it is accordingly necessary to have a definition of the concept of controlling undertaking relating solely to this Directive and not prejudging definitions of the concepts of group or control which might be adopted in texts to be drafted in the future;

Whereas the mechanisms for informing and consulting employees in such undertakings or groups must encompass all of the establishments or, as the case may be, the group's undertakings located within the Member States, regardless of whether the undertaking or the group's controlling undertaking has its central management inside or outside the territory of the Member States;

Whereas, in accordance with the principle of autonomy of the parties, it is for the representatives of employees and the management of the undertaking or the group's controlling undertaking to determine by agreement the nature, composition, the function, mode of operation, procedures and financial resources of European Works Councils or other information or consultation procedures so as to suit their own particular circumstances;

Whereas, in accordance with the principle of subsidiarity, it is for the Member States to determine who the employees' representatives are and in particular to provide, if they consider appropriate, for a balanced representation of different categories of employees;

Whereas, however, provision should be made for certain subsidiary requirements to apply should the parties so decide or in the event of the central management refusing to initiate negotiations or in the absence of agreement subsequent to such negotiations;

Whereas, moreover, employees' representatives may decide not to seek the setting-up of a European Works Council or the parties concerned may decide on other procedures for the transnational information and consultation of employees;

Whereas, without prejudice to the possibility of the parties deciding otherwise, the European Works Council set up in the absence of agreement between the parties must, in order to fulfil the objective of this Directive, be kept informed and consulted on the activities of the undertaking or group of undertakings so that it may assess the possible impact on employees' interests in at least two different Member States; whereas, to that end, the undertaking or controlling undertaking must be required to communicate to the employees' appointed representatives general information concerning the interests of employees and information relating more specifically to those aspects of the activities of the undertaking or group of undertakings which affect employees' interests; whereas the European Works Council must be able to deliver an opinion at the end of that meeting;

Whereas certain decisions having a significant effect on the interests of employees must be the subject of information and consultation of the employees' appointed representatives as soon as possible;

Whereas provisions should be made for the employees' representatives acting within the framework of the Directive to enjoy, when exercising their functions, the same protection and guarantees similar to those provided to employees' representatives by the legislation and/or practice of the country of employment; whereas they must not be subject to any discrimination as a result of the lawful exercise of their activities and must enjoy adequate protection as regards dismissal and other sanctions;

Whereas the information and consultation provisions laid down in this Directive must be implemented in the case of an undertaking or a group's controlling undertaking which has its central management outside the territory of the Member States by its representative agent, to be designated if necessary, in one of the Member States or, in the absence of such an agent, by the establishment or controlled undertaking employing the greatest number of employees in the Member States;

Whereas special treatment should be accorded to Community-scale undertakings and groups of undertakings in which there exists, at the time when this Directive is brought into effect, an agreement, covering the entire workforce, providing for the transnational information and consultation of employees;

Whereas the Member States must take appropriate measures in the event of failure to comply with the obligations laid down in this Directive,

HAS ADOPTED THIS DIRECTIVE:

SECTION 1

GENERAL

Article 1

Objective

1. The purpose of this Directive is to improve the right to information and to consultation of employees in Community-scale undertakings and Community-scale groups of undertakings.

2. To that end, a European Works Council or a procedure for informing and consulting employees shall be established in every Community-scale undertaking and every Community-scale group of undertakings, where requested in the manner laid down in Article 5(1), with the purpose of informing and consulting employees under the terms, in the manner and with the effects laid down in this Directive.

3. Notwithstanding paragraph 2, where a Community-scale group of undertakings within the meaning of Article 2(1)(c) comprises one or more undertakings or groups of undertakings which are Community-scale undertakings or Community-scale groups of undertakings within the meaning of Article 2(1)(a) or (c), a European Works Council shall be established at the level of the group unless the agreements referred to in Article 6 provide otherwise.

4. Unless a wider scope is provided for in the agreements referred to in Article 6, the powers and competence of European Works Councils and the scope of information and consultation procedures established to achieve the purpose specified in paragraph 1 shall, in the case of a Community-scale undertaking, cover all the establishments located within the Member States and, in the case of a Community-scale group of undertakings, all group undertakings located within the Member States.

5. Member States may provide that this Directive shall not apply to merchant navy crews.

Article 2

Definitions

1. For the purposes of this Directive:

(a) 'Community-scale undertaking' means any undertaking with at least 1,000 employees within the Member States and at least 150 employees in each of at least two Member States;

(b) 'group of undertakings' means a controlling undertaking and its controlled undertakings;

(c) 'Community-scale group of undertakings' means a group of undertakings with the following characteristics:
  - at least 1,000 employees within the Member States,
  - at least two group undertakings in different Member States, and
  - at least one group undertaking with at least 150 employees in one Member State and at least one other group undertaking with at least 150 employees in another Member State;

(d) 'employees' representatives' means the employees' representatives provided for by national law and/or practice;

(e) 'central management' means the central management of the Community-scale undertaking or, in the case a Community-scale group of undertakings, of the controlling undertaking;

(f) 'consultation' means the exchange of views and establishment of dialogue between employees' representatives and central management or any more appropriate level of management;

(g) 'European Works Council' means the council established in accordance with Article 1(2) or the provisions of the Annex, with the purpose of informing and consulting employees;

(h) 'special negotiating body' means the body established in accordance with Article 5(2) to negotiate with the central management regarding the establishment of a European Works Council or a procedure for informing and consulting employees in accordance with Article 1(2).

2. For the purposes of this Directive, the prescribed thresholds for the size of the workforce shall be based on the average number of employees, including part-time employees, employed during the previous two years calculated according to national legislation and/or practice.

Article 3

Definition of 'controlling undertaking'

1. For the purposes of this Directive, 'controlling undertaking' means an undertaking which can exercise a dominant influence over another undertaking ('the controlled undertaking') by virtue, for example, of ownership, financial participation or the rules which govern it.

2. The ability to exercise a dominant influence shall be presumed, without prejudice to proof to the contrary, when, in relation to another undertaking directly or indirectly;

(a) holds a majority of that undertaking's subscribed capital; or
(b) controls a majority of the votes attached to that undertaking's issued share capital; or
(c) can appoint more than half of the members of that undertaking's administrative, management or supervisory body.

3. For the purposes of paragraph 2, a controlling undertaking's rights as regards voting and appointment shall include the rights of any other controlled undertaking and those of any person or body acting in his or its own name but on behalf of the controlling undertaking or of any other controlled undertaking.

4. Notwithstanding paragraphs 1 and 2, an undertaking shall not be deemed to be a 'controlling undertaking' with respect to another undertaking in which it has holdings where the former undertaking is a company referred to in Article 3(5)(a) or (c) of Council Regulation (EEC) No 4064/89 of 21 December 1989 on the control of concentrations between undertakings[6].

5. A dominant influence shall not be presumed to be exercised solely by virtue of the fact that an office holder is exercising his functions, according to the law of a Member State relating to liquidation, winding up, insolvency, cessation of payments, compositions or analogous proceedings.

6. The law applicable in order to determine whether an undertaking is a 'controlling undertaking' shall be the law of the Member State which governs that undertaking.

Where the law governing that undertaking is not that of a Member State, the law applicable shall be the law of the Member State within whose territory the representative of the undertaking or, in the absence of such a representative, the central management of the group undertaking which employs the greatest number of employees is situated.

7. Where, in the case of a conflict of laws in the application of paragraph 2, two or more undertakings from a group satisfy one or more of the criteria laid

---

[6] OJ No L 395, 30.12.1989, p. 1.

down in that paragraph, the undertaking which satisfies the criterion laid down in point (c) thereof shall be regarded as the controlling undertaking, without prejudice to proof that another undertaking is able to exercise a dominant influence.

SECTION 2

ESTABLISHMENT OF A EUROPEAN WORKS COUNCIL OR AN EMPLOYEE INFORMATION AND CONSULTATION PROCEDURE

Article 4

Responsibility for the establishment of a European Works Council or an employee information and consultation procedure

1. The central management shall be responsible for creating the conditions and means necessary for the setting up of a European Works Council or an information and consultation procedure, as provided for in Article 1(2), in a Community-scale undertaking and a Community-scale group of undertakings.
2. Where the central management is not situated in a Member State, the central management's representative agent in a Member State, to be designated if necessary, shall take on the responsibility referred to in paragraph 1.

In the absence of such a representative, the management of the establishment or group undertaking employing the greatest number of employees in any one Member State shall take on the responsibility referred to in paragraph 1.
3. For the purposes of this Directive, the representative or representatives or, in the absence of any such representatives, the management referred to in the second subparagraph of paragraph 2, shall be regarded as the central management.

Article 5

Special negotiating body

1. In order to achieve the objective in Article 1(1), the central management shall initiate negotiations for the establishment of a European Works Council or an information and consultation procedure on its own initiative or at the

written request of at least 100 employees or their representatives in at least two undertakings or establishments in at least two different Member States.

2. For this purpose, a special negotiating body shall be established in accordance with the following guidelines:

(a) The Member State shall determine the method to be used for the election or appointment of the members of the special negotiating body who are to be elected or appointed in their territories.

   Member States shall provide that employees in undertakings and/or establishments in which there are no employees' representatives through no fault of their own, have the right to elect or appoint members of the special negotiating body.

   The second subparagraph shall be without prejudice to national legislation and/or practice laying down thresholds for the establishment of employee representation bodies.

(b) The special negotiating body shall have a minimum of three and a maximum of 17 members.

(c) In these elections or appointments, it must be ensured:
   - firstly, that each Member State in which the Community-scale undertaking has one or more establishments or in which the Community-scale group of undertakings has the controlling undertaking or one or more controlled undertakings is represented by one member,
   - secondly, that there are supplementary members in proportion to the number of employees working in the establishments, the controlling undertaking or the controlled undertakings as laid down by the legislation of the Member State within the territory of which the central management is situated.

(d) The central management and local management shall be informed of the composition of the special negotiating body.

3. The special negotiating body shall have the task of determining, with the central management, by written agreement, the scope, composition, functions, and term of office of the European Works Council(s) or the arrangements for implementing a procedure for the information and consultation of employees.

4. With a view to the conclusion of an agreement in accordance with Article 6, the central management shall convene a meeting with the special negotiating body. It shall inform the local managements accordingly.

   For the purpose of the negotiations, the special negotiating body may be assisted by experts of its choice.

5. The special negotiating body may decide, by at least two-thirds of the votes, not to open negotiations in accordance with paragraph 4, or to terminate the negotiations already opened.

Such a decision shall stop the procedure to conclude the agreement referred to in Article 6. Where such a decision has been taken, the provisions in the Annex shall not apply.

A new request to convene the special negotiating body may be made at the earliest two years after the abovementioned decision unless the parties concerned lay down a shorter period.

6. Any expenses relating to the negotiations referred to in paragraphs 3 and 4 shall be borne by the central management so as to enable the special negotiating body to carry out its task in an appropriate manner.

In compliance with this principle, Member States may lay down budgetary rules regarding the operation of the special negotiating body. They may in particular limit the funding to cover one expert only.

Article 6

Content of the agreement

1. The central management and the special negotiating body must negotiate in a spirit of cooperation with a view to reaching an agreement on the detailed arrangements for implementing the information and consultation of employees provided for in Article 1(1).

2. Without prejudice to the autonomy of the parties, the agreement referred to in paragraph 1 between the central management and the special negotiating body shall determine:

(a) the undertakings of the Community-scale group of undertakings or the establishments of the Community-scale undertaking which are covered by the agreement;

(b) the composition of the European Works Council, the number of members, the allocation of seats and the term of office;

(c) the functions and the procedure for information and consultation of the European Works Council;

(d) the venue, frequency and duration of meetings of the European Works Council;

(e) the financial and material resources to be allocated to the European Works Council;

(f) the duration of the agreement and the procedure for its renegotiation.

3. The central management and the special negotiating body may decide, in writing, to establish one or more information and consultation procedures instead of a European Works Council.

The agreement must stipulate by what method the employees' representatives shall have the right to meet to discuss the information conveyed to them.

This information shall relate in particular to transnational questions which significantly affect workers' interests.

4. The agreements referred to in paragraphs 2 and 3 shall not, unless provision is made otherwise therein, be subject to the subsidiary requirements of the Annex.

5. For the purposes of concluding the agreements referred to in paragraphs 2 and 3, the special negotiating body shall act by a majority of its members.

Article 7

Subsidiary requirements

1. In order to achieve the objective in Article 1(1), the subsidiary requirements laid down by the legislation of the Member State in which the central management is situated shall apply:

-   where the central management and the special negotiating body so decide, or
-   where the central management refuses to commence negotiations within six months of the request referred to in Article 5(1), or
-   where, after three years from the date of this request, they are unable to conclude an agreement as laid down in Article 6 and the special negotiating body has not taken the decision provided for in Article 5(5).

2. The subsidiary requirements referred to in paragraph 1 as adopted in the legislation of the Member States must satisfy the provisions set out in the Annex.

SECTION 3

MISCELLANEOUS PROVISIONS

Article 8

Confidential information

1. Member States shall provide that members of special negotiating bodies or of European Works Councils and any experts who assist them are not

authorised to reveal any information which has expressly been provided to them in confidence.

The same shall apply to employees' representatives in the framework of an information and consultation procedure.

This obligation shall continue to apply, wherever the persons referred to in the first and second subparagraphs are, even after the expiry of their terms of office.

2. Each Member State shall provide, in specific cases and under the conditions and limits laid down by national legislation, that the central management situated in its territory is not obliged to transmit information when its nature is such that, according to objective criteria, it would seriously harm the functioning of the undertakings concerned or would be prejudicial to them.

A Member State may make such dispensation subject to prior administrative or judicial authorization.

3. Each Member State may lay down particular provisions for the central management of undertakings in its territory which pursue directly and essentially the aim of ideological guidance with respect to information and the expression of opinions, on condition that, at the date of adoption of this Directive such particular provisions already exist in the national legislation.

Article 9

Operation of European Works Council and information and consultation procedure for workers

The central management and the European Works Council shall work in a spirit of co-operation with due regard to their reciprocal rights and obligations.

The same shall apply to co-operation between the central management and employees' representatives in the framework of an information and consultation procedure for workers.

Article 10

Protection of employees' representatives

Members of special negotiating bodies, members of European Works Councils and employees' representatives exercising their functions under the procedure referred to in Article 6(3) shall, in the exercise of their functions, enjoy the same protection and guarantees provided for employees' representatives by the national legislation and/or practice in force in their country of employment.

This shall apply in particular to attendance at meetings of special negotiating bodies or European Works Councils or any other meetings within the framework of the agreement referred to in Article 6(3), and the payment of wages for members who are on the staff of the Community-scale undertaking or the Community-scale group of undertakings for the period of absence necessary for the performance of their duties.

Article 11

Compliance with this Directive

1. Each Member State shall ensure that the management of establishments of a Community-scale undertaking and the management of undertakings which form part of a Community-scale group of undertakings which are situated within its territory and their employees' representatives or, as the case may be, employees abide by the obligations laid down by this Directive, regardless of whether or not the central management is situated within its territory.

2. Member States shall ensure that the information on the number of employees referred to in Article 2(1)(a) and (c) is made available by undertakings at the request of the parties concerned by the application of this Directive.

3. Member States shall provide for appropriate measures in the event of failure to comply with this Directive; in particular, they shall ensure that adequate administrative or judicial procedures are available to enable the obligations deriving from this Directive to be enforced.

4. Where Member States apply Article 8, they shall make provision for administrative or judicial appeal procedures which the employees' representatives may initiate when the central management requires confidentiality or does not give information in accordance with that Article.

Such procedures may include procedures designed to protect the confidentiality of the information in question.

Article 12

Link between this Directive and other provisions

1. This Directive shall apply without prejudice to measures taken pursuant to Council Directive 75/129/EEC of 17 February 1975 on the approximation of

the laws of the Member States relating to collective redundancies[7], and to Council Directive 77/187/EEC of 14 February 1977 on the approximation of the laws of the Member States relating to the safeguarding of employees' rights in the event of transfers of undertakings, businesses or parts of businesses[8].

2. This Directive shall be without prejudice to employees' existing rights to information and consultation under national law.

Article 13

Agreements in force

1. Without prejudice to paragraph 2, the obligations arising from this Directive shall not apply to Community-scale undertakings or Community-scale groups of undertakings in which, on the date laid down in Article 14(1) for the implementation of this Directive or the date of its transposition in the Member State in question, where this is earlier than the abovementioned date, there is already an agreement, covering the entire workforce, providing for the transnational information and consultation of employees.

2. When the agreements referred to in paragraph 1 expire, the parties to those agreements may decide jointly to renew them.

Where this is not the case, the provisions of this Directive shall apply.

Article 14

Final provisions

1. Member States shall bring into force the laws, regulations and administrative provisions necessary to comply with this Directive no later than 22 September 1996 or shall ensure by that date at the latest that management and labour introduce the required provisions by way of agreement, the Member States being obliged to take all necessary steps enabling them at all times to guarantee the results imposed by this Directive. They shall forthwith inform the Commission thereof.

2. When Member States adopt these measures, they shall contain a reference to this Directive or shall be accompanied by such reference on the occasion of

---

[7] OJ No L 48, 22.2.1975, p. 29. Regulations as last amended by Directive 92/56/EEC (OJ No L 245, 26.8.1992, p. 3).
[8] OJ No L 61, 5.3.1977, p. 26.

their official publication. The methods of making such reference shall be laid down by Member States.

Article 15

Review by the Commission

Not later than 22 September 1999, the Commission shall, in consultation with the Member States and with management and labour at European level, review its operation and, in particular examine whether the workforce size thresholds are appropriate with a view to proposing suitable amendments to the Council, where necessary.

Article 16

This Directive is addressed to the Member States.
　　Done, at Brussels, 22 September 1994.

For the Council
The President
N. BLUM

ANNEX

SUBSIDIARY REQUIREMENTS

referred to in Article 7 of the Directive

1. In order to achieve the objective in Article 1(1) of the Directive and in the cases provided for in Article 7(1) of the Directive, the establishment, composition and competence of a European Works Council shall be governed by the following rules:

(a)　The competence of the European Works Council shall be limited to information and consultation on the matters which concern the Community-scale undertaking or Community-scale group of undertakings as a whole or at least two of its establishments or group undertakings situated in different Member States.

　　In the case of undertakings or groups of undertakings referred to in Article 4(2), the competence of the European Works Council shall be limited to those matters concerning all their establishments or group undertakings situated within the Member States or concerning at least two of their establishments or group undertakings situated in different Member States.

(b) The European Works Council shall be composed of employees of the Community-scale undertaking or Community-scale group of undertakings elected or appointed from their number by the employees' representatives or, in the absence thereof, by the entire body of employees.

The election or appointment of members of the European Works Council shall be carried out in accordance with national legislation and/or practice.

(c) The European Works Council shall have a minimum of three members and a maximum of 30.

Where its size so warants, it shall elect a select committee from among its members, comprising at most three members.

It shall adopt its own rule of procedure.

(d) In the election or appointment of members of the European Works Council, it must be ensured:
  - firstly, that each Member State in which the Community-scale undertaking has one or more establishments or in which the Community-scale group of undertakings has the controlling undertaking or one or more controlled undertakings is represented by one member.
  - secondly, that there are supplementary members in proportion to the number of employees working in the establishments, the controlling undertaking or the controlled undertakings as laid down by the legislation of the Member State within the territory of which the central management is situated.

(e) The central management and any other more approriate level of management shall be informed of the composition of the European Works Council.

(f) Four years after the European Works Council is established it shall examine whether to open negotiations for the conclusion of the agreement referred to in Article 6 of this Directive or to continue to apply the subsidiary requirements adopted in accordance with this Annex.

Articles 6 and 7 of this Directive shall apply, *mutatis mutandis*, if a decision has been taken to negotiate an agreement according to Article 6 of the Directive, in which case 'special negotiating body' shall be replaced by 'European Works Council'.

2. The European Works Council shall have the right to meet with the central management once a year, to be informed and consulted, on the basis of a report drawn up by the central management, on the progress of the business

of the Community-scale undertaking or Community-scale group of undertakings and its prospects. The local managements shall be informed accordingly.

The meeting shall relate in particular to the structure, economic and financial situation, the probable development of the business and of production and sales, the situation and probable trend of employment, investments, and substantial changes concerning organization, introduction of new working methods or production processes, transfers of production, mergers, cut-backs or closures of undertakings, establishments or important parts thereof, and collective redundancies.

3. Where there are exceptional circumstances affecting the employees' interests to a considerable extent, particularly in the event of relocations, the closure of establishments or undertakings or collective redundancies, the select committee or, where no such committee exists, the European Works Council shall have the right to be informed. It shall have the right to meet, at its request, the central management, or any other more appropriate level of management within the Community-scale undertaking or group of undertakings having its own powers of decision, so as to be informed and consulted on measures significantly affecting employees' interests.

Those members of the European Works Council who have been elected or appointed by the establishment and/or undertakings which are directly concerned by the measures in question shall also have the right to participate in the meeting organized with the select committee.

This information and consultation meeting shall take place as soon as possible on the basis of a report drawn up by the central management or any other appropriate level of management of the Community-scale undertaking or group of undertakings, on which an opinion may be delivered at the end of the meeting or within a reasonable time.

This meeting shall not affect the prerogatives of the central management.

4. The Member States may lay down rules on the chairing of information and consultation meetings.

Before any meeting with the central management, the European Works Council or the select committee, where necessary enlarged in accordance with the second paragraph of point 3, shall be entitled to meet without the management concerned being present.

5. Without prejudice to Article 8 of the Directive, the members of the European Works Council shall inform the representatives of the employees of the establishments or of the undertakings of a Community-scale group of undertakings or, in the absence of representatives, the workforce as a whole, of the content and outcome of the information and consultation procedure carried out in accordance with this Annex.

6. The European Works Council or the select committee may be assisted by experts of its choice, in so far as this is necessary for it to carry out its tasks.

7. The operating expenses of the European Works Council shall be borne by the central management.

The central management concerned shall provide the members of the European Works Council with such financial and material resources as enable them to perform their duties in an appropriate manner.

In particular, the cost of organizing meetings and arranging for interpretation facilities and the accomodation and travelling expenses of members of the European Works Council and its select committee shall be met by the central management unless otherwise agreed.

In compliance with these principles, the Member States may lay down budgetary rules regarding the operation of the European Works Council. They may in particular limit funding to cover one expert only.

Community Charter of the Fundamental Social Rights of Workers

THE HEADS OF STATE OR GOVERNMENT OF THE MEMBER STATES OF THE EUROPEAN COMMUNITY MEETING AT STRASBOURG ON 9 DECEMBER 1989[1]

Whereas, under the terms of Article 117 of the EEC Treaty, the Member States have agreed on the need to promote improved living and working conditions for workers so as to make possible their harmonization while the improvement is being maintained;

Whereas following on from the conclusions of the European Councils of Hanover and Rhodes the European Council of Madrid considered that, in the context of the establishment of the single European market, the same importance must be attached to the social aspects as to the economic aspects and whereas, therefore, they must be developed in a balanced manner;

Having regard to the Resolutions of the European Parliament of 15 March 1989, 14 September 1989 and 22 November 1989, and to the Opinion of the Economic and Social Committee of 22 February 1989;

Whereas the completion of the internal market is the most effective means of creating employment and ensuring maximum well-being in the Community; whereas employment development and creation must be given first

---

[1] Text adopted by the Heads of State or Government of 11 Member States.

priority in the completion of the internal market; whereas it is for the Community to take up the challenges of the future with regard to economic competitiveness, taking into account, in particular, regional imbalances;

Whereas the social consensus contributes to the strengthening of the competitiveness of undertakings, of the economy as a whole and to the creation of employment; whereas in this respect it is an essential condition for ensuring sustained economic development;

Whereas the completion of the internal market must favour the approximation of improvements in living and working conditions, as well as economic and social cohesion within the European Community while avoiding distortions of competition;

Whereas the completion of the internal market must offer improvements in the social field for workers of the European Community, especially in terms of freedom of movement, living and working conditions, health and safety at work, social protection, education and training;

Whereas, in order to ensure equal treatment, it is important to combat every form of discrimination, including discrimination on grounds of sex, colour, race, opinions and beliefs, and whereas, in a spirit of solidarity, it is important to combat social exclusion;

Whereas it is for Member States to guarantee that workers from non-member countries and members of their families who are legally resident in a Member State of the European Community are able to enjoy, as regards their living and working conditions, treatment comparable to that enjoyed by workers who are nationals of the Member State concerned;

Whereas inspiration should be drawn from the Conventions of the International labour Organization, and from the European Social Charter of the Council of Europe;

Whereas the Treaty, as amended by the single European Act, contains provisions down the powers of the Community relating *inter alia* to the freedom of workers (Article 7, 48 to 51), the right of establishment (Article 52 to 58), the social field under the conditions laid down in Articles 117 to 122 – in particular as regards the improvement of health and safety in the working environment (Article 118a), the development of the dialogue between management and labour at European level (Article 118b), equal pay for men and women for equal work (Article 119) – the general principles for implementing a common vocational training policy (Article 128), economic and social cohesion (Article 130a to 130e) and, more generally, the approximation of legislation (Articles 100, 100a and 235); whereas the implementation of the Charter must not entail an extension of the Community's powers as defined by the Treaties;

Whereas the aim of the present Charter is on the one hand to consolidate the progress made in the social field, through action by the Member States, the two sides of industry and the Community;

Whereas its aim is on the other hand to declare solemnly that the implementation of the Single European Act must take full account of the social dimension of the Community and that it is necessary in this context to ensure at appropriate levels the development of the social rights of workers of the European Community, especially employed workers and self-employed persons;

Whereas, in accordance with the conclusions of the Madrid European Council, the respective roles of Community rules, national legislation and collective agreements must be clearly established;

Whereas, by virtue of the principle of subsidiarity, responsibility for the initiatives to be taken with regard to the implementation of these social rights lies with the Member States or their constituent parts and, within the limits of its powers, with the European Community; whereas such implementation may take the form of laws, collective agreements or existing practices at the various appropriate levels and whereas it requires in many spheres the active involvement of the two sides of industry;

Whereas the solemn proclamation of fundamental social rights at European Community level may not, when implemented, provide grounds for any retrogression compared with the situation currently existing in each Member State,

HAVE ADOPTED THE FOLLOWING DECLARATION CONSTI-TUTING THE 'COMMUNITY CHARTER OF THE FUNDAMENTAL SOCIAL RIGHTS OF WORKERS':

TITLE 1

Fundamental social rights of workers

Freedom of movement

1. Every worker of the European Community shall have the right to freedom of movement throughout the territory of the Community, subject to restrictions justified on grounds of public order, public safety or public health.
2. The right to freedom of movement shall enable any worker to engage in any occupation of profession in the Community in accordance with the principles of equal treatment as regards access to employment, working conditions and social protection in the host country.

3. The right of freedom of movement shall also imply:

(i)　harmonization of conditions of residence in all Member States, particularly those concerning family reunification;

(ii)　elimination of obstacles arising from the non-recognition of diplomas or equivalent occupational qualifications;

(iii)　improvement of the living and working conditions of frontier workers.

Employment and remuneration

4. Every individual shall be free to choose and engage in an occupation according to the regulations governing each occupation.

5. All employment shall be fairly remunerated. To this end, in accordance with arrangements applying in each country:

(i)　workers shall be assured of an equitable wage, ie. a wage sufficient to enable them to have a decent standard of living;

(ii)　workers subject to terms of employment other than an open-ended full-time contract shall benefit from an equitable reference wage;

(iii)　wages may be withheld, seized or transferred only in accordance with national law; such provisions should entail measures enabling the worker concerned to continue to enjoy the necessary means of subsistence for him or herself and his or her family.

6. Every individual must be able to have access to public placement services free of charge.

Improvement of living and working conditions

7. The completion of the internal market must lead to an improvement in the living and working conditions of workers in the European Community. This process must result from an approximation in these conditions while the improvement is being maintained, as regards in particular the duration and organization of working time and forms of employment other than open-ended contracts, such as fixed-term contracts, part-time working, temporary work and seasonal work.

The improvement must cover, where necessary, the development of certain aspects of employment regulations such as procedures for collective redundancies and those regarding bankruptcies.

8. Every worker of the European Community shall have a right to a weekly rest period and to annual paid leave, the duration of which must be progressively harmonized in accordance with national practices.

9. The conditions of employment of every worker of the European Community shall be stipulated in laws, a collective agreement or a contract of employment, according to arrangements applying in each country.

Social protection

According to the arrangements applying in each country:

10. Every worker of the European Community shall have a right to adequate social protection and shall, whatever his status and whatever the size of the undertaking in which he is employed, enjoy an adequate level of social security benefits.

Persons who have been unable either to enter or re-enter the labour market and have no means of subsistence must be able to receive sufficient resources and social assistance in keeping with their particular situation.

Freedom of association and collective bargaining

11. Employers and workers of the European Community shall have the right of association in order to constitute professional organizations or trade unions of their choice for the defence of their economic and social interests.

Every employer and every worker shall have the freedom to join or not to join such organizations without any personal or occupational damage being thereby suffered by him.

12. Employers or employers' organizations, on the one hand, and workers' organizations, on the other, shall have the right to negotiate and conclude collective agreements under the conditions laid down by national legislation and practice.

The dialogue between the two sides of industry at European level which must be developed, may, if the parties deem it desirable, result in contractual relations in particular at inter-occupational and sectoral level.

13. The right to resort to collective action in the event of a conflict of interests shall include the right to strike, subject to the obligations arising under national regulations and collective agreements.

In order to facilitate the settlement of industrial disputes the establishment and utilization at the appropriate level of conciliation, mediation and arbitration procedures should be encouraged in accordance with national practice.

14. The internal legal order of the Member States shall determine under which conditions and to what extent the rights provided for in Articles 11 to 13 apply to the armed forces, the police and the civil service.

Vocational training

15. Every worker of the European Community must be able to have access to vocational training and to benefit therefrom throughout his working life. In the conditions governing access to such training there may be no discrimination on grounds of nationality.

The competent public authorities, undertakings or the two sides of industry, each within their own sphere of competence, should set up continuing and permanent training systems enabling every person to undergo retraining more especially through leave for training purposes, to improve his skills or to acquire new skills, particularly in the light of technical developments.

Equal treatment for men and women

16. Equal treatment for men and women must be assured. Equal opportunities for men and women must be developed.

To this end, action must be intensified to ensure the implementation of the principle of equality between men and women as regards in particular access to employment, remuneration, working conditions, social protection, education, vocational training and career development.

Measures should also be developed enabling men and women to reconcile their occupational and family obligations.

Information, consultation and participation for workers

17. Information, consultation and participation for workers must be developed along appropriate lines, taking account of the practices in force in the various Member States.

This shall apply especially in companies or groups of companies having establishments or companies in two or more Member States of the European Community.

18. Such information, consultation and participation must be implemented in due time, particularly in the following cases:

(i)   when technological changes which, from the point of view of working conditions and work organization, have major implications for the workforce, are introduced into undertakings;

(ii) in connection with restructuring operations in undertakings or in cases of mergers having an impact on the employment of workers;

(iii) in cases of collective redundancy procedures;

(iv) when transfrontier workers in particular are affected by employment policies pursued by the undertaking where they are employed.

Health protection and safety at the workplace

19. Every worker must enjoy satisfactory health and safety conditions in his working environment. Appropriate measures must be taken in order to achieve further harmonization of conditions in this area while maintaining the improvements made.

These measures shall take account, in particular, of the need for the training, information, consultation and balanced participation of workers as regards the risks incurred and the steps taken to eliminate or reduce them.

The provisions regarding implementation of the internal market shall help to ensure such protection.

Protection of children and adolescents

20. Without prejudice to such rules as may be more favourable to young people, in particular those ensuring their preparation for work through vocational training, and subject to derogations limited to certain light work, the minimum employment age must not be lower than the minimum school-leaving age and, in any case, not lower than 15 years.

21. Young people who are in gainful employment must receive equitable remuneration in accordance with national practice.

22. Appropriate measures must be taken to adjust labour regulations applicable to young workers so that their specific development and vocational training and access to employment needs are met.

The duration of work must, in particular, be limited – without it being possible to circumvent this limitation through recourse to overtime – and night work prohibited in the case of workers of under 18 years of age, save in the case of certain jobs laid down in national legislation or regulations.

23. Following the end of compulsory education, young people must be entitled to receive initial vocational training of a sufficient duration to enable them to adapt to the requirements of their future working life; for young workers, such training should take place during working hours.

Elderly persons

According to the arrangements applying in each country:

24. Every worker of the European Community must, at the time of retirement, be able to enjoy resources affording him or her a decent standard of living.

25. Any person who has reached retirement age but who is not entitled to a pension or who does not have other means of subsistence, must be entitled to sufficient resources and to medical and social assistance specifically suited to his needs.

Disabled persons

26. All disabled persons, whatever the origin and nature of their disablement, must be entitled to additional concrete measures aimed at improving their social and professional integration.

These measures must concern, in particular, according to the capacities of the beneficiaries, vocational training, ergonomics, accessibility, mobility, means of transport and housing.

TITLE 2

Implementation of the Charter

27. It is more particularly the responsibility of the Member States, in accordance with national practices, notably through legislative measures or collective agreements, to guarantee the fundamental social rights in this Charter and to implement the social measures indispensable to the smooth operation of the internal market as part of a strategy of economic and social cohesion.

28. The European Council invites the Commission to submit as soon as possible initiatives which fall within its powers, as provided for in the Treaties, with a view to the adoption of legal instruments for the effective implementation, as and when the internal market is completed, of those rights which come within the Community's area of competence.

29. The Commission shall establish each year, during the last three months, a report on the application of the Charter by the Member States and by the European Community.

30. The report of the Commission shall be forwarded to the European Council, the European Parliament and the Economic and Social Committee.

MAASTRICHT PROTOCOLS

Protocol on Social Policy

THE HIGH CONTRACTING PARTIES,

Noting that eleven Member States, that is to say the Kingdom of Belgium, the Kingdom of Denmark, the Federal Republic of Germany, the Hellenic Republic, the Kingdom of Spain, the French Republic, Ireland, the Italian Republic, the Grand Duchy of Luxembourg, the Kingdom of the Netherlands, the Portuguese Republic, wish to continue along the path laid down in the 1989 Social Charter; that they have adopted among themselves an Agreement to this end; that this Agreement is annexed to this Protocol; that this Protocol and the said Agreement are without prejudice to the provisions of this Treaty, particularly those which relate to social policy which constitute an integral part of the 'acquis communautaire':

1. Agree to authorise those eleven Member States to have recourse to the institutions, procedures and mechanisms of the Treaty for the purposes of taking among themselves and applying as far as they are concerned the acts and decisions required for giving effect to the abovementioned Agreement.
2. The United Kingdom of Great Britain and Northern Ireland shall not take part in the deliberations and the adoption by the Council of Commission proposals made on the basis of this Protocol and the abovementioned Agreement.

    By way of derogation from Article 148(2) of the Treaty, acts of the Council which are made pursuant to this Protocol and which must be adopted by a qualified majority shall be deemed to be so adopted if they have received at least forty-four votes in favour. The unanimity of the members of the Council, with the exception of the United Kingdom of Great Britain and Northern Ireland, shall be necessary for acts of the Council which must be adopted unanimously and for those amending the Commission proposal.

    Acts adopted by the Council and any financial consequences other than administrative costs entailed for the institutions shall not be applicable to the United Kingdom of Great Britain and Northern Ireland.

3.   This Protocol shall be annexed to the Treaty establishing the European Community.

Agreement on Social Policy concluded between the Member States of the European Community with the exception of the United Kingdom of Great Britain and Northern Ireland

The undersigned eleven HIGH CONTRACTING PARTIES, that is to say the Kingdom of Belgium, the Kingdom of Denmark, the Federal Republic of Germany, the Hellenic Republic, the Kingdom of Spain, the French Republic, Ireland, the Italian Republic, the Grand Duchy of Luxembourg, the Kingdom of the Netherlands and the Portuguese Republic (hereinafter referred to as 'the Member States'),

Wishing to implement the 1989 Social Charter on the basis of the 'acquis communautaire',

Considering the Protocol on social policy,

Have agreed as follows:

Article 1

The Community and the Member States shall have as their objectives the promotion of employment, improved living and working conditions, proper social protection, dialogue between management and labour, the development of human resources with a view to lasting employment and the combatting of exclusion. To this end the Community and the Member States shall implement measures which take account of the diverse forms of national practices, in particular in the field of contractual relations, and the need to maintain the competitiveness of the Community economy.

Article 2

1. With a view to achieving the objectives of Article 1, the Community shall support and complement the activities of the Member States in the following fields:

- improvement in particular of the working environment to protect workers' health and safety;
- working conditions;
- the information and consultation of workers;
- equality between men and women with regard to labour market opportunities and treatment at work;
- the integration of persons excluded from the labour market, without prejudice to Article 127 of the Treaty establishing the European Community (hereinafter referred to as 'the Treaty').

2. To this end, the Council may adopt, by means of directives, minimum requirements for gradual implementation, having regard to the conditions and technical rules obtaining in each of the Member States. Such directives shall avoid imposing administrative, financial and legal constraints in a way which would hold back the creation and development of small and medium-sized undertakings.

The Council shall act in accordance with the procedure referred to in Article 189c of the Treaty after consulting the Economic and Social Committee.

3. However, the Council shall act unanimously on a proposal from the Commission, after consulting the European Parliament and the Economic and Social Committee, in the following areas:

- social security and social protection of workers;
- protection of workers where their employment contract is terminated;
- representation and collective defence of the interests of workers and employers, including co-determination, subject to paragraph 6;
- conditions of employment for third-country nationals legally residing in community territory;
- financial contributions for promotion of employment and job-creation, without prejudice to the provisions relating to the Social Fund.

4. A Member State may entrust management and labour, at their joint request, with the implementation of directives adopted pursuant to paragraphs 2 and 3.

In this case, it shall ensure that, no later than the date on which a directive must be transposed in accordance with Article 189, management and labour have introduced the necessary measures by agreement, the Member State concerned being required to take any necessary measures enabling it at any time to be in a position to guarantee the results imposed by that directive.

5. The provisions adopted pursuant to this Article shall not prevent any Member State from maintaining or introducing more stringent preventive measures compatible with the Treaty.

6. The provisions of this Article shall not apply to pay, the right of association, the right to strike or the right to impose lock-outs.

Article 3

1. The Commission shall have the task of promoting the consultation of management and labour at Community level and shall take any relevant measure to facilitate their dialogue by ensuring balanced support for the parties.
2. To this end, before submitting proposals in the social policy field, the Commission shall consult management and labour on the possible direction of Community action.
3. If, after such consultation, the Commission considers Community action advisable, it shall consult management and labour on the content of the envisaged proposal. Management and labour shall forward to the Commission an opinion or, where appropriate, a recommendation.
4. On the occasion of such consultation, management and labour may inform the Commission of their wish to initiate the process provided for in Article 4. The duration of the procedure shall not exceed nine months, unless the management and labour concerned and the Commission decide jointly to extend it.

Article 4

1. Should management and labour so desire, the dialogue between them at Community level may lead to contractual relations, including agreements.
2. Agreements concluded at Community level shall be implemented either in accordance with the procedures and practices specific to management and labour and the Member States or, in matters covered by Article 2, at the joint request of the signatory parties, by a Council decision on a proposal from the Commission.

The Council shall act by qualified majority, except where the agreement in question contains one or more provisions relating to one of the areas referred to in Article 2(3), in which case it shall act unanimously.

Article 5

With a view to achieving the objectives of Article 1 and without prejudice to the other provisions of the Treaty, the Commission shall encourage co-operation between the Member States and facilitate the co-ordination of their action in all social policy fields under this Agreement.

Article 6

1. Each Member State shall ensure that the principle of equal pay for male and female workers for equal work is applied.

2. For the purpose of this Article, 'pay' means the ordinary basic or minimum wage or salary and any other consideration, whether in cash or in kind, which the worker receives directly or indirectly, in respect of his employment, from his employer.

Equal pay without discrimination based on sex means:

(a) that pay for the same work at piece rates shall be calculated on the basis of the same unit of measurement;

(b) that pay for work at time rates shall be the same for the same job.

3. This Article shall not prevent any Member State from maintaining or adopting measures providing for specific advantages in order to make it easier for women to pursue a vocational activity or to prevent or compensate for disadvantages in their professional careers.

Article 7

The Commission shall draw up a report each year on progress in achieving the objectives of Article 1, including the demographic situation in the Community. It shall forward the report to the European Parliament, the Council and the Economic and Social Committee.

The European Parliament may invite the Commission to draw up reports on particular problems concerning the social situation.

Declarations

1. **Declaration on Article 2(2)**
    The eleven High Contracting Parties note that in the discussions on Article 2(2) of the Agreement it was agreed that the Community does not intend, in laying down minimum requirements for the protection of the safety and health of employees, to discriminate in a manner unjustified by the circumstances against employees in small and medium-sized undertakings.

2. **Declaration on Article 4(2)**
    The eleven High Contracting Parties declare that the first of the arrangements for application of the agreements between management and labour Community-wide - referred to in Article 4(2) - will consist in developing, by collective bargaining according to the rules of each Member State, the content of the agreements, and that consequently this arrangement

implies no obligation on the Member States to apply the agreements directly or to work out rules for their transposition, nor any obligation to amend national legislation in force to facilitate their implementation.

Protocol concerning Article 119 of the Treaty establishing the European Community

THE HIGH CONTRACTING PARTIES,

Have agreed upon the following provision, which shall be annexed to the Treaty establishing the European Community:

For the purposes of Article 119 of this Treaty, benefits under occupational social security schemes shall not be considered as remuneration if and in so far as they are attributable to periods of employment prior to 17 May 1990, except in the case of workers or those claiming under them who have before that date initiated legal proceedings or introduced an equivalent claim under the applicable national law.

Commission Recommendation on the protection of the dignity of women and men at work

THE COMMISSION OF THE EUROPEAN COMMUNITIES

Having regard to the Treaty establishing the European Economic Community and the second indent of Article 155 thereof;

Whereas unwanted conduct of a sexual nature, or other conduct based on sex affecting the dignity of women and men at work, including the conduct of superiors and colleagues, is unacceptable and may, in certain circumstances, be contrary to the principle of equal treatment within the meaning of Articles 3, 4 and 5 of Council Directive 76/207/EEC of 9 February 1976 on the implementation of the principle of equal treatment for men and women as regards access to employment, vocational training and promotion and working conditions[1], a view supported by case law in some Member States;

Whereas, in accordance with the Council Recommendation of 13 December 1984 on the promotion of positive action for women[2],

---

[1] OJ No L 39, 14.2.1976, p. 40 (see Appendix ?, p. ?).
[2] OJ No L 331, 19.12.1984, p. 34.

many Member States have carried out a variety of positive action measures having a bearing, *inter alia*, on respect for the dignity of women at the workplace;

Whereas the European Parliament, in its resolution of 11 June 1986 on violence against women[3], has called upon national governments, equal opportunities committees and trade unions to carry out concerted information campaigns to create a proper awareness of the individual rights of all members of the labour force;

Whereas the Advisory Committee on Equal Opportunities for Women and Men, in its opinion of 20 June 1988, has unanimously recommended that there should be a Recommendation and code of conduct on sexual harassment in the workplace covering harassment of both sexes;

Whereas the Commission in its Action Programme relating to the implementation of the Community Charter of Basic Social Rights for workers undertook to examine the protection of workers and their dignity at work, having regard to the reports and recommendations prepared on various aspects of implementation of Community law[4],

Whereas the Council, in its resolution of 29 May 1990 on the protection of the dignity of women and men at work[5], affirms that conduct based on sex affecting the dignity of women and men at work, including conduct of superiors and colleagues, constitutes an intolerable violation of the dignity of workers or trainees, and calls on the Member States and the institutions and organs of the European Communities to develop positive measures designed to create a climate at work in which women and men respect one another's human integrity;

Whereas the Commission, in its Third Action Programme on Equal Opportunities for Women and men, 1991-1995 and pursuant to paragraph 3.2 of the said Council resolution of 29 May 1990, resolved to draw up a code of conduct on the protection of the dignity of women and men at work[6], based on experience and best practice in the Member States, to provide guidance on initiating and pursuing positive measures designed to create a climate at work in which women and men respect one another's human integrity;

Whereas the European Parliament, on 22 October 1991, adopted a Resolution on the protection of the dignity of women and men at work;

Whereas the Economic and Social committee, on 30 October 1991, adopted an Opinion on the protection of the dignity of women and men at work;

RECOMMENDS AS FOLLOWS;

[3] OJ No C 176, 14.7.1986, p. 79.
[4] COM (89) 568 Final, 29.11.1989.
[5] OJ No C 157, 27.6.1990, p. 3.
[6] COM (90) 449 Final, 6.11.1990.

Article 1

It is recommended that the Member States take action to promote awareness that conduct of a sexual nature, or other conduct based on sex affecting the dignity of women and men at work, including conduct of superiors and colleagues, is unacceptable if:
(a) such conduct is unwanted, unreasonable and offensive to the recipient;
(b) a person's rejection of or submission to such conduct on the part of employers or workers (including superiors or colleagues) is used explicitly or implicitly as a basis for a decision which affects that person's access to vocational training, access to employment, continued employment, promotion, salary or other employment decisions; and/or
(c) such conduct creates an intimidating, hostile or humiliating work environment for the recipient;
and that such conduct may, in certain circumstances, be contrary to the principle of equal treatment within the meaning of Articles 3, 4 and 5 of Directive 76/207/EEC.

Article 2

It is recommended that Member States should take action, in the public sector, to implement the Commission's Code of practice on the protection of the dignity of women and men at work, annexed hereto. The action of the Member States, in thus initiating and pursuing positive measures designed to create a climate at work in which women and men respect one another's human integrity, should serve as an example to the private sector.

Article 3

It is recommended that Member States encourage employers and employee representatives to develop measures to implement the Commission's Code of Practice on the protection of the dignity of women and men at work.

Article 4

The Member States shall inform the Commission within three years of the date of this Recommendation of the measures taken to give effect to it, in order to allow the Commission to draw up a report on all such measures. The Commission shall, within this period, ensure the widest possible circulation of the Code of Practice. The report should examine the degree of awareness of the Code, its perceived effectiveness, its degree of application and the extent of its use in collective bargaining between the social partners.

Article 5

This Recommendation is addressed to the Member States.

Protecting the Dignity of Women and Men at Work

A Code of Practice on measures to combat sexual harassment

1. Introduction

This Code of Practice is issued in accordance with the Resolution of the Council of Ministers on the protection of the dignity of women and men at work[1], and to accompany the Commission's Recommendation on this issue.

Its purpose is to give practical guidance to employers, trade unions, and employees on the protection of the dignity of women and men at work. The Code is intended to be applicable in both the public and the private sector and employers are encouraged to follow the recommendations contained in the Code in a way which is appropriate to the size and structure of their organisation. It may be particularly relevant for small and medium-sized enterprises to adapt some of the practical steps to their specific needs.

The aim is to ensure that sexual harassment does not occur and, if it does occur, to ensure that adequate procedures are readily available to deal with the problem and prevent its recurrence. The Code thus seeks to encourage the development and implementation of policies and practices which establish working environments free of sexual harassment and in which women and men respect one another's human integrity.

The expert report carried out on behalf of the Commission found that sexual harassment is a serious problem for many working women in the

---

[1] OJ No C 157, 27.6.90, p. 2, s.3.2.

European Community[2] and research in Member States has proven beyond doubt that sexual harassment at work is not an isolated phenomenon. On the contrary, it is clear that for millions of women in the European Community, sexual harassment is an unpleasant and unavoidable part of their working lives. Men too may suffer sexual harassment and should, of course, have the same rights as women to the protection of their dignity.

Some specific groups are particularly vulnerable to sexual harassment. Research in several Member States, which documents the link between the risk of sexual harassment and the recipient's perceived vulnerability, suggests that divorced and separated women, young women and new entrants to the labour market and those with irregular or precarious employment contracts, women in non-traditional jobs, women with disabilities, lesbians and women from racial minorities are disproportionately at risk. Gay men and young men are also vulnerable to harassment. It is undeniable that harassment on grounds of sexual orientation undermines the dignity at work of those affected and it is impossible to regard such harassment as appropriate workplace behaviour.

Sexual harassment pollutes the working environment and can have a devastating effect upon the health, confidence, morale and performance of those affected by it. The anxiety and stress produced by sexual harassment commonly leads to those subjected to it taking time off work due to sickness, being less efficient at work, or leaving their job to seek work elsewhere. Employees often suffer the adverse consequences of the harassment itself and short-and long-term damage to their employment prospects if they are forced to change jobs. Sexual harassment may also have a damaging impact on employees not themselves the object of unwanted behaviour but who are witness to it or have a knowledge of the unwanted behaviour.

There are also adverse consequences arising from sexual harassment for employers. It has a direct impact on the profitability of the enterprise where staff take sick leave or resign their posts because of sexual harassment, and on the economic efficiency of the enterprise where employees' productivity is reduced by having to work in a climate in which individuals' integrity is not respected.

In general terms, sexual harassment is an obstacle to the proper integration of women into the labour market and the Commission is committed to encouraging the development of comprehensive measures to improve such integration[3].

---

[2] "The dignity of women at work: a report on the problem of sexual harassment in the Member States of the European Communities", October 1987, by Michael Rubenstein, ISBN 92-825-8-8764-9.
[3] Third Action Programme on Equal Opportunities for Women and Men, 1991-1995, COM(90) 449, 6.11.1990.

2. Definition

Sexual harassment means "unwanted conduct of a sexual nature, or other conduct based on sex affecting the dignity of women and men at work".[4] This can include unwanted physical, verbal or non-verbal conduct.

Thus, a range of behaviour may be considered to constitute sexual harassment. It is unacceptable if such conduct is unwanted, unreasonable and offensive to the recipient; a person's rejection of or submission to such conduct on the part of employers or workers (including superiors or colleagues) is used explicitly or implicitly as a basis for a decision which affects that person's access to vocational training or to employment, continued employment, promotion, salary or any other employment decisions; and/or such conduct creates an intimidating, hostile or humiliating working environment for the recipient.

The essential characteristic of sexual harassment is that it is *unwanted* by the recipient, that is for each individual to determine what behaviour is acceptable to them and what they regard as offensive. Sexual attention becomes sexual harassment if it is persisted in once it has been made clear that it is regarded by the recipient as offensive, although one incident of harassment may constitute sexual harassment if sufficiently serious. It is the unwanted nature of the conduct which distinguishes sexual harassment from friendly behaviour, which is welcome and mutual.

3. The law and employers' responsibilities

Conduct of a sexual nature or other conduct based on sex affecting the dignity of women and men at work may be contrary to the principle of equal treatment within the meaning of Articles 3, 4 and 5 of Council Directive 76/207/EEC of 9 February 1976 on the implementation of the principle of equal treatment for men and women as regards access to employment, vocational treatment and promotion and working conditions. This principle means that there shall be no discrimination whatsoever on grounds of sex either directly or indirectly by reference in particular to marital or family status[5].

In certain circumstances, and depending upon national law, sexual harassment may also be a criminal offence or may contravene other obligations

---

[4] Council Resolution on the protection of the dignity of women and men at work, OJ No C 157, 27.6.1990, p. 2, s.1.
[5] OJ No L 39, 14.2.1976, p. 40, Article 2.

imposed by the law, such as health and safety duties, or a duty, contractual or otherwise, to be a good employer. Since sexual harassment is a form of employee misconduct, employers have a responsibility to deal with it as they do with any other form of employee misconduct as well as to refrain from harassing employees themselves. Since sexual harassment is a risk to health and safety, employers have a responsibility to take steps to minimise the risk as they do with other hazards. Since sexual harassment often entails an abuse of power, employers may have a responsibility for the misuse of the authority they delegate.

This Code, however, focuses on sexual harassment as a problem of sex discrimination. Sexual harassment is sex discrimination because the gender of the recipient is the determining factor in who is harassed. Conduct of a sexual nature or other conduct based on sex affecting the dignity of women and men at work in some Member States already has been found to contravene national equal treatment laws and employers have a responsibility to seek to ensure that the work environment is free from such conduct[6].

As sexual harassment is often a function of women's status in the employment hierarchy, policies to deal with sexual harassment are likely to be most effective where they are linked to a broader policy to promote equal opportunities and to improve the position of women. Advice on steps which can be taken generally to implement an equal opportunities policy is set out in the Commission's Guide to Positive Action[7].

Similarly, a procedure to deal with complaints of sexual harassment should be regarded as only one component of a strategy to deal with the problem. The prime objective should be to change behaviour and attitudes, to seek to ensure the prevention of sexual harassment.

4. Collective bargaining

The majority of the recommendations contained in this Code are for action by employers, since employers have clear responsibilities to ensure the protection of the dignity of women and men at work.

Trade unions should also have responsibilities to their members and they can and should play an important role in the prevention of sexual harassment in the workplace. It is recommended that the question of including appropriate clauses in agreements is examined in the context of the collective bargaining process, with the aim of achieving a work environment free from unwanted conduct of a sexual nature or other conduct based on sex affecting

---

[6] Council Resolution on the protection of the dignity of women and men at work, OJ No C 157, 27.6.1990, p. 2, s.2.3(a).
[7] "Positive action: equal opportunities for women in employment – a guide", OPCE, 1988.

the dignity of women and men at work and free from victimisation of a complainant or of a person wishing to give, or giving, evidence in the event of a complaint.

5. Recommendations to employers

The policies and procedures recommended below should be adopted, where appropriate, after consultation or negotiation with trade unions or employee representatives. Experience suggests that strategies to create and maintain a working environment in which the dignity of employees is respected are most likely to be effective where they are jointly agreed.

It should be emphasised that a distinguishing characteristic of sexual harassment is that employees subjected to it often will be reluctant to complain. An absence of complaints about sexual harassment in a particular organisation, therefore, does not necessarily mean an absence of sexual harassment. It may mean that the recipients of sexual harassment think that there is no point in complaining because nothing will be done about it, or because it will be trivialised or the complainant subjected to ridicule, or because they fear reprisals. Implementing the preventative and procedural recommendations outlined below should facilitate the creation of a climate at work in which such concerns have no place.

A. Prevention

(i) Policy statements

As a first step in showing senior management's concern and their commitment to dealing with the problem of sexual harassment, employers should issue a policy statement which expressly states that all employees have a right to be treated with dignity, that sexual harassment at work will not be permitted or condoned and that employees have a right to complain about it should it occur.

It is recommended that the policy statement makes clear what is considered inappropriate behaviour at work, and explains that such behaviour, in certain circumstances, may be unlawful. It is advisable for the statement to set out a positive duty on managers and supervisors to implement the policy and to take corrective action to ensure compliance with it. It should also place a positive duty on all employees to comply with the policy and to ensure that their colleagues are treated with respect and dignity.

In addition, it is recommended that the statement explains the procedure which should be followed by employees subjected to sexual harassment at work in order to obtain assistance and to whom they should complain; that it contain an undertaking that allegations of sexual harassment will be dealt with seriously, expeditiously and confidentially; and that employees will be protected against victimisation or retaliation for bringing a complaint of sexual harassment. It should also specify that appropriate disciplinary measures will be taken against employees found guilty of sexual harassment.

(II) Communicating the policy

Once the policy has been developed, it is important to ensure that it is communicated effectively to all employees, so that they are aware that they have a right to complain and to whom they should complain; that their complaint will be dealt with promptly and fairly; and so that employees are made aware of likely consequences of engaging in sexual harassment. Such communication will highlight management's commitment to eliminating sexual harassment, thus enhancing a climate in which it will not occur.

(iii) Responsibility

All employees have a responsibility to help to ensure a working environment in which the dignity of employees is respected and managers (including supervisors) have a particular duty to ensure that sexual harassment does not occur in work areas for which they are responsible. It is recommended that managers should explain the organisation's policy to their staff and take steps to positively promote the policy. Managers should also be responsive and supportive to any member of staff who complains about sexual harassment; provide full and clear advice on the procedure to be adopted; maintain confidentiality in any cases of sexual harassment; and ensure that there is no further problem of sexual harassment or any victimisation after a complaint has been resolved.

(iv) Training

An important means of ensuring that sexual harassment does not occur and that, if it does occur, the problem is resolved efficiently through the provision of training for managers and supervisors. Such training should aim to identify the factors which contribute to a working environment free of sexual harassment and to familiarise participants with their responsibilities under the employer's policy and any problems they are likely to encounter.

In addition, those playing an official role in any complaints procedure in respect of sexual harassment should receive specialist training, such as that outlined above.

It is also good practice to include information as to the organisation's policy on sexual harassment and procedures for dealing with it as part of appropriate induction and training programmes.

B. Procedures

The development of clear and precise procedures to deal with sexual harassment once it has occurred is of great importance. The Procedures should ensure the resolution of problems in an efficient and effective manner. Practical guidance for employees on how to deal with sexual harassment when it occurs and with its aftermath will make it more likely that it will be dealt with at an early stage. Such guidance should of course draw attention to an employee's legal rights and to any time limits within which they must be exercised.

(i) Resolving problems informally

Most recipients of harassment simply want the harassment to stop. Both informal and formal methods of resolving problems should be available.

Employees should be advised that, if possible, they should attempt to resolve the problem informally in the first instance. In some cases, it may be possible and sufficient for the employer to explain clearly to the person engaging in the unwanted conduct that the behaviour in question is not welcome, that it offends them or makes them uncomfortable, and that it interferes with their work.

In circumstances where it is too difficult or embarrassing for an individual to do this on their own behalf, an alternative approach would be to seek support from, or for an initial approach to be made by, a sympathetic friend or confidential counsellor.

If the conduct continues or if it is not appropriate to resolve the problem informally, it should be raised through the formal complaints procedure.

(ii) Advice and assistance

It is recommended that employers should designate someone to provide advice and assistance to employees subjected to sexual harassment, where possible, with responsibilities to assist in the resolution of any problems, whether through informal or formal means. It may be helpful if the officer is designated with the agreement of the trade unions or employees, as this is likely to enhance their acceptability. Such officers could be selected from personnel departments or equal opportunities departments for example. In some organisations they are designated as "confidential counsellors" or "sympathetic friends". Often such a role may be played by someone from the employee's trade union or by women's support groups.

Whatever the location of this responsibility in the organisation, it is recommended that the designated officer receives appropriate training in the best means of resolving problems and in the detail of the organisation's policy and procedures, so that they can perform their role effectively. It is also important that they are given adequate resources to carry out their function, and protection against victimisation for assisting any recipient of sexual harassment.

(iii) Complaints procedure

It is recommended that, where the complainant regards attempts at informal resolution as inappropriate, where informal attempts at resolution have been refused, or where the outcome has been unsatisfactory, a formal procedure for resolving the complaint should be provided. The procedure should give employees confidence that the organisation will take allegations of sexual harassment seriously.

By its nature sexual harassment may make the normal channels of complaint difficult to use because of embarrassment, fears of not being taken seriously, fears of damage to reputation, fears of reprisal or the prospect of damaging the working environment. Therefore, a formal procedure should specify to whom the employee should bring a complaint, and it should also provide an alternative if in the particular circumstances the normal grievance procedure may not be suitable, for example because the alleged harasser is the employee's line manager. It is also advisable to make provision for employees to bring a complaint in the first instance to someone of their own sex, should they so choose.

It is good practice for employers to monitor and review complaints of sexual harassment and how they have been resolved, in order to ensure that their procedures are working effectively.

(iv) Investigations

It is important to ensure that internal investigations of any complaints are handled with sensitivity and with due respect for the rights of both the complainant and the alleged harasser. The investigation should be seen to be independent and objective. Those carrying out the investigation should not be connected with the allegation in any way, and every effort should be made to resolve complaints speedily – grievances should be handled promptly and the procedure should set a time limit within which complaints will be processed, with due regard for any time limits set by national legislation for initiating a complaint through the legal system.

It is recommended as good practice that both the complainant and the alleged harasser have the right to be accompanied and/or represented, perhaps by a representative of their trade union or a friend or colleague; that the alleged harasser be given full details of the nature of the complaint and the opportunity to respond; and that strict confidentiality be maintained throughout any investigation into an allegation. Where it is necessary to interview witnesses, the importance of confidentiality should be emphasised.

It must be recognised that recounting the experience of sexual harassment is difficult and can damage the employee's dignity. Therefore, a complainant should not be required to repeatedly recount the events complained of where this is unnecessary.

The investigation should focus on the facts of the complaint and it is advisable for the employer to keep a complete record of all meetings and investigations.

(v) Disciplinary offence

It is recommended that violations of the organisation's policy protecting the dignity of employees at work should be treated as a disciplinary offence; and the disciplinary rules should make clear what is regarded as inappropriate behaviour at work. It is also good practice to ensure that the range of penalties to which offenders will be liable for violating the rule is clearly stated and also to make it clear that it will be considered a disciplinary offence to victimise or retaliate against an employee for bringing a complaint of sexual harassment in good faith.

Where a complaint is upheld and it is determined that it is necessary to relocate or transfer one party, consideration should be given, wherever practicable, to allowing the complainant to choose whether he or she wishes to remain in their post or be transferred to another location. No element of penalty should be seen to attach to a complainant whose complaint is upheld and in addition, where a complaint is upheld, the employer should monitor the situation to ensure that the harassment has stopped.

Even where a complaint is not upheld, for example because the evidence is regarded as inconclusive, consideration should be given to transferring or rescheduling the work of one of the employees concerned rather than requiring them to continue to work together against the wishes of either party.

6. Recommendations to trade unions

Sexual harassment is a trade union issue as well as an issue for employers. It is recommended as good practice that trade unions should formulate and issue clear policy statements on sexual harassment and take steps to raise awareness of the problems of sexual harassment in the workplace, in order to help create a climate in which it is neither condoned nor ignored. For example, trade unions could aim to give all officers and representatives training on equality issues, including dealing with sexual harassment and include such information in union-sponsored or approved training courses, as well as information on the union's policy. Trade unions should consider declaring that sexual harassment is inappropriate behaviour and educating members and officials about its consequences is recommended as good practice.

Trade unions should also raise the issue of sexual harassment with employers and encourage the adoption of adequate policies and procedures to protect the dignity of women and men at work in the organisation. It is advisable for trade unions to inform members of their right not to be sexually harassed at work and provide members with clear guidance as to what to do if they are sexually harassed, including guidance on any relevant legal rights.

Where complaints arise, it is important for trade unions to treat them seriously and sympathetically and ensure that the complainant has the opportunity of representation if a complaint is to be pursued. It is important to create an environment in which members feel able to raise such complaints knowing they will receive a sympathetic and supportive response from local union representatives. Trade unions could consider designating specially-trained officials to advise and counsel members with complaints of sexual harassment and act on their behalf if required. This will provide a focal point for support. It is also a good idea to ensure that there are sufficient female representatives to support women subjected to sexual harassment.

It is recommended too, where the trade union is representing both the complainant and the alleged harasser for the purpose of the complaints procedure, that it be made clear that the union is not condoning offensive behaviour by providing representation. In any event, the same official should not represent both parties.

It is good practice to advise members that keeping a record of incidents by the harassed worker will assist in bringing any formal or informal action to a more effective conclusion; and that the union wishes to be informed of any incident of sexual harassment and that such information will be kept confidential. It is also good practice for the union to monitor and review the union's record in responding to complaints and in representing alleged harassers and the harassed, in order to ensure its responses are effective.

7. Employees' responsibilities

Employees have a clear role to play in helping to create a climate at work in which sexual harassment is unacceptable. They can contribute to preventing sexual harassment through an awareness and sensitivity towards the issue and by ensuring that standards of conduct for themselves and for colleagues do not cause offence.

Employees can do much to discourage sexual harassment by making it clear that they find such behaviour unacceptable and by supporting colleagues who suffer such treatment and are considering making a complaint.

Employees who are themselves recipients of harassment should, where practicable, tell the harasser that the behaviour is unwanted and unacceptable. Once the offender understands clearly that the behaviour is unwelcome, this may be enough to put an end to it. If the behaviour is persisted in, employees should inform management and/or their employee representative through the appropriate channels and request assistance in stopping the harassment whether through informal or formal means.

INDEX

Index compiled by Alex Corrin

Wiley Series in
EUROPEAN LAW